Key Sociological Thinkers

Also by Rob Stones:

Sociological Reasoning: Towards a Past-modern Sociology

Key Sociological Thinkers

Edited by

Rob Stones

NEW YORK UNIVERSITY PRESS
Washington Square, New York

Selection and editorial matter, Introduction and Conclusion © Rob Stones 1998
Chapter 1 © Bob Jessop 1998   Chapter 11 © Robin Williams 1998
Chapter 2 © Lawrence Scaff 1998   Chapter 12 © Nicos Mouzelis 1998
Chapter 3 © Whitney Pope 1998   Chapter 13 © John Heritage 1998
Chapter 4 © Ian Craib 1998   Chapter 14 © Ted Benton 1998
Chapter 5 © Patrick Watier 1998   Chapter 15 © William Outhwaite 1998
Chapter 6 © Ken Plummer 1998   Chapter 16 © Loïc J.D. Wacquant 1998
Chapter 7 © Robert Holton 1998   Chapter 17 © Karin A. Martin 1998
Chapter 8 © Alan Sica 1998   Chapter 18 © Simon J. Williams 1998
Chapter 9 © Mary Evans 1998   Chapter 19 © Lawrence Barth 1998
Chapter 10 © Jason Hughes 1998   Chapter 20 © Michèle Barrett 1998
                Chapter 21 © Ira J. Cohen 1998
The translation of Chapter 5: *Georg Simmel* by Patrick Watier © Phil Brew
                       and Rob Stones 1998

First published in the U.S.A. in 1998 by
NEW YORK UNIVERSITY PRESS
Washington Square
New York, N.Y. 10003

This book is printed on paper suitable for recycling and
made from fully managed and sustained forest sources.

Library of Congress Cataloging-in-Publication Data
Key sociological thinkers / edited by Rob Stones.
p. cm.
Includes bibliographical references and index.
ISBN 0–8147–8115–2. — ISBN 0–8147–8116–0 (pbk.)
1. Sociology. 2. Sociologists. I. Stones, Rob, 1957–
HM51.K43 1998
301—dc21   98–7514
                                                  CIP

Printed in Great Britain

For
Apinya, Chaiyan, Jamaree and Anan
Department of Sociology and Anthropology
University of Chiang Mai

Contents

PART III

Contents   203

'Seeing Things Differently'

This is an alternative contents list, focusing just on the section appearing within most chapters, entitled 'Seeing Things Differently'. In this section authors relate how the perspective of their key thinker has made them see the social world in a new and illuminating way, drawing their attention to aspects of the world that otherwise would have passed them by. In this section they do not draw directly on examples given in the work of their thinker, but use examples from everyday life, literature and film, or from the work of subsequent sociologists working within the tradition of that thinker. The examples tend to be graphic and colourful. Thus, the idea of giving a separate contents list here is that the relatively greater accessibility of these sections means that readers may wish to get an initial feel for a thinker new to them (or even to those not so new to them) by going first to this section before returning later to read the chapter from the beginning. I have taken the liberty of providing my own individual titles for the sections. In one or two cases authors did not include a section explicitly entitled 'Seeing Things Differently'; where this is the case I have selected an analogously colourful or illustrative section of their chapter towards which to direct the reader, inventing an appropriate heading. In these cases I have followed my heading with the author's own section heading in brackets.

Acknowledgements

I would like to thank Catherine Gray at Macmillan for coming up with the very bright idea for a collection on key sociological thinkers and for her advice and support throughout the editorial process. Thanks also to Diane Streeting for help in the early stages of the book, relaying messages for a good six months between myself in Bangkok and invited contributors whom I had asked to use my address at the University of Essex. Also, without the invaluable help of Sue Aylott in formatting chapters, entering in editorial changes, preparing contents pages and bibliographies, and much more, the book would have been much the poorer, and published much later. Aardvark Editorial, for their part, provided their unfailing combination of skill and lightning efficiency. Thanks also to my brother, Mike Stones, for designing and illustrating the book's cover with his usual patient enthusiasm. I am grateful also to Phil Brew for co-translating with me Patrick Watier's chapter on Simmel, and for improving my French in the process. Thank you, Klong, Pimai and Ja for stepping carefully – sometimes – over the piles of papers. And finally, of course, I would like to express my appreciation to the contributory authors of each chapter for making the book as good as it is.

Notes on Contributors

Michèle Barrett is Professor of Sociology at City University, London. She is author of *Virginia Woolf: Women and Writing* (1979), *Women's Oppression Today: Problems in Marxist Feminist Analysis* (1980 and 1988), and *The Politics of Truth: From Marx to Foucault* (1991), a co-authored book (with Mary McIntosh) *The Anti-Social Family* (1982 and 1988), and an edited collection (with Anne Phillips) *Destabilizing Theory: Contemporary Feminist Debates* (1992). A new collection of essays will be published in 1998.

Lawrence Barth is completing his PhD in Urban Planning in the School of Public Policy and Social Research at the University of California, Los Angeles. His thesis, 'The Rule of the Metropolis', explores the advent of the Los Angeles metropolitan region in the first decades of the twentieth century. He currently resides in London where he lectures part time at the Architectural Association and Birkbeck College, University of London. He has also written on the implications of Jean Francois Lyotard's philosophy for urban social theory in 'Immemorial Visibilities: Seeing the City's Difference', *Environment and Planning A* (1996), and has applied Michel Foucault's work to problems of nineteenth- and twentieth-century urbanism, *Economy and Society* (1998, forthcoming).

Ted Benton is Professor of Sociology, University of Essex. His current interests are in environmental issues and modern social theory, especially in links between socialist and 'green' perspectives. Publications include *Philosophical Foundations of the Three Sociologies* (1977), '"Objective" Interests and the Sociology of Power', *Sociology* (1981), *The Rise and Fall of Structural Marxism* (1984), *Natural Relations: Ecology, Animal Rights and Social Justice* (1993), (with M. Redclift, eds) *Social Theory and the Global Environment* (1994) and (ed.) *The Greening of Marxism* (1996).

Ira J. Cohen is Professor of Sociology, teaching social theory as a member of the Graduate Faculty in Sociology at Rutgers Univesity in New Brunswick and in the Department of Sociology, Rutgers University in Newark. He has published works on a broad range of themes in classical and contemporary social theory including *Structuration Theory: Anthony Giddens and the Constitution of Social Life* (1989), 'Structuration Theory and Social Order: Five Issues in Brief' in Clarke, Modgil and Modgil (eds) *Anthony Giddens: Consensus and Controversy* (1990), 'Theories of Action and Praxis' in B. Turner (ed.) *The Blackwell Companion to Social Theory* (1996), and (with Mary F.

Rogers) 'Autonomy and Credibility: Voice as Method', *Sociological Theory* (1994).

Ian Craib is Professor of Sociology, University of Essex and is a psycho-analytic group therapist. His publications include *Existentialism and Sociology: A Study of Jean-Paul Sartre* (1976), *Modern Social Theory: From Parsons to Habermas* (2nd edn, 1992), *Psychoanalysis and Social Theory: The Limits of Sociology* (1989), *Anthony Giddens* (1991), *The Importance of Disappointment* (1994) and *Classical Social Theory* (1997). An edition of his collected papers is due to be published in 1998 and he is currently working on an introduction to psychoanalytic theory and practice.

Mary Evans is Professor of Women's Studies and Sociology at the University of Kent at Canterbury. In the past 25 years she has taught and written on various issues within feminism and sociology, but her current research interests are in auto/biography and morality. These interests arise out of previous work on Simone de Beauvoir, Jane Austen and the impact of feminism on a range of disciplines. Publications include *Simone de Beauvoir* (1996) and *Introducing Contemporary Feminist Thought* (1998).

John Heritage is Professor of Sociology at the University of California, Los Angeles. He has published extensively in the fields of ethnomethodology and conversation analysis, including *Garfinkel and Ethnomethodology* (1984), *Structures of Social Action: Studies in Conversation Analysis* (co-edited with Max Atkinson) (1984), (with David Greatbatch) 'On the Institutional Character of Institutional Talk: The Case of News Interviews' in D. Boden and D. H. Zimmerman (eds) *Talk & Social Structure: Studies in Ethnomethodology and Conversation Analysis* (1991), *Talk at Work* (co-edited with Paul Drew) (1992) and *Practising Medicine* (co-edited with Doug Maynard, 1998, forthcoming).

Robert Holton is Associate Professor of Sociology and Director of the Centre for Multicultural Studies at Flinders University of South Australia. He is author of a number of books and articles on social theory, historical sociology, immigration and ethnicity, including *Cities, Capitalism, and Civilisation* (1986), *Talcott Parsons on Economy and Society* (1986) and *Max Weber on Economy and Society* (1989) (both with B.S. Turner), *Economy and Society* (1992) and 'Classical Social Theory' in *The Blackwell Companion to Social Theory* (1996).

Jason Hughes is a Lecturer at the Centre for Labour Market Studies, University of Leicester. He recently completed his PhD thesis, 'From Panacea to Pandemic: Towards a Process Sociological Understanding of Tobacco Use in the West' which will be published shortly. He is currently working on a co-authored book with Professor Eric Dunning on the contribution of the work of Norbert Elias to contemporary debates in sociological theory. His research interests range from the process sociology of Norbert Elias, through cross-cultural comparisons of the relationship between work and stress, to the general relationship between theory and empirical research.

Bob Jessop is Professor of Sociology at the University of Lancaster. He has written extensively on Marxism, theories of the state, political sociology and political economy. His publications include *The Capitalist State: Marxist Theories and Methods* (1982), *Nicos Poulantzas: Marxist Theory and Political Strategy* (1985), *State Theory: Putting Capitalist States in their Place* (1990), *Strategic Dilemmas and Path Dependency in Post Socialism* (1995) and *Regulation Theory: Putting Capitalist Economies in their Place* (1996). He is also the co-author of *Thatcherism: A Tale of Two Nations* (1988).

Karin A. Martin is Assistant Professor of Sociology and Women's Studies at the University of Michigan. Her PhD was from the University of California at Berkeley where Nancy Chodorow was her advisor. She is the author of *Puberty, Sexuality and the Self: Girls and Boys at Adolescence* (1996). Her current research continues to be around the issues of gender, bodies and sexuality.

Nicos Mouzelis is Professor of Sociology at the London School of Economics. He has written widely on issues of sociological theory, theories of underdevelopment and organisation theory. His most recent publications include *Post-Marxist Alternatives: The Construction of Social Orders* (1990), *Back to Sociological Theory: The Construction of Social Orders* (1991), *Sociological Theory: What Went Wrong?* (1995) and 'Social and System Integration: Lockwood, Habermas, Giddens', *Sociology* (1997).

William Outhwaite is Professor of Sociology in the School of European Studies at the University of Sussex. His research interests include the philosophy of the social sciences (especially realism), social theory (especially critical theory and contemporary European social theory), political sociology and the sociology of knowledge. He is the author of *Understanding Social Life: The Method Called Verstehen* (1975 and 1986), *Concept Formation in Social Science* (1983), *New Philosophies of Social Science: Realism, Hermeneutics and Critical Theory* (1987) and *Jürgen Habermas: A Critical Introduction* (1994). Edited books include *The Habermas Reader* (1996) and (with Tom Bottomore) *The Blackwell Dictionary of Twentieth-century Social Thought* (1993).

Ken Plummer is Professor of Sociology at the University of Essex and has been a regular visiting Professor at the University of California (Santa Barbara). In addition to a long-standing interest in the teaching of introductory sociology his major research interests lie in the fields of sexuality, stigma, methodology and symbolic interactionist theory He is the author of *Sexual Stigma* (1975), *Documents of Life* (1983), and *Telling Sexual Stories* (1995), as well as the editor of *Symbolic Interactionism*, vols I and II (1991), *Modern Homosexualities* (1992) and *The Chicago School* (1997, 4 vols). He is also currently the editor of a new journal, *Sexualities*.

Whitney Pope is Professor of Sociology at the University of Indiana, Bloomington. In addition to publishing articles on sociological theory and on suicide, he is the author of what is widely regarded as the finest book-length examination of Emile Durkheim's study of suicide, *Durkheim's 'Suicide': A Classic Analysed* (1976), and *Alexis de Tocqueville: His Social and Political Theory*. His current research interests include Tocqueville's theory of freedom, assessing the asserted trade-off between economic growth and equality, and relations between the state and the market in the United States from colonial times to the present.

Lawrence A. Scaff is Professor of Political Science and Head of Department at Pennsylvania State University. He is the author of *Fleeing the Iron Cage: Culture, Politics and Modernity in the Thought of Max Weber* (1989) and he has written extensively on topics in modern social theory and German social thought including 'Weber before Weberian Sociology', *British Journal of Sociology* (1984), 'Life contra Ratio: Music and Social Theory', *Sociological Theory* (1993) and 'Social Theory, Rationalism and the Architecture of the City: Fin-de-Siècle Thematics', *Theory, Culture and Society* (1995).

Alan Sica is Professor of Sociology and Director of the Graduate Program in Social Thought at Pennsylvania State University. Until recently he was editor of *Sociological Theory*, the theoretical journal of the American Sociological Association. His publications include 'Hermeneutics and Social Theory: The Contemporary Conversation', *Current Perspectives in Social Theory* (1981), *Weber, Irrationality, and Social Order* (1988), 'Gabel's "Micro/Macro" Bridge: the Schizophrenic Process Writ Large', *Sociological Theory* (1995), and *Weberian Social Theory* (1998).

Rob Stones is Lecturer in Sociology and Director of Undergraduate Studies at the University of Essex. His publications include 'A Tale of Three Cities: Government-finance Relations in Britain 1964–67', *Economy and Society* (1990), 'Strategic Context Analysis: a New Research Strategy for Structuration Theory', *Sociology* (1991), (with Bob Jessop) 'Old City and New Times: Economic and Political Aspects of De-regulation' in L. Budd and S. Whimster (eds) *Global Finance and Urban Living: the Case of London* (1992), *Sociological Reasoning: Towards a Past-modern Sociology* (1996) and 'Social Theory: Beyond "Blind Date" with "The Felt and Plastic Bird Kit"', in M. Haralambos (ed.) *Developments in Sociology: An Annual Review*, vol. 14 (1998).

Loïc Wacquant is Associate Professor of Sociology at the University of California, Berkeley. He has written widely on the sociological writings of Pierre Bourdieu, on ethnographic and qualitative methods, and on the inner-city 'ghetto'. Writings include (with Pierre Bourdieu) *An Invitation to Reflexive Sociology* (1992), 'On the Tracks of Symbolic Power: Prefatory Notes to Bourdieu's "State Nobility"', *Theory, Culture and Society* (1993), 'The New Urban Color Line: The State and Fate of the Ghetto in PostFordist America' in C. Calhoun (ed.) *Social Theory and the Politics of Identity* (1994), 'Durkheim et

Bourdieu: le socle commun et ses fissures', _Critique_ (1995) and 'The Pugilistic Point of View: How Boxers Think and Feel about their Trade', _Theory and Society_ (1995).

Patrick Watier is Professor of Sociology at the University of Strasbourg and Director of the Institute of the Sociology of European Culture, CNRS, Strasbourg. His publications include _G. Simmel, la sociologie et l'expérience du monde moderne_ (1986), 'The war writings of Georg Simmel', _Theory, Culture and Society_ (1991), _La sociologie et les représentations de l'activité sociale_ (1996), _Une introduction à la sociologie compréhensive_ (1998) and _G. Simmel et les Sciences Humaines_ O. Rammstedt and P. Watier [dir] (1992).

Robin Williams is a Senior Lecturer in Sociology at the University of Durham. His interests are in the sociology of interaction and the history of sociological theory and research methods. He is the author of a number of publications on the sociology of Erving Goffman, on the interpretative tradition in sociology and in social constructionism. These include 'Goffman's Sociology of Talk', in _The View from Goffman_ (Ditton, ed., 1980) and 'Understanding Goffman's Methods' in _Erving Goffman, Exploring the Interaction Order_ (Drew and Wooton, eds, 1988). He is currently completing a book on the concept of identity to be published by Polity Press in 1998.

Simon J. Williams is a Warwick Research Fellow in the Department of Sociology at the University of Warwick, and co-director of the Centre for Research in Health, Medicine and Society, University of Warwick. With Gillian Bendelow he has written 'Emotions and Health: The "Missing Link" in Medical Sociology' in (James and Gabe, ed., 1996) _Health and the Sociology of Emotions_, 'Emotions and "Sociological Imperialism": A Rejoinder to Craib', _Sociology_ (1996) and has edited _Emotions in Social Life: Critical Themes and Contemporary Issues_ (1998). His current projects include a forthcoming book on _Emotions and Social Theory_ (Sage).

Introduction: Society as More Than a Collection of Free-floating Individuals

Rob Stones

The Sociological World-view

Thinking Like Grown-ups Should Think

I once read that the celebrated radical historian E.P. Thompson, author of *The Making of the English Working Class* (that outstanding, innovatory, testament to the lives of people who had been silenced by traditional history) had wondered why it was that the level of sophistication and attention demanded by *Gardeners' Question Time* on British radio was so far above that required by the politics and current affairs programme *Any Questions*. The latter, he thought, would be an insult to children, the former could stretch adults as they should be stretched. People were equipped to take responsibility for their gardens but not for the societies in which they – and their gardens – existed. If E.P. Thompson was right, and I think he was, then it cannot be because of a lack of raw intelligence on the part of the people that appear on the panel of *Any Questions*, for many of them are clearly bright and articulate, they clearly 'know their stuff'. But could it, we may ask, have something to do with the 'kind of stuff they know'? For, quite simply, most of us think about society and social life without having had any schooling in how to think about society and social life. Indeed, the dominant culture seems to hold dear the belief that we do not require any schooling. We are part of social life – so this belief runs – and so we must quite obviously possess all the understanding required. Intimately connected to this attitude is a positive resistance to any suggestion that sociologists – 'experts' in looking at society – may have something to teach ordinary people. Against this view, every single chapter in this book is premised on the view that we all do have something to learn from a range of sociological thinkers who have taken the time and made the (disciplined, patient, dogged, generous) effort to think long and hard about a whole variety of significant aspects of society that most of us will have barely sensed let alone spent as much time and energy

1

considering. We are complex beings and the social life that we, and past generations, have collectively constructed is complex too. Given this complexity, it should come as no surprise to anyone but the blinkered or the philistine that its workings are not transparent. Without a specialist socio-logical training we – and our alter egos on *Any Questions* – typically approach social issues in terms of one of a number of impoverished, and often rather childlike, variants of moral outrage and Utopian wish fulfilment. One of the more popular variants is to think in terms of individual heroines and heroes, villains and villainesses, without any sense of how one should place their actions within the social pressures, constraints and possibilities of their social context. In such scenarios, much-lauded heroes often become villains overnight because they fail to accomplish a task that a sociologically informed assessment would have easily revealed to be impossible to accom-plish. The hero could be shown not to be a villain because, quite simply, he did not have the power to do the thing that he is being upbraided for not doing. Conversely, a real heroine might fail to be recognised as a heroine because the social constraints and obstacles that she overcame to do what she did were not even remotely appreciated by a culture unable to think in these terms. In other words, the 'stuff' that our asociological culture knows is only a little bit of the stuff we need to know in order to think responsibly and maturely about society. And it is not only that we need to 'know more stuff', it is that we need to know how to order 'the stuff we know' in a systematic and rigorous manner. In other words we need theory, and so we need thinkers. We need theories about society, ways of thinking about society. We need sociological thinkers.

Sociological thinkers have long told us that society is more than a collec-tion of individuals. That is, while individuals and groups are clearly part of what society is, there is much more to society than this. To just scrape the surface, there are, first, socially structured interactions between individuals in which social actors make creative (while constrained and structured) adjust-ments to social situations (cf. **Simmel**, Chapter 4; **Blumer**, Chapter 6; **Goffman**, Chapter 11) that have been constituted in large part before they have arrived on the scene (cf. **Durkheim**, Chapter 3; **de Beauvoir**, Chapter 9; **Bourdieu**, Chapter 16). Second, there are those socially structured ways in which social actors cannot make the impact on society that they want to make because *either* they do not fully understand how they could have that impact, *or* because they simply do not have the power to do so when faced with the intractable weight of the society-building of previous generations – the dead weight of crystallised social structure (cf. **Marx**, Chapter 1; **Merton**, Chapter 8; **Giddens**, Chapter 21). There is a lot to understand about the workings of society that is as much about the social situations in which individuals find themselves as it is about their immediate interactions (let alone about them as individuals).

These social situations provide the terrain that constitutes the pressures, constraints and opportunities mentioned above. And, in terms of social responsibility, we cannot think very deeply about what we should do about social issues without also thinking about what it is possible to do. We will never be able to think responsibly about society and social action, social policies, political decisions until we understand how inadequate it is to think in terms of the will-power and ideals of supposedly 'free' individuals – of a free-floating world of heroines and villains. We are always free to a degree, but the extent to which we are free is a moot point. Society itself moulds, structures and constrains individuals. This is ignored in the dominant way of thinking about social responsibility, certainly in the USA and in Britain, as we reach the beginning of a new millennium, the way of thinking that we can call 'spontaneous individualism' – the unstated belief (and such an absurd belief relies for its continued efficacy on not being stated out loud) that social life is produced by nothing but the will of unique free-floating individuals who have spontaneously developed all their own skills, culture, education, language, understanding and social life chances. They have done this, somehow, without reference to the particular social circumstances that they were born into – to the particular parents (employed or unemployed? working class or professional? literate or illiterate? with social connections or without?), part of town (inner-city no-go area or plush and leafy suburban?), part of the world (the fuel-consuming 'developed' North, the boom-slump-boom world of the Asian Tigers and Dragons, or the poor South?) they were born to be a part of. 'Spontaneous individualism' ignores all these things – because it does not know how to consider them – just as it ignores the particular socialisation that individuals acquire in terms of education, gender, ethnicity, class and geographical region. Just as it ignores, also, the particular cultural images, stories and messages of television, films, politics, magazines, newspapers, comics and advertisements that are dominant in particular cultures and sub-cultures. I could go on. The free-floating (spontaneous) individuals of this untutored way of thinking would be, if they existed, if we ever met them, unrecognisable as human beings. Humans are social beings and they, their opportunities and their life chances, even their deepest aspirations and unconscious attachments, frustrations and longings, are shot through and through with the marks and traces of social structuring, social influencing and social content.

The onus is on us to work hard to be able to move beyond the misleading cultural common sense that imagines the social world to be made up of free-floating heroes and villains. In order to take any sort of responsibility for our lives and for the lives of those whose fates are inextricably linked with our own, then our thinking about society must rise above the level of *The Oprah Winfrey Show*, *Kilroy* or any other talk show based on entertainment and the quick fix of righteous but badly informed – sociologically anaemic – opinion. In fact, as the memory of E.P. Thompson reminds us, there is no need to start so low. What about news and documentary? What about serious news interviews or question and answer programmes? If we are reduced to sound bites and simplistic rhetoric then we are lost. But if we get something more than this, something better, then how do we know that we are getting something better? How do we judge the adequacy of the knowledge we receive, the quality of the thinking about society that we are offered by politicians and society's salaried administrators? We need, to repeat, to be able to judge how much of the stuff we need to know is included in the stuff they are offering to us. And to work this out we need the intellectual resources to order that knowledge, that information (those floating facts and figures) in a rigorous and systematic fashion. The key sociological thinkers covered in this book have spent their lives – or did spend their lives – producing the intellectual resources that we require in order to enable us to make such judgements. Their commitment has produced a quality of thinking about society that should also provide a benchmark as to the quality of thinking that we too should aspire to.

The asociological nature of the dominant culture means that there are more than a few central themes or considerations of sociological thought – all covered in this book – that may, on first acquaintance, seem strange and forbidding. Here are some of these considerations:

a. of the ways in which society helps to create individuals;
b. of the way in which social events are structured by a series of conditions and trends that mesh together for moments, years or centuries;
c. of the complicated nature of intended and unintended consequences of actions that structure the social conditions for the next round of social actions;
d. of the nature of social constraints and opportunities;
e. of the relation between small and local 'micro' events in society and large, national or global 'macro' events in society; the ways in which seemingly 'micro' events can, in fact, turn out to be 'macro' events because everybody – or nearly everybody – in a society tends to do the same 'local' thing (like shaking hands to greet rather than, for example, bowing in the two-handed prayer-like greeting used by the Thais, known as a *wai*; or like paying their salary cheques into the bank at the end of the month; like being sexist or racist in similar ways; like putting a cross next to a name on a ballot paper in many different booths right across a geographical space) in many local places, and many local places make a country, a nation, a society;
f. of the relation between the systemic 'parts' of society and the 'people' in society.

The very fact that these considerations so often seem strange and forbidding is a testament to our inability to think in more than very superficial ways about society. It would be all too easy to dismiss these themes as the vehicles of so much unnecessary jargon, so much mystification of the essentially simple processes of society. But this would be a grave mistake. A retreat into common-sense superficiality may make us feel better in the short term, reassure us, cheaply, that we know as much as the experts about the social life we inhabit, but it is a false comfort. There is a large price to pay for anti-intellectualism, for social philistinism. The great sociological themes all speak to important dimensions of society that we do not routinely speak about, that we do not have an everyday language for. Those themes listed above, and others, will appear and reappear throughout the book, approached in remarkably different ways by different key thinkers. We will have come a long way if ever these themes, and the language in which they are expressed by the key thinkers, make their way into everyday thinking about society, into everyday language.

Each key thinker gives the social world his or her own distinctive perspective, shining a torch on parts of that world and leaving other parts in the dark, leaving them ready for the arrival of another theorist holding her torch at a slightly different angle. Each of them colours the social world with the sort of quirky and obsessional brilliance that is necessary in order to illuminate aspects of our social world that would otherwise go by unnoticed. They are the chemists and physicists of the social world, perceiving and describing social elements, forces, particles and compounds, explaining reactions, behaviours and mechanisms, mapping the statics of social orders and disorders that need a creative, technical, specialist eye to fathom.

Clarity, Accessibility and a Spirit of Openness

The aim of *Key Sociological Thinkers* is to introduce readers to these riches of sociological thought by providing a clear, accessible and manageable overview of many of the major developments in the area from Marx onwards, and to do so in a manner that will create a thirst to read and study more sociology and to be able to make connections between its lessons and everyday lives. The relative brevity of the individual chapters is designed to make it easier for readers new to the field, or new to particular thinkers, to stay the course, while also allowing them to develop a clear idea of the particular significance of a given key theorist. While the chapters have been kept short enough to be accessible to the sociological beginner, readers are nevertheless also encouraged to dig further and a reading list is provided at the end of each chapter in order to facilitate this. The common format for the chapters that contributors were asked to follow, as far as they felt was appropriate, was structured with an eye more on capturing the imagination of readers rather than on any attempt at an exhaustive coverage of topics. It was felt that if the former is achieved then a broader and more protracted engagement with a range of related topics will naturally follow as far as individual readers are concerned. It was also hoped that dispensing with any injunction to be exhaustive would enable contributors to have more fun while writing the individual chapters.

All of the chapters have been specially commissioned for this volume from writers with a close knowledge of their subject. The striking quality of the contributions can perhaps be best conveyed by simply noting that the majority of these contributors – all those of 'a certain age', if they will forgive me – are themselves routinely counted as among the most innovative sociological theorists of their generation. The list of contributors also bears the mark of a conscious editorial decision to approach only those writers who had an enthusiasm for their key thinker in the hope that this would be conveyed to the reader and, conversely, that one would avoid the almost inevitable problem of single-authored textbooks in which the author is at best lukewarm and at worst downright dismissive towards thinkers with whom he or she differs. A closely related syndrome in textbooks is the one that induces a feeling of 'why bother?' in students when they are introduced to a thinker only to have any initial excitement at new insights undermined by an immediate hard and fast critique that seems to dispense with that 'so-called thinker' once and for all. An interminable succession of new bodies of thought is strangled at birth by an equally interminable array of murderous critiques. My own belief is that it is much better to run along with the excitement of the new perspective as far as is possible and for as long as is possible until one begins to sense *for oneself* the obstacles and limitations that it cannot overcome, at least by itself. Then is a good time to read the critiques. Then is a good time to see if they can tell you something about your own growing problems with this thinker. The critics, at this stage, no longer seem so murderous; the best ones seem to be like you, to be fellow travellers who have arrived at the borders of this particular landscape. They, like you, want to see more, to discover more, and they try to work out why they feel like this, what it is about the familiar landscape that means it cannot fulfil their needs.

But this is to get ahead of ourselves. This is not the fare to be served up in the first few days in a new land. *Key Sociological Thinkers* is, first, about new days in new lands. Indeed, it aims to provide a succession of new days in many new lands. Second, however, the book also attempts to convey a spirit of openness within the sociological enterprise whereby one does not necessarily always have to make a choice between these different lands, these different theories. Rather, most of these theories have developed out of a spectrum of concerns with a rich and varied range of quite disparate questions and problematics. One can very often find interesting and fruitful overlaps but very rarely an identical focus. The different theorists have tended to select different parts of social reality to ask questions about. It follows that if two thinkers are attempting to provide answers to different questions then there is no need to rubbish one in order to laud the other. Starting from this premise the various chapters of the book can be seen as introducing major contributions to a gradual deepening and widening of the sociological world-view. This sense of openness and mutual exploration can exist quite easily with an acknowledgement that sometimes overlapping theories do clash and that their points of conflict do constitute an essential site for argument and debate in the reformulation of ideas.

A Canon?

A Rich Resource for Later Generations

The question of whether a discipline such as sociology should have a discernible and recognisable canon of works or thinkers that in some sense provide a core to that discipline is a vexed one. It would be disingenuous of me, not to say somewhat self-defeating, to pretend that I did not think that the key thinkers represented in this book are all in their very different ways important and central to the development of sociology. They provide a rich resource for later generations to draw upon, and they provide sociologists with common reference points in relation to which they can discuss ways of approaching new problems. Their existence means that one does not always have to start entirely from scratch. Figures 1 and 2 below give a selective, and rough and ready, indication of the continuing influence of the first wave of classic sociological thinkers (those included in Part I of this volume) on the second and third wave of thinkers (those included in Parts II and III of this volume). They show that sociological thinkers, no less than anyone else, are dependent on influences from elsewhere – they are not spontaneous individualists, geniuses who somehow spin their new theories out of thin air. Sociological thinkers, like other people, are structured and moulded by many influences in many areas of their life, but in that area of their life in which they think and write sociologically they are usually intensely and intensively indebted to sociologists who have come before them. If they had really to start from scratch – from thin air – then our ability to understand society would be impoverished indeed.

The work of Karl Marx, for example, continues to have a profound influence on many of today's key theorists. His theories of the role of the capitalist system in forging the shape of contemporary societies and the lives that are led within them is as powerful a point of reference as his parallel emphasis on the role of social and economic class as a structuring force on the shape of society and the consciousness of individuals. Figure 1 indicates various ways (a, b, and c) in which Marx's theories have been influential for later theorists covered in this volume. Marx's theories have acted as a starting point for:

a. Marxist theorists who have wanted to build upon and improve his theories (and to correct what they saw as misunderstandings about what Marx had been saying all along).

b. Non-Marxist theorists who have found his work insightful but needing to be synthesised with other theories and built upon in a way that is not distinctively Marxist.
c. Others who see themselves as building upon Marx in a way that maintains the radical spirit of social critique that inspired Marx, and as certainly wanting to acknowledge their debt to that tradition, but as having gone beyond Marxism. These writers sometimes refer to themselves as 'Post-Marxist'.

		a. **Louis Althusser** (Chapter 14)
		a. **Jürgen Habermas** (Chapter 15)
KARL MARX (Chapter 1)	➡	b. **David Lockwood** (Chapter 12)
		b. **Anthony Giddens** (Chapter 21)
		c. **Stuart Hall** (Chapter 20)

Figure 1

To reinforce this point about the influence of the first wave of classics we can note that the work of Emile Durkheim also continues to have a significant bearing on some of today's most influential theorists (see Figure 2). **David Lockwood's** work has not only been moulded by his concern with the role of the capitalist system and class conflict in social disorder but also, through Durkheim, by a preoccupation with the role of social solidarity and collective rituals in the sustaining of social order. The influence of Durkheim on the work of Pierre Bourdieu, **Michel Foucault** and **Stuart Hall,** respectively, has been mediated by Durkheim's influence on the intellectual development of structuralism, and then post-structuralism. The key figure in the 'take-off' of structuralism was the Swiss linguist, Ferdinand de Saussure (1857–1913). Saussure's notion of language – the language we use in everyday life – as a thing in itself, as having its own autonomous level of reality, to be studied as a system – contains much more than an echo of Durkheim's insistence that society was a thing in itself, that society has a *sui generis* reality (a reality that is specifically social; society has a reality of its own) that is not reducible to the individuals that inhabit it, or to the interactions between these individuals. Society, for Durkheim, had its own level of reality and society as a thing to be studied could therefore be distinguished quite clearly from psychology (which dealt with what went on in the minds of individuals) and from biology.

Foucault and Hall are both prepared to give language a great deal of autonomy (although never a total autonomy) as a moving social force in its own right, with practices of representation (or 'signification', in structuralist language) being able to mould the way that race, gender, class, politics, sexuality, punishment, madness, and so on and so on, are perceived within society. Perceptions, in turn, mould social practices and both Foucault and Hall, in their different ways, attempt to look at how language combines with other aspects of social life within embodied practices. Bourdieu is also concerned with language and the symbolic as an autonomous realm but – and here the fact that Bourdieu's work has spanned the divide between sociology and anthropology is probably telling – he is much more concerned with the social constraints created by the tensions between, on the one hand, these structuring languages or discourses that are embodied in people who have been socialised into particular social milieux (for example, the way they speak or dress), and, on the other hand, alien social milieux – of culture, class, status, economy or ethnicity – that are less hospitable to these inherited languages, skills and ways of doing things. The main influence of Durkheim on the work of Giddens is, quite straightforwardly, in the latter's insistence that the structure of society has a reality all of its own that provides the conditions, opportunities and the constraints for social actors when they act. Both Bourdieu and Giddens draw from a range of other sources besides Durkheim, but without the legacy he bequeathed to structuralism their theories would be unrecognisable.

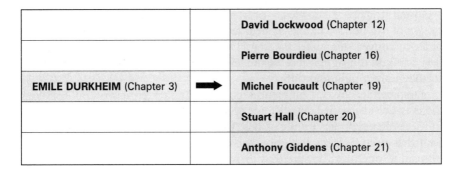

		David Lockwood (Chapter 12)
		Pierre Bourdieu (Chapter 16)
EMILE DURKHEIM (Chapter 3)	→	Michel Foucault (Chapter 19)
		Stuart Hall (Chapter 20)
		Anthony Giddens (Chapter 21)

Figure 2

An Expansive, Self-critical and Flexible Canon

It is always useful to have previous attempts, successes and failures to learn from. Some of the older 'classics' (for example Marx, **Weber** [Chapter 2], Durkheim), although still extremely powerful in their ability to offer insights into many contemporary phenomena, will be more relevant to some questions than to others – this much is fairly obvious. Some new problems – at least 'new' in the sense that the general recognition of them as areas of interest is new – are just too new, too novel, for many of the 'older' traditions to have much to offer (for example, to de Beauvoir and feminism, Hall and post-colonialism, **Hochschild** on the sociology of emotions, Giddens on – at least some of the 'novel' aspects of – late modernity). Here an *intellectual space* opens up for new classics, new traditions, to take hold and begin to explore those questions. While it is important to be very aware of how often this intellectual space is denied any *institutional space* within academia, and that this is often not unrelated to the vested interests – academic and non-academic – of those trained in and wedded to the existing canon, it is also important to recognise that this does not necessarily add up to an all or nothing choice between the old and the new, or to a choice *between* an old traditional canon *and* a rejection of all canons of any hue or colour. This is not the only choice. One can have a canon without it being cast in stone (or metal!). Canons can be useful for the reasons already mentioned, but their value will be all the greater if they are treated expansively, self-critically, and with flexibility. Also, just as the older classics will always be open to new critiques and developments so the neophyte traditions of responses to new issues will soon also be open to critiques and developments and will through time, all things being equal, increase their level of sophistication and deepen and broaden the extent of their coverage. It follows from this that not only should one be prepared to give a certain degree of latitude – a benefit of the doubt – to the newer traditions in the early stages of development, but also that, in order to do this, one should distinguish clearly between, on the one hand, a new area of study and the importance of exploring it, gaining knowledge of it, and, on the other hand, the issue of the *quality* of the understanding gained, and the quality of the work produced in order to convey this understanding. That is, one should make a clear distinction between the significance of the area of study itself and the quality of the sociological thought about this area.

Despite the obvious differences between literary criticism and sociology there is an instructive parallel to be drawn here with controversy in the former. Whatever one thinks of the American Nobel Prize winning novelist Saul Bellow's much quoted quip that 'when a Zulu writes a great novel then I'll read it' one must be sure that there is a difference between reading litera-ture for its quality as literature and reading it in order to increase our know-ledge about a particular subject matter (for example the Zulu way of life in a particular era). Let us suppose that our main desire is to increase the breadth of our knowledge. In this case, 'if' there are no *great* novels written by a Zulu about the Zulu way of life then one might still want to read the novels that Zulus or non-Zulus *have* written about the Zulu way of life but which are not great. This would seem to be the best on offer and is a way of increasing one's knowledge of a neglected area. Likewise, 'if' there are no 'classic' quality sociological works on the body or emotions or time and space or post-colonialism then perhaps we will want to read and teach sub-classic or 'yet to be judged as' classic texts on these subjects in order to begin to establish the institutional space and intellectual traditions within which future 'classic' texts can be written. The work of key theorists such as de Beauvoir, Hochschild (Chapter 18) and Hall, for example, could only have made their marks within a flexible and expansive enough intellectual environment. Without this intellectual space the rigidities of institutional traditions would not even have been noticed, let alone assailed. The logic of this argument entails the imaginative setting of new questions, the definition of key terms, the development of new typologies, the consideration of the range of social influences involved, the comparison of seemingly similar processes in different cultures and historical eras, and so on. But, equally, the logic in no way implies any disregard for the rigours of systematic thought, and for the attempt to forge standards of intellectual excellence in a particular sphere in order that the problems at hand can be addressed in the best of all available ways. Alongside *the imaginative moment* would be *the moment of discipline*. There is no reason why the widening of the canon to take in new issues should not entail an expansion in the range of both imagination and discipline.

The Sociological Canon and the Strengths of Inter-disciplinarity

One can approach theoretical perspectives on the basis of 'great or 'key' individuals or on the basis of the perspective considered as a tradition or a school. Different books do different things, some choose one way, some the other.[1] They are different ways of organising the field while in many ways not being very different at all. Most theoretical perspectives are associated with key figures, founders. However, while it is true that theoretical perspectives often come to be associated very quickly with particular individuals, and in the early days of their life it is very hard to shift the popular sense of that perspective into a more collective enterprise (structuration theory and its ready association with Anthony Giddens is a good example here, and an even better one – because older in years – is **Parsonian** [Chapter 7] sociology) it is also true to say that eventually most 'successful' perspectives, those that take hold and become established, make a gradual transition from person to school. The person is not erased but the relative weight of her or his individual contribution to the whole body of significant literature within that perspective is seen to be a steadily diminishing one. Occasionally – and perhaps this will become the norm rather than the exception as the broadening and deepening of sociological thought continue – it is quite difficult to identify one particular thinker as the primary founder of a tradition without doing a great injustice to what was essentially a collective enterprise.

Feminism, for example, has had a much greater sense of collectivity about it, with a legion of significant figures – often in disciplines other than sociology – and a fair degree of debate about the most significant. Perhaps this dual sense of collectivity and dispersion is partly because feminism from

its first appearances in academia has cut across traditional disciplinary boundaries, and has thus made its mark slowly but surely in so many domains, in a
way that, say, the Weberian or Durkheimian traditions cannot be said to have
done to anywhere near the same extent, notwithstanding the significance of
the former in some branches of political science and of them both in anthropology. The particular genealogy of feminism in this respect is partly reflected
in the choice of feminist thinkers for this volume in that Simone de Beauvoir
is usually associated first and foremost with philosophy and literature, even
though her impact on feminist thinking within sociology, not least through
her innovative and wide-ranging volume *The Second Sex,* has been enormous.
Likewise, **Nancy Chodorow** (Chapter 17), in writing books such as *The
Reproduction of Mothering: Psychoanalysis and the Sociology of Gender* and *Feminism and Psychoanalytic Theory* is thinking about a domain that cuts plainly
across the margins that divide the formal disciplines of psychoanalysis and
sociology. And Arlie Hochschild's work on the sociology of emotions has
drawn on a range of sources that cross interdisciplinary boundaries (see
Figure 3), with, in some cases, the influence of a discipline being carried by a
significant individual figure and, in other cases, a range of thinkers from a
discipline all contributing a little to what cumulatively amounts to a significant influence from that disciplinary world-view.

Stuart Hall's work in cultural studies and colonialism has, likewise, drawn
upon cross-disciplinary influences – literature, film, philosophy, sociology,
politics and linguistics – so that it is very difficult to pigeon-hole his work in
any of the established disciplines, including sociology. His work certainly has
sociological dimensions, and is important for sociology, but it cuts across
sociology just as it also cuts across other domains of knowledge. As Michèle
Barrett points out in her chapter on Hall, cultural studies has now become
another discipline in its own right. Certainly some universities, even as I
write, are currently rethinking their whole approach to traditional humanities
and social science demarcations in the light of recent developments in cultural
studies. Some of the major influences on Hall's work are represented in
Figure 4. What strikes one about this list of influences is that not only has
Hall found it necessary to draw upon a series of cross-cutting sources in order
to properly focus upon the things he believes are significant in contemporary
life, but that a number of those writers he has drawn upon had themselves
already felt it necessary to do the same.

Sociology needs to understand both that it cannot, and should not want
to, create a discipline that is sealed off hermetically from the influence of
other disciplines. Sociology is, and always has been, shot through with
'outside' influences. On the other hand, it is well to remember what
sociology (however constituted) is particularly and uniquely well equipped to
do. We should remember the power that emanates from sociology's specific
focus on society and social life as such, and, within this focus, from its ability
to see society as more than a collection of individuals. We can see this easily

Various: **Heidi Hartmann, Dorothy Smith Nancy Chodorow** (Feminism)		
C. Wright Mills (Sociology)		
Erving Goffman (Sociology)		
Sigmund Freud (Psychology – primary sociology – secondary)	➡	**ARLIE HOCHSCHILD** Sociology of emotions
Charles Darwin (Biology)		
Various: **Ruth Benedict, Mary Douglas, Hildred Geertz** (Anthropology)		
John Dewey (Philosophy)		

Figure 3

Antonio Gramsci (Marxist philosophy and politics)		
Ferdinand de Saussure (Linguistics)		
Michel Foucault (Philosophy, history of ideas, sociology)	➡	**STUART HALL:** Cultural studies and the sociology of culture
Jacques Derrida (Philosophy, post-structuralism, literature)		
Jacques Lacan (Psychoanalysis)		
Judith Butler (Feminism, gay and lesbian studies, psychoanalysis, post-structuralism, philosophy)		

Figure 4

by means of a brief comparison with cultural studies itself. One of the major recent developments in cultural studies (one in which Hall – see Chapter 20 – was a leading force) has involved an attempt to move out from studies that focused on just the meanings contained within the text (whether this text was a film, a television programme, an advertisement, a speech or the written word) to an interest also in the production of the text and the audience's understanding and interpretation of that text. Indeed, one of Hall's major innovations was to argue for the linking together of these 'moments' of production, text and audience reception into one 'circuit'. Marxists and others involved in the sociology of art and literature had, for a long time, been interested in the production of texts and images and, as Barrett notes (Chapter 20) their analyses had been fairly crude, reducing works of art and culture to a mere reflection or expression of historical class or sociological forces, leaving little room for individual and contextual creativity, innovation, talent and expertise within the cultural form at issue. While it is probably true that previous sociological studies tended, to a greater or lesser extent, to be inadequately sensitive to the degree of autonomy possessed by the cultural level in society, it is also true that cultural studies have found it necessary to return to sociology – to the production (to the social contexts and structured institutional practices within which films, news, radio debates, novels, advertisements and all the rest are produced) and the reception (to the social backgrounds of class, gender, ethnicity, profession or trade, region, and cultural understandings of different audiences) of texts.

Sociology, it should be obvious, is the domain *par excellence* of the *production* of social practices. Every single chapter in this volume has something to say that is relevant here. So much is clear. But it is also the case that sociology has much to offer in the domain of the *reception* of texts. In fact, it is difficult to see how a non-superficial analysis of the reception of messages could be carried out without the benefit of sociological thought. For we are dealing here with understandings *in situ,* with understandings that are not socially determined but which most definitely are socially structured. If you are a street cleaner in Cardiff's Tiger Bay you will have a different set of cultural and social preconceptions than if you are a street cleaner in downtown Los Angeles. If you are a lone mother running for senate then you will have social perceptions that diverge from those possessed by a lone mother stuck in a damp one-room flat with no hot water, unmanageable debts and no opportunities for decent employment. We are dealing here with sociology's domain, with an area in which sociology has long been very much at home. Sociology has many resources to draw upon here – beyond a Marxist reductionism of the cultural – from Max Weber's first path-breaking insights into the importance of different types of understandings in social life, through Herbert Blumer's insistence on the significance of symbols and Erving Goffman's foregrounding of the workings of the interaction order, to the documentary method of interpretation pioneered by **Harold Garfinkel** (see Chapter 13). Stuart Hall's emphasis on the whole cultural circuit points to a major role for sociology, it moves beyond the reductionism of the previous dominant sociological approaches to the cultural realm, and it draws on the Marxist tradition – in the shape of the work of Antonio Gramsci (see also Chapter 14, for Gramsci's influence on **Althusser**) – in a way which is not reductionist. It would be fascinating to see a synthesis of Hall's work with the wider sociological tradition, including those thinkers just cited, that cultural studies has not yet drawn upon.

What to Expect from the Chapters – and a Choice of Places to Start

The twenty-one individual chapters on the key sociological thinkers have been divided into three broad sections (see Contents, p. vii) for the purpose of providing a rough sense of chronology and in order to allow the reader some markers in order to give an initial sense of orientation. The ordering is a rough and ready attempt to combine the bare facts of the years when the key theorist was writing, or still is writing, with a sense of the timing of their most significant impact on sociological thought.

Outline of the Common Format for the Individual Chapters

Contributors were asked to follow the common format outlined below as far as this was possible and where it was not possible (or desirable) to follow it to the letter then to adhere to its spirit. In most cases contributors were happy to follow this format very closely.

Section 1. Driving Impulses

What were the driving impulses and influences – both intellectual influences and those of social milieu (society, politics, culture) – that motivated the thinker to spend so much time and energy attempting to come to terms with a given particular range of issues? Where did the simmering passion come from, the obsessive inquisitiveness necessary to fuel the discipline of thought and writing over decades? This section is not a generalised review of the intellectual and social climate within which the theorist was writing but, rather, a more specifically focused placing of the intellectual and social influences on those particular preoccupations of the theorist that are singled out for elaboration in the next section.

Section 2. Key Issues

Four or five issues which were central to the work of this theorist. These are philosophical, methodological or substantive. There is usually a mixture of these with the majority being substantive. The restriction to five is obviously arbitrary but has the advantage of deflecting the emphasis away from an exhaustive coverage of topics and towards providing a manageable nucleus of information designed to be more inspiring than daunting.

Section 3. Seeing Things Differently

Authors provide a graphic sense of how the ideas of this key thinker have illuminated their own view of society by providing a substantive example/illustration taken from either the wider sociological literature (that is, not an example from this thinker's own work, as this could come in Section 2), or from another source such as a novel, a movie, a documentary or everyday life.

Section 4. Legacies and Unfinished Business

This section addresses such questions as: what are the major intellectual and social legacies of this thinker? Which later thinkers/schools of thought has he or she influenced? Which parts of the intellectual legacy are still being investigated, still bearing fruit, or have still to be fully investigated? Are there paths started along by this thinker which should have been explored further but have been neglected thus far? Are there themes which have been critiqued, reworked and reformulated by later thinkers in such a way that they shed more light on the problematic that motivated this thinker? Which later thinkers have taken up themes and issues explored by this theorist and have carried them further?

Section 5. Further Reading

A short reading list of, for example, three books and three journal articles through which the reader could take his or her interest further.

Variations on the Guidelines

A small number of the contributors felt that they could best treat their thinker by departing somewhat from the letter of the guidelines, while remaining faithful to the spirit of their objectives. Thus, for example, the Key Issues section in Mary Evans's chapter on Simone de Beauvoir follows the guidelines in outlining a number of key themes but it does not approach them serially, one by one, as other contributors have done. Rather, these themes are woven into a discussion which is organised around some other topics, the key themes are more or less relevant to each topic, they criss-cross each other, sometimes coming together and at other times appearing separately and independently. The themes are seen to be enduring preoccupations, their presence never far from the topic of de Beauvoir's current concern. As the sub-headings of this Key Issues section relate to the topics rather than the key issues themselves, I have included a summary listing the four key issues at the start of this section for easy reference.

Likewise, Alan Sica's elegantly written chapter on Robert K. Merton departs quite substantially from the general format. Sica finds his own compelling way to convey his enthusiasm and respect for his subject, a way that politely eschews the path of elaboration and exemplification of key concepts and, instead, lures the reader deeper into the Merton universe (on the fringes of which, Sica tells us, many of us have already been for many years, albeit unwittingly) by dangling delicious promises of what we will find there. He directs us, for example, to books or articles of Merton's that analyse the American society of the 1930s and 1940s and asks us to compare what we find there with what we see around us today. He invokes comparisons of Merton with magicians and jugglers, speaks of the regal elegance of his 'many fertile expressions', and sums him up with the word 'quality', his most enduring characteristic being his 'sheer intelligence and energetic application, over 60 years, of mindfulness to the disentangling of social phenomena'. He succeeds in making us want to 'read further'.

The Contents Pages: A User-friendly Guide to Sections and a Choice of Places to Start

In addition to the standard contents page giving the names of the key thinkers and the authors of the individual chapters, there are also separate, more extended, contents pages at the beginning of Parts I, II and III respectively. These include a list of all the headings and sub-headings within each chapter in order that readers can see at a glance the issues that are covered. It is also hoped that these headings can act as a useful *aide-mémoire* to readers who, at a later date, wish to refresh their memories as to the contents of a particular chapter. The alternative contents list, organised around the 'Seeing Things Differently' sections, provides the reader with another point of entry into chapters, one that will immediately give an impression of how the more abstract and conceptual thinking of that key thinker can be applied to real-world situations, informing and illuminating the way in which these are apprehended. It is hoped that this avenue into the chapters may prove tempting to readers who might otherwise miss out on thinkers who could well turn out to have a lot to say to them. Finally, roughly half the chapters contain one or two glossary boxes which, with the agreement of the contributors, I have introduced in order to clarify central concepts that may be unfamiliar or difficult for readers new to a field to understand. These boxes are highlighted clearly in the text and they are indicated in bold type in the index at the back of the book.

PART I

1

Karl Marx

Bob Jessop

Driving Impulses

It is odd to begin a book on key sociological thinkers with Karl Marx. He had two career ambitions as a student: journalism or university teaching. After disruptions due to censorship, suppression, and political activism, he did eventually eke a living from extensive economic and political reporting. He never secured an academic post. Even had he succeeded, he would not have practised sociology. For he dismissed this discipline as 'rubbish' on reading its founding father, Auguste Comte; and its real intellectual 'take-off' occurred much later in the nineteenth century.[1] Moreover, contrary to what one might infer from the history of Marxism after his death, Marx had little political or theo-retical influence in his own lifetime. The *Communist Manifesto*, intended as a popular account of scientific socialism, had little impact when published. His collaborator, Engels, was better known than Marx in the 1840s and 1850s – especially for his damning account of the condition of the English working class; and, even after *Capital* was published, it was Engels's popularizing works on historical materialism that stimulated study and debate in international socialism. In short, for a leading sociologist, Marx seems to have been both an apostate and a resounding failure.

Yet Marx is often heralded as a founder of sociology and his studies (or influential, if often distorted, accounts of them) have been the main foil against which much in sociological theory and sociological research has subsequently been developed. **Max Weber** and **Emile Durkheim** often debated with Marx's ghost in developing their own sociological approaches – offering bourgeois analyses to counter those of the communist thinker. And, although Marxism has frequently been declared moribund, it has equally often been revived and integrated into current sociological thinking. Thus Marx certainly counts as a 'key sociological thinker'.

Marx was born in 1818 in the Westphalian town of Trier, close to France. He studied humanities at Bonn University and then law and philosophy in Berlin. There he joined a Young Hegelian club devoted to literary and philosophical issues and aiming to develop the radical potential of Hegel's philosophy against the conservative cast its master had given it The initial battle ground against Right Hegelianism was the nature of religion; later, under the influence of Feuerbach, attention shifted to the differences between idealism and materialism. Marx's writings in this period mainly concerned philosophy, law, and politics and expressed radical democratic and republican opinions. Only in the mid-1840s did he begin to study political economy, develop his 'scientific socialism', and advocate communism.

This shift depended on political and theoretical factors. Disillusioned with his fellow philosophers for merely interpreting the world, instead of changing it, Marx became increasingly involved in political activities in Germany and France. He also turned from campaigning for a radical extension of democracy and social equality to place his faith in the revolutionary potential of the proletarian masses. Marx saw them as uprooted and dispossessed by industrialization and urbanization and condemned to a life of poverty, oppression, and alienation. Since they had no stake in society and were subject to all its ills, they would sooner or later combine to overthrow it. While Marx initially saw in this 'proletariat' – literally those whose only property was their children – merely the massed ranks of suffering humanity, his later research on English economists (notably Smith and Ricardo) and the English economy (then the most advanced capitalist economy) led him to see it very differently. It actually comprised a distinct class with distinct interests exploited by the dominant capitalist class in an expanding but inherently contradictory capitalist mode of production. Thus Marx came to emphasize both the world-transforming revolutionary dynamic of capitalism and its creation of an expanding, world-wide class of dispossessed waged labour which would sooner or later overthrow it.

This brief account may explain why Marxism is said to have three sources: German philosophy, French politics (especially French socialism), and English economics. But Marx's capacity to combine them to produce Marxism depended on the driving impulse of his close identification with the working class and his attempts to give it solid intellectual foundations and political direction. In developing his critique of capitalism, Marx also helped to trigger the development of sociology. The latter provided an alternative account of modern industrial societies as the basis for economic, social, and political reforms that might prevent the revolution Marx predicted and for which a growing working-class movement was mobilizing.[1]

Key Issues

The first central issue in Marx's work concerns the nature of the social world and is expressed in the philosophical dispute between idealism and materialism. The second concerns the methodological lessons he drew from his version of materialism (sometimes called 'historical materialism') and its implications for social analysis. The more substantive core of a Marxist 'sociology' can be presented in terms of three further themes: capitalism as a mode of production; class relations and class struggle; and the relative autonomy of the state in class societies.

A Materialist Social Ontology

Philosophy and the social sciences both involve a long-running debate about the relation between mind and matter. This debate is organized around two poles (idealism and materialism) but seems to have endless permutations. It is enough for now, however, to contrast Hegelian idealism and Marxian materialism.

Hegel's ideas are difficult to comprehend on first encounter but it is important to have at least a rough general sense of his position. He treated the self-consciousness of the mind as a substantive, really existing, disembodied entity and regarded individual minds as fragments of the one true mind (or Absolute Spirit). In separating spirit, ideas, values from the natural world, he could treat the latter as the result of the self-realization of the Absolute Spirit. He could also claim that 'the real is rational'. That it often appeared less than rational was counter-claimed by the Young Hegelians, who condemned poverty, misery, and political oppression. In true idealist fashion, however, they attributed these evils to the grip of unsound ideas – especially mystification and illusions produced by religion. Thus human emancipation would depend on overcoming such false consciousness.

Marx soon broke with the Young Hegelians and would later claim to have turned Hegel, whom he saw as standing on his head, rightside up. Marx started from the analysis of real human activity, arguing that consciousness is a product of that activity. Thus Marx proposed that 'it is not the consciousness of men that determines their existence, but their social existence that determines their consciousness'.[2] The essence of man's being was his social nature – man could only develop his capacities and realize his full potential in a free society. If poverty, misery, and political oppression existed, the pathological organization of society was to blame rather than aberrant ideas. Human emancipation required the material transformation of society rather than a mere change in consciousness. In this context Marx also argued that the key feature of societies was how they organized material production. He analysed this in different ways. But, in general, he understood the material world in terms of a materialist *ontology of labour*, that is, man was a social animal who produced himself and society in and through active social labour (sometimes broadly understood to include all social practices). Thus, whereas Hegel viewed the intellectual world of reason, ideas, and spirit as the ultimate determinant of history, Marx held that it was the economic world broadly understood that provided the key to understanding and transforming historical development.[2]

Ontology

A philosophical or abstract view on the sorts of entities that are in the world, that the world is made up of. Ontologies are typically very general, referring to all times and all places or, at least, to vast periods of history when the sorts of things that are in the world are held to have stayed the same. Examples are the nature of human beings, the nature of the most basic aspects of human life and human societies, the nature of structure and agency, time and space, or the human body. Ontologies can include views on the relative importance of ideas, on the one hand, and the material dimensions of social life, on the other. A materialist social ontology is thus a view of the nature of the social world that gives a lot of emphasis to material aspects. A materialist ontology of labour is thus a view of labour (that is, a view on the sort of entity that labour is) that emphasizes its relationship to the material world.

Historical Materialism

Marx developed a distinctive method for analysing this development: historical materialism. Its precise content is controversial. For some, it simply inverts Hegelian idealism by explaining all of history in terms of the discontinuous development of material production. For others, it involves applying Hegelian dialectics to the internal relations and contradictions of capitalism. The first view holds more for the young Marx and his later broad historical analyses, the second applies more to the mature Marx and his abstract critique of capitalism. In addition, Marx tried different ways of presenting historical materialism. The popular view in the *Communist Manifesto* (1848), for example, contrasts clearly with the more abstract accounts in Marx's work on capitalism. Later, Engels would dispute more extreme interpretations of historical materialism which overemphasized the determining role of technology and/or the economy more generally.

The *Manifesto* argues with forceful elegance that 'the history of all hitherto existing societies is the history of class struggle'. Class struggle is the motor of history. To understand the course of history, one must analyse the class relations that typify different historical epochs, the antagonisms and forms of class struggle embodied in such class relations, the development of class consciousness and revolutionary movements to challenge the dominant class(es), and the role of successful revolutions in developing new *modes of production* and forms of social organization.

Mode of Production

The mode of production in Marx's writings is broadly speaking the same as the economic structure or base. It includes two main elements: (1) the social relations of production; and (2) the forces of production. The social relations of production refer to the way that production is organized in a particular society, including, most importantly, the ownership of the means of production and control over the labour process (for example lord and serf/peasant; capitalist owners and proletarian propertyless workers; communist state ownership). The forces of production refer to all those material and social factors used or drawn upon by owners and/or workers for the production, distribution and circulation of goods and services. These include: instruments of production (tools, machinery, and so on); raw materials; labour power (physical strength, skills, co-operation, information) and infrastructure (roads, the information superhighway, electricity, and so on).

Economic Base, and Political and Ideological Superstructure

Marx's 1859 *Preface* (see below) suggests that there is a very close relationship between the economic base or mode of production of a society (for example capitalist) and the political and ideological aspects of that society. It is a much debated question as to how far the economic base strictly determines and moulds the politics and ideas of a society. For some Marx implies a total determination and for others he is thought to believe that the political and ideological levels have a 'relative autonomy' of their own in relation to the economic base.

An alternative account of historical development, more obviously indebted to the Hegelian dialectic, emphasized the self-destructive contradictions and 'laws of motion' of specific modes of production. Marx advanced two versions of this approach: one in the 1859 *Preface to the Contribution to the Critique of Political Economy*, the other version in *Capital*.

The *Preface* argues that society's economic organization (or its mode of production) consists in a distinctive pattern of forces and relations of production; this is the foundation (or base) on which arises a complex political and ideological superstructure and definite forms of social consciousness; initially, for each mode of production, the relations of production facilitate the development of the productive forces; they later act as a fetter on this development; this initiates an era of social revolution in which the dominant relations of production (and their legal expression in property rights) are challenged; any resulting changes in the economic basis sooner or later lead to superstructural changes. This pattern holds for all societies from primitive communism through antiquity and feudalism to contemporary capitalism – which is described as the last antagonistic mode of production. *Capital* was more concerned with the genesis and dynamic of capitalism and made fewer claims of a transhistorical nature. It refers to class struggle mainly in the context of the struggle between capital and labour within capitalism rather than over its supersession. In this sense, then, it presents a critical political economy of the capitalist system and its antagonisms rather than a popular political sociology of revolutionary class struggle. In contrast to the *Manifesto*, both texts focus on the unfolding logic of a system rather than class struggle.[3]

The Critique of Capitalism

Capital was less concerned to forecast how capitalism would be overthrown (although Marx still believed this would occur) than to consider how it had developed and how it functioned. Much of Marx's illustrative material came from England. But he forecast other countries would undergo the same experiences because capitalism had an inherent logic independent of its instantiation in specific countries. The key to understanding this logic was the 'commodity' form of social relations – a form that was most fully developed only in capitalism.

Marx analysed capitalism as a mode of production which had two key features. First, goods and services are produced as *commodities*, that is, are produced for sale with a view to monetary profit rather than for the immediate consumption of the producers. Second, the individual's *labour-power* (capacity to work) acquires the form of a commodity to be bought and sold in the labour market. Marx regarded the commodification of labour-power as the distinguishing feature of capitalism. Slaves could certainly be bought and sold; but slave-owners relied on coercion to extract surplus from their slaves and had to maintain them regardless of their output. Wage-labourers retain their personal liberty and are free, in principle, to choose for whom to work; hence capitalism involves free exchange rather than coercion. Without alternative means of subsistence, however, workers must sell their labour-power to one capitalist or another to survive. In this sense they are 'wage-slaves'.

Marx claimed that 'value added' (to use modern jargon) is entirely due to labour-power. Machines, tools, buildings, and so on, merely transfer part of their value as they are used up in production. Individual capitalists may gain above-average profits through innovation or market fluctuations. But these mechanisms simply redistribute the surplus value produced by the working class as a whole. As innovations are adopted by all producers or as supply and demand are re-equilibrated, these advantages disappear and workers' productivity and wage costs once again become crucial. In short, considering capitalism as a whole, only labour-power can add value.

Whether or not labour-power actually does so, however, depends on capital's ability to control workers in the labour process. It is not so much the hours workers spend at work but their productivity that matters. Thus the struggle between capital and labour to increase productivity (by extending the working day, intensifying effort during this time, or boosting output through cost-effective labour-saving techniques) is the fundamental basis of the economic class struggle in capitalism. Class struggle is not simply about relative shares of the capitalist cake. It is rooted in the organization of *production* itself (the labour process) and not just in *market relations* (including struggles over wages) or *distribution* (including redistribution through the state). It concerns not only the accumulation of money as capital but also the overall reproduction of capital's domination of wage-labour in the economy and the wider society.

Marx analysed many different aspects of capitalism from this viewpoint: the nature of commodities, money, capital, wages, competition, prices, profits, ground rent, and so on. But these were all related to the organization of the labour process as a process of *valorization* or 'value-adding'. He also defined some fundamental laws rooted in the commodification of labour-power and its integration into the operation of capitalism. These laws do not operate independently of the class struggle and with unbending necessity. Instead they are *tendencies* realized in and through the class struggle in specific conjunctures.[4]

Class as a Social Relation

Marx returned many times to the analysis of class relations and struggles, not only in the economy but also in politics, religion, the family, morality, and so forth. Yet Marx never completed a text devoted to class as such and, although his theoretical work and political action were explicitly developed from a proletarian viewpoint, he wrote little directly about this class in contrast to the bourgeoisie, landowners, petty bourgeoisie, peasants, and lumpenproletariat. Moreover, when Marx's *Capital* was about to discuss classes in capitalism, there appears the tantalizing sentence: 'at this point the manuscript breaks off'.

Marx denied he had discovered classes or class struggle. He did claim credit for showing that 'the *existence of classes* is merely linked to *particular historical phases in the development of production*'.[3] In particular, Marx identified the secret of capitalist economic exploitation and why it produced specific forms of class struggle. Only in capitalism are classes demarcated in terms of relations of production which are disembedded from broader institutional forms (such as the family or kinship, political bonds, or religion). In introducing market relations and the cash nexus into all spheres of society and throughout the world, it overturned the traditional social bonds among society's members. Thus social relations in capitalist societies are largely shaped by the capital–labour relation and the dynamic of accumulation.

The *Manifesto* presents the clearest statement of this view. It claims that capitalism creates its own gravediggers by creating the industrial proletariat. As capitalism consolidates its hold around the globe, non-capitalist classes are eliminated and the proletariat expands. It is also concentrated in ever-larger numbers as factories and industrial cities grow in size. As individuals, then groups of workers in a factory or trade, and, eventually, all workers in a nation-state (even the world economy) mobilize to resist capitalist exploitation, they grow more conscious of their shared class position and common interest in overthrowing capitalism. Their economic struggles are resisted by the state as well as capitalists. The working classes then move on from trade unionism to party political organization and more revolutionary consciousness. Communists should provide intellectual and political leadership here without regard to immediate party advantage or national differences. As economic conditions worsen and the proletariat gain strength, revolution will eventually occur. The proletariat will then use state power to dispossess capital of the means of production and subject the economy to social control.

The *Manifesto* has provided the basis for others to construct a sociological theory of class formation, class consciousness, and political action. It was already said to have been falsified within fifty years (for example, in the work of Bernstein, a German social democrat).[4] But Marx himself modified this approach in his more scientific works as well as his more detailed historical analyses of specific political conjunctures. Thus *Capital* qualified arguments about the growing polarization of class relations. For Marx indicated that, as capitalism developed, it would require a growing middle class of clerks, engineers, managers, accountants, and so on. His historical studies also described several significant classes or class fractions as well as non-class movements that could play important historical roles in making or breaking revolutions. Later observation of democratic experiences in the USA, Britain, and Germany led Marx to suggest that a parliamentary road to socialism might be possible. Conversely, his studies of Russia encouraged him to believe that a peasant-based revolution might establish a different form of communism rooted in surviving social patterns of rural community life.

The State and Politics

Marx's work on the state and politics are equally fragmented, incomplete, and inconsistent. Neither he nor Engels provided a coherent theory of the state as an organ of class domination, of the party as a form of organization, of the strategy and tactics of revolution (especially whether it must always be violent or could assume a more parliamentary form), or of the nature of the 'dictatorship of the proletariat' and 'withering away of the state' which would supersede the capitalist form of the state. Given that their project was as much political as theoretical, these are surprising and serious omissions.

In simplified terms, Marx and Engels developed two broad views of the state. One sees it as an instrument of class rule wielded more or less successfully by the economically dominant class to secure continuing economic exploitation and political control. The other sees the state as a potentially autonomous authority which could regulate the class struggle in the public interest or even manipulate it to the private advantage of the political stratum. The former view is clearly expressed in the *Manifesto*, the latter is illustrated in Marx's analyses of the French state under Louis Bonaparte. Building on this twofold division, some commentators suggest the first view characterizes more normal periods of class struggle, the latter 'exceptional' periods in which the class struggle is stalemated and/or can be portrayed as threatening a social catastrophe. This interpretation has since been applied by Marxists to fascism, military dictatorships, and the Soviet Union. A third view of the state should be added. Rooted in Marx's earliest critiques of Hegel, it was reworked during subsequent studies and most clearly restated in the light of the regime established by the Paris Commune in 1870. This view is that the state is always an alienated form of political organization because it is based on a separation of rulers and ruled. Only when this separation is abolished through the self-organization of society will political alienation disappear.[5]

Seeing Things Differently

This section considers two contrasting views on the future of capitalism. If Marxism tends to privilege the relations of production in explaining the dynamic of capitalism, some sociologists give more weight to the forces of production. Thus stages in social development are distinguished not by class relations but by the material basis of production. Two key historical breaks are identified: the transition from agrarian to industrial societies; and thence to post-industrialism. Such theorists also argue that, whereas industrial societies depended on the exploitation of waged labour, post-industrial growth relies on the production and utilization of knowledge. Marxists see this as deeply misleading. An interesting test case is provided by the contrasting predictions in the 1970s of a Belgian Marxist, Ernest Mandel, and an American sociologist, Daniel Bell, about the future of capitalist societies.[5] Whereas Mandel forecast that 'late capitalism' would develop on a global scale with increased inequalities and instabilities, Bell expected the demise of industrial society based on economic exploitation and a narrow concern with private profit-and-loss in favour of a knowledge-based, post-industrial society orientated to co-operation and the public interest.

Bell predicted that the economy would change from one largely producing goods to one in which services such as health, education, research, and government became increasingly important activities. The university would replace the business firm as the core institution. In occupational terms, there would be a decisive shift towards the professional and technical class – especially scientists and engineers. Organizing material production would become less important than mastery of theoretical knowledge for purposive innovation and social control. As such knowledge developed, post-industrial society would be able to assess its technological needs and plan and control its technological growth. Market forces would decline in favour of public planning based on a new 'intellectual technology' for rational decision-making. Knowledge would be freely accessible and could be used to expand leisure for all.[6]

With hindsight, Bell got many predictions wrong. This is partly because he extrapolated empirically from the USA as the leading capitalist nation,[7] thereby ignoring the global nature of capital accumulation. Simply because

US firms transfer industry abroad to exploit lower costs and/or new markets but retain headquarters functions at home, they do not stop being capitalist. Instead they spread the logic of capital more widely. Indeed, observing today's world, one finds much to confirm Marx's predictions that capitalism entails the destruction of pre-capitalist relations, increasing polarization, a growing reserve army of labour, and recurrent crises. Bell also erred because he believed technological development would create a situation where people could choose between economic exploitation under capitalism and social emancipation in a planned, learning society. But this ignores capital's capacity to exploit new technological developments to reinforce its economic, political, and social control and deprive people of such a choice. In this sense his views are reminiscent of the Young Hegelians who believed that a change in social consciousness would be enough to effect the material transformation of the world.

Some of Mandel's predictions also proved wrong. But he did explain how profit drives technological development and how the logic of accumulation shapes the wider society. For Mandel the multinational firm (not the university) would become the core institution of late capitalism; and it would be reflected in increasing antagonism between American, Japanese, and European capitalists. Moreover, whereas Bell took technological innovation for granted, Mandel employed Marxism to explain its wave-like development over long periods. This was linked in late capitalism to a great increase in R&D, the expansion of skilled and intellectual labour, the growth of producer services as well as the commodification of working-class leisure, and so on. Mandel also suggested that technological progress would become a major theme in late capitalist ideology (a prediction reflected ideologically in Bell's own work). New forms of global expansion of capitalism would be reflected in new forms of state intervention as national economies became more open and competition grew more intense. If his analyses erred in some respects, it is because he was too committed to the Marxist view that the logic of capitalism could explain most changes in economic, political, and socio-cultural organization.

A more balanced Marxist analysis should be able to show where both Bell and Mandel erred. In particular it would reveal that the contradiction between the information society and information economy is a particular form of the contradiction between the forces and relations of production. Bell seems to believe that, once knowledge is the principal force for economic expansion, it could become the property of all and a basis for democratic control. But capital seems bent on asserting property rights in all forms of information and knowledge. Thus intellectual property rights have become a key stake in international conflicts (for example, with the USA, Bell's paradigmatic post-industrial society, leading the fight). Likewise, there is a growing struggle by capital to extend property rights (and hence the right to private profit) to include the human genome, wild plants, animals, tribal medicines, outer space, the deep sea, and so on. An interesting case is the current struggle to commodify the Internet – an anarchic cyberspace originally free from both government and private economic control and now subject to growing attempts to censor it and/or turn it into a marketing channel.

Legacies and Unfinished Business

Issues raised by Marx still dominate much sociological enquiry into the nature, history, overall logic, and future development of capitalism. But the reception of his work is often ambivalent and politicized. Intellectually, this is due to its richness, complexity, and discontinuities, the incompleteness of some texts, and the posthumous appearance of others. Politically, it is due in part to Marx's critique of capitalism, his support for socialism, and his confusing advocacy both of democracy and 'dictatorship of the proletariat'; and, in part, to the subsequent appropriation of his name (if not always his ideas) by Marxism-Leninism and its association with Stalinism. However, even where Marx's actual or alleged ideas provoke disagreement, they often provide major reference points in social analysis. This is evident from work within the Durkheimian and Weberian traditions, in functionalist sociology, in arguments about the transition from industrialism to post-industrialism, and in the development of various postmodern sociologies.

Marx's standing as a 'key sociological thinker' is best linked to his work on the political economy of capitalism rather than his commitment to the grave-digging role of the proletariat. In particular his analysis of the commodity form (especially its generalization to wage-labour) is still essential to understanding the dynamic of capitalism. Problems arise when this critique is applied to the analysis of society as a whole. The central importance of labour-power and the labour process within capitalism does not mean that capitalism (even if broadly defined) is necessarily just as central in turn for the explanation of the dynamic of entire societies. This must surely be something open to empirical investigation. Indeed there is growing belief among social scientists that no one system (whether it be the economy, the state, law, religion, or some other system) can determine the overall logic of societal development or become so powerful that it can effectively master all forms of resistance. Taken to extremes this can lead into the morass of a postmodernism where anything goes. More cautiously and carefully interpreted, however, it provides a basis for studying the complex interdependence and co-evolution of different institutional orders within the context of an emerging global society.

Despite the century and a half of continuing debate on Marx's work, there is still much unfinished business. If we consider Marx first and foremost as the theorist of the capitalist mode of production, at least two issues remain contentious. The first involves difficult and often esoteric debates about the 'labour theory of value', that is, the view that the value of any commodity is the sum of the values of the commodities that enter into its production. This allegedly holds for labour-power itself so that its value depends on the value of the commodities needed to renew its capacity to labour. This view has few defenders today. For some, the problems are more empirical. Thus wages have risen above minimal subsistence levels and so contain a larger 'moral and historical component'. The labour theory of value is also said to ignore the role of upaid (and typically female) domestic labour in reproducing labour-power. The role of so-called unproductive labour paid for by the state to provide (until recently) non-commodified educational, health, and other services also poses a problem for a 'labour theory of value'. For others, the problem is more theoretical, namely, that it concludes from the fact that living labour-power is bought and sold that it must have the same commodity char-acter as an inert machine. In both regards, however, it is sufficient to regard labour-power as a *fictitious commodity*, that is, as having the external form but not the real substance of a commodity, to derive most of Marx's conclusions about the labour process, capitalist exploitation, class conflict, and the overall logic of capital.

Second, there is increasing recognition that, while capitalism may have a distinctive dynamic, its future remains open. Marx's own detailed analyses of capitalist development implied nothing inevitable about its rise or demise and the 1859 *Preface* emphasized that no mode of production ever ended before its full potential had been exhausted. Capitalism is not moving inexorably towards some predetermined revolutionary crisis (even if its growth dynamic appears to have fundamental ecological limits) but has instead shown remark-able regenerative capacities. This is reflected in competition between different ways of organizing capitalism and of embedding it in wider social relations. For example, there is a struggle today between Anglo-American, Continental European, and Confucian capitalisms. Marx's own work also noted different paths of development as well as the crucial mediating role of class struggle.

As a theorist of society rather than capitalism, Marx is sometimes accused of seeking to explain everything in terms of class relations or, worse still, of technological development; or else of being so vague about the interaction of base and superstructure that his views are open to almost any interpretation. There is still scope for discussion of the relative importance in different contexts of class as compared to gender, ethnic, national, and relations, class consciousness as compared to other identities, and class struggles as compared to other social movements. Likewise there is much scope for debate over the relative importance of the capital relation as opposed to technology, the inter-state system, patriarchy, struggles in civil society, and so on, for the future of contemporary society. In these respects Marx has left us a rich research agenda to be explored on many levels and in many domains.

Further Reading

For Marx's own works see the references in the main body of the chapter. The following are excellent commentaries either on Marx's work as a whole or on central specialized aspects of his work.

S. Avineri, *The Social and Political Thought of Karl Marx* (Cambridge: Cambridge University Press, 1968).

D.J. Friedman, 'Marx's Perspective on the Objective Class Structure', *Polity*, 6, (1974), 318–44.

Eric Hobsbawm, 'Marx and History', *New Left Review*, **143**, (1984), 39–50.

D. McLellan, *Karl Marx: His Life and Thought* (Basingstoke: Macmillan, 1974).

Ralph Miliband, 'Marx and the State', *Socialist Register,* 1965, (London: Merlin Press, 1965), 278–96.

2

Max Weber

Lawrence A. Scaff

Driving Impulses: Life and Orientation

Max Weber is one of the Promethean figures of social thought. Born in 1864 into a Protestant upper-middle-class family, his ancestors included German merchants and businessmen on his father's side of the family and French Huguenots on his mother's side. A successful lawyer and National Liberal politician in Berlin, Weber's father, Max Weber Senior, introduced his son to the exhilarating world of European politics and statesmanship in the age of Bismarck. An educated woman with strong religious beliefs and commitments to social welfare, his mother, Helene, encouraged his intellectual and spiritual development. The poles of young Max's existence were thus clearly marked: either pursuit of power and a life of public affairs, or devotion to **Geist** and the life of the mind. These alternatives shaped the entire course of Weber's life and work, culminating in his brilliant last testimonial: the speeches on politics and science as vocations.

Completing his dissertation and habilitation in 1889 and 1891 on topics in economic history at the Humboldt University of Berlin, Weber reluctantly entered the university world of teaching and scholarship, while expressing a longing for a life of political engagement. But hopes for either career were dashed in his thirties, when he suffered a psychological collapse in 1898, brought on by overwork and family strife having the outward characteristics of a classic **Freudian** oedipal conflict, as his colleague, Friedrich Meinecke, later pointed out. Weber's convalescence was painfully slow, and after a dazzling start at the universities of Freiburg and Heidelberg, he eventually returned to teaching at Vienna and Munich only during the last two years of his life. All the major work for which he is known today, from *The Protestant Ethic and the Spirit of Capitalism* (1904–5) to the unfinished text of *Economy and Society* (published posthumously in 1922), was written in the diaspora, so to speak, of two decades outside the protected environment of academia. This mature work can be seen as a labor of recovery and a triumph of self-mastery.

Weber's social and cultural world was marked by deep conflicts and irreconcilable tensions, as if to mirror his personal turmoil. It is well known that the industrial revolution hit the continent full force after Germany's unification in 1871, leading to massive social dislocations, rapid urbanization, incipient class conflict, and the formation of revolutionary political movements. But we often need to be reminded that by the turn of the century new cultural movements were underway as well – in art and architecture, literature and drama, and in the conventions concerning sex and gender. Weber felt these tensions deeply and observed them at close range. Because of his temperament, interests, and personal relationships, he found himself placed at the center of the raging cross-currents, often attempting to understand them, respond to them, or resist them. Why do people conduct their lives as they do, often in such different ways? What material forces restrict or enlarge their life opportunities? What moral powers do they call upon in facing up to the demands of the world? Even his comparative and historical scholarship that may seem most remote from the present, such as the studies of society and religion in China and India, radiates an intense curiosity about these questions, which ultimately concern the fate of civilizations.

During the last year of his life in 1920, following a heated student-sponsored debate with Oswald Spengler, who expounded his 'decline of the West' thesis, Weber remarked that the intellectual world of his time had been formed in large measure by the writings of **Marx** and Nietzsche. They had defined the major themes for the twentieth century: the question of social justice, the nature of the capitalist economy, the fate of western civilization, the problem of our relationship to history and knowledge, modernity and its discontents. Weber read their work, addressed their themes, and sustained a dialogue with their followers. Like Marx, he identified himself throughout his life as a political economist. Much of his discussion of the relationship between economics and religion can be seen as a sustained inquiry into the validity of the 'materialistic conception of history' popularized by the man he called 'the great thinker'.[1] And like Nietzsche, Weber was fascinated with the expressions and problems of culture, both traditional and modern, and particularly its effects on our personalities and the way we conduct our lives. Much of his cultural science and sociology thus took the form of a critical response to what he called Nietzsche's 'brilliant' constructions.[2]

Had Weber added Freud to his citation, then his remark on the occasion of the Spengler debate would have encompassed our own times as well. Indeed, Weber read some of Freud's essays, and he knew the work of the experimental psychologists, such as Wundt and William James. But he had little patience with the 'talking cure' and other new therapies. Instead, what he took from the debates about subjectivity and the psyche was the problem of rationalism, that 'superficially simple concept' he once said[3] – its nature, varieties, and consequences. Weber's life-work was an effort to map this contested terrain.

Key Issues

Weber thought deeply about an unusually wide range of subjects, covering the sweep of world civilization and the nature of human inquiry. The leading question of his three-volume study of the world religions – why is it that we have capitalism in the West? – served as a focal point for a comparative *tour de force* of the relationship between religion and economics. Weber then used these studies to probe the nature of what he called the 'disenchantment of the world' and the 'rationalization' of life – that is, in general the tendency of our activities and practices to become intellectualized, calculable, defined by technique, and subjected to means–ends tests. In the course of these investigations he also sought clarity about the character of work and vocation in the modern world, just as he puzzled over the nature of authority and power, and the problem of knowledge and the knowledge-seeker in the human sciences.

On the Relationship between Religion and Economics

Weber's reputation is owed above all to his studies of *The Protestant Ethic and the Spirit of Capitalism* (1904–5). Provoking an instant debate and numerous follow-up investigations, which show little sign of diminishing, Weber proposed a thesis that connected the dynamic 'capitalist' system of production and exchange with a religiously inspired *ethos* of work and self-control. Weber called the latter a kind of asceticism orientated toward acting in the here and now, which he found especially characteristic of members of the Protestant sects. With respect to the hypothetical connection between this particular economic system and a particular religion, Weber claimed only to have unearthed an 'elective affinity' that helped identify one reason for the emergence and success of modern capitalism. Making a point that is often overlooked, he denied proposing a causal connection or a specification of necessary and sufficient conditions for the rise of capitalism. But he did contend that one of the important factors favoring the kind of dynamic, market-orientated economies typical of the West resided in the Reformation and the creation of anti-traditional belief systems that sanctioned work, savings, investment, entrepreneurial success, or in short, the systematic creation of wealth *as a calling*. Commitment to a 'calling' or 'vocation' was an unconditional duty, a matter of attempting to fulfill the demands of a practical ethic and way of life. Originating in the search for religious salvation, the idea of the calling came to be extended over time to the search for worldly achievement and recognition.

Of course, Weber understood that concealed beneath the banner of 'capitalism,' that 'most fateful force in our modern life',[4] as he called it, are a variety of quite different characteristics. Like most abstract nouns in the lexicon of science, capitalism (and feudalism, mercantilism, socialism, and so on) can only be a pure or 'ideal' type, not a real entity, that the investigator constructs from complex events for analytic purposes. As production for a market, capitalism had appeared elsewhere in history – in ancient Rome, for example. As entrepreneurial activity aimed at amassing savings, it achieved prominence in the Italian city-states of the Renaissance. Or as forcible seizure of booty, it could be found throughout world history. But Weber's point was that this particular modern configuration of forces – production for a market, separation of the enterprise from the household, the rational organization of formally 'free' labor, technical means of bookkeeping, rational calculation of profits for re-investment – amounted to a new, dynamic *system,* that once set in motion would transform traditional societies everywhere around the globe. He saw that an important starting point for this transformation (though not the only one) was located in changes in the moral order – specifically, the predominance of asceticism orientated toward action in this world and mundane achievement. This orientation toward action, or *ethos,* formed the groundwork for the distinctive character of western culture as a whole – its 'specific and peculiar rationalism' in Weber's words.5 Thus, the ethos affected not only western culture's modes of production and exchange, but also its science and technology, legal and political orders, administrative systems, and its cultural life as a whole.

Weber's comparative studies of the world religions – religion in China and India, in ancient Judaism, and a planned study of Islam that remained unfinished – were carried out with the aim of showing exactly why and how conditions for the indigenous emergence of modern capitalism were missing in these contrasting settings. The combinations there of mysticism and asceticism focused on another world, a heaven or nirvana, were associated with different consequences for civilization. Indeed, Weber considered asceticism and mysticism to be radically opposed practices for achieving the goals of life, just as he perceived a principled opposition between action orientated toward the world in which we live and toward another imagined world beyond human experience and time. The consequences of such different orientations have been far reaching, to say the least, for as we have seen repeatedly, the extension of western forms into other contexts has typically provoked a clash – both rejection and emulation of these forms – in all kinds of traditional orders.

The Disenchantment of the World and the Rationalization of Life

From Weber's perspective his inquiry into the capitalist world-order elaborated primarily a historical thesis, although he was alert to its implications for the present and future: What does such a thesis mean for us today, living centuries after the Reformation and the scientific revolution of the Enlightenment? The answer to this question opens on to one of Weber's great themes, announced on the famous concluding pages of *The Protestant Ethic and the Spirit of Capitalism*. For there he noted that 'Limitation to specialized work, with a renunciation of the Faustian universality of man which it involves, is a condition of any valuable work in the modern world.' In a previous age the 'Puritan wanted to work in a calling; we are forced to do so.' Today the modern economic order is 'bound to the technical and economic conditions of machine production' that determine our lives with the power of an unavoidable fate, a fatality that threatens to confine us within an 'iron cage'. Gazing further into our century, Weber intoned in phrases recalling Nietzsche:

> No one knows who will live in this cage in the future, or whether at the end of this tremendous development entirely new prophets will arise, or there will be a great rebirth of old ideas and ideals, or, if neither, mechanized petrification, embellished with a sort of convulsive self-importance. For of the last stage of this cultural development, it might well be truly said: 'Specialists without spirit, sensualists without heart; this nullity imagines that it has attained a level of civilization never before achieved.' 6

The metaphor of the 'iron cage' is one of Weber's most arresting images for describing the condition of humankind in a bureaucratized world, or more abstractly stated, the constriction of opportunities and possibilities in a world dominated by 'purposive' or 'instrumental rationality' (*Zweckrationalität*), a type of rationality orientated exclusively toward the efficient maximization of practical goals. Such a prospect suggests the depth to the problem of work and calling in the modern age, and indeed, much of Weber's attention was given to reflection on the conditions of vocational activity and the internal demands on the character or personality placed upon representative figures like the scientist, teacher, scholar, cleric, politician, official, administrator, lawyer, journalist, artist, intellectual, or entrepreneur. In 'Science as a Vocation' and 'Politics as a Vocation' Weber pronounced his last words on this theme, issuing in both texts an eloquent appeal for personal moral engagement – a call to integrity and an 'ethic of responsibility' – and for the contributions of knowledge to 'self-clarification.'7

If this response to the 'iron cage' sounds unsurprising and uncomplicated, then it is important to recognize that Weber raised the stakes for an answer considerably higher than previous social theorists. Unlike either Marx or **Durkheim**, for example, he understood the practice of science or the pursuit of knowledge as both a progressive, beneficial activity, but also a 'disenchanting' activity – in his words, 'the most important fraction of the process of intellectualization which we have been undergoing for thousands of years'.8 Just as politics had to face up to the 'diabolical' consequences of the use of power, so science had to confront the disenchanting consequences of 'intellectualist rationalization'.

Weber chose dramatic and theologically weighted language to state his case for his commitment to a 'disenchanting' science and against a naive belief in progress:

> The fate of an epoch which has eaten of the tree of knowledge is that it must know that we cannot learn the *meaning* of the world from the results of its analysis, be it ever so perfect; it must rather be in a position to create this meaning itself. It must recognize that a *Weltanschauung* can never be the product of advancing empirical knowledge, and that therefore the highest ideals, which move us most powerfully, are formed for all time only in the struggle with other ideals which are just as sacred to others as ours are to us.[9]

In this view one consequence of disenchantment was the dominion of technique, the certainty that the human mind could master nature by calculation. But the hubris of world-mastery also meant, as he said, that 'the bearing of humankind has been disenchanted and denuded of its mystical and inwardly genuine plasticity', and that 'the ultimate and most sublime values have retreated from public life either into the transcendental realm of mystic life or into the brotherliness of direct and personal human relations'.[10] The dilemma is that science is only one of the orders of life, and although it is uniquely qualified to gain knowledge about nature and the human world, its competence *qua science* does not extend to answering our most urgent questions: What should we believe in? How should we conduct ourselves? What kinds of lives should we lead? The vital, but disenchanting order of science cannot answer our questions about the 'meaning' of life and the world. Other orders and spheres of value have a powerful say in these matters, according to Weber, and the different answers they give are joined in an irreconcilable, endless struggle with each other.

Method and the Philosophy of Science

What conclusions can be drawn from this position? In his writings on method and the philosophy of science, Weber developed a complex, nuanced answer that unfortunately is often misconstrued. Briefly put, on the one hand he articulated the notion that science should aim for 'objectivity' in the sense of creating a conversation in which personal bias and ideological distortion are held in check. This was a prescriptive ideal for *disinterested* inquiry. But on the other hand he acknowledged that western experimental science as practiced in the modern age is historically and culturally determined. It is an all too human activity and a product of a particular concatenation of circumstances, not a quest rooted in the nature of things. Nevertheless, arrayed against alternatives, science still offers the best possible means for searching for the 'truth' about ourselves, our history, and our possible future.

Stated abstractly, then, the body of knowledge known as 'science' was provisional in the sense of being conditioned by cultural values, social interests and historical developments. But it was also 'valid' because formulated through critical and self-corrective methods and rational standards of inquiry, subjected to the controlling debates of the scientific community. 'For scientific truth is precisely what is *valid* for all who *seek* the truth' is Weber's shorthand way of stating the idea.[11] This position should underscore the **voluntarist,** rather than the **relativist** consequences of science in the Weberian mold. Emphasizing the significance of conscious choosing, Weber surely would have agreed with J.S. Mill's assertion that 'The human faculties of perception, judgement, discriminative feeling, mental activity, and even moral preference, are exercised only in making a choice.'[12]

Voluntarist and Relativist

Weber's attitude to the status of knowledge claims was **voluntarist** because he believed that the most adequate forms of knowledge were produced by means of the social scientific community applying their own voluntary codes and standards of critical analysis, debate and evidence. Such standards were always the result of hard-fought, and ongoing, battles between differing positions. The voluntarism refers to the clear choices that have to be made within such a process. While Weber would readily concede that such standards were culturally and historically situated his position still differs from **relativism** because the latter attitude to knowledge is simply that any claim is as good as any other. A relativist does not believe that some knowledge claims are more adequate than others. She or he does not recognize the qualitative difference between an unsubstantiated opinion, on the one hand, and a belief that has been subjected to critical and self-corrective methods and rational standards of inquiry, on the other. Weber certainly did recognize this difference.

Notwithstanding the intense effort Weber expended on these topics, he remained an extraordinarily skeptical philosopher of science, believing that no important scientific problem is ever solved by purely methodological or philosophical interventions alone. It is fitting to emphasize, therefore, that his substantive work recorded a passion for historical knowledge and an understanding of social action and institutional forms – as he liked to remark, the clear-sighted investigation of 'what is' that is the substance of his essays in the sociology of religion and his later sociology and social economics in *Economy and Society*.

Authority or 'Legitimate Domination'

One of the most important aspects of Weber's later work was the analysis of authority or 'legitimate domination' – *Herrschaft* in the original terminology. The centerpiece of this widely cited contribution – the threefold typology of **legal-rational**, **traditional**, and **charismatic authority** – was used by Weber as a general scheme for analyzing specific configurations of power. It was also the general framework for much that he had to say in different areas of sociological investigation which he helped to found: studies of bureaucracy, law, leadership, the state, social stratification, and the city as a political community. Though simplified and overly schematic, the categories in Table 2.1 indicate something about the scope of these efforts and the kind of terminology Weber employed.

Legal-Rational, Traditional and Charismatic Authority

In the section entitled 'The Three Pure Types of Authority' in *Economy and Society* Weber writes: 'There are three pure types of legitimate domination. The validity of the claims to legitimacy may be based on:

1. Rational grounds – resting on a belief in the legality of enacted rules and the rights of those elevated to authority under such rules to issue commands (legal authority).

2. Traditional grounds – resting on an established belief in the sanctity of immemorial traditions and the legitimacy of those exercising authority under them (traditional authority); or finally,

3. Charismatic grounds – resting on devotion to the exceptional sanctity, heroism or exemplary character of an individual person, and of the normative patterns or order revealed or ordained by him (charismatic authority).' (*Economy and Society*, Berkeley, University of California Press, 1978, p. 215.)

Weber was fascinated by the tensions and contradictions among the different bases for legitimation and power in social life, and he thought it important to take account of the different ways in which these bases could be rationalized:

> Bureaucratic authority is specifically rational in the sense of being bound to intellectually analysable rules; while charismatic authority is specifically irrational in the sense of being foreign to all rules. Traditional authority is bound to the precedents handed down from the past... [whereas] within the sphere of its claims, charismatic authority repudiates the past, and is in this sense a specifically revolutionary force.[13]

Table 2.1   Basic characteristics of the three pure types of authority or 'legitimate domination' (adapted from Weber, *Economy and Society*)

	Organization	*Membership*	*Law*	*Responsibility*	*Leadership*
I. LEGALITY					
Instrumental Rationality	bureaucratic	specialized	legal formalism	impersonal	monocratic
Value Rationality	professional	rational competence	promulgation of natural law	public service	collegial/ democratic
II. TRADITION					
Patriarchy/ Patrimony	none/ gerontocracy/ personal staff	birth, honor	prescription precedent	personalistic	monocratic/ collegial
Estates	personal staff	fealty, personal loyalty	prescription	personalistic	collegial (estate collegiality)
III. CHARISMA	voluntaristic	personal devotion	substantive legal principles	commitment to a cause	monocratic/ democatic

Every society contained a complex mixture of the three types, and yet there was also a dynamic relationship among them that could be observed: ordinary tradition and legal forms challenged by extraordinary charisma, but then charisma itself transformed into 'rational' rule-governed routines. Social change came about in part because of such clashes between competing structures of power, expressed on the surface of social reality by competing claims to legitimation. From Weber's perspective, to trace the dynamic relationships and process in different spheres of action was the point of the specialized sociologies of bureaucracy, the law, or the state.

Unlike Durkheim or Marx, Weber fathered no coterie of disciples or specific school of thought. But even so, aspects of his political sociology have achieved a powerful grip on the modern imagination: instrumental rationality as a potent agent of change, bureaucracy as an immensely effective mechanism of control, professionalism as a standard of conduct, and 'charisma' as a mythic quality of personality and leadership. From worries about 'bureaucracy' to the quest for 'charisma' we have learned to speak in Weberian formulae. One reason is that despite the way the present overshadows the past and dominates our vision, the late twentieth century still shares important resemblances with its *fin-de-siècle* points of origin.

Seeing Things Differently

Resemblances are not difficult to locate. To take one example, applications and evidence of Weber's insights are commonplace because of the managed environments we experience daily. The lessons of the tendencies and characteristics Weber discussed under the heading of rationalization seem to be everywhere – in popular culture and entertainment, in the economic trends associated with 'globalization', in the marketing of everything from political candidates to spiritual beliefs, and in the workings of modern organizations of all kinds.

Consider a typical experience: recently one of my students accepted a well-paid position in a prominent firm in the burgeoning 'service' economy. Shortly after her arrival the firm moved into new corporate headquarters equipped with the latest electronic paraphernalia and design features. One management innovation was use of the open-plan office – that is, a large space, sealed off and soundproofed against the outside world, occupied by numerous employees, and partitioned only by cubicles separating open work areas, rather than floor-to-ceiling walls with windows and connecting passageways. The expressed aim, of course, was improved communication, better consultation, and higher levels of productivity. But in practice employees experienced the environment as a sterile and noisy capsule, paradoxically creating a feeling of isolation, yet without a sense of privacy. To regain a sense of freedom and equilibrium required flight into other spaces. The corporate response was not to humanize the means or reassess the appropriate ends for the work environment, but rather to employ more sophisticated instrumentalities: background 'white noise' was piped into the office space to simulate a 'normal' human environment, which otherwise had been suppressed. Weeks of 'fine tuning' ensued, in which painfully shrill static was modulated into something less recognizable and more tolerable. 'In a world now devoid of meaning,' as Jacques Attali remarks, 'background noise [is] increasingly necessary to give people a sense of security'; 'it is a means of silencing, a concrete example of commodities speaking in place of people, of the monologue of institutions.'[14]

What is striking about such cases is the irrationalism associated with instrumental rationality, the way in which human requirements are contravened by the rationalization of activity as a goal-orientated enterprise. Consider the situation that sometimes prevails in the contemporary university. It was not so long ago that universities were institutions in which at least some of the time 'collegial' principles prevailed, using Weber's category. That is, authoritative decision-making depended in some important ways and in some settings on discussion, deliberation, and often rather messy efforts to form or approximate a consensus. Governance could have been interpreted using the model of 'communicative action' that **Jürgen Habermas** has promoted in his work. Moreover, there were some areas of scholarly activity and student life that had little to do with rational ends, such as 'efficiency' or 'effectiveness'. But as the imperatives of 'planning', 'productivity', and 'efficiency' have taken hold, the modern university has come to resemble any enterprise subjected to means–ends rationalization. In Weber's terminology this kind of rationalization signifies the deployment of instrumental rationality in the service of bureaucratic domination. In the marketplace of university policies it means the deployment of 'total quality management' teams to eliminate inefficiencies, the use of productivity metrics for the evaluation of scholarship, the assignment of targets and quotas for future accomplishments, the application of 'algorithms' to yield judgments about policy, the treatment of students as 'consumers' of a product or 'customers' shopping for goods and services, the understanding of teachers as service 'providers' or facilitators, and the measurement of learning 'outcomes' to justify continued financial support.

Humans are inventive creatures and thus respond with an impressive array of efforts to adapt, exploit, subvert, or outwit these languages and mechanisms of control. Knowledge and its application offer the only way out in such circumstances. Before intelligence arrives, however, the institutional lives we lead may end up still more impoverished than before, and the tensions between life and vocation, of which Weber was acutely aware, may be left in an even more severe state of crisis.

Weberian Legacies

Weber's work has grown in stature over the decades, affecting studies in the sociology of religion, political and historical sociology, sociology of law and the state, the methodology and philosophy of the social sciences, the theory of social action (from **Parsons** to Habermas), and even moral and political philosophy. Weber's thinking about disenchantment, rationalization, and the relationship between ideas and material interests also influenced discussions within the Frankfurt School and in some branches of revisionist Marxism, as represented by Lukács and the early Michels. Today the 'Weberian approach' to social theory has a distinctive imprimatur, and it is commonly thought to refer to multicausal, comparative analyses that give special attention to the interaction between structural factors and subjective beliefs and intentions. Stated in this manner, it is important to see that the older disputes pitting materialism against idealism, positivism against historicism, or formal theory against empirical history, have ended in the victory of neo-Weberian approaches. Work that focuses on large-scale comparative historical questions dealing with institutional change, political and economic transformation, the global expansion of modern capitalism, or the dynamic relationship between state and civil society rest implicitly on Weberian foundations. The effort 'to bring the state back in' follows in the footsteps of Weber's thought, as does the 'new institutionalism' or work in the field of economic sociology that Weber helped define.[15] Working with explicit models of rationality and different kinds of explanatory hypotheses, contemporary scholarship has continued along the path set forth by Weber.

It is also the case, however, that some aspects of Weber's work have been either poorly understood or neglected. As someone who emerged as a political economist at the intersection between historicism and positivism, rejecting both and attempting to find a new synthesis, Weber staked out independent positions that were often difficult to grasp, even for his contemporaries.

Today there are two relatively new areas of inquiry in which Weber's work may prove useful and thought-provoking: economic sociology or social economics, and cultural sociology. With regard to the former, it is usually overlooked that Weber devoted considerable effort in *Economy and Society* to specifying 'categories of economic action' which would guide our understanding of rational action that is both social and economic, and thus serve as a bridge between two disciplines.[16] Interest in types and models of rational action has always been central to the social sciences. If modern economics now launches an effort, in Robert Solow's words, 'to look to sociology as a way of escaping from the narrow idea of rationality',[17] then Weber's categories and approach should deserve revisiting.

Similarly, much of Weber's actual writing and most innovative thinking, such as his unfinished essay on music,[18] addressed themes and issues in cultural sociology. There has been a tendency, however, to assimilate this work to specialized topics within sociology's disciplinary boundaries.[19] But the current revival across the human sciences of a more broadly configured interest in 'culture' should spell an opportunity to extend this aspect of Weber's perspective into areas such as art and literature that he only began to consider.[20] Exploring the emergence, development, and rationalization of a particular sphere of culture, such as music or painting, is one of those grand civilizational themes that represents the most challenging extension of the Weberian legacy.

Further Reading

There is an extensive and growing literature on Weber's life and work. A good brief introduction is Dirk Käsler, *Max Weber* (tr. 1988). Randall Collins, *Weberian Sociological Theory* (1986), surveys his sociological interests. Lawrence Scaff, *Fleeing the Iron Cage* (1989), addresses the theme of culture and modernity. Among recent studies, Peter Breiner, *Max Weber and Democratic Politics* (1996), probes political topics, while Stephen Kalberg, *Max Weber's Comparative-Historical Sociology* (1994), aims to systematize the contribution to comparative studies.

3

Emile Durkheim

Whitney Pope

Driving Impulses

Emile Durkheim sought to establish a new, scientific sociology capable of helping France overcome its moral crisis, a crisis reflected in the turmoil, violence, and discontent pervading French society. Ever since the French Revolution the nation had been wracked by conflict between monarchists and antimonarchists, Catholics and their secular opponents, and capital and labor. Intellectuals debated the nature of the crisis and possible cures. Conservatives longed for a return to the religion, authority, hierarchy, and community of a more stable past; liberals believed in individual freedom and rights and the use of peaceful means to achieve a free, secular, democratic republic; and radicals felt that a revolutionary transformation was necessary to achieve social justice. The lower orders of society demanded greater equality even as the upper orders sought to retain or regain their power and privileges. Different kinds of government succeeded one another: the First Republic, the First Empire, the Houses of Bourbon and then Orleans, the Second Republic, the Second Empire, and finally the Third Republic (1871–1940). Defeated by Germany in the war of 1870 and torn by the Dreyfus scandal at the end of the century which exacerbated social fissures to the extent of bringing the country to the brink of civil war, France was devastated by World War I in which six of the eight million men mobilized for military service became war casualties.[1] At the individual level rising suicide rates reflected a growing sense of malaise. Durkheim's goal was to develop a sociology which would help France overcome its continuing moral crisis.

In doing so he incorporated many themes of his predecessors, often acknowledging his intellectual debt to them. Auguste Comte recognized the *sui generis* nature of society which he defined as a living organism and championed the development of a scientific sociology using the same methods employed in the natural sciences. Charles Montesquieu analyzed the way in which customs vary from society to society. Alexis de Tocqueville advocated the proliferation of secondary groups as sources of community and the strengthening of local power which would promote freedom by counterbalancing the power of the

46

national government. Even though Durkheim emphasized these and other French origins of sociology, he was also influenced by German thinkers. He was impressed by the empirical foundations of experimental German psychology and felt that those German scholars who emphasized the importance of the collective moral life – who understood that rules, customs, and morality, and not reason and individual interests, are the bases of social life – were on the right track.[2] The English philosopher and sociologist, Herbert Spencer, whose thought was a powerful intellectual current of the times both in Europe and the USA, helped pioneer the structural-functional approach to sociology which Durkheim further developed.

Even while building on other disciplines, Durkheim sought to differentiate sociology by eliminating their shortcomings. He thought that philosophy was too abstract and lost in endless metaphysical speculations, with philosophers too prone to counter one speculation with another and to deductively derive the conclusions implied in their general premises rather than beginning with the facts and then proceeding inductively. Although sociologists should emulate those psychologists who based their work on empirical evidence, psychology's focus on the individual failed to recognize that social phenomena must be explained in terms of other social phenomena. The economists also suffered from beginning and ending their explanations with individuals, thereby incorrectly seeking to derive the social from the individual. In employing a far too general conception of an abstract, universal, profit-seeking individual the economists also failed to recognize that individuals vary, depending on the society and their place within it.[3] Durkheim's intellectual passion, then, was to develop a new science of sociology which, shorn of the shortcomings of competing approaches to social life, would help France overcome its version of the general European crisis which he boldly defined as history's greatest moral crisis.[4]

Key Issues

Legitimating the Discipline: Sociology, Science, and Emergence

Establishing sociology as a legitimate scientific discipline required, first, that sociology have its own distinctive subject matter and, second, that it be studied scientifically, a powerful combination which would differentiate sociology from the other academic disciplines with which it was most likely to be confused and establish it as a legitimate science worthy of taking its place alongside such established sciences as physics and chemistry.

Durkheim's definition of sociology's distinctive province is based on the doctrine of emergence which distinguishes levels of reality. The interaction, organization, structural relations, and interconnectedness of phenomena at one level of reality give rise to new, emergent phenomena at the next higher level: most importantly, the physical to the chemical, chemical to biological, biological to psychological, and psychological to sociological. Emergent phenomena must be explained in terms of causes at their own level of reality and cannot be explained in terms of, that is, reduced to, causes at some lower level. Just as water cannot be explained in terms of the characteristics of oxygen and hydrogen taken separately, social phenomena cannot be explained in terms of the characteristics of individuals. Rather, both water and society are emergent phenomena relative to the characteristics of the parts (individuals) whose interactions and relations constitute them.

He viewed social phenomena as natural phenomena, parts of nature. As such they should be studied using the same scientific methods which have proven to be so powerful in the disciplines which study other aspects of nature such as physics, chemistry, and biology. Science explains effects in terms of their respective causes in an effort to discover the laws and theories governing these cause-and-effect relationships. Scientists should not proceed deductively, applying preconceived conceptions and conclusions to the facts. Rather, they must begin with the natural world itself, with empirical reality, by carefully observing, defining, gathering, comparing, and classifying facts and only then proceeding inductively to identify the cause-and-effect relationships these facts reveal.

The Relationship between the Individual and Society: Images of Society

Durkheim made effective use of two images of society, one of which, using the language and imagery of the natural sciences of his day, views the individual and the social as opposed forces. This opposition provides a basic source of conflict, tension, and energy in Durkheim's theory. The more powerful given systems of causes and effects, the greater the importance of the science which studies them. Accordingly, in showing how social forces overcome individual forces and direct, coerce, contain, control, and socialize the individual, Durkheim demonstrated not only sociology's independence from psychology but also the power of social, relative to individual, forces and therefore sociology's scientific legitimacy.

The 'individual' in this formulation is a theoretical construct quite different from the individuals actually encountered in society. It refers to the unsocialized component of the individual's personality, the individual divorced from social life and, sometimes, to the individual in pursuit of egoistic interests. In contrast, the individuals who populate any society are eminently social beings guided by moral rules. Indeed, Durkheim felt we got all the best in ourselves, and all the things that distinguish us from other animals, from our social existence. Thought, language, world-views, rationality, morality, aspirations, in short, culture, derive from society. Thus, the unsocialized 'individual', the 'individual' divorced from society, the beast within us, is a poor approximation of the highly socialized beings who constitute societies.

Durkheim's second image of society is borrowed, not from the physical sciences, but from biology: like the human body, society is a structural-functional system of interacting, exchanging, mutually adjusting and supportive parts which make necessary contributions toward the survival of the whole. Structures (parts) are analyzed in terms of their effects or functions, that is, the services they perform for the system. The family gives birth to, legitimates, and socializes children; religion integrates society; the state enforces laws, adjudicates disputes, and makes decisions binding on the entire society; and the economy provides the goods and services necessary for survival.

Three Studies of Social Solidarity

The Division of Labour in Society

In a number of studies of social solidarity developing these perspectives Durkheim pursued his goal of establishing a useful scientific sociology. His first major book, *The Division of Labor in Society,* employs his evolutionary functionalism to examine the changing bases of social solidarity as primitive societies integrated by the similarities underlying mechanical solidarity evolve into advanced societies integrated by the differences underlying organic solidarity. Primitive societies are composed of a small number of similar individuals who constitute a homogeneous, undifferentiated mass. The strong emotional reactions to infractions of the strict, unforgiving moral code embodied in the collective conscience – that is, shared, strongly held beliefs, values, and sentiments – and the repressive law at its core underlie the harsh justice and severe punishments which perpetuate the similarities underlying mechanical solidarity.

Over time societies may grow in size, heightening pressure on increasingly scarce resources. Durkheim felt that this intensified struggle for existence produced the specialization and division of labor which permit the same resources to support more people. Society undergoes structural and functional differentiation, as different individual activities are grouped into different institutions specializing in their respective functions. Individuals and institutions relate to one another on the basis of the complementary differences which make them mutually dependent on one another. The collective conscience becomes weaker and more abstract, permitting the development of greater individuality and freedom. Mechanical solidarity based on likenesses and a powerful collective conscience is increasingly supplanted by a division of labor producing an organic solidarity based on the mutual interdependence of individuals and groups. Repressive law is largely replaced by restitutive law which calls not for revenge but rather for the return of things to the conditions which would have prevailed had the legal offenses not occurred. In sum, the course of social evolution is marked by a transition from small, simple, homogeneous tribal societies integrated by likenesses and a powerful, concrete collective conscience to large, modern, differentiated industrial societies integrated by the interdependence of individuals and structures created by the division of labor.

The contrasts between mechanical and organic solidarity coexist with some basic similarities. Diagrammatically:

Mechanical Solidarity

| Likenesses Similarities | → | Interaction | → | Moral Rules Powerful, concrete collective conscience Repressive law | → | Integration |

Organic Solidarity

| Mutually Complementary Differences (Division of Labor) | → | Interaction | → | Moral Rules Weaker, more abstract collective conscience Restitutive law | → | Integration |

One difference between mechanical and organic solidarity lies in the impetus to interaction: similarities versus differences. Another is the change in morality embodied in the changing nature of the collective conscience and the transition from repressive to restitutive law. Beyond these differences the causal chains are the same, and both mechanical and organic solidarity are proportional to rates of interaction and therefore the strength of the moral rules which integrate society.

Suicide

Durkheim's most famous work, *Suicide*, pursues the study of social solidarity. The choice of suicide was brilliant because studying it permitted him to meet psychology on its own ground. People have their own individual reasons for killing themselves, making suicide a preeminently personal act. To prove that this was nonetheless a social phenomenon with social causes would be a powerful demonstration of the importance of social factors and another feather in sociology's hat. Above all, then, Durkheim sought to develop a sociological theory of suicide which meant that suicide had to be explained in terms of social causes. Durkheim did not seek to explain individual instances of suicide. He did not appeal to individual differences in motivation, personality, depression, or mental health to explain why one person committed suicide but another did not. Rather, he sought to explain variation in suicide rates, for example, why rates were lower in one group than another, why a given group's rates changed over time, or why rates for people in one social condition were higher than those for another.

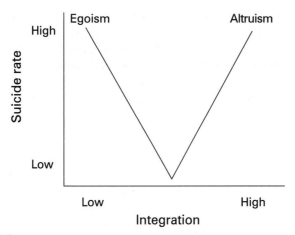

Figure 3.1

Durkheim explains suicide in terms of two independent variables, integration and regulation. Too much or too little of either causes suicide. Thus both high levels of integration (altruism) and low levels of integration (egoism)(see Figure 3.1) cause suicide, just as do high levels of regulation (fatalism) and low levels of regulation (anomie) (see Figure 3.2).

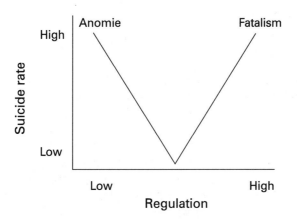

Figure 3.2

Egoism and anomie are the main causes of suicide in the modern world. Applying his theory of egoism to religious, familial, and political 'society', Durkheim argued that each instance revealed the same relationship: the greater the egoism, the higher the suicide rate. Compared to more integrated groups, egoistic groups have lower rates of interaction, people think about themselves more than others and are less bound to one another, there is less community, and social control is weaker. Anomie is weak regulation or norm-lessness. Chronic anomie is produced by a gradual weakening of social control in contrast to acute anomie which is caused by sudden changes either in the situation of a given individual, for example divorce or widowhood, or in social institutions, for example economic booms and busts. Applying his theory of chronic anomie to marriage and to economic institutions, Durkheim argues that the gradual diminution of social control in each had produced higher suicide rates. Applying his theory of acute anomie to the widowed and divorced and to times of rapid economic change, Durkheim asserts that these sudden changes weaken social control, because, given the new circumstances, the old rules no longer apply and new ones have not had time to develop, thereby leading to higher suicide rates for both widowed and divorced persons, compared to the still married, and to higher suicide rates during both economic busts *and* booms, compared to times of economic stability. To explain how anomie leads to higher suicide rates Durkheim pointed to uncon-trolled appetites and aspirations. As social beings humans acquire desires and goals. But these are inherently expandable and their attainment simply stimu-lates the desire for more. The only thing that can restrain inherently insatiable desires is social regulation. Hence, when social regulation is weak, desires outstrip attainment, leaving people frustrated, unhappy, and prone to suicide.

More than one hundred years after its publication in 1897, *Suicide* remains a landmark: it is widely regarded as sociology's exemplary piece of research, because it skillfully interrelates theory and data, using data to test and develop theory and using theory to explain the data, an approach which allowed Durkheim to reject competing biological and psychological theories while validating his sociological theory of variation in suicide rates. Numerous later studies have repeatedly confirmed most of Durkheim's basic findings; and, indeed, sociology has found it difficult to move substantially beyond the theory and findings so persuasively presented in *Suicide*.

The Elementary Forms of the Religious Life

Durkheim's final major work, *The Elementary Forms of the Religious Life,* one of the greatest works of the twentieth century, deepens his account of inter-action as the source of integration by extending his analysis of emotions and, more importantly, by demonstrating the importance of symbols. Durkheim assumed that religion's essential nature would be most visible in the simplest religion which would be found in the simplest societies. Accordingly, he made extensive use of studies of a tribe of primitive Australian aborigines, the Arunta. Durkheim observes that religion cannot be defined in terms of the supernatural, the idea of which is a late development in human thought, or of conceptions about gods and spirits, because such beliefs are secondary or absent in some great religions such as Buddhism and Jainism. Rather, he defined religion in terms of what he regarded as the most basic distinction known to humans, that between the sacred and the profane. Religious symbols are sacred objects; religious beliefs are about sacred objects; and religious practices are orientated toward sacred objects.

Identifying religion as the basic source of moral rules and social integration among the Arunta, Durkheim analyzed it as a cyclical process. As people pursue their secular lives religious sentiments weaken and would die without periodic renewal. Reminded by religious symbols of their beliefs and obligations, people gather to perform religious ceremonies. During these ceremonies, with high rates of interaction and common focus, participants publicly engage in ceremonial behavior symbolizing their religious beliefs. This common affirmation strengthens these beliefs by bringing them to the forefront of consciousness. Collective rituals also generate intense emotion which, in becoming attached to the beliefs symbolized in the ceremonies and to their participants, strengthens them, while bonding the participants to each other. Religious ceremonies, then, integrate society, both by strengthening collective beliefs and morals and by mutually bonding their participants. The function of religion is to integrate society.

Religion is a system of mutually reinforcing beliefs, rites (behavior), and symbols (which include both objects and the rites themselves). Beliefs cause the rites by reminding people of their religious duties. As visible physical enactments (symbols) of beliefs, the rites reinforce beliefs. Within a wide range of beliefs, content is secondary; rather, what is essential is that they cause believers to enact the rites which strengthen the common beliefs and sentiments which integrate society. Symbolic objects are important because, while society cannot be continuously gathered in performance of rites, such objects can serve as constant reminders of religious beliefs and obligations.

Durkheim's perspectives explain both the extrinsic sacredness of religious symbols and the intimate link between groups and symbols. The Arunta are organized into clans (kinship groups), each represented by its own sacred religious symbol or totem (emblem). But what is the source of the totem's sacredness, the feelings of respect and awe which it inspires? Durkheim rejects the argument that the inherent qualities of what the totems ostensibly represent inspire these feelings, because the totems represent not awesome forces of nature such as thunder and lightning but the most ordinary, mundane objects of everyday existence, such as plants or more typically animals like kangaroos or crows. Furthermore, these things themselves are not sacred; only their symbolic representation, the totem, is. Clearly, the totem's sacredness is not intrinsic but superimposed. But by what? Participants feel the power and emotion generated by religious ceremonies. Unable to explain the origin of that power, they attribute it to some object in their presence which thereby becomes sacred. Furthermore, Durkheim argued, if the totem stands for the clan, is that not because the clan and the totem are ultimately the same thing, because the totem represents the power of society which is especially manifest during collective religious ceremonies? Durkheim concluded that religion is simply society worshipping itself. Durkheim's first book, *The Division of Labor,* emphasizes the role of interaction in creating social solidarity; his last book, *The Elementary Forms,* emphasizes how a particularly intense form of interaction, religious or ritual interaction, creates an especially powerful form of integration.

Seeing Things Differently

We may use Durkheim's perspectives to analyze sports as a system of mutually reinforcing beliefs, rites, symbols, and emotions bonding people into communities. Doing so will help us understand the importance of sports, why people talk so much and feel so strongly about them, the depth of attachment to favorite teams, the emotional impact of attending the game, and why fans who do not know each other often find it easier to talk about sports than anything else. Although our example is American collegiate football, Durkheim's perspectives suggest the more general importance of what is ostensibly simply an entertaining pastime.

As the big event approaches there is increasing talk about the game, with ever more heartfelt expressions of support for the home team. Friday night's pep rally fires up fans and team alike. Saturday morning university banners appear on homes and lawns throughout the area and on the parade of vehicles heading toward the stadium, as people publicly remind themselves and others of their loyalties. Tailgate parties reinforce these shared commitments. Fans experience a further rise in excitement as the expectant crowd fills the stadium, grouping themselves into two opposing factions which, although unequal in size, are nonetheless equally enthusiastic and outfitted in team colors and hats, symbolizing their loyalties. The home crowd is pleased to see its team logo emblazoned on the field itself, with the university's name prominently written in both endzones. Each group roars as its team returns to the field shortly before kickoff, dressed in distinctive uniforms with helmets featuring the team's logo. After booing or chanting 'Who cares?' after the introduction of each member of the visiting team's starting line-up, the home crowd roars its support for the home team's line-up. Immediately before the game everyone participates in another ritual, honoring the country's flag and singing the national anthem. As this temporary interruption reinforcing their common commitment to the larger national community ends, the crowd yells in happy anticipation of the game and collectively produces the characteristic crescendo accompanying kickoffs. During the game fans energetically take advantage of numerous opportunities to collectively participate in the common activities demonstrating their shared beliefs, emotions, and togetherness: cheering their team, standing to cheer after scores and for especially important plays, yelling at referees, waving team banners as they participate in cheers led by cheerleaders dressed in team colors, booing opponents, and cheering still more, as cheerleaders race around the stadium carrying a large university flag waving in the breeze. Half-time performances by the two university bands, dressed in school colors, include opportunities for supporters to sing school songs. After the game the crowd files out, supporters of the losing team unhappy and subdued, supporters of the winning team talking boisterously and perhaps lingering to prolong the moment.

In short, sporting events exemplify the conditions of religious ritual: high rates of group interaction, focus on sacred symbols, and collective ritual behavior symbolizing group membership and strengthening shared beliefs, values, aspirations, and emotions. People experience the general excitement which builds in anticipation of the game, the stimulation and sheer joy of being surrounded by others sharing their enthusiasm, and the ebb and flow of emotions following the waxing and waning fortunes of their team. Regardless of whether they have just shared the thrill of victory or the agony of defeat, fans continue to assert their common hopes for their team and experience a reinforced emotional commitment to it and the sport itself.

Just as Durkheim analyzed the waxing and waning strength of religion among the Arunta as a function of the cycle of religious life, so the intensity of commitment to spectator sports is a function of cycles. The weekly cycles begin with concern about the upcoming game which peaks during the game itself. The seasonal cycle finds fans increasingly involved, as games cumulate, influencing chances for winning the league championship and for post-season play. Additionally, interest grows in the annual 'big game' with a traditional, especially reviled, rival, the winner of which keeps the game's symbol – an ax, an old oaken bucket, or some other trophy – for a year until the next big game. Finally, there is the yearly cycle with interest diminishing in the off-season.

If sporting events are very much what they seem to be – entertainment for millions of followers – they are also much more. They create groups and subgroups. Fans support their team against all rivals but will then support another league team in its post-season play against a non-league team and support any national team in international competition. Although divided into partisans of different teams, fans also constitute a larger group of people who follow the sport and enjoy talking about it. Game crowds constitute emotional groups with common sentiments who bond together as they relish the spectacle and their many shared activities in the presence of sacred symbols. In sum, like other sporting events, football games unite believers into a community of fans.

Legacies and Unfinished Business

Durkheim had his greatest immediate influence in France, where he offered the first French university course in social science and was the driving force behind institutionalizing sociology within the academy. Through the force of his personality, the power of his ideas, the persuasiveness of his arguments, the range and originality of his writings, the charisma of his teaching, the influence of his students, and the extensiveness of his contacts both within and outside of the academy, his influence extended well beyond sociology into numerous related disciplines, especially anthropology, history, and linguistics. In England his greatest influence was on British social anthropology, notably the works of A.R. Radcliffe-Brown, an influence suggested in the title of a collection of his essays, *Structure and Function in Primitive Society*. Durkheim also had great influence on American sociology both before and especially after World War II. His initial influence was on functionalism and its leading theorists, **Talcott Parsons** and **Robert K. Merton**. Parsons' first major work, *The Structure of Social Action*, sought to synthesize the works of Durkheim and **Weber** (and several others) into a theory of action. Later, Parsons greatly expanded this theory by synthesizing it with a structural-functional image of society, addressing a basic Durkheimian question: How do social institutions do all those things necessary for society to survive? Parsons' most famous student, Merton, built on Durkheim's theory of anomie to develop his own theory of anomie and deviance. Whereas Durkheim's general concepts of the collective conscience and solidarity (*Division*), integration and regulation (*Suicide*), and collective representations (*The Elementary Forms*) fail to differentiate between norms and goals, making this distinction allowed Merton to identify four kinds of deviance – innovation, ritualism, retreatism, and rebellion – in what remains one of sociology's most influential theories of conformity and deviance.[5]

Perpetuating Durkheim's focus on interaction, another American sociologist, **Erving Goffman** asks: What selves, motivations, and strategies do people bring to interaction; how do these affect the interaction itself; and how are they reinforced or altered by interaction? Goffman's analysis of deference and demeanor builds on Durkheim's insight that in the modern world the individual is sacred.[6] On the one hand, as sacred beings we are entitled to the deference demanded by all sacred objects; on the other, since we must be so treated, we also experience the pressure to display demeanor worthy of such respect. Goffman extends his analysis by showing how what appear to be simply everyday encounters can be analyzed as sacred ceremonies. When two people meet, each experiences the pressure to appropriately acknowledge the other. Both ask, 'How are you?' not because they necessarily care but to fulfill the requirements of the greeting ceremony. After marking the end of the ceremony with 'good-byes,' each finds it awkward to quickly re-encounter the other. Having gone through and appropriately ended the greeting ceremony, repeating it seems unnecessary but ignoring the other person also seems inappropriate. Similarly, after having thanked the host and said their 'good-byes', people find it awkward to return to a party to retrieve something left behind. Defining these everyday encounters as sacred ceremonies helps Goffman penetrate beneath the surface to expose their underlying dynamics.

Perhaps the most influential American sociological theorist of his generation, Randall Collins extends Durkheim's and Goffman's analyses of ritual interaction. Distinguishing a vertical and horizontal dimension of social interaction, Collins uses the first to build his theory of social stratification. Giving orders makes people proud and self-confident and encourages them to identify with the organization in the name of which they give orders and which supports them. In contrast, taking orders makes people less self-confident, more passive, and more cynical about and alienated from the organizations in which they take orders. Order-givers share the upper-class culture structured by their place in the social hierarchy just as order-takers share their working-class culture. This vertical dimension of social interaction is crosscut by the horizonal dimension, ritual density, which itself includes two components: first, how much of the time is the individual in the presence of other people and, second, are these other people the same or different people? High rates of interaction with the same people create robust group solidarity with high levels of conformity and a strong sense of insiders versus outsiders (Durkheim's mechanical solidarity). In contrast, where people spend less time with others, giving them more privacy, and interact with a variety of people, there is less solidarity and conformity, greater individuality, and people think more relativistically and abstractly. Collins, then, uses two dimensions of interaction, vertical and horizontal, to explain group solidarity, how interaction affects world-views, and how individuals with similar world-views perpetuate distinctive class structures. In this way Collins develops the perspectives of a classic consensus, functionalist theorist (Durkheim) which he then introduces into the heart of his contemporary conflict theory.[7]

Even such a brief overview of Durkheim's legacy in American sociology suggests the range of his influence, which extends from functionalists like Parsons to conflict theorists like Collins, who emphatically reject functionalism. We can see the application and extension of his ideas to society as in Parsons; to conformity and deviance as in Merton's theory of anomie and deviance; to ritual interaction as in Goffman; and to beliefs, rituals, emotions, bonding, class cultures, and stratification as in Collins. Durkheim's deep, multifaceted theory retains its power to inspire successive generations of sociologists as they theorize about everything from social structure to human agency to the relationship between the two.

Further Reading

R. Collins and M. Makowsky, *The Discovery of Society*, 5th edn (New York: McGraw-Hill, 1993), pp. 272–9.

E. Durkheim, 'The Dualism of Human Nature and Its Social Conditions'. *Emile Durkheim on Morality and Society*. (Chicago: The University of Chicago Press, 1973), pp. 149–63.

E. Goffman, *Interaction Ritual* (Garden City, NY: Anchor Books, 1967).

S. Lukes, *Emile Durkheim: His Life and Work* (New York: Harper & Row, 1972).

R. Merton, 'Social Structure and Anomie'. *Social Theory and Social Structure*, rev. and enl. edn (Glencoe, IL: The Free Press, 1957), pp. 131–60.

W. Pope, *Durkheim's 'Suicide'* (Chicago: The University of Chicago Press, 1976).

4

Sigmund Freud

Ian Craib

Driving Impulses

Freud is comparable only really to **Marx** among the thinkers discussed in this volume; his ideas have not only influenced those in his own discipline, he did in fact found a discipline, and he has influenced thinkers across all the social sciences and humanities, medicine and biology. More than this, however, he has changed our common-sense understanding of vital aspects of our lives; it is not just that his most crucial ideas are present in our everyday references to 'Freudian slips', but our views about sexuality, childhood, mental health and illness and psychological therapy have been permeated by his thought to the point where even those who regard themselves as critical of, or opponents of, psychoanalysis, do not realise how profoundly they have been influenced by his ideas. Like Marx he changed the world, and like Marx, a century after his ideas were formulated, he is subjected not only to intellectual criticism but also to personal vilification – he was a cocaine addict, dishonest, he was scared of making public what he knew about incest, he developed an essentially fraudulent treatment for which gullible people pay large sums of money. A good rule of thumb in intellectual life is that somebody who comes under such sustained personal attack for a century or so probably has something important to say.

Freud was born in Freiberg in Moravia in 1856, the son of a Jewish wool merchant, and the family moved to Vienna when Freud was four. Families are always complex networks and thanks to Freud we now know the emotional energy and intellectual creativity that we devote as children and as adults to making sense of our place in the family. In the late twentieth century it is divorce, step-parenting and single-parenting which add to the complexities of the fantasy we have of a 'normal' family; in the mid-nineteenth century, it was death and disease which created step-parenting and single-parenting. Freud's mother was his father's third wife, 20 years younger than his father and younger than Freud's oldest half-brother. He had his work cut out.

Growing up in what was then Austria, Freud was able to make use of some three to four decades of liberalism in which to develop his ideas, but anti-

Semitism was always in the air and towards the end of the nineteenth century it grew ever stronger. To add to his confusion Freud's early years in his profoundly Jewish family were complicated by an influential Roman Catholic nursemaid. But his mother was all important: she adored Freud and thought he was destined for great things, as had apparently been predicted at his birth. Freud adored his young and beautiful mother and perhaps thought he was a more suitable partner for her than was his ageing father.

It is not unusual for children adored in such a way to feel that they are special, and will achieve great fame. Given that he also had to sort out his place in a complicated family, and that his family, as did many middle-class Jewish families, encouraged disciplined study and that during his years of education it was still possible for middle-class Austrian Jews to build successful careers, it is not surprising that Freud was an immensely successful student. When he went to university to study medicine, it was not through any great desire to ease suffering but through what he described as a 'greed for knowledge'. There is still an ambivalence in psychoanalysis between a desire to know and a desire to help and although Freud made his living through practising as an analyst it was his search for knowledge which really drew his energy; he did not have a very high opinion of many of his patients.

In his medical studies Freud moved to neurology, and then through studying under Charcot, the renowned French psychologist in Paris, he became absorbed in psychology. It is difficult to pinpoint precise intellectual influences on Freud – he read widely and voraciously in philosophy and liter-ature as well as medicine and the natural sciences and while one can see, for example, Marx emerging from the Hegelian tradition, Freud created his own tradition, becoming increasingly aware that he was opening up new fields of knowledge. He jealously organised his followers to protect it from early attacks. It developed outside of universities and even today in Europe (and especially in Britain) the major training organisations are private institutions, just beginning to form links with universities, and the institutions still carry the sectarian inheritance of Freud's fierce protective defences of his ideas. It is a pleasing paradox that, after a lifetime of splitting from close colleagues – most notably Jung – to protect his ideas, he escaped the Nazis by moving to England rather than America for the least sectarian of reasons: he disagreed profoundly with the American requirement that psychoanalysts should first undergo a medical training. He thought it vital that analysts should come from a wide range of disciplines. He spent his last few years practising in London, dying in 1939.

Rather than seeing Freud as emerging from an intellectual background, it might be more useful to see him as emerging from a particular social devel-opment: the development of the city and modern metropolitan life. From a more sociological point of view **Simmel** (1971) has talked about the way urban life bombards the individual with stimuli and involves each of us in short-term shallow relations – something which the development of late capitalism has accentuated. In such situations we build protective shells around ourselves. This is not quite what psychoanalysts call defence mechanisms but we can regard Freud as looking at what goes on under the defences, under the shell.

Key Issues

It is often thought that Freud's psychology is the opposite of sociology, that it is concerned with the individual rather than society. It should be clear that this is a profound mistake, but, more than this, even when he is most concerned with individual psychology Freud has an important message for sociology.

The Unconscious

His most important 'discovery' was the unconscious; I put 'discovery' in inverted commas because, as Freud pointed out, the existence of an unconscious dimension to the human psyche had been apparent to philosophers and artists for centuries. What distinguishes Freud is his attempt to give the unconscious a content, to bring it into the range of a scientific or rational understanding. The unconscious consists of wishes and desires, ideas which are too socially or personally dangerous to allow into consciousness – literally the 'unthinkable'. Freud thought these ideas were primarily sexual but later analysts have added destructive ideas, and our awareness of our vulnerability to the list.

The unconscious is, of course, not quite unconscious. At some level we know what is going on. One modern analyst refers to the 'unthought known', something we know but do not allow to enter our thoughts. Of course it pushes through into consciousness despite our attempts to push it down. Freud refers to the unconscious desire as an unwanted party guest: you turn her away from the door and then she goes around the house trying to attract attention by tapping on the windows; when you draw the blinds you hear her climbing up to the roof and trying to get down the chimney; if you light a fire, she starts tunnelling in the garden.

The unconscious desire sneaks through in unexpected ways, hence the famous Freudian slip. A real Freudian slip is acutely embarrassing, when you find you have said something revealing about yourself and that you know you mean but which you would never consciously have revealed. My favourite personal example happened a few years ago when I was seriously ill: a colleague with whom I had once had an argument sent me a postcard offering me sympathy on my demise; this person would, I am sure, have been quite mortified had he realised what he had written.

The unconscious also appears through dreams, but the meaning of dream symbols is less obvious than Freudian slips. Freud suggests that the unconscious has no history, that it does not change and that unconscious desires demand immediate satisfaction: there is a sense in which a part of each of us is a screaming baby demanding that those around us fulfil our needs. He also suggests that the unconscious does not follow the laws of logic: that we can demand contradictory things at the same time, love and hate the same person, accept and reject intimacy and so on. In dreaming we are closer to the unconscious than we are in waking life. But dream symbols still have to be decoded, we need to find the latent content underneath the manifest content that we remember when we wake up. Freud found that his patients regularly told him their dreams and if he asked them to 'free associate' – just say whatever came into their mind as they thought about the dream symbol – they would undo the coding which had resulted from the 'dream-work' which attempted to hide the meaning of the dream. The dream-work involves a process of:

(a) condensation – of bringing together different meanings in one symbol, so that, for example, if I dream of a policeman, it could stand for my father and my boss, and my psychoanalyst, not to mention my own super-ego (see below);

(b) displacement – the dream symbol is a displacement of the unconscious object which occurs through similarity or some contingent conjunction or some linguistic connection. Similarity covers the case of the train going through a tunnel signifying sexual intercourse that seems to be so well known. Contingent conjunction covers my dreaming about the table rather than the very attractive woman I saw standing next to it; the linguistic dimension is illustrated by the recent dream of a colleague: that her work was being rubbished by a Dr Martin whom she knew. The connection here is to the Dr Marten who produces boots – the dream figure was 'putting the boot in';

(c) symbolization or turning an idea into pictures; here the example is of a colleague who dreamt he was laying a table with knives and forks which had no handles – carrying the idea that he could not handle a particular situation.

(d) secondary revision – the 'story' of the dream which Freud thought was constructed as we awake to hide the dream's meaning, although most contemporary analysts would see the story as important.

Thus the unconscious is not just a repository for unwanted guests. Seen in this context, dreaming is an act of our imagination, a creative act undertaken during sleep, motivated by our need to live with ourselves. It is also an aspect of our lives which also goes on, usually unbeknownst to ourselves, when we are awake, investing our relationships and our surrounding world with levels of meaning which stretch back into our past and our parents' past.

Psychic Structure

Returning to the idea of the unwanted guests, Freud suggested that we develop an internal psychic structure to deal with their presence. The crucial psychological problem for any individual to deal with is the demand for immediate satisfaction in an external world where immediate satisfaction is not possible. This involves us in a constant internal conflict and negotiation.

Freud suggests that there are three crucial internal psychic structures. In the first English translation of Freud these were given Latin names in an attempt to gain respectability with the medical profession, but Freud used everyday German words which convey the meaning more clearly.

The basis is the 'id' or the 'it', the source of our drives which demand satisfaction. It is important to understand that Freud is not talking about biological instincts but about biological energies which are attached to psychological symbols – the instinct is biological, the drive is psychological and already to some degree social since symbols have a social origin and are given individual meanings. The 'it', like the other structures, is partly conscious and partly unconscious – I know that I have a sexual drive but I do not know all its dimensions and complexities, particularly its less salubrious aspects. The 'it' is most closely connected with our bodies – it is the thing that we are despite ourselves and which sometimes seems to take control and push us forward into actions where we do not feel that we have any choice.

At the other end of the psyche, so to speak, there is the super-ego, the 'over-I', in part representative of external authority and external reality. Its function is to control our drives by suppression and repression.

In between there is the 'ego', the part of my psyche that I refer to when I use the word 'I', the part which tries to mediate between my internal drives and the requirements of the outside world. It is common these days to find the word 'psychodynamic' used to describe psychoanalytic theories and this word offers a grasp of the way our psyches are constantly in movement – the three structures behaving like three warring armies, forming and breaking alliances in our internal conflicts.

These three structures are only the basis of the internal dynamics of the psyche; Freud also talks about the 'objects' of our drives, by which he means the people towards whom our drives are directed. They are 'objects' because at the most basic level – as babies – we simply require them to satisfy our needs. As we grow we can perhaps begin to treat our objects as people, but there is always a dimension in any relationship in which we use the other person for our own satisfaction. However, the objects of our desires are also 'introjected'. This is a concept with a stronger sense than 'internalisation' which is usually used in sociological accounts of socialisation and usually refers to ideas. We introject people, primarily parents and siblings, through identifying with them and giving over part of our internal world to them, and in this way we carry our families and their loves and hates, alliances and fights around with us as part of ourselves for the rest of our lives and they become involved in the dynamics of id, ego and super-ego. Freud did not develop this object relations part of his work very far, but it was taken much further by Melanie Klein and by the main school of British psychoanalysts. Some people see it as an alternative to Freud's emphasis on drives but I do not think the two are incompatible, and together they comprise a complex depth model of the human psyche.

Freud and Society

There is enough here to be able to begin looking at Freud's conception of society and social life. This operates on two levels, one a **meta-theoretical**, almost metaphysical level and the other the micro-level of day-to-day relationships.

Meta-theoretical

This refers to a conception arrived at by philosophical or abstract reflection. Both ontology (conceptions of the sorts of things there *are* in the world – known as the 'theory of being') and epistemology (conceptions of how we *know* that there are these sorts of things in the world – known as the 'theory of knowledge') are aspects of meta-theory.

Freud's notion of drives demanding immediate satisfaction and the necessity of their repression leads to the meta-theory. He suggests a process by means of which the unacceptable object – the idea to which it is attached (for example in some societies homosexuality) – of a drive is repressed and the energy (the biological component of the drive) is attached to something else (same sex friendships). This may take the form of a neurosis – if for example I deal with my desire for oral satisfaction by overeating – or it may take the form of a socially useful activity (sublimation), for example I might become an opera singer. Some people manage both outcomes at the same time. It is interesting that the activities we regard as socially useful and those we regard as a sign of mental illness bear the same structure and there is a thin and movable line between the two. Some theorists have argued that society itself is a form of neurosis.

However I do not want to follow this line of argument here. The important point is the relationship between society, civilisation and misery. Perhaps Freud's most important insight is that in order to live together with each other we sacrifice something, we cannot get all that we want when we want it. The more complex the society, the more sophisticated the level of civilisation, the more satisfaction we have to give up and the more misery we have to bear. This eliminates the possibility of a perfect society. If we compare Freud and Marx, the latter suggested that the foundation of human society is co-operative labour and what distinguishes the human species is that we change our environment and then change ourselves to adjust to the new environment. Freud suggests that labour is not basic but an achievement: in order to spend our days working we have to give up other satisfactions we want more urgently. The Marxist philosopher Herbert Marcuse (1969) argued that different societies require different levels of repression, of misery and the development of capitalism requires a particularly high level of repression. The more developed capitalist system can relax the repression, and sexual urges in particular are channelled into consumption.

This type of analysis seems suggestive, although it is not very popular these days. There have been various radical attempts to equate sexual liberation with political liberation. In the 1920s and 1930s, for example the German communist psychoanalyst Wilhelm Reich (1957) made a very direct connection between the two and saw sexual education and especially the teaching of an ability to reach a full orgasm as an important part of socialist education. Both Reich and Marcuse effectively lose the insight that civilisation and misery are closely linked and that, as Freud pointed out, a radical reorganisation of property rights and wealth might make life easier but would not change fundamentally the human destructive urge which is generated by the sacrifice of immediate satisfaction. At its best this destructiveness can be put to use in the battle against threats from nature and human enemies of one's own society. After the First World War Freud developed a theory of a 'death drive' to explain the fact that so many apparently rational people can engage in mass destruction without rebelling. Later in the century, Melanie Klein gave this a very precise clinical meaning with her concept of envy.

On a micro-level we get a rather different picture, based on the object-relations dimensions of Freud's work. Again he himself did not develop this very far and we can find most of what he has to say directly about the issue in his discussion of groups. Here he talks about the way in which a group member surrenders part of him or herself – the ego-ideal – to the group leader. We also find in his development of a therapeutic technique his identification of 'transference', where the patient comes to perceive the analyst as he or she once perceived a parent and tries to solve early problems by projecting certain qualities on to the analyst. The treatment involves working through these projections.

What this offers is an understanding of everyday interaction which can take us into the less rational aspects of our behaviour. Primarily sociological conceptions of action assume that we act out our social roles and that our actions can be understood as a result of our ideas about the world, and there is a more or less rational connection between our ideas and our actions.

Sociology has a distinct cognitive bias in the way it understands people's actions, it focuses on knowledge, whereas psychoanalysis takes us into the depths of our emotional attachment to our world, the forces which can push or pull us into actions which might have little to do with what we consciously think about ourselves.

Sex and Gender

It is not possible to write about Freud without saying something about his conception of sexuality and his view of women. It is impossible to think about modern conceptions of sexuality without some reference to Freud. I hope I have already said enough to show that he is not some form of sexual determinist, that the important point is that our sexual drive is always attached to some idea, some symbolic object. In this we are unlike other animals. Human sexuality is always in the head as well as the body and can in principle be attached to any object – members of the same sex, members of the opposite sex, other animals, physical objects and so on. The human infant is at least bisexual, if not, in Freud's felicitous phrase, 'polymorphously perverse'. Part of each of us remains so throughout our lives, whether or not we are conscious of it, whether or not we act out the more peculiar forms of sexuality.

If a society is to survive, it must make sure that enough of its members are attracted to the opposite sex enough of the time to allow the society to reproduce itself. Freud's theory of sexual development is about how the baby, whose first love object is the mother whether we are talking about a boy or a girl, comes to move its desire towards a member of the opposite sex – a different member of the opposite sex in the case of a little boy. It is in describing this process that Freud sometimes writes as if women are less able than men simply because they do not possess a penis. Largely, however, modern feminists have gone beyond simply condemning him for these statements. In her classic text *Psychoanalysis and Feminism* (1975) Juliet Mitchell has argued that Freud can be seen as showing how patriarchy reproduces itself, whereas **Nancy Chodorow** has used more modern object relations theories to argue that women's oppression is rooted in the relational consequences of women being assigned a central role in child rearing.

Seeing Things Differently

I have deliberately presented a fairly open account of Freud's ideas because I think that the way in which his work has been developed by the best modern psychoanalysts emphasises the depth and complexity of our conception of what we are, and encourages an openness and tolerance which often seems to be becoming rarer as we move further into late modernity, or as I would prefer to call it, late capitalism. Freud himself changed the way we think about sexuality, and this was recognised while he was still alive. More recently it has been argued that Freud can be put into a line of major figures who have 'decentred' our conception of humanity. First there was Galileo, who showed that the earth was not at the centre of the universe, but just one planet among others. Then much later Darwin showed that human beings were not the centre of God's creation, but rather a possibly random result of a long evolutionary process. Then Marx showed that human beings were not creators of society but its creatures, and finally Freud showed that even as individuals we are not unitary, centred beings but complex entities subjected to internal forces that we struggle to control.

One way of reading Freud in the contemporary world is that of **Foucault** who sees him as developing yet another technique of social control; there is a degree of truth in this and psychoanalysts who see themselves as experts aiming to cure people would certainly fall under such a description. But I also think that there is a more radical way of using Freudian ideas which enables us to change our conceptions of ourselves and our relationships and make the best use of our limited freedoms and abilities.

The complexity of the human psyche, its various structures, desires and internal objects is something that is common to us all; what varies, from society to society, from historical period to historical period and from individual to individual is our ability to tolerate that complexity and the rich content of being human. A good example of the effect of looking at the world in this way is the way in which it changes our understanding of contemporary arguments about crime and morality. On the one hand there is the 'moral' argument about individual responsibility, good and evil, the necessity for firm moral guidelines and clear social duties. Crime is a matter of evil, or badness, and should be punished. On the other hand there is what we might call the sociological argument (or at least the argument with which sociologists might be expected to sympathise) that modern societies are inevitably pluralist and that there can be no firm common morality, and we must see crime primarily as a product of poverty and unemployment. This argument tends to lead to a concern for reforming rather than punishing the criminal. There is in fact much evidence to support the sociological arguments, but many people, if not most, have a gut reaction in favour of the moralistic argument, especially when it comes to violent crime, and the brutal and senseless murders which gain so much publicity.

The Freudian ideas I have discussed here enable us to develop a critical approach to both sides in this argument. I will start with the moral arguments, and ask why they seem to draw on such energy in the individuals who hold them, often fuelling demands for corporal punishment, capital punishment and imprisonment involving punitive prison regimes. Now the Freudian argument suggests that no person is exclusively good or evil (just as no individual is solely heterosexual or homosexual), and that we all have capacities for good and evil actions. If we are disturbed by our capacity for evil then one way of dealing with it is by projecting it on to others and trying to deal with it there, by suppressing or punishing it. The same mechanisms underlie homophobia. The rage of the moralistic argument fulfils the function of dealing with our own 'evil' desires – in other words one of its prime functions is to make its supporters feel better. If we are aware of this emotional force, and allow for it, we can create the space to see the force of some of the socio-logical counter-arguments – that modern societies are too complex and varie-gated to develop a unifying morality except at the most general and therefore most meaningless level, and there are clear connections between levels of poverty and levels of crime.

The same sort of argument can be made on the other side in that the socio-logical arguments should leave us the space to understand our own psycho-logical reactions and processes. In a complex and often a contradictory world morality raises difficult problems that seem hard, often impossible to think through. The moral relativism and the easy determinism that sociology tends to foster ease the anxiety posed by such problems and ease the anxiety posed by our own internal reactions. If the moral relativism argument is right, we do not have to worry too much about guilt or moral constraints on our actions; and if the deterministic arguments are right, then we do not have to worry about moral ambiguities and judgments. In other words the sociolog-ical arguments make us feel better in a different way from the moralistic argu-ments but they still make us feel better. And again, if this can be realised, it is possible to recognise some of the force of the moral arguments, for example, that it is not possible to lead a coherent life without some form of morality which joins and subordinates the individual to the social community, and that not everyone who is poor or unemployed becomes a criminal.

Once we recognise the limitations of both arguments we can ask intelligent questions about the basis of moral communities in modern societies – are they geographically based, professionally based, class or gender based, and is there some overall or totalising way of looking at this problem which requires elaboration of a morality to which we argue that everybody should be subjected. It is here that **Habermas'** (1984, 1987) 'procedural ethics' becomes important: what matters is not so much the content of our collec-tive decisions about public life but the way in which these decisions are arrived at, whether the procedure involves the informed participation of all those who will be affected by the outcome. We can also ask questions about the psychological bases of individual morality and the social conditions which enable a moral sensibility to develop, and the social conditions which tend to blunt such a sensibility – which are perhaps similar to those conditions which are associated with increases in the crime rate.

Legacies and Unfinished Business

Perhaps much of the last section would not have been what the reader might have expected from his or her knowledge of Freud. The legacy of Freud has not always been as open as the ideas I have discussed here – all too often psychoanalysis has been dogmatic, exclusive and even bigoted (most notably in its attitudes to homosexuality which are only now changing). All too often it has adopted a conformist approach to existing social conditions and those in power. Both traditions, the radical and open and the closed and conservative, can be found in the history of sociology.

Developmental Psychology

Simply that branch of psychological thought that is concerned with the development of the psychology of babies and children as they grow and mature.

On the radical side there are first the thinkers I have already mentioned who have tried to equate sexual repression and social oppression, and second those who have employed Freud's **developmental psychology** to develop a critique of modern family structures and the way they are undermined by the development of the market and modern capitalism. Critical theory in the form of Adorno and other writers argued in the middle of this century that changes in social structure (the development of modern technology and large-scale bureaucratic organisations including the modern state) were undermining both the role of the father in the family and the effective working of the family itself as an agent of socialisation. The weakened family structure was producing the sort of personality that responds to authoritarian political leadership. More recently, in the same tradition, Christopher Lasch (1980) has argued that the continuation of these changes has tended to produce a typical narcissistic, dependent person unable to develop a moral, political or intellectual independence. Such personalities tend to close down their internal psychic space. I have suggested that the implications of Freud's arguments is that we have to open up our internal space and accept things about ourselves that we do not want to accept. In this sense Freud offers a standard, of intellectual and emotional openness, by which we make judgments about contemporary societies.

The conservative side of psychoanalysis has developed in sociology through its employment in theories of socialisation, most notably by **Talcott Parsons** (see for example Parsons 1973). In effect Parsons managed to change Freud's work on socialisation into something more closely approaching the ideas of G.H. Mead (Mead 1934). Socialisation must control biological drives and encourage their sublimation into socially useful activity and this achieves the integration of the individual into the social system. The result of this for Parsons seems to be the suppression of the conflict between individual desires and social constraints, and the suppression of internal conflict and complexity.

While it seems to me that the contributions of psychoanalysis to social theory as a whole are suggestive and interesting, its contributions to micro-social analysis and to the sociological understanding of the personality have yet to be realised. I suspect that one of the reasons for the failure to explore this area is life is much easier for the sociologist if he or she believes that people are not complex entities but creatures whose actions are based on knowledge and rationality; perhaps it is feared that if this were not the case, any sort of general sociological understanding on a structural or cultural level would be undermined. I do not believe that this is so. The more general levels of analysis tell us about the scenery within which we act, but the scenery tells us nothing of the depths of the ways that we relate to each other within its confines.

Further Reading

A fairly straightforward introduction to a psychoanalytic conception of the self can be found in R. Stevens (ed.) *Understanding the Self* (London: Sage, 1996). This book provides a useful comparison with other conceptions of the self.

Accessible discussions of Freud, psychoanalysis, society and sociology can be found in:

R. Bocock, *Freud and Modern Society* (Walton-on-Thames, Surrey: Nelson, 1976).
I. Craib, *Psychoanalysis and Social Theory* (Brighton: Harvester Wheatsheaf, 1989).
I. Craib, *The Importance of Disappointment* (London: Routledge, 1994).

A stimulating and controversial use of psychoanalytic ideas to criticise modern societies can be found in:

C. Lasch, *The Culture of Narcissism* (London: Sphere Books, 1980).

5

Georg Simmel

*Patrick Watier**

Driving Impulses

Georg Simmel has always occupied a special place in the pantheon of the founders of sociology. Lewis Coser's characterisation of him as a stranger, an outsider within the academy, seems appropriate only if one looks just to his formal position within academia. It does not, however, take into account the position of Simmel in the wider intellectual domain, nor his role in the institutional consolidation of sociological research: he occupied an ambiguous position, at one and the same time marginal from the point of view of academic standing and central within the intellectual milieu. Many factors, including no doubt the apparent eclecticism of his work – ranging from historiography through psychology and sociology to aesthetics – contributed to this and to the reception of his work. Simmel's *Soziologie* (1992) ran to over 700 pages but he never for a second believed, as did Comte, that sociology should be the queen of the sciences, the pinnacle of the intellectual enterprise. Paradoxically, those things that assured Simmel a central place in the history of ideas in the early years of the twentieth century, his imaginative, bold and exploratory journeys back and forth across the borders of sociology, philosophy and aesthetics, together with his reflections on culture, are what contributed, at least in part, to his lack of recognition in the academic world.

Born of upper-middle-class parents in Berlin in 1858 in a house which stood at the intersection of two of the city's busiest thoroughfares, Friedrichstrasse and Leipzigerstrasse, Simmel converted from Judaism to Christianity and was educated at the Werder Gymnasium and then at the university from which he graduated in 1885. It was while in Berlin that he laid the foundations for his subsequent career. He was appointed *Privatdozent* in 1895, and *Ausserordentlicher* Professor in 1901, but he had to wait until 1914 to be appointed as a full professor at the University of Strasbourg, which at that time was part of Germany, Alsace having been annexed at the end of the 1870

---

*Translation by Phil Brew and Rob Stones © Phil Brew and Rob Stones

Franco-Prussian War. Simmel spent the last years of his life here, regretting that Strasbourg did not possess an intellectual milieu comparable with that of Berlin. It is important to note that his academic career met with considerable resistance. Some of his colleagues believed that his teaching would have a destructive effect on his students, and he would certainly have encountered recurrent anti-Semitism. His life in Berlin, one of the world's great cities, was clearly instrumental in developing his interest in the new social relations individuals of necessity evolve when the majority of their dealings are with people they do not know, strangers in the broadest sense, people who were not part of one's circle of acquaintances.

Key Issues

A Plurality of Approaches, a Plurality of Forms

From as early as his 1894 volume, *The Problem of Sociology,* Simmel insisted on the necessity of drawing boundaries around the domain of the new discipline. But it would be simplistic to see Simmel as just a sociologist, confining himself within these boundaries, and an examination of his work as a whole, and of the range of themes that he dealt with, reveals that he covered much more than the sociological domain. His *oeuvre* included erudite discussions on values, money, culture, the individual, the artistic personality and fashion. It raised questions about the transformation of large cities and the implications of this for the lives of individuals, and explored the new relations between the sexes arising out of modern forms of association. Simmel, through all his probings into social and cultural questions, attempted to capture the spirit of the times, to describe the transformation of the soul of modern society. He was sensitive to the question of women and to the feminist movement, and speculated on the possibility of a specifically feminist culture, and on the relations between the claims of women and the struggles of workers. Noting the arrival and institutionalisation of a social world brought increasingly under the aegis of the calculable and the intellectual, he made a connection between this and the lifestyles of modern man, and wondered what new relations might emerge between the objective and subjective cultures. He began to sketch out a sociology of feelings and insisted on the recognition that psycho-social categories such as loyalty and gratitude were essential supports of socialisation. In short he attempted to describe the liaisons which individuals construct within forms of socialisation. It is also worth emphasising that from 1890 to 1918 Simmel attempted to envisage both the possibilities for liberation and emancipation and the limitations placed on the development of individuals, at least in part, by the ever-growing significance assumed by technology, and by the attendant interminable focus on a succession of technical means whose ends were no longer clear.

The modes of relations between individuals and society, the relations between the subjective culture and the objective culture, emerged more and more distinctly to Simmel as posing the central questions of social development. He attempted to capture this in his coining of the expression 'the tragedy of culture': life and creativity seek expression but can find it only within forms characterised by a distancing from these very wellsprings.

That Simmel's work was so rich and varied can be understood if one accepts his view that the social world and its reality can be envisaged from a number of different angles of attack. Distinct forms of investigation can be applied to it, as he points out in *The Philosophy of Money,* where he developed a number of fundamental epistemological categories. The tentative and fragmented character of some of his work, his always nuanced and hypothetical pronouncements, his relativist conceptions, his interest in seemingly trivial phenomena, are all easily explained once one grasps the spirit of this central idea of a plurality of forms of investigation. It was a historico-social form, for example, that cleared a pathway for the emergence of what Simmel refers to as a 'pure form', money, whose impact on modern society and styles of living he was able to theorise in these terms. Money was itself the condition of the transformation of forms of association, but, seen from another angle, it was the transformation of these social forms that allowed the development of a money economy.

The changes are analysed by a chain of elegant and plausible reasoning that can be seen as hypothetical, and it is understandable that many more conventional sociologists should have found themselves confused by his idiosyncratic artistry. The variety of topics studied, combined with the confusion created by the conception of a plurality of forms of investigation, mentioned above, was liable to puzzle, and indeed certainly did puzzle, many readers. Within this plurality of forms, Simmel came to place greater and greater importance on art and religion. The centre of his problematic shifted towards a cultural analysis of the modern world and the contradictions that cut across it.

Before going on to present Simmel's sociology in more detail I would first like to dispose of a familiar accusation often levelled at it, which is that it is unbridled speculation, and a hopelessly vague and woolly conception of sociology. This accusation has come primarily from professional sociologists, most notably from **Durkheim.** It took a good deal of courage for Célestin Bouglé to end his review of *Soziologie* for *L'Année Sociologique* with the words: 'these observations and unsubstantiated jottings, they too have their place within the domain of sociology in the broadest sense'. But in saying this did not Bouglé stray into the terrain of Simmel's opponents, surrendering to them far too much ground in terms of the importance of proof, which the Simmelian perspective precisely did not concern itself with? Was not the domain of sociology in this broader sense a reference to that very specific kind of social philosophy that always had such a bad press within the Durkheimian school? Is it not accurate to say that this was in fact outside the scope of

Simmel's ambition given that he aimed at the creation of a 'pure sociology' which he clearly distinguished from the more speculative domain of socio-philosophical questions? In attempting to justify a place for Simmel within sociology, it seems to me that Bouglé has consigned him to quarters that fail to encompass the formal sociology that constituted the very core of what Simmel sought to establish.

The Sociological Point of View

From his first works Simmel tried to establish a new type of analysis that rested on a determinate point of view, a specific perspective on the facts. If it proved possible to isolate such a level of abstraction, then sociology would rest on an analysis of the *forms of socialisation* seen from such a perspective (letter of 22.11.1896 from Simmel to Bouglé, in which he speaks of the acquisition of a sociological point of view): and on a particular abstraction of social reality that consists of separating the form of socialisation from its content, and that views society from a certain distance, which enables one to recognise association and reciprocal action as the fundamental constituents of that within society which is pure society and nothing more.

These three terms – the sociological point of view, abstraction and variable distance – indicate the intellectual activity of configuring social reality, and thus of constituting a sociological object that does not pre-exist. Simmel believed that, in order to constitute itself as a science of social reality, sociology must reject all notion of realism. To develop this point he drew upon respected arguments concerning the constitution of historical knowledge. Indeed, *The Problems of the Philosophy of History* (Simmel, [1907], 1977) directly addresses the question of realism in its first chapter, which deals with the 'intrinsic conditions of historical research'. Simmel argues here that 'all knowledge is the translation of the immediate givens of experience into a new language, a language with its own inherent forms, categories and rules'.[1] The problem of sociology is precisely that of constituting a language, of creating categories through which reality – both facts and social experience – acquires the status of knowledge. In this sense, knowledge is always a second-order construction, it is not a mirror-image or a carbon copy of the real, which realism had always claimed it to be. Sociology must, then, forge those *a priori* instruments that all areas of knowledge require to enable them to organise their subject-matter, since it is clear that 'in the last resort, the content of any science doesn't rest on simple objective facts, but always involves an interpretation *(Deutung)* and a shaping *(Formung)* of them according to categories and rules that are the *a priori* of the science concerned'.[2]

Form and Content

Taking as his starting point previous sociological scholarship, the results of epistemological studies carried out in relation to historical knowledge, and the relativist theory of knowledge developed in *The Philosophy of Money*, Simmel returns in his great *Soziologie* to the questioning of sociology itself and the determination of its field of study. The procedures of abstraction that Simmel's 'pure sociology' applies to those elements within society that are purely societal and nothing more involve the separation of the form from the content of socialisation. Socialisation is the configuration from within which a number of individuals engage in reciprocal action, and the reciprocal action can only have its source in the expression of certain instincts or the desire to achieve certain goals. The social level that Simmel endeavoured to make intelligible is necessarily the result of interactions between individuals, but it develops specific properties and consequences of its own into which no research had been carried out. Such a project would require clear distinctions to be made between, on the one hand, the instincts, interests, tendencies, and targets or goals manifested by individuals and that are the *content* or the material of socialisation, and, on the other hand, the *forms* in which individuals, in order to realise this content, are socialised. Time and again Simmel emphasised the heuristic character of the form–content distinction. It is a distinction which belongs to the group of categories designed to help the human intellect to organise what is given in immediate experience: 'Just as the forms of sociology are formulated on the basis of an unlimited number of contents, in the same way the forms themselves develop out of the most general and the most profoundly rooted fundamental psychic functions. Everywhere, form and content are *relative* concepts, categories of knowledge developed in order to cope with phenomena and to organise them intellectually. Thus a feature seen as it were from above as form in one relationship, will in another, seen from below, need to be described as content.'[3]

Contents, motives, dispositions, such as hunger, love, work, religion or the impulse to sociability, are not in themselves social. They exist in society because they are to be found in individuals, and in this sense they provide the conditions for all socialisation, but they become really social only through the forms of reciprocal action through which, and within which, individuals associate with and influence one another. The notion of 'liaison' is fundamental, because sociology studies the forms that come into being when individuals reciprocally influence each other through interaction and form social unities. Not hesitating to play with the elasticity of the word 'liaison', especially pronounced in popular German, and the range of the activities that it can include, Simmel writes:

> The more decisive a purely sociological concept is (which is not to say a substantive or particularistic concept, but rather one referring to a simple form of relation-

ship), the more readily it will define linguistically its own content and realisations. ... Such is the character of that most purely sociological word: 'liaison'. In its general use in popular language where it has the meaning of an erotic relationship, the word's ability to be stretched this way and that has been exploited to the maximum. Lovers 'have' a liaison, they 'are', as a sociological unit, a liaison, and finally, he is 'her liaison' and she his. (*Soziologie*, p. 710)

Simmel takes as his starting point the existence of dispositions, which have a flexibility that enables them to enter into different forms of socialisation. To take some examples: devotion is one of those dispositions that is seen within family relationships, in the relationships that individuals may have with a group, or workers with their party, or again, that individuals have with their native country. These dispositions can be present in numerous relations but in many ways only reach complete fulfilment when they constitute the principal basis of the socialisation currently active. The same goes for sociability. It is present in numerous relations but will only acquire its full accomplishment within the interplay of pure sociality, in the way that devotion will only acquire its ultimate fulfilment when it takes on religious expression. The sociology of meals shows how such socialisation takes for granted that the content, the hunger that needs to be satisfied, becomes to some degree secondary, passing into the background, compared with the links which are formed reciprocally between fellow guests or within the family. Hunger becomes form within the configuration of the meal, the particular orientation of the participants towards one another. The individuals are thus linked together by this form, which then, as the currently dominant mode of reciprocal orientation, serves to guide the mutual activities which take place within it.

Socialisation in the broadest sense, whatever the content involved, corresponds to a form 'that manifests itself in a thousand different ways, and within which individuals, because of their interests – sensual or ideal, transient or enduring, conscious or unconscious, causally or teleologically driven – become a unit within which these interests are realised'.[4] The relevance of this analytical distinction, between content and form (which cannot of course be separated in social reality) is demonstrated to the extent that it is possible to show that different contents can be socialised by and within the same form, and, conversely, that the same content can give rise to very different forms of socialisation. Love or economic advantage, for example, can be used to illustrate that this is possible. These contents can indeed give rise to diverse forms of reciprocal action, such as in a range of different commercial or family relationships. But as exchanges they are also liable to be exemplars of some general overarching form. On the other hand, formal relationships such as imitation or competition can be instrumental in the socialisation of individuals towards a range of goals and interests as varied as those that characterise political parties or religious communities. Similarly, the religious impulse as content can give rise to non-religious forms of socialisation, just as, in its purest form, it can express itself as religion.

Reciprocal action is the realisation of a unit, a society, or of a socialisation. Simmel suggested that it would therefore be more appropriate to speak of the process of socialisation, the 'pure forms of socialisation', rather than of society. It is to be noted from the outset that socialisation can have varying degrees of intensity according to the type and depth of intimacy of reciprocal action, and also that it is not possible to think of even the most minimal of relations between humans as having no importance.

Micro-relations

One of Simmel's central contributions is undoubtedly the following: that the sociological point of view reveals socialisation as process, a web of relationships between individuals that forms, dissolves and reforms anew, allowing us to glimpse the 'microscopic molecular processes' that connect us to each other. Célestin Bouglé in his critical review of *Soziologie,* saw very clearly that sociology for Simmel

> must encompass more than simply... collective practices and habits. It finds its subject matter whenever any relation whatsoever is formed between people, anywhere where a reciprocal action takes place between one person and another. In sum, the analysis of interactions is, for Monsieur Simmel, as for Tarde (one recognises just how many similarities there are between the styles and sensibilities of these two thinkers), the very essence of sociology. It must of course concern itself with the great institutions – churches, political powers, commercial organisations – that dominate individuals and which, once established, seem to take on a life of their own. But even more fruitful is the study of what Monsieur Simmel calls association 'in its incipient state', that is, relations between individuals, the effect they exert upon each other.[5]

The discipline of sociology had until then, in his view, concentrated its attention exclusively on those massive socialisations which crystallised in the largest social forms, whereas the very smallest liaisons between individuals run right through all these large social forms.

Seemingly insignificant micro-forms are the focus of Simmel's attention because they give society its flexibility, its viscosity. Through all these processes – a meal taken together, a walk, an exchange of glances, a pavement conversation – society becomes increasingly 'society', and social beings are thereby fortified. A Durkheimian would recognise that the number and the intensity of the relationships contribute to the moral density of society. What Simmel clearly added was the possibility of personal development and fulfilment for the individual.

Forms of socialisation are society in process, and it follows that one can study the varying degrees to which people create social units, how through the multiple associations that form it socially the 'same group becomes more "society" than it was before'.[6] So, for example, a group will strengthen its own societal character through the socialising reciprocal action of struggle with another group, and this same consolidation can also be achieved by forms of secret socialisation, just as it can through fashion or by taking a meal together. If a secret society is a form of socialisation, it is because 'the secret determines the reciprocal relations of those that share it'.[7] Sharing a secret leads to specific relations with neighbouring groups, of self-protection for example, as well as affecting the relations within the group. These examples illustrate the gradual character that Simmel attributes to socialisation, that is, different socialisations bind the members of groups to varying degrees, create differing degrees of cohesion between individuals. Furthermore, the degree to which the members of the group are conscious of the forms themselves will also vary. The content of a socialisation activity can become so deeply embedded within the consciousness of the members of a group that the individuals actually forget the formal fact and the nature of the socialisation. According to Simmel, the content of the activity in which members of a group engage often makes them forget the form of socialisation within which it takes place. This, he claims, is a very general phenomenon. On the other hand, any group formed within a wider circle, particularly where there is a clearly defined boundary, as with the sharing of a secret or a creed, strengthens the boundary and accentuates the awareness of the members as to the fact of their forming a society. Most socialisations, nevertheless, come about through processes based on implicit knowledge, and the attention devoted to the goals of the activity masks the socialisation within which it takes place. Forms of socialisation can therefore be differentiated according to the degree of consciousness of the formal ties that unite participants. The higher the degree, the more the accent placed on the reciprocal ties will be explicitly valued compared with the pure content, that is, the material activity of the association.

Forms of socialisation are based on contents that are not in themselves social, but part of the psycho-physical constitution of human beings. They presuppose the possibility of psychic relations that enable people to collaborate or to act against one another, and in so doing form associations, unions and societies. One of the most fruitful aspects of Simmel's sociology is his detailing of the presuppositions on which associations are founded and his emphasis on the role played within forms of socialisation by psycho-social drives such as trust, loyalty, gratitude, devotion, and belief in human nature. Micro-sociology allows us to get very close to everyday life, to perceive both the dense web of reciprocal obligations, and the importance of certain forces and dispositions that make society possible. While one cannot speak of rules or norms, individuals interact with one another according to certain dispositions, imbuing their relations with goodwill, trust and confidence. The absence of these social sentiments would make social relations impossible.

Such dispositions are not however immutable and it must be noted that the increasing objectivisation of culture is modifying the ways in which trust is given and this, in turn, modifies what is known and not known by individuals about one another. 'The modern shop keeper who enters into a business relation with another shop keeper; the researcher who embarks on a research project in collaboration with another researcher; the leader of a political party who makes a pact with another party leader over electoral issues or legislative proposals – all know, with the exception of a few minor gaps, just what they need to know about their partner in order to set up the relationship they wish to establish.'[8] This shift in the distribution of knowledge and non-knowledge results from the qualitative and quantitative evolution of relations and often we know only very little of the individuals with whom we are in relation.

The greater the number of liaisons, the more a psychologically differentiated individual can realise the multiple potentialities inscribed within a many-faceted personality. In his earliest writings on social differentiation Simmel examined the ways in which modern society differs from traditional societies, and he emphasised the proliferation of possible affiliations and new interconnections between social circles. The interlacing of social circles is a model of social differentiation that leads us to a description of society characterised by more flexible memberships, no longer structured in a pattern of concentric circles, but criss-crossing, intersecting and overlapping with each other, out of which each individual is assumed to be able to construct his or her individuality. Such a model widens the margins of individual liberty, but also produces new moral complications, for, being less subject to the close surveillance of any single group, the individual is confronted with potential contradictions resulting from these multiple memberships. This type of model that draws our attention so clearly to both gains and losses is very common in Simmel's work. He is thus neither purely and simply an apologist for, nor a one-sided critic of, modernity.

The Simmelian perspective differs from classic approaches in that it is on the forms of socialisation in their incipient state that he focuses his attention. The study of society is therefore that of all forms of socialisation and cannot be confined to the analysis of large institutions which orchestrate social relations. This is because the large institutions themselves are shot through with mutual ties and reciprocal actions, with the seemingly insignificant forms of liaison through which individuals are socialised, forming societies whose existence is more or less ephemeral, more or less durable.

Such an objective necessitates the prior analysis of the potentiality conditions of society – society's conditions of possibility – and, in a digression in Chapter 1 of *Soziologie,* Simmel makes a notable contribution to the analysis of this problem of the constitution of society.

The A Priori *of Socialisation*

> ### A Priori
>
> An *a priori* is a basic belief about something that is derived from philosophical or abstract reflection rather than from direct experience or from some kind of direct contact with the empirical world. Few people now believe that we can have any direct unmediated experience of the empirical world because, following the philosopher Immanuel Kant, it is generally believed that all experience is at least partly structured by pre-existing beliefs or presuppositions we have about the world (we know that the ball is a long way off and that it will take some time to retrieve it because, not least, we implicitly work with conceptions of time and space). Time and space are two *a priori* categories by which we make sense of sense experience, that are fundamental preconditions for the very possibility of sense experience as we know it. Another basic category is that of substance. It would be impossible for us to experience the ball as something of substance unless we first understood the general concept or category of substance. Analogously, Simmel wants to investigate the preconditions for socialisation. If socialisation happens then what preconditions must be in place in order to allow it to happen? These preconditions are the *a priori* of socialisation. Thus there are *a priori* or preconditions for being able to gain knowledge about society, and also for being able to practically reproduce or constitute society.

The digression which forms part of Chapter 1 of *Soziologie* summarises those *a priori* which underpin the study of the forms of socialisation. It is based on the distinction formulated by the sociological point of view between the form and content of socialisation, but in order to properly execute this stage it is necessary first to satisfy a requirement that is at once both ontological and epistemological: that is, to analyse those specific relations between the conditions for the constitution of society and the conditions for gaining knowledge of it. The purpose of the 'Digression on the question: How is society possible?' is precisely to show that the answer to such a question requires a type of investigation different from that required to answer the question 'How is nature possible?' Society's existence presupposes that those elements that constitute it have knowledge of it and recognise it, but not in the sense of knowing it from the outside as an observer of the physical world might gain knowledge of its phenomena, but from the inside, as members of society itself. In fact Simmel specified that he preferred to speak of ability or practical skill (*savoir*) rather than knowledge in a passive sense (*connaissance*), for the constitution of society presupposes at the very least a practical ability (a knowing 'how to') that individual subjects use to establish relations with one another. The analysis of the conditions for the constitution of any society must examine both the modes of knowledge and the modes of actualisation of society. The *a priori* involved relate not only to knowledge of society but also touch, fundamentally, on the very existence of society itself. More precisely, they concern the modes of formation of social liaisons. The existence of societies presupposes the activation by its potential members of their abilities and skills, feelings and perceptions of reciprocal relations, in other words of their socialisation skills.

In addition one must bear in mind the very special position that these constituent elements occupy in socialisation, that is to say that liaisons at one and the same time include and embrace individuals and yet never include them totally, nor perfectly. For social relations to exist supposes a minimum hermeneutic threshold in a general sense, at least the tacit practical ability of individuals to interpret the actions and reactions of other individuals. The status of this type of interpretation and the bases from which it derives must be the focus of investigation. Society as the sum of reciprocal actions is possible only through the incessant socialising activities of individuals. In interpreting Simmel's work, and in steering it a little towards ethnomethodological conceptions (cf. **Garfinkel,** Chapter 13), one can say that society is only made possible by the reciprocal activities of individuals (*Verbindungen*), who have to understand one another, activate a particular knowledge of those activities, and make use of the practical abilities through which they know, recognise and produce society. All social liaison, as reciprocal action, on the one hand consists of a process of people influencing each other, of orientating themselves towards one another – a theme that social psychology was to develop, and Simmel can in this sense be considered as one of the founders of that discipline – and on the other, comes into being through a self-awareness of the social unit being formed, a consciousness of socialisation as process. Indeed, the unit is produced through the 'multiplicity of specific relations, and through the feeling and the knowledge that one determines others and is determined by them'.[9]

The content of *Soziologie*, Simmel tells us, still within the 'Digression on the question: How is society possible?' is an investigation into the modes and processes of socialisation. The forms of socialisation are at once the setting and the outcome of the socialising activities of individuals. Socialisation itself actualises social energy and this is why Simmel defines society as a becoming and not simply as a state. Society is in this sense always in the process of being created and re-created. People are social beings by definition and therefore engage in reciprocal activities from the start with certain inbuilt dispositions, but it is those particular reciprocal orientations peculiar to socialisation that create society. What we normally refer to as 'society' is therefore the result, precarious and in a perpetually unstable equilibrium, of all forms of socialisation. Sociology within Simmel's perspective concentrates on the processes at work in the creation of societies, on the totality of social liaisons which we, abstractly, constitute into society. He seeks to prove their importance by the simple means of a thought experiment: if you were to try to imagine them not existing, what is revealed is the disappearance of society in any normal sense of the word.

One can say, using the admittedly different vocabulary and perspective of Alfred Schutz (cf. Garfinkel, Chapter 13), that Simmel sets himself the objective of describing the implicit presuppositions of people's comprehension of one another on the basis of 'the natural attitude', for without the latter, reciprocal actions could not occur. He explains that we are led to construct the other as a personality, as a psychological unity, and that in doing so we draw on *a priori* representations that consist in attributing an assembly of fragmentary perceptions to one person. Such a procedure we call comprehension. Comprehension and attribution are connected since the personality that we understand and to which we attribute such and such an intention is an ideal type construction, or, to use Schutz's term, a typification. The understanding of the other through typification is an *a priori* of socialisation, whose value lies in its usefulness for gaining knowledge and undertaking action, above all of course, in our routine day-to-day lives. All forms of socialisation presume mutual anticipations and norms of conduct. The processes of reciprocal influence or action thus pass necessarily through the psychology of persons. Socialisation is a psychic unit that is produced by separate spatial elements forming a new unit but, more importantly, having an awareness of forming this new unit. It is this which differentiates social units from natural phenomena. For the latter, spatial coexistence is not accompanied by an awareness of coexistence as a unit, or of at least the possibility of such. Once this difference is accepted it leads to the conclusion that for its interpretation and comprehension, society requires a psychological knowledge *that is nevertheless not a psychology.* Unless the psychic dimension of socialisation is taken into account, society 'would be a mere puppet theatre, no more meaningful than the merging of one cloud into another or the entanglement of the branches of a tree. So psychological motivations – feelings, thoughts, needs – must be recognised, not simply as the underpinning of any socialisation, but as its very essence *and as the only form of knowledge which really interests us.*'[10] All socialisation presumes psychological knowledge and interactive skills, an exchange between I and you, 'an exchange alternating between the me and the you,' and just as reciprocal action characterises socialisation, the latter can only be created on the basis of the construction of psychological skills. Social life would not be as we know it if individuals did not orientate themselves on the basis of expectations, suppositions, anticipations and typifications that are the mental representations of their mutual behaviour.

All socialisation brings into play mechanisms for the interpretation of others and of situations, mechanisms that are tied to the functioning of the mind and that produce, beyond the individual units, a social form which serves as a kind of mould for the orientation of individuals. Pursuing a comparison with the themes of **Erving Goffman,** socialisation consists in the agreement on a common line of conduct. This agreement may be achieved with varying degrees of familiarity, varying degrees of novelty, but it always demands attention and mutuality. Socialisation between strangers clearly requires more adjustments, a greater sensitivity and practical skills than that between an old married couple where a long shared past provides a framework for current typifications. The establishment of a relation between strangers involves each tentatively advancing towards the other seeking the reassurance of a shared framework; whereas between acquaintances and, *a fortiori*, between intimates, this is taken for granted. Typification proceeds according to the requirements of the activity or the objective being pursued, drawing on a knowledge of background assumptions or, again, that which **Max Weber** referred to as a nomological knowledge of habitual ways of behaving within typical situations.

It follows from these remarks that comprehension plays a central role in social life. In this respect Simmel is interested in comprehension in the social sciences not simply as a method, but takes as his theme what Schutz later developed in his phenomenological sociology. When we speak here of comprehension, we are led towards the ordinary, everyday level of understanding and knowledge we all have of one another, based on typifications. Comprehension as the practical actualisation of a synthesis of typifications, prior to being a method of the social sciences, is a mode of thinking by which individuals become aware of their relations and, *a fortiori*, of social reality.

Simmel did not produce a systematic sociology but the sociological perspective that he brought to bear on reciprocal relations between individuals has proved extremely fruitful, and for some time now he has once more been recognised as a thinker whose contribution is still insightful and fresh enough to inspire research into today's contemporary world.

Further Reading

D. Frisby, *Simmel and Since: Essays on Georg Simmel's Social Theory* (London: Routledge & Kegan Paul, 1991).

H. Helle, *Simmel on Religion* (Yale University Press [in press])

D. Levine, *Georg Simmel: On Individuality and Social Forms* (Chicago: Chicago University Press, 1971).

G. Oakes, *Essays on Interpretation in the Social Sciences* (Totowa, NJ: Rowman & Littlefield, 1980).

G. Simmel, *Conflict and the Web of Group Affiliations* (Glencoe, IL: The Free Press, 1955).

K. Wolff, *The Sociology of Georg Simmel* (Glencoe, IL: The Free Press, 1950).

6

Herbert Blumer

Ken Plummer

> His work was lodged in the tradition of American Pragmatism, of James, Dewey and Mead. Indeed, it could be said that Herbert Blumer was the last sonorous voice of that tradition in this century. (Duster 1987, p. 16)

> Though we seldom recognise his enormous impact, few sociologists are untouched by his thought. (Becker 1988, p. 15)

Driving Impulses

The Trouble with Sociology

Herbert Blumer – 'an inspiring teacher, engaging writer, talented adminis-trator, charismatic personality, and forceful intellectual'[1] – is probably the soci-ologist who is least known about by the students who read this book. Yet he is the carrier of a very distinctive sociological tradition – symbolic interac-tionism; with a very specific set of practical concerns – to do sociology 'natu-ralistically'. This brief article aims to introduce some of his ideas.

Throughout much of the twentieth century Blumer was driven by an irri-tation with many of the sociological orthodoxies of his day, and sought to develop his own humanistic, pragmatist approach – now popularly known as 'symbolic interactionism' (a term he coined in 1937). Blumer was a perpetual and ardent critic of all the major traditions of sociological reasoning from the start of his career to the end of it. At one extreme, he stood opposed to the trivial and quite misleading reduction of social life to surveys and measure-ments as if they actually told us anything; and at the other extreme, he ques-tioned the superimposition of abstract and reified concepts like culture, structure, attitude or industrialisation on to social life, as if they somehow explained something. For him, the appropriate stance for sociology was to look closely and carefully at human group life and collective behaviour through 'action': 'action must be the starting point (and the point of return)

for any scheme that purports to treat and analyse human society empirically'
(Blumer 1969, p. 6).

In one discussion he put it like this:

> More and more over the years, as I have had occasion to reflect on what is going
> on in sociology, the more convinced I have become of the inescapable need... of
> recognising that a human group consists of people who are living. Oddly enough
> this is not the picture which underlies the dominant imagery in the field of
> sociology today. They think of a society or group as something that is there in the
> form of a regularised structure in which people are placed. And they act on the basis
> of the influence of the structure on them. This is a complete inversion of what is
> involved... (instead) there are people who engaged in living, in having to cope with
> situations that arise in their experience, organising their behaviour and their
> conduct in the light of those situations they encounter, coming to develop all kinds
> of arrangements which are ongoing affairs... The metaphor I like to use is just
> 'lifting the veil' to see what is happening. (Blumer, in Lofland 1980, pp. 189–90)

Here we have the kernel of his thought, still relevant today. Most sociology
cuts out the living lives in process and turns instead to grander schemes of
analysis: from structures and variables to discourse and advanced methodologies. Blumer wants to bring back the huffing and puffing human being in
action.

This is not a fashionable view today; and we must be careful not to misread
Blumer. As Becker says, 'he was never anti-theoretical, anti-empirical, or anti-
measurement' (1988, p. 14). And he always saw the importance of social
organisation, power and history. But his concern was that theories and observations had to be about real things in the world. 'Empirical research (should)
pay attention to the nature of what was being studied; and... we (should)
measure real quantities' (1988, p. 14). This was his abiding concern: he urged
sociologists to talk about 'real' things with 'real' evidence! If you wanted to
understand drug user activity, for example, you had to explore and inspect
these worlds closely and carefully from every angle you could, building your
understanding out of this. It was hopelessly misconceived to cut short the
work of intimately familiarising yourself with 'drugs' by constructing abstract
theoretical schemas about it; and likewise it was a gross error to think you
could simply 'measure' drug life from abstracted interviews and questionnaires conducted aloofly. One of his students, Howard S. Becker, produced
the classic study of marijuana use, in his *Outsiders* (1963), precisely because
of this first-hand involvement in a social world, followed by his subsequent
close attention to conceptual building (a litany of powerful theories and
concepts are developed in his book: labelling, 'motives', 'culture', 'moral
crusaders', 'becoming and careers').[2] And the same was true of race relations,
or trade union activity, or the industrialisation process in Latin America – all
areas he worked on. His passion was to improve sociology and to do this he

adopted the perpetual mantle of critic. He was against thoughtless measurement and obscure abstract theory equally. And insofar as he was, he was opposed to the two major strands of doing sociology. It remains the case today that sociology can largely be divided into those who theorise with little empirical content and those who produce elaborate data sets with very little theory. What he complained about for sixty years has still not been rectified!

On Background and Style

To understand Herbert Blumer's work, he should be seen as the mantle bearer of two important, connected, North American intellectual traditions which he found at the University of Chicago, the foremost sociological centre for much of the earlier part of this century (Plummer 1997).

One source of Blumer's passion clearly lay in his admiration for his great teacher, the Chicago philosophical pragmatist George Herbert Mead. Blumer attended his lectures, assisted in their posthumous publication, and became the major sociological proselytiser on Mead's behalf for many years after Mead's death (most notably, in two key publications: Blumer, 1966, 1979b). For Blumer, Mead was probably 'the only "true genius" he had ever met, and he clearly had a profound impact upon him. He was teaching his ideas throughout his life...'[3] For both Mead and Blumer, 'science' was the major form of thought for the modern world, a science grounded in the pragmatic attitude.

Another source of his passion lay more generally in his being part of the Chicago School of Sociology. He was trained there; gained his PhD from there in 1928; taught there from 1931; and when he left in 1953 to chair the Department of Sociology at the University of California at Berkeley, he took this inheritance with him. The core concerns of Chicago sociology – in the work of W.I. Thomas, Robert Park and others – was to study the city as a mosaic of social worlds; to get away from the library and to do real research in the city; and to build out of this a conceptually and theoretically grounded view of the social world. The philosophical strain of Mead and the empirical obsessions of 'Chicago' left a marked impact on Blumer.

I think this dual background generated tensions in Blumer's work. For the Meadian influence was not always compatible with the fieldwork Chicago inheritance. The former, after all, highlighted a philosophical issue; the latter an empirical one.[4] One paradox concerns his advocacy for empirical work yet his general failure to do it. For from his earliest doctoral work on method in social psychology to his last ruminations, he is obsessively concerned with finding out the best way to study everyday collective behaviour and group experience – doing it as scientifically as possible; yet at the same time he often seems reluctant to actually do it himself. There are some studies of media, fashion, race and industrialisation but in the main doing empirical work was not his strength – even though he advocated it all the time. As a critic said to him in the early 1950s: 'you seem to advocate a lingering intellectual hypochondria in which we dwell upon all the dire things which may go wrong if we do attempt research' (Abbott and Gaziano 1995, p. 248). It may indeed well be that he saw the doing of sociology as so difficult, as so fraught with problems in 'getting it right' that he incapacitated himself (cf. Hammersley 1989). While, ironically, he is something of a 'scientific absolutist' (cf. Abbott and Gaziano 1995, p. 253) and his work reeks of a sureness about what sociology most surely is and indeed surely should be, he also advocates a deep scepticism and a critical approach to all things. He is, if you like, sure about being unsure!

He was also against systematising and synthesising. Much of his work reads like scattered fragments; his most famous book, *Symbolic Interactionism,* was only written under duress, encouraged by his students. He was against providing coda, recipes, models. Others have tried to do this for him – but it is clear he did not personally like it. Codification and abstraction strain against pragmatism (cf. Rock 1979). But Becker, for instance, one of his foremost students, remarked after his death that Blumer's work in fact harboured a deductive axiomatic theory – one organised around the idea of the collective act: 'any human event can be understood as the result of the people involved continually adjusting what they do in the light of what others do, so that each individual's line of activity "fits" into what the others do' (Becker 1988, p. 18).

Key Issues – Theorising in the Empirical World: Sampling Blumer's Work

While Blumer is probably best known for his writings on George Herbert Mead and his development of the theory of symbolic interactionism (SI) there is so much more to him than this. A full-length appraisal of his work must still be awaited. Among his accomplishments were the development of a distinctive methodological style; the exploration of key areas of social life – industrial relations, race and racism, the mass media, collective behaviour, social movements, social problems; as well as a concern with industrialisation, social structure, social change, and comparative sociology, especially within Latin America. (Some of these latter interests are not commonly recognised: see Maines 1988.) Although he personally never swerved from the position of interactionism which he championed, his chairmanship at Berkeley was characterised by a wide-ranging support for a variety of styles of doing sociology. In a short review I can only briefly highlight a few of his contributions.

Creating Symbolic Interactionism and Developing a Theory of the Self

For Blumer:

> Human group life consists of the fitting together of the lines of action of the participants; such aligning of actions takes place predominantly by the participants indicating to one another what to do and in turn interpreting such indications made by the others; out of such interaction people form the objects that constitute their worlds; people are prepared to act towards their objects on the basis of the meaning these objects have for them; human beings face their world as organisms with selves, thus allowing each other to make indications to himself; human action constructed by the actor on the basis of what he notes, interprets and assesses; and the interlinking of such ongoing action constitutes organisations, institutions, and vast complexes of interdependent relations. To test the validity of these premises one must go to a direct examination of actual human group life... (Blumer 1969, p. 49)

Here we have a litany of sensitising concepts: selves, joint actions, objects, interactions, interpretations, organisations, interdependencies.[5] What lies at the heart of SI is an image of the world that says:

- always look for the processes, the changes, how lives, groups and whole societies emerge. Nothing is ever fixed and static: social life is always emergent. 'The empirical world is continuously recast' (Blumer 1969, p. 23)
- always look for the meanings, the symbols, the languages in which social life gets done. It is this which makes human life truly distinctive, and why it needs special kinds of methods to 'dig out' these shifting meanings
- always look for the interactions and interconnections. There is no such thing as an individual in this view, as individuals are always in interaction with others. Societies are interactive webs of people 'doing things together' (cf. Becker 1986).

One key concept which binds much of this together is the concept of the self, developed from Mead. What makes human beings distinctive is that they develop reflective and reflexive ideas of who they are through communication with themselves and others. People are able to indicate who they are; they are able to see themselves through the eyes of others; they are able to indicate to others who they are; they are able to make, present, transform and work on 'selves'. Selves, for Blumer and Mead, are processes contingent upon language, communications, role taking and interaction with others.

It is crucial to see that Blumer's work neither ignores nor minimises the importance of wider social forces, power, history or the economic. He is certainly opposed to grand theory in the abstract and had he lived he would have been no friend at all to the current whirl of discourse analysis that so often becomes cut off from empirically observable language. But he is not opposed to a wider sense of social structure insofar as a society is constituted through symbolic interaction. 'Human society is to be seen as consisting of acting people, and the life of a society is to be seen as consisting of their actions' (Blumer 1969, p. 85).

For Blumer, society is 'the framework inside of which social action takes place and is not a determinant of that society' (Blumer 1962, p. 189). Collective actions are the concern. Blumer always stresses the 'group setting' in which all of social life is conducted.

Building a Methodological Stance of 'Naturalistic Rigour'

Closely allied is his work on methods. Blumer developed the 'pragmatic turn' which highlighted the importance of grounding analysis in concrete sets of experience. Pragmatism is a general philosophical position which shuns grand abstractions, dualisms and split thinking in favour of directly and practically looking at the limited and local truths as they emerge in concrete experience.[6] The much heralded self, for instance, was one major way around the classic dualist split of subject and object, individual and society. Neither should be given priority; both were always present and in dialectical tension with each other. By looking at the self in concrete situations, it was manifest that self was both subject and object: only abstract philosophy could say otherwise!

For Blumer, then, it becomes a *sine qua non* that 'an empirical world exists as something available for observation, study and analysis'. Moreover, 'it *stands over against* the scientific observer with a character that has to be dug out'. 'Reality for empirical science exists only in the empirical world, can be sought only there, and can be verified only there' (Blumer 1969, pp. 21–2). The obdurate empirical world has to be the focus of study.

This leads to much of Blumer's work being about methods.[7] One of his most famous contributions to such debates comes in his (book-length) review of a sociological classic in 1939. At this time in the USA, there was an evaluation of the state of USA sociology, and the study by W.I. Thomas and F. Znaniecki, *The Polish Peasant in Europe and America,* had been adjudicated the best example of good sociological work. Some 2,000 pages long, it charted the migration of Polish peasants from the old communities to the new cities in the USA. It used life histories, letters, documents of many kinds as a way of collecting data. And Blumer was asked by the Social Science Research Council to provide a review of it. While he was, as usual, very critical of this study, he also praised the range of methods, and the concern with detail, and the importance given to subjective factors. This is never to suggest that he denied 'objective factors'; but he is concerned with any sociology that does not take seriously the fact that humans 'always act in social situations', 'actors are always oriented and guided in situations by subjective dispositions'

(Blumer 1979b, p. 85). Sympathetically drawing from Thomas and Znaniecki, he says:

> (1) Group life consists *always* of the action of human actors; (2) such action always takes place as an adjustment of human actors to social situations; and (3) action in situations is always in the form of actors expressing their dispositions. Ergo, sociological research has to ferret out the play of subjective dispositions, and sociological propositions have to incorporate the record of that play. (Blumer 1979b, p. 86)

Human documents, naturalistic study, life histories: these are the tools Blumer favoured to get at these subjective dispositions. And this agreed, they then need their own methodological logic: much of the standard talk about representativeness, data adequacy, reliability and decisive theoretical validation leads up wrong paths once 'subjective dispositions' become the issue. For instance, representativeness is usually seen to raise the problem of sampling. But for Blumer modern sampling theory usually overlooks the fact that 'not all people who are involved in the given area of social action under study are equally involved, nor are they equally knowledgeable about what is taking place; hence they cannot be regarded as equally capable of supplying information on the form of social action under study. Some of the people... are in the periphery; others... may be in the mainstream... (but) poor observers. To include them... may weaken the study' (1979b, p. 94). If grasping subjectivity is the issue, representativeness changes its character. For instance, in his research on labour arbitration, Blumer suggests not a random sample of workers but rather the need to listen closely to the 'key informants' who know much better what is going on. Not everyone does! All this means that standard views on 'representative samples' need challenging.

Studying the Empirical World: An Example – Going to the Movies

Blumer researched a number of areas, but he was one of the first to conduct audience research on the movies, and as such he anticipated the much later development of 'audience ethnography' found in such works as Janice Radway's *Reading the Romance*. As part of a widespread concern about the impact of movies on young people, a series of investigations were set up in the late 1920s and early 1930s (popularly known as the Payne Studies, they were initiated by a pro-movie censorship group, the Motion Picture Research Council). Blumer was involved with one of these that looked at young people. Straightforwardly, he asked some one and a half thousand young people to write 'motion-picture autobiographies', backed up with more selective interviews, group discussions and observations. In all of this, he demonstrated his commitment to the empirical world – effectively to know what impact media had on young people's lives, it is best to simply ask them. And following on from this, much of his ensuing book *Movies and Conduct* is given over to young people's first-hand accounts of the films they have seen – how they provide the basis of imitation, play, daydreams, emotional development, and 'schemes of life'. For Blumer, the task is not to impose some preordained theoretical framework on his subjects (as so much contemporary audience ethnography chooses to do – usually from a psychoanalytic frame), but rather to let the people speak for themselves. One entry – dealing with stereotypes – reads:

> *Female, 19, white college senior:* ...One thing these pictures did was to establish a permanent fear of Chinamen in my mind. To this day I do not see a Chinese person but what I think of him as being mixed up in some evil affair. I always pass them as quickly as possible if I meet them in the street, and refuse to go into a Chinese restaurant or laundry... (Blumer 1933, p. 145)

Quite rightly, others more recently have been critical of his straightforward naïvety of approach. Just ask people! Denzin, for example, has recently been very critical of Blumer's work in this area, suggesting that while progressive in method it is shrouded with Blumer's assumptions ('pro-middle class and anti-film') (Denzin 1992, p. 107), was open to being used to crusade against movie content, and viewed texts unproblematically (Clough 1992). True, Blumer's initial studies in the 1930s now look somewhat simple: but he was the first to take audience responses seriously.

Creating a Public Philosophy: An Example – the Problem of Race Relations

Lyman and Vidich, in their analysis of the work of Herbert Blumer, suggest his work should be seen as the embodiment of an emerging new creative 'public philosophy' in North America during this century. Suggesting the bankruptcy of past ideas, and especially those of social science, and drawing from the pragmatic mode of Chicago philosophers, Blumer saw the need for the systematic investigation of problems in American public life: from race to industrial relations; from media to the consequences of industrialisation. This work *is* less well known than his account of the Meadian self; but it is all part of a co-ordinated, seamless approach.[8] His was not a counsel of despair in the face of so many social problems; and neither was it a plea for revolutionary change. Instead, a public philosophy – pragmatic, populist, democratic – had to be forged that recognised the empirical world and opened debates around it. As Lyman and Vidich comment:

> His approach emphasizes the collective construction of meaning that imparts definitions to the various schemes of social reality, repudiates the allegedly irrevocable

effects of structural arrangements, and allows for – indeed, expects and encourages – opposition, individuality and idiosyncrasy within the social order. (1988, p. 7)

An example of all this can be found in his abiding concern with race relations – the big issue of North American sociology. From some of his earliest writings, and under the influence of Robert E. Park, Blumer took an active interest in the study of race relations (although contemporary studies more or less systematically ignore all his work). For him, 'race prejudice has a history, and the history is collective'.[9] 'The defining process must be seen as central in the career of race relations.'[10] Starting with a paper in 1937 on 'the Nature of Race Prejudice' and ending with a summary paper in 1980 on 'Theories of Race and Social Action' (co-authored with Troy Duster) Blumer evolved a comprehensive theory of race relations. It was a fully social theory – he dismissed biological accounts of race, saw the whole process as a social one involving relationships and categorisations, and urged public debates to change and weaken segregation and discrimination. Using Blumer's own words, the following could be taken as a summary of his position:

1. Race prejudice is fundamentally a matter of relationships between racial groups (and not as a set of feelings which members of one racial group have towards the members of another racial group)... this directs us immediately to a sociological level and not a personal one.
2. Race prejudice is directed towards a 'conceptualised group' or abstract category; it exists as an attitude towards what is logically an abstraction (the Jew, the Oriental, the Negro)... this directs us to a concern with the abstraction, categorisations and defining systems surrounding groups.
3. Racial prejudice is a highly variable, changing and complex phenomenon; it differs a great deal from time to time and from place to place... this directs us to its changing historical nature, its variability amongst different groups and times, to the fact that nothing is permanent about it. One group like 'the Jew' may appear at one time for one group; another like 'the Negro' may appear at other times for other groups; and others like the 'Arab' or the 'Moslem' may appear at yet another.[11]
4. Race prejudice is a collective process though which racial groups form images of themselves and of others; it is a process in which two groups define their position in relation to each other; it is the sense of social position emerging for this collective process of characterisation which provides the basis of racial prejudice... this directs us to concerns with labelling, racialisation and the creation of 'others'.
5. Race prejudice is a collective process which involves four patterns in the dominant group: (1) a feeling of superiority, (2) a feeling that the subordinate race is intrinsically different and alien, (3) a feeling of proprietary claim to certain areas of privilege and advantage and (4) a fear and suspi-

cion that the subordinate race harbours designs on the prerogatives of the dominant race... this directs us to hierarchy, dominance, difference and privilege as bases of race prejudice.

6. The source of race prejudice lies in a felt challenge to this sense of group position. Race prejudice has its origins in many sources. One of them undoubtedly is the general ethnocentrism of groups, but of more importance is a sense of threat where a dominant group feels insecure and has its status, or economic position, threatened... this directs us to the fact that the conflict is group based not individual based.

This is only a very provisional summary of Blumer's position. But like so much of his work, if followed through, these ideas are highly suggestive for public change.

Seeing Things Differently

Blumer brings to sociology a perspective for seeing the world that has influenced a great many studies: from illness and dying to occupations and classroom interaction; from social movements and collective behaviour to the patterning and organisation of social problems; from crime and deviance to labour and industrial relations; from media studies to life history research; from self theory to race relations. Blumer's overarching concern with staying true to the empirical world and providing a rigorous methodology for inspecting and exploring it has guided a great many sociologists. Wittingly or unwittingly, a large corpus of work has flowed from Blumer's seminal ideas.

I read Blumer in 1970, shortly after embarking upon a PhD which was to explore the sociology of sexuality. The major intellectual influences on me at that time had been Howard S. Becker's *Outsiders* and David Matza's *Becoming Deviant* which had both introduced me to the key ideas of labelling theory; it turns out that both had been strongly shaped by Blumer's ideas. Yet these were both 'substantive' or topic-based studies, and it was only really when I read Blumer's *Symbolic Interactionism* that the full weight of his arguments became clearer. The book itself has major flaws: there is repetition (as one might expect from a series of largely previously published essays); it was dated in parts (much of it draws from the 1930s and 1940s – which to a child of the 1960s could have been seen as *very* old fashioned!); and there is very little in the way of referencing, footnoting or acknowledging to guide the reader any further. But it came to me as a serious exhortation to think about what I was trying to do sociologically. It gave me a series of themes (process, symbols, interaction), an image of society (as a precarious network of interactions) and human beings (as symbolic, active creators of social worlds who inhabit co-ordinates of repetitive social actions), a view of methodology (which largely reiterated the old Park dictum to 'get off the seat of your pants and see what is going on' but tempered it with a concern for the logic of method), and a sense of required techniques for studying society (those which advocated intimate familiarity with the social world – through field research and life histories in particular). All of these themes helped shape my view of sociology, but also of sexuality in general and homosexuality (as it was then called) in particular.

There have been several major traditions for the study of sexuality: Kinsey's surveys, Masters and Johnson's therapies, psychodynamic theories turn to the unconscious, anthropological travel notes about patterns of sexual behaviour in remote islands. As a graduate student I read through these studies assiduously, but felt something was lacking in each. Overwhelmingly, they suggested the importance of biology, the natural and an essentially uncontested notion of sexuality: it was a given and remained untheorised socially. Only the anthropological approach came near to capturing the distinctly human features of sexuality. Blumer's ruminations hence came as a brilliant even shocking set of tips for how human sexuality could be studied. In effect he told me to go and look at sexualities in naturalistic settings (a bit like the anthropologists) and to build up life stories of people's sexualities (while being aware of how 'damn hard this was to do). He suggested to me that human sexuality should be approached as a massive symbolic enterprise, as something that emerges in human interactions, and that it is something we effectively piece together as joint actions. It is patterned but creative; symbolic while being biologic; and always social – varying in meaning in time, places and encounters (cf. Plummer 1975, 1995).

I was not alone in these realisations. A little earlier in the pathbreaking work of Gagnon and Simon (1973), they had come to similar conclusions and developed an approach to sexuality that they called a sexual scripting approach. It provided the foundations of what some now call (perhaps inappropriately) the constructionist approach to sexualities.

Legacies and Unfinished Business – Blumer at Century's Turn

Blumer was a sociologist for the twentieth century. His influence – primarily as the founder of symbolic interactionist theory – has been enormous. Not a prolific writer or researcher himself, he seems to have trained whole generations of sociologists in his distinctive view of the world.[12] He gave them all the pragmatist inheritance.

Nevertheless, by the time he died, many of his ideas had been moved on. We had entered a 'Post-Blumerian World' (Fine 1990). It is true that symbolic interactionism had become a strong force with its own journal, yearbook, professional body and conferences.[13] Likewise, many of his leads were continuing to be developed. Thus, the theory of action continues to be refined (for example Strauss 1993; Joas 1997). Mead and Blumer's abiding concern with self and identity as processual and changing has become a widespread concern of more and more scholars (indeed in the 1990s, identity theory became highly fashionable). Ethnographic and life history work continues, and becomes more sophisticated. And some have significantly reworked the theory so that it can now look better at emotions, structures and semiotics. Others have not just developed it: they have pushed it into hitherto unknown territories. For some it has become the harbinger of post-modern social theory (Denzin 1992). Feminism (Deegan and Hill 1987), gay activist theory (Plummer 1995) and the politics of race (Lal 1990) have all recently been linked further to it. Yet although Blumer may not have approved of all these developments, he would certainly not have been surprised. Sociologists come and go, as do sociological 'fashions' – indeed, this was yet another area he studied! – and Blumer would have been the last to claim that new generations should stick to old orthodoxies. Since Blumer saw change as rapid and inevitable, he would not have been overly puzzled by them. As he remarked, 'Social change is woven into the very fabric of modern life... It represents modern society in action (1962, p. 356). We have to transform our mentality to suit the new world (and) you are hereby enjoined to begin the change' (p. 359). He has left us a rich legacy with which to further this change.

Further Reading

H. Blumer, *Symbolic Interactionism: Perspective and Method* (Englewood Cliffs, NJ: Prentice-Hall, 1969).

H. Blumer and T. Duster, 'Theories of Race and Social Action', in *Sociological Theories: Race and Colonialism* (Paris: UNESCO, 1980), pp. 211–38.

N. Denzin, *Symbolic Interactionism and Cultural Studies* (Oxford: Blackwell, 1992).

G.A. Fine (ed.), Special issue on Herbert Blumer's legacy, *Symbolic Interaction*, **11**(1), Spring (1988).

S. Lyman and A. Vidich, *Social Order and Public Philosophy: The Analysis and Interpretation of the Work of Herbert Blumer* (Fayetteville, AR: University of Arkansas Press, 1988).

G.H. Mead, *Mind, Self and Society* (Chicago: University of Chicago Press, 1934).

Talcott Parsons

Robert Holton

Driving Impulses

Talcott Parsons (1902–1979) is regarded by some as the leading American sociologist of the twentieth century, by others as a theorist whose work is deeply flawed. What few scholars dispute is that Parsons took up the challenge of tackling the central questions posed by nineteenth-century sociology, while at the same time responding to contemporary intellectual and political issues. From the earlier period he took up the problem of social order, striving to find an answer to the question 'How is it that societies hold together?' His search for an answer led him to reject the economists' emphasis on self-interest, and to assert the importance of norms and values in social life. Meanwhile Parsons was also deeply concerned with political issues faced by the world in which he lived. These included the struggle between capitalism and communism, the advent of Fascism and world war, racial and ethnic conflict, and the lack of a stable global environment for political security.

Born into a religious milieu,[1] Parsons maintained an interest in the big questions that define the human condition, together with the ambition of bringing such issues within a single overarching framework of theory and explanation. These concerns engendered an abiding concern to construct theories about the social system, amounting to a truly comprehensive mapping of human society. This was designed to include both the social structures within which individuals find themselves, and the actions of individuals and organisations seeking to choose meaningful courses of action in pursuit of their goals. Some sociologists have focused predominantly on the 'macro', or large-scale phenomena such as markets or bureaucracies, while others have been mostly concerned with 'micro' or small-scale phenomena, such as intimate interpersonal relations and personality formation. In Parsons' case he attempted to look at both, bridging what has often been called the 'macro-micro' divide in social thought.

Parsons' mapping of the contours of social life also led him to reject the excessive development of intellectual specialisation. This meant economists were experts on the economy, political scientists on the political system and psychologists on the personality. The problem with this was that it failed to address the interactions and exchanges between the different parts of society, including, for example, the ways in which political and cultural phenomena influenced the economy and vice versa. One key task for sociology was to explain such interconnections. This required syntheses bringing together elements from a range of disciplines, including economics, social psychology, psychiatry and political science as well as sociology, as well as a range of thinkers such as **Weber, Durkheim, Freud**, Alfred Marshall and Keynes.[2]

Parsons was a theorist, dealing with big questions at a high level of generality. Yet, this does not mean he never conducted research, or took an interest in particular events around him. On the contrary, his theoretical work was also designed to unravel the mysteries and resolve the puzzles surrounding the practical everyday life of individuals and societies. Situations that Parsons explored included illness and interactions between doctor and patient and divisions of labour and responsibility within the family between men and women. Underlying these concerns was a resolve to understand both the nature of modern society, and the direction of contemporary social changes.

While Parsons' thought is highly relevant to real-world situations, it is clear that his primary significance is as a grand theorist. Most of his work is intentionally written in a highly abstract language, and organised within conceptual frameworks that are complex and often unfamiliar. For some this renders much of his work unreadable, but those prepared to dig deeper have often been rewarded with profound insights into the nature of social life. The justification for theoretical abstraction as pursued by Parsons, and certain other key thinkers in this volume, is that it may offer pathways of understanding that are unavailable in common sense.

An intellectual passion to comprehend human society as a systematic entity was certainly a driving force in Parsons' sociology. But alongside that was a moral concern for the desirability of social reform. Parsons took a stand for liberal-democratic values against totalitarianism and racism. A key element in this moral vision was that of social inclusion. No individual or social group should be denied full membership of what he called 'the societal community', on the basis of characteristics ascribed to that person or group on account of their social status or race. Similarly, no political authority should so dominate the non-governmental institutions of society, such as business, the professions or the universities, that their capacity to advance personal autonomy, professional ethics and intellectual freedom would be undermined. Parsons' sociological account of how modern society operated was also an account of how social life should be organised so as to realise the values he believed in.

Key Issues

Social Action and Social System

The basic building blocks of Parsons' general theory of social life are very generalised and abstract. Yet they are worth the effort required to understand them because they deal with nearly all the major theoretical questions that sociology has considered hitherto. A useful starting point involves the twin concepts of social action and social system. One of the most fundamental issues in sociology is the so-called structure/agency problem. Are the actions of individuals and groups determined by the large structures of social life? Or do actors make voluntary choices according to their own values or objectives? Examples of structural determination include **Marx**'s emphasis on the mode of production, or Durkheim's emphasis on modes of social solidarity. Examples of voluntary choice include economists' emphasis on the market sovereignty of consumers following their preferences.

Parsons' initial approach to this problem was to think in terms of what he called a voluntaristic theory of action.[3] Social action did indeed involve voluntary choices by individuals and groups in pursuit of their objectives. Social action, in this sense, must be meaningful to those involved. Yet the matter could not be left there, because three vital additional elements were necessary to any general mapping of social life.

First, there was the problem of the component parts of voluntaristic action, including its characteristic forms of motivation. The dominant utilitarian model held by economists emphasises the importance of self-interest in pursuit of personal tastes or preferences, developed outside society. Parsons did not doubt the importance of self-interest, but rejected the proposition that this was at the centre of social action. One of the difficulties here was that self-interest deals only with the means by which actors may seek to realise their ends, rather than with the origins of their ends, by which is meant the things they value. Utilitarianism, in effect, produced an incomplete and excessively narrow account of social action, leaving out the ways that the values and social rules embodied within human interaction influence individual wants and desires. Fashion is a classic case of socially derived wants.

A second, related point arises here. The problem with utilitarianism is not simply its abbreviated account of the cultural richness of human life. Where it also fails is in its inability to account for social order. Parsons here raises what he calls the utilitarian dilemma.[4] If the ends of social action are random and arbitrary, contingent on the biology or psychology of the individual, then how is it possible for such individual actions to be reconciled with each other in an orderly and predictable way? If self-interest rules, then society would be in a constant state of war, as individuals clashed with each other.

One way that utilitarians tried to resolve this difficulty was to portray social action as a rational response to the external environment faced by the actor.

Given the constraints of the situation they faced, such as limited natural resources, rational individuals acted in a self-interested way to maximise benefits and minimise costs. For economists, the institution of the market was one means by which the rational pursuit of self-interest would generate order and pattern. Within given external conditions, equilibrium between supply and demand would occur through the price mechanism. Order would eventuate, as if by the operation of a hidden hand, rather than any deliberate construction of regulatory rules or laws.

This kind of reply did not satisfy Parsons. First, he disputed the proposition that rationality and self-interest necessarily resulted in the harmonisation of different actions. People made choices for a range of different value-driven reasons, and according to a range of social definitions of the situation they found themselves in. Neither rationality nor self-interest were sufficient to produce integration into a stable pattern of rules. Second, Parsons felt that undue emphasis on the given conditions under which action took place threatened to undermine the voluntaristic approach to action. In other words, once you start to explain individual actions in terms of the surrounding environment you start to undermine the idea of individual choice or autonomy, and reinstate the importance of structural determination.

The way out of this dilemma for Parsons was to bring social values and rules of conduct (or norms) fully into the picture. This helps sociology to go one better than economics by explaining where the ends of action come from. They derive not from innate individual tastes and desires, but from society. Social order arises from the rules that regulate self-interest, and from the development of shared value systems that provide individuals with meaningful ways of selecting between courses of action.

In emphasising the normative as well as the self-interested side of social action, Parsons accepted that there were indeed social constraints on social action. A third element was then needed to complete a general mapping of social life, namely some way of systematising both the types of social action individuals engaged in, and the types of constraint or challenge that all human societies must face. These questions led Parsons to speak of the social system,[5] and not simply social action.

A system may be regarded as any entity that is relatively free-standing in relation to other entities. To say that nations are social systems is to say that they exhibit socially generated patterns in the way they function, and in the way the various component parts, such as the economy, government, the law and so forth mesh with one another. Parsons' idea of the social system drew on his earlier interest in biology, and in particular the human body. Just as the body comprised a range of different organs (heart, lungs, liver and so on) to perform the vital functions necessary for its survival and growth, so society requires institutions (for example households, firms, government and so on) capable of fulfilling functions necessary for society's equilibrium and development. The attraction of this model was that it emphasised the key importance of differentiation between specialised types of social function and organisation. Different institutions perform different functions.

The next step was to identify the basic social functions that social systems must successfully perform if they are to survive. Parsons focused on four. The first involved adaptation (A) to the external or natural environment from which scarce physical resources derive, or, put more simply, the economic function. The second was called goal attainment (G), meaning the political utilisation of resources to meet particular ends. The third function of integration (I) refers to the achievement of legitimate rules or norms to regulate the entire system, reflected, for example, in law. The fourth function, latent pattern maintenance (L), is to do with the transformation of values that are personal to the individual into value patterns that are shared and stable within a given system.

This four-function theory is often referred to by the acronym AGIL. Taken as a whole it is intended as a comprehensive account of the challenges faced by actors in any social system, large or small. Any social entity may then be regarded as a social system, provided it meets the test of being autonomous from the broader environment. Parsons is not talking only of the social system of nation-states, but of more micro-level organisational social systems, as well as the most macro-level system, namely global society.

The patient reader is at this point entitled to ask whether this vast theoretical edifice is really capable of being applied to real-world situations. Parsons, as we shall see below, was convinced it could.

Evolution and Modernity

Like earlier generations of sociologists Parsons struggled to understand the distinctive character of modern society as it had emerged in western Europe and North America since the sixteenth century. Most western thinkers until recently have approached this enterprise in evolutionary terms. Social evolutionism refers to the theory that human society contains within it an unfolding potential to develop new institutions and ways of life. This potential is realised insofar as social arrangements emerge that are somehow better able to meet human needs than those which went before. Evolutionary change typically takes place through a series of stages. These are usually regarded as progressive, lending to evolutionism a strongly normative as well as scientific tone. Put more simply, progress is good.

Parsons' sociological predecessors had focused on a wide-ranging set of indicators of modernity, from the dominance of society over nature through technological change, to a greater autonomy for individuals in relation to social rules. Parsons incorporated many of these earlier strands of analysis, but came to the view that a more complex and multidimensional approach to evolutionary change was required.[6] Human history was not simply a matter of one single evolutionary process, such as technological change, or economic individualism, but involved a far wider set of elements. At a system level these encompassed every aspect of the AGIL framework, including economic, political, legal and cultural institutions. At the level of social interaction within the real world, changes were also evident in the challenges and choices faced by individuals in giving meaning to their actions.

Parsons tried to bring 'system' and 'action' together, within four sets of **pattern variables**,[7] namely **universalism/particularism, achievement/ascription, specificity/diffuseness** and **neutrality/affectivity**. Modernity was defined in terms of contrasts between the former and the latter terms in each of these pairs. It meant universalism rather than particularism, an emphasis on achievement rather than ascription, specificity rather than diffuseness in social roles and greater neutrality rather than affectivity.

Pattern Variables

1. **Particularism versus Universalism:** Actors have to decide whether to judge a person by general criteria (universalism) or criteria unique to that person (particularism).

2. **Achievement versus Ascription:** Actors have to decide whether to judge people by performance criteria (such as educational qualifications, professional credentials, business 'success', and so on) or in terms of qualities that are ascribed on the basis of heredity of other forms of endowment (such as age, sex, race, caste and so on) that lack a performance standard.

3. **Specificity versus Diffuseness:** Actors have to choose, in any particular situation, whether to engage with others in a holistic way concerned with many aspects of that person's activities or well-being, or only for specific restricted purposes. An example of the latter is the dentist's concern with a patient's teeth to the exclusion of any other aspect of that person's life.

4. **Neutrality versus Affectivity:** Actors can either engage in a relationship for instrumental reasons without the involvement of feelings (neutrality) or for emotional reasons (affectivity).

Sources: Derived from: N. Abercrombie, S. Hill and B. Turner (eds) *The Penguin Dictionary of Sociology* (2nd edn) (Harmondsworth: Penguin, 1988, p. 178), and P. Hamilton, *Talcott Parsons* (London: Ellis Horwood & Tavistock, 1983, p. 103).

If this is what modernity comprises, how then may the historical development of modernity be understood? Parsons' argument was that social systems, which developed institutions capable of better performing all four AGIL functions, had an evolutionary advantage over those who did not. This argument was applied to western history, wherein Parsons located key institutions which gave particular societies an evolutionary advantage over others.[8] Examples included the development of common law in seventeenth-century England, which provided a universal set of norms that helped secure individual rights and property rights free from the arbitrary personal intervention of monarchs. He felt this innovation provided a better solution to society's integration (I) problems than previous forms of law, and gave England an evolutionary advantage over other places where law was less secure. Law and integration, rather than the customary focus on technological change, help explain why the first Industrial Revolution occurred in England.

Professions

A more concrete contemporary interest of Parsons was the evolution of the professions as a key aspect of modernity.[9] It was from a study of the professions that Parsons first developed the 'pattern variables' mentioned above. In line with his general emphasis on the normative basis of social action, Parsons regarded the professions not primarily as self-interested economic actors, but rather as occupations regulated by a normative code of conduct towards clients. The professional relationship with the client was regarded as an example of characteristics such as universalism and neutrality, whereby professional services would be guaranteed to the client on a standardised basis, and in a detached manner, irrespective of the particular ascribed status or social characteristics of the client. What mattered was not which social group the client came from, but rather their exposure to universalistic professional knowledge by a provider motivated by more than self-interest.

This argument, based on evidence gathered in a US context of limited state involvement in health care, took the market-based context of health delivery as the norm for its analysis of the professions. This served to highlight Parsons' more general argument about the limits of self-interest as a basis for social order. Markets dominated by individual self-interest could not explain the stable rule-bound patterns of social interaction that we see when we look at the operation of professional–client relations. These depend rather on normative commitments, such as the idea of the service ethic or vocation for their articulation. According to Parsons, the rewards to individual professionals accrue not primarily in terms of money. Nor do they depend on the ascribed social background of the professional, as in the case of members of families of traditional healers. They arise instead from individual achievement measured against professional standards. The compliance of the client in such interactions is dependent upon the professional acting in accordance with these standards.

Parsons applied this model of the professions more generally to modern society. He saw it as one more manifestation of the limits of self-interest and the importance of normative rules of behaviour in generating social order. The hardest challenge he faced in this respect was to apply the model to economic life in general, and the operation of large corporations in particular. Where once the functions of ownership and management had been conducted by family members within the family firm, the modern corporation was now typically a limited liability company, owned by a mass of shareholders, but operated by specialist managers.

For Parsons this had two points of significance. The first was that older forms of divisive class conflict between capitalist owners and a propertyless proletariat would no longer be central to modern society.[10] The old schism between capital and labour was reminiscent of the social and economic divide between lord and peasant. It was being superseded by opportunities for upward social mobility created by mass access to education, and processes of occupational specialisation.

The second point of significance for Parsons was that he expected the increasing autonomy of management as a profession to generate the same kinds of normative rules of behaviour that he had found in the medical profession. Self-interest and profit seeking within the corporation would certainly not be undermined, but they would, in his view, be subjected to a more ethical discipline emanating from managers. This particular argument was, however, based more on expectation than observation, as Parsons was the first to admit.

The Sick Role

A final substantive aspect of Parsons' sociology is his major contribution to the analysis of health and illness. This work is of great significance because it shows Parsons claiming for sociology areas of investigation conventionally allocated to biology and medicine. The principal feature of this claim was his notion of the sick role.[11]

For Parsons, sickness was not only a biological state, but also a matter of social significance. One did not become sick independent of the social system, rather one was socially defined as sick. The social definition of sickness was elaborated in his idea that sickness was a social role with a particular set of features.

Four such features of the sick role were identified. The first was that it justified the withdrawal of the sick person from normal work and family duties. Second, the person was not seen as responsible for his or her condition, and hence could not become well without outside intervention. Third, there was a responsibility on the sick person to become well, withdrawal only being legitimate if subsequent return was accepted as a duty. Fourth, the person should seek professionally competent health care and therapy.

These role expectations were also connected to broader analyses of social order, linking social action at the individual level, with the wider social system. Illness in this sense was regarded by Parsons as a kind of deviancy, where normative controls, such as the obligation to get well through medical therapy, were essential to the restoration of the normal functioning of both the individual and the society. Yet it is a misreading of Parsons to suggest he believed all sick people would take up the obligations of the sick role and seek recovery. On the contrary, he felt that certain kinds of chronic sickness, and much mental illness, were responses to social tensions where individuals felt unable to cope. Sickness in this sense offered a legitimate role, by permitting withdrawal from stressful situations.

In Parsons' discussion of the sick role we see both his general theoretical ambitions and his concern for concrete interactions of daily life at work. At one and the same time he is challenging the idea that 'the invading microbe' is the root cause of all sickness, while at the same time claiming for sociology a part in the fine-grained analysis of health and illness, within – not outside – society.

Seeing Things Differently

Great social thinkers are noteworthy not only for the array of concepts and theories they develop, but also for their creative capacity to assist us to see things differently. Sometimes we do not become aware of the potential insights contained in their work until faced with a personal experience which we have tried to make sense of. The following autobiographical episode illustrates that sociologists are sometimes the last to apply sociology to themselves, but that a key thinker like Parsons may sometimes belatedly come to the rescue.

University teachers spend a good deal of time in committees, trying to exercise forms of self-government appropriate to their professional autonomy. In the university where I work we periodically have staff meetings to discuss our teaching and research, and a host of questions to do with resources like rooms and computers. I sometimes feel these meetings are an interruption to my work as a sociologist.

As I sit in these meetings, I hear colleagues debating with each other. Some bring their values to bear in a very open way, declaring this or that teaching philosophy to be good and others to be flawed in some way. They seek a consensus of values, but are often frustrated when value conflict seems irresolvable. Another way of debating is to speak instead of particular policies which it is felt will realise the complex set of goals present among a dozen or so strongly willed individuals. If a majority vote for a particular policy, say to devote more resources to teaching first-year and less to upper-year topics, then this will generally carry legitimacy. It is hard to get very far with this kind of discussion, however, without being aware of the level of human and financial resources which we have at our disposal to meet our policy pronouncements. Morally and politically driven arguments about where the department should go and what it should prioritise are fine, but can we really afford to do them?

And of course it sometimes gets a bit heated, although no more so than any other body of people who care about what they do. At this point, some attempt is often made to keep things civil and fair, ensuring the more vocal and opinionated do not drown out others. There is no written set of rules which enshrine such rules of debate and decision-making, but they have a reality nonetheless, some kind of sense of obligation to the department as such that usually puts a rein on excesses of moralising or political self-interest.

Department meetings are fine, but I am usually pleased when they are over and I can get back to teaching and research. And then one day it hit me. The department was a social system in its own right, inasmuch as it is able to determine within limits the direction it will take. But more than that it has a range of subsystems in operation, dealing with something like the AGIL functions that any system must successfully perform to survive and develop. If we pursue the G (policy-setting) and L (value-forming) functions too hard without thought of A (resources) or I (the overall integration of the department) functions then we will get into trouble. This may take the form of an A (resource) crisis, or an I (integration) crisis. Since the department has just celebrated its 20th birthday, however, I guess any such crises along the way have been overcome.

When I attend the departmental meeting then, I am not suspending an engagement with sociology for the next two hours! No, the sociological way of seeing things remains relevant all the time, and in all circumstances. Yet it took Parsons' highly abstract AGIL system theory for me to see this reality in my everyday work life.

Legacies and Unfinished Business

There are few fields in which the legacy of Parsons has not been felt. But his most significant impact has been twofold. First, he made major contributions in social theory and system theory. Much of this work drew on Parsons' synthesis of European and American strands of social thought. To assist this work, Parsons translated texts written in other languages into English, such as Max Weber's *Protestant Ethic and the Spirit of Capitalism*.[12] Parsons' general theories of action and the social system have influenced other key thinkers in the post-war period, even though they have taken social theory in different directions from Parsons. This applies to the critical theorist **Jürgen Habermas,** who has produced a more radical version of system theory that emphasises crisis as much as equilibrium.[13] It also applies to the psychoanalytic feminist **Nancy Chodorow,** who has developed a gendered analysis of personality formation, that goes beyond Parsons' very conservative account of child socialisation and the nuclear family.[14]

The second kind of impact made by Parsons was in more specific areas such as the sociology of the professions, the family, medical sociology, sociology of education, economic sociology and social stratification. Research in each of these areas has taken Parsons' work as a major reference point, although it would be equally true to say that a good deal of what he wrote has become obsolete in the light of further study. One of the major reasons for this is the weakness of his work in discussing power and inequality. A range of critics across all the areas listed make the same general point.[15] Sociologists of the professions, for example, claim Parsons underestimates professional self-interest and power over clients, while exaggerating the impact of normative rules in regulating professional action. Economic sociologists, meanwhile, argue that Parsons prematurely announced the demise of capitalism, countering his rather benign view of economic life with an emphasis on continuing inequalities of power and personal life-chances deriving from economic property rights.

While Parsons became the dominant theoretical figure in American sociology during the 1950s and early 1960s, the rising tide of criticism that greeted his work in the late 1960s and early 1970s led to a rapid process of eclipse.[16] This occurred in the context of radical social upheaval in American society, linked to student protests against the Vietnam War and the military–industrial complex, explosions of black protest in the inner city, and the emergence of feminist movements to challenge the gender division of labour and conventional forms of sexuality. Many similar processes were evident in other western societies. The net effect was to render Parsons' discussion of social order, achieved through value consensus and commitment to normative integration, very shaky. Sociologists returned to what was now called conflict theory, in contrast with Parsons' emphasis on order.

Between the mid-1970s and the mid-1990s, however, the USA and western society went a long way towards restabilisation. Institutions such as the regulated market, the democratic polity, and the rule of law, which Parsons regarded as conferring evolutionary advantage on social systems, experienced a revival in the restabilised West, boosted also by the collapse of Soviet Communism in Russia and eastern Europe. These social trends helped to encourage a revival in Parsonian sociology, which has continued apace.[17]

One notable feature of contemporary theory is the attempt to confront and reconcile Parsons with his critics. This involves returning to Parsons' texts to identify previously unperceived strengths as well as weaknesses. One such underappreciated resource is Parsons' nuanced account of socialisation. This was previously regarded as an almost automatic effect of the operation of the social system, drawing the criticism that Parsons operated with an over-socialised conception of human actors. Put another way, it was assumed Parsons' theory of the social system left individuals as robots programmed by an all-powerful set of rules.

This interpretation of Parsons is, however, wide of the mark. What he was trying to say was more subtle than his critics supposed. At one level socialisation did operate in systemic ways through the core institutions of society founded on rules and values. Yet Parsons also wanted to leave space for the individual and for individualism which he saw as such a crucial feature of modern society. He reconciled individual autonomy with the social system by claiming that we learn to be individuals, but this learning process is never automatic nor is it without tensions and conflicts. One reason for this is that one can never be socialised into the social system as such, only into particular patterns of life, within the home, the school and the workplace. The processes operating here do not create robots but rather individuals with particular biographies and trajectories through life. Socialisation is never smooth, perfect or trouble free.[18]

Many of the conflicts of the 1960s, for example, were regarded by Parsons as integration (I function) problems, stemming from the continuing exclusion of particular groups (for example blacks or students), from the goal-setting (G function) political process. Democracy was the most satisfactory way of meeting goal-setting (G) functions, but not if significant parts of society were excluded. Insofar as extensions of citizenship rights and new political participation structures achieve greater inclusion of the excluded, so too will reintegration occur.

The net effect of the Parsons revival has been to encourage a more open, less partisan sociology that moves beyond polarised opposites, such as conservative Parsonian versus radical sociology, or order versus conflict sociology. The search for a more persuasive synthesis of different sociological traditions is entirely within the spirit of Parsons' work, and that of the key thinkers before him such as Marx and Weber. Parsons legacy is therefore rich, stimulating and still highly relevant. It remains a legacy worth embracing.

Further Reading

P. Hamilton, *Talcott Parsons* (London/Chichester: Tavistock/Horwood Ellis, 1983).

P. Hamilton (ed.), *Talcott Parsons: Critical Assessments*, 4 vols (London: Routledge, 1992).

R. Holton, 'Talcott Parsons and the Integration of Economic and Sociological Theory', *Sociological Inquiry*, 61(1), (1991), 102–14.

R. Robertson and B.S. Turner (eds), *Talcott Parsons: Theorist of Modernity* (London: Sage, 1991).

D. Wrong, 'The Oversocialised Conception of Man in Modern Sociology', *American Sociological Review*, **26**, (1961), 183–93.

PART II

8

Robert K. Merton

Alan Sica

Approaching Merton

The list of entire books and articles principally committed to explaining or elaborating Robert K. Merton's contributions to social science is long and distinguished. His core work, *Social Theory and Social Structure,* has been translated into a dozen languages since 1949, when it first appeared in English, and has required 30 printings to fill the global market's demand.[1] Along with perhaps one other book from the same period – Gerth and Mills' 1946 compilation, *From Max Weber* – this collection of Merton's earlier essays is as close to a Bible as one is likely to come when surveying social theories that provided inspiration and conceptual guidelines for the most fruitful social research undertaken since the Second World War.

While this intense veneration is surely gratifying for Merton and his legion of followers, it presents a serious dilemma for the expositor hoping to give a newcomer some sense of the process whereby Merton's name has become synonymous with analytic brilliance, conceptual creativity, and intellection at the highest level. Simply put, there is too much Merton to compress within the confines of a brief chapter – too many of his own books, articles, essays, introductions; too many ideas, research strategies, programs for projects still waiting to be carried out; too many extraordinary students, commentators, and researchers who have 'fine-tuned' aspects of Merton's thinking or empirical work. (As only one piece of evidence from among dozens that exist indicating Merton's *nonpareil* position in the field, consider that in 1990, 52 years after his dissertation saw print, an entire volume was dedicated to analyzing its *continuing* significance by means of chapters written by 18 scholars, and including by Merton himself four reprints, plus one new entry!)[2]

Thus, a simplifying choice must be made in order to render an economical presentation of his accomplishments. Such a reduction will necessarily 'privilege' one avenue over a host of possible others, in an effort to offer what some readers might nevertheless regard as an artificially tidy description of Merton's sociological world and, just as interestingly, his world-view. Therefore, this chapter does not purport to present, or even to describe in broad terms, all of

Merton's achievements in sociology or its theories. Rather, it highlights his special use of theoretical language, the creation of which uniquely marks his work as superior to that of any other American social theorist in the realm of conceptualization *qua* linguistic innovation.

It should therefore be emphasized that this is not Merton's own preferred mode of exposition in the realm of theory work. As he wrote nearly 50 years ago, 'The *distinctive* intellectual contributions of the sociologist are found primarily in the study of unintended consequences (among which are latent functions) of social practices as well as in the study of anticipated consequences (among which are manifest functions).' Reprinted in 1991 as part of a source-book of pregnant sociological quotations which Merton himself co-edited,[3] this could well be taken as his own sociological self-image, and bears notably small concurrence with the partial evaluation of his work expressed in what follows.

As a propaedeutic to this heterodox way of understanding Merton's special place in the history of contemporary theory, it might be useful to recall some 'textual history'. In 1949, still just 39, Merton pointedly distinguished his goals as a theorist and scientific researcher from those of the artist, writing a passage on 'paradigms' (anticipating Kuhn's usage) that has become famous among his many readers:

> Contributing to the tendency for sociological exposition to become lengthy rather than lucid is the tradition – inherited slightly from philosophy, substantially from history, and greatly from literature – of writing sociological accounts vividly and intensely to convey all the rich fullness of the human scene. The sociologist who does not disavow this handsome but alien heritage becomes intent on searching for the exceptional constellation of words that will best express the *particularity* of the sociological case in hand, rather than on seeking out the objective, generalizable concepts and relationships it exemplifies – the core of a science as distinct from the arts. Too often, this misplaced use of genuine artistic skills is encouraged by the plaudits of a lay public, gratefully assuring the sociologist that he writes like a novelist and not like an overly domesticated and academically henpecked Ph.D. Not infrequently, the sociologist pays for this popular applause, for the closer one approaches eloquence, the farther one retreats from methodical sense... If true art consists in concealing all signs of art, true science consists in revealing its scaffolding as well as its finished structure.[4]

For my purposes, the most intriguing and telling words in this bold passage disclose Merton's belief that sociologists who embrace 'this handsome *but alien* heritage' (my emphases) – springing, as it does, from artistically inspired prose – run the serious risk of losing their credentials as 'scientists' in search of 'objective, generalizable concepts'. And yet Merton's very name has become synonymous with unrivalled sociological prose. It is around this apparent contradiction that what follows is composed, in an effort to illuminate part of Merton's continuing appeal and importance for devout students of social thought on the one hand, and social researchers on the other.

The Uniqueness of Merton's Sociology

It would be hard to compose a better summary tribute to Robert K. Merton's 60-year record as a sociologist and social theorist than that provided by Piotr Sztompka, one of Merton's most informed expositors, in his opening paragraph to the latest collection of the latter's work:

> Rarely has the heritage of sociology been so deeply savored and dramatically enriched as in the life and work of Robert K. Merton. Nourished by a bountiful range of classical authors and guided by a succession of remarkable mentors, Merton opened up fruitful areas of inquiry along lines that he and generations of others would pursue for decades. The self-fulfilling prophecy, focussed interview (whence 'focus groups'), opportunity structure, middle-range theory, manifest and latent function, role-sets and status-sets, social dysfunctions, locals and cosmopolitans, scientific paradigms, the Matthew effect, accumulation of advantage and disadvantage, self-exemplification of sociological ideas, strategic research site, reconceptualization, and the serendipity pattern in research are some of his ingenious generative concepts. Some of these concepts in turn have proven so useful that, once adopted in sociology, they have then entered the common parlance in ways that obscure their origins, a process Merton describes colorfully as 'obliteration by incorporation'.[5]

Among the most famous and thoroughly 'obliterated' of all Merton's analytic expressions – having been successively reduced, in unacknowledged form, from scientific prose into journalistic cant – is 'the unanticipated consequences of social action'. It began as the inspired notion of a 26-year-old graduate student at Harvard, who had the wit to crystallize this widespread socio-cultural process in the first volume of the *American Sociological Review,* which has since become the top journal in the discipline.[6]

Merton has always been extremely wise, as well as fortunate, in his timing, professional affiliations, and the corresponding reception of his ideas. Along with the journal article just mentioned, he also produced several brief, pithy 'classics' – a weary word nowadays, to be sure, but one well earned in this case – before he reached his 30th year. These included one that elaborated **Durkheim**'s theory of anomie, and was reprinted 28 times before 1975,[7] and another on bureaucratic personality which was reproduced in 19 subsequent loci after its initial appearance.[8] When one adds to this a masterful dissertation that became a foundational work in the sociology of science,[9] an additional 15 well-received articles and book chapters, plus 50 or so book reviews, all in print before 1940 when Merton turned 30, a sociological virtuoso (in Weber's sense) was obviously in the making.

Thus, it can truly be said, amplifying Sztompka's remarks, that if any single scholar personifies the best about American sociology during its most optimistic period of intellectual and professional development (roughly 1937 until

1970),[10] this person would be Merton. There are many reasons for this, as many psychological as sociological, historical as well as political. But a key identifying characteristic, something uniquely his own, that has granted Merton's work its singular durability and appeal over the last 60 years, for social scientists of all types, concerns the quality not only of his analysis and sheer knowledge, but of his extraordinary attention to questions of language. Because so many sociologists of his generation and after chose to emphasize the 'scientific' nature of their enterprise, they slighted prose in order to accentuate their skill with enumeration. Merton, as much a historian and linguist as sociologist, never took that route, which gave him the opportunity to speak far beyond the perimeters of sociology, and directly to the concerns of scholars who normally regard his discipline with hostility or dismissal. Merton's induction into honorary scholarly societies world-wide has as much to do with his cultivated gracefulness, in thought and word, as with what might in a simpler writer be termed 'his ideas *per se*'. Somehow this hackneyed phrase jangles even louder than usual when applied to him.

The way that Merton transferred to students his great regard for the language and practices of systematic discovery was well remembered by the mathematical sociologist, James S. Coleman, nearly 40 years later: 'Merton was not content to develop his theoretical categories and show us their meaning', but also put them directly to analytic and empirical use.[11] In addition, and under the lifelong inspiration of his teacher at Harvard, George Sarton, Merton directed sociology graduate students in Coleman's cohort at Columbia to work their way through studies of scientific discovery and the maturation of various fields, in order to understand where exactly on the disciplinary continuum sociology lay. Sarton's legendary rigor as a historian of science gave Merton license to expect similar dedication from his charges. Yet at the same time he asked them to march through **Parsons'** newly published *The Social System* with a level of hermeneutic care which at the time was scarce in American sociology, and has only rarely occurred since. Modern sociologists had not, until Merton's arrival, normally aspired to become great readers of difficult texts; 'close reading' did not appear in their methodology handbooks. Among the many innovations Merton can fairly claim *vis-à-vis* the role of language in social theory is this insistence upon vigorous hermeneutic practices within an influential graduate program. Interestingly, the obvious connection between Merton's innovative pedagogy at Columbia and the venerable hermeneutic tradition, hundreds of years old, has seldom been noted as such.

One could go on interminably about Merton's lifelong love affair with linguistic innovation and creativity (most famously documented in his book best known to nonsociologists, *On the Shoulders of Giants*[12]). What was said 40 years ago about the great popular historian of the Middle Ages, Henry Osborn Taylor – who also taught, although briefly, at Columbia – applies equally well to Merton:

[He] was a literary craftsman. The times change, of course, and new historical evidence requires new syntheses. Grace of style is not enough in any age to give a book permanence. A book, however, which combines the gift of clear prose with a truly cultivated thoughtfulness can have a timelessness all its own.[13]

That Merton has applied throughout his career 'a truly cultivated thoughtfulness' in combination with prose of memorable lucidity has become almost a platitude among careful readers. Even his (relatively few) detractors admit to the seductive quality of his writings, not only on readers predisposed to agreement with him, but also upon skeptics.

Here is a sample of typical Merton prose from an important essay, one that has been fixed on graduate school reading lists for nearly 30 years:

The same point was made recently by the physicist, A. A. Moles, who said that scientists are 'professionally trained to conceal from themselves their deepest thought' and to 'exaggerate unconsciously the rational aspect' of work done in the past. What must be emphasized here is that the practice of glossing over the actual course of inquiry results largely from the mores of scientific publication which call for a passive idiom and format of reporting which imply that ideas develop without benefit of human brain and that investigations are conducted without benefit of human hand.[14]

Many of what became standard aspects of Mertonian rhetoric are here: tantalizing opening reference to an obscure foreign savant whom no one in sociology should know; ironic detachment (often noted by Merton students) in the author's attitude toward the common practices of researchers more intent on covering their tracks than giving frank self-exposure to their mental processes of discovery; clean, bracing English prose, yet within a multiclausal sentence of almost Germanic construction; and, beneath it all, the promise of revelation – what one would expect from a magician or magus – about mysteries, the existence of which most readers had not yet even noted, but which the author had identified and also begun to solve, by means of brilliant textwork and even more arresting footnotes and asides.

Great acting depends on hiding technique from the audience so that only the portrayed character is perceivable. Much the same is true of accomplished writing. Merton, writer and teacher, seemed outwardly clear and indubitable, almost serene, about his desires and discoveries. But upon closer study, the quicksilver quality of his thinking, and the writing that carried it into the public sphere, becomes maddeningly evident, so that what Merton in 'clear and distinct' fashion might mean for one earnest party – in an ironic hermeneutic twist – seems wholly wrong-headed to another. For instance, if Merton was truly serious that the history and systematics of theorizing could profitably be separated, and ultimately that the palm goes to the latter as sociology evolves toward 'real' science, why did he spend such energy pursuing historical detail, not only within sociology proper, but from a half-dozen other fields as well?[15] It is easy to see that by using him as an exemplar, his readers could become with equal pride either historians of ideas or survey researchers, while simultaneously claiming his intellectual paternity. It is this very ambiguity of message that has, in part, contributed to the Merton mystique and helped sustain his influence over the last five decades.

Merton's Genesis

Only recently – when he was nearly 84 – did Merton sketch his early years, claiming that his memory for personally significant incident is as imprecise as his memory for scholarly detail is exacting. Born in 'the slums of South Philadelphia' on 4 July, 1910, Meyer R. Schkolnick absorbed the city's many cultural offerings within walking distance of his home, including Stokowski's world-renowned symphony orchestra and a 10,000-volume Carnegie library. Through the encouraging complicity of the resident librarians, he regarded the latter as his 'private' store of knowledge. All of this and more, taken together, is what Merton has called 'public capital', a necessary ingredient in an 'opportunity structure'[16] that would emancipate himself and countless others from what was later dubbed 'the social order of the slum'.[17] His self-transformation, at 14, into Robert K. Merlin (a stage name for his developing magic act) almost immediately became 'Merton', a less predictable name for a magician, and this was how he was known when he entered Temple College (within Temple University) several years later. As with many other upwardly mobile 'ethnic' youths, an 'American-sounding' name seemed important to Merton in the 1920s, as he explains: 'Names in the performing arts were [then] routinely Americanized; that is, to say, they were transmuted into largely Anglo-American forms. For this, of course, was the era of hegemonic Americanization, generations before the emergence of anything resembling today's multiculturalism.' By now it is almost trite to observe that the improbable metamorphosis of this son of poor immigrants into the world's most respected sociologist is itself a special act of (American) magic, the generalized processes of which have occupied Merton's imagination for some years.

Merton's startling trajectory through Temple and then Harvard has been well documented, and as Sztompka noted above, he was blessed with several excellent teachers and 'role-models', not to mention a stellar set of peers once he got to Cambridge. His luck began with his Temple sociology teacher, George E. Simpson, who, among many kindnesses, made certain during a professional meeting that Merton would meet the head of the young sociology department at Harvard, the volcanic Pitirim Sorokin, whose monumental *Contemporary Sociological Theories* (1928) Merton had read. Sorokin's daredevil escape from Bolshevik Russia, his pronounced cosmopolitanism, and his theory book made it clear to Merton that 'plainly he was the teacher

I was looking for'.[18] Miraculously, or so it seemed, a scholarship was granted Merton, and he entered the enchanted and 'serendipitous environment'[19] at Harvard. Despite the fact that neither scholar gave nor asked for any quarter when it came to intellectual matters, and remembering that Sorokin was twice his student's age, their relationship bore remarkable fruit. Merton was primarily responsible for the science and technology chapters in Sorokin's masterpiece, *Social and Cultural Dynamics* (1937–1941 in four large volumes), published two articles with him (one regarding medieval Arabian intellectual development, the other about 'social time'), and along the way also copy edited Parsons' first and probably best book, *The Structure of Social Action* (1937).

Meanwhile, Merton took full advantage of the phenomenal liveliness of scholarly life in Cambridge during that period, and crossed disciplinary borders without compunction. His most important deviation from sociology proper involved persuading George Sarton, olympian historian of science, to work closely with him, which included opening to this precocious young scholar the pages of *ISIS*, Sarton's journal for the history of science. From him Merton learned about the human background to scientific procedure and discovery, which new knowledge helped Merton initiate 'the sociology of science' in its American version.[20] In sum, the cadre of top-flight teachers and students at Harvard during Merton's tenure there was of such unusual quality that social science began to revolve around many of them, with Merton quickly at the head of this new legion. He had, not for the last time, been at the right place at the right time, largely, one could argue, owing to his own gifts and energy, but also through the luck of fortuitous meetings, readings, and writings. A more Mertonian rendering would emphasize structurally opened possibilities that transcend the merely psychological. But a number of people, it could be shown, came upon very similar lines of opportunity between 1930 and 1940, and only one became Merton. Nevertheless, of the 'serendipitous', yet no less telling, nature of certain events throughout his career – from Temple to Harvard, on to Tulane for two years, and then to Columbia for more than fifty – he became only too aware.

Merton's Ideas and Their Legacy

Speaking Merton for Forty Years Without Knowing it: the Plenitude of Mertonian Notions

Already 30 years ago one could hear the slightly premature remark from sociologists who thought they were 'knowing' – one of Merton's favorite adjectives – that he had become 'the victim of his own success'; that the unintended consequence of his precocious brilliance, stylistic and substantive, had led to his own premature obliteration by ingestion, as it were. In a mythic move that Merton, knowing Frazer and **Freud**, would have understood, the children had consumed the father along with his heritage. His manifold theoretical 'interventions' (as they might now be termed) beginning in the late 1930s, whether pertaining to the sociology of knowledge, mass communications, social psychology, sociology of science, or the history of theorizing, had become by 1970 so much the coin of the realm that ever fewer readers knew their precise origin. And since sociology was riding a popular wave of societal and collegiate enthusiasm, giving due credit did not seem as important as it would later on when the dust had begun to settle, and the contributions of Merton's generation were beginning to be evaluated more carefully.

What this now means is that every introductory sociology textbook incorporates without acknowledgement a plentitude of Mertonian notions, those specifically his own or elaborated by his students, so that, along with Molière's 'cit', Mr Jordan, one might also exclaim, 'For more than 40 years I have been talking Merton without knowing it!'[21] Worse by far, the linguistic flotsam bequeathed by journalism to the 'educated' person's vocabulary includes regular use of 'self-fulfilling prophecy' and 'dysfunction' in such diluted form that the slogan 'I'm dysfunctional, you're dysfunctional' has become a nightclub joke.[22] All this suggests that Merton's contribution to sociological thought has proved so engaging that it has virtually disappeared *as such* – at least those epigrammatic aspects of it which most readily lend themselves to capsule summary and transmission.

Although theory writers today dare not invoke certain terms without a nod to proper authorities – for example **Bourdieu**'s 'cultural capital', **Giddens**' 'structuration', 'communicative competence' from **Habermas**, or **Foucault**'s 'regimes of power–knowledge–pleasure' – the same cannot be said for Merton. Since 'everyone knows' about manifest and latent functions, role-sets, and functional requisites, it would now be considered pedantic – for those who do know – to acknowledge these concepts' true progenitor. As well-put by a man of Merton's generation who assayed the history of American theory with unusual perspicacity,[23] Merton's 'reputation will rest not upon any general systematic theory but rather upon the many fertile expressions he has introduced into the literature – expressions such as theories of the middle range, paradigms, unanticipated consequences of purposive social action, sociological ambivalence, the role-set, manifest and latent functions, the self-fulfilling prophecy, anticipatory socialization, reference group (in fact, Herbert Hyman's term, systematized by Merton and Alice S. Rossi) and many more.'[24] In marked opposition to Sztompka, Bierstedt believes that Merton's enormous list of publications, including as it does no single *magnum opus* 'about society' as such, but, rather, scores of essays addressed to an unfettered range of theoretical and substantive topics, makes it difficult to gauge Merton's long-term significance as a theorist. As much a master prose stylist as Merton, Bierstedt summarizes his view of this unique situation in memorable imagery: 'The first merit badge to be pinned on [Merton] is precisely this almost incredible range of interests, his moving with the speed and grace of a humming bird from one blossom to the next, never still but always seemingly in flight.'[25] Sztompka, while quoting this very line from Bierstedt elsewhere, argues forcefully for a contrary position, as have others.[26]

Of course, living well into one's ninth decade does pose for an author certain 'copyright' limitations to deference practices. Yet it is possible that by the time most of these younger theorists have reached Merton's current age, their terminological innovations will have become 'a collection of stale cream-puffs'. So Ezra Pound designated his early poems when they were reissued, 55 years after their revolutionary detonation of Edwardian stuffiness.[27] Drawing an analogy between these two linguistic innovators is not so far-fetched after one considers the unschooled rhetoric of sociology in the 1930s, and Merton's studied remove from it. Bierstedt's opinion, that Merton's 'many fertile expressions' rather than a single, embracing theory, are what will propel his reputation into the future, is on its face more plausible, at least for the nontheory specialist, than the opposing view – even if the term 'expressions' does not properly convey the analytic labors that have gone into Merton's conceptual refinement over the last five decades.

Yet, leaving terminological precision aside, a thorny issue is indeed raised by observations of this sort, concerning phenomena about which Merton is, ironically enough, the leading expert: 'OBI' (obliteration by incorporation) and eponymy (naming discoveries for their notable predecessors in a given discipline). At what point do ritual citations become little more than attempts to legitimate current research, rather than, as they should be, attentive rethinking of foundational ideas? Put more prosaically, how frequently do scholars today read with hermeneutic alertness the essays Merton composed in the 1930s, 1940s, and 1950s to which they give automatic obeisance in their bibliographies? Though hardly peculiar to Merton's legacy, in his case these questions become more troubling than might usually be the case for the very reason that he has systematically investigated these practices *as a social and intellectual process.*

Conceptual Virtuosity and Linguistic Elegance

That said, if opinions like Bierstedt's are not entirely wrong, at least two more questions arise. They pertain to the apparent course that sociality and literacy may well take under the influence of electronic communication, and the fate of 'traditional' scholarship that must come to terms with it. In the new world of the so-called postmodern, words carry less significance than images, and exacting attention to language *as representing a consensually acceptable reality* becomes ever rarer – or so one reads in standard analyses of postmodernity. Thus, the sort of conceptual virtuosity and nearly Aristotelian concern for categorization and fine distinction, for which Merton has long been famous, accordingly loses some of its luster. The same, of course, applies to any number of other theorists, but is particularly apt in Merton's case for the very reason that he exercised such care when creating his works. This claim on my part is based more on a study of recent cultural theory, which claims to have knowledge of contemporary conditions that surpasses the obvious, than on any 'empirical' investigation, and should be appraised accordingly.

He has often claimed in private correspondence to be a slow writer, with the implication that painstaking precision (meant literally) goes into his pronouncements. As he put it once in an influential essay from 1949: '*Too often, a single term has been used to symbolize different concepts, just as the same concept has been symbolized by different terms*. Clarity of analysis and adequacy of communication are both victims of this frivolous use of words.'[28] In a dictionary of antonyms, 'frivolous' and 'Merton' could well serve to illuminate each other. Yet just as 'the postmodern condition' emphasizes the 'play' of words and the ludicy of social life[29] in lieu of the measured and restrained, the virtues Merton already cultivated as a young author – rigor, exactness, sobriety, inclusiveness – fall to the debit side of the ledger, becoming as detractive to the contemporary ear and eye as they were seductive to those of his mentors and peers 60 years ago.

Consider, for example, this bit of regal elegance from his dissertation, composed circa 1935:

> it is evident that the formal organization of values constituted by Puritanism led to the largely unwitting furtherance of modern science. The Puritan complex of a scarcely disguised [*sic*] utilitarianism; of intramundane interests; methodical, unremitting action; thoroughgoing empiricism; of the right and even the duty of *libre examen*; of anti-traditionalism – all this was congenial to the same values in science. The happy marriage of those two movements was based on an intrinsic compatibility and even in the nineteenth century, their divorce was not yet final.[30]

Would anyone entertain or expect this kind of writing today from a 25-year-old graduate student in sociology? 'Intramundane' is a word not in my word processor's dictionary, and captures better than standard translations do **Weber**'s idea of the Puritan's 'this-worldly orientation'; 'unremitting' is also not currently much used among 'social scientists', it being too 'hot' a term for 'cool' analysis, in McLuhan's terms; *libre examen,* of course, is approaching extinction, in word and deed; and few social scientists would now allow themselves metaphorical reference to the pained condition of 'divorce', which during Merton's youth was as rare as today it is rampant. Most importantly, the authorial voice heard loud and clear in this characteristic passage shares none of the coy hesitancy common to today's 'theoretical' or speculative dissertations of the broad gauge. In a way, reading vintage Merton is not unlike listening to Caruso on 78-rpm 'vinyl': the voice is unapologetically bold, eager to take risks, and marvelously from another world.

Nor is it that with age he changed very much. In a 1970 preface to his reissued dissertation, he recalls his juvenile labors in the third person:

> The inquiry began as he was rummaging about in seventeenth-century England, trying to make some sense of the remarkable efflorescence of science at that time and place, being directed in the search by a general sociological orientation. The orientation was simple enough: various institutions in the society are variously interdependent so that what happens in the economic or religious realm is apt to have some perceptible connections with some of what happens in the realm of science, and conversely. In the course of reading the letters, diaries, memoirs and papers of seventeenth-century men of science, the author slowly noted the frequent religious commitments of scientists in this time, and even more, what seemed to be their Puritan orientation. Only then, and almost as though he had not been put through his paces during the course of graduate study, was he belatedly put in mind of that intellectual tradition, established by Max Weber, Troeltsch, Tawney, and others, which centered on the interaction between the Protestant ethic and the emergence of modern capitalism. Swiftly making amends for this temporary amnesia, the author turned to a line-by-line reading of Weber's work to see whether he had anything at all to say about the relation of Puritanism to science and technology. Of course, he had.[31]

When one considers that this entire process occurred between 1933 and 1935 – while Merton was taking classes, helping Sorokin, learning to teach at Harvard, beginning married life, and otherwise doing what graduate students during the Depression had to do to survive – his claims of 'temporary amnesia' and 'belated' self-reminder of Weber's usefulness to his thesis almost approaches false modesty. Yet again, the rhetoric of this passage, and the effort it describes – a kind of heroic hermeneutic enterprise that now seems quite impossible for one so young – 'brings into sharp relief' (a cliché of the sort Merton would not allow himself) the conditions of his intellectual labors versus those of our own time, even among the best young scholars.

Sociological Inspiration from a World Now Lost

The other intriguing question prompted by thoughts about Merton's virtuosic writing is more sociological than linguistic, and therefore more in keeping with his own preferred domain of analysis. In a passage of mature Mertonian confidence, he writes (his italics): '*The sociological theory deals with the processes through which social structures generate the circumstances in which ambivalence is embedded in particular statuses and status-sets together with their associated social roles.*'[32] If one patiently studies this sentence, and also goes down the long list of concepts Merton left in his wake, the suspicion begins to emerge, however slowly, that he was analytically inspired by a social world not precisely commensurate with today's. Would it be too much of an exaggeration to note that the world which gave birth to his congeries of concepts and definitions has begun to seem as distant from our own as Katharine Hepburn's *ingénue* roles in *Bringing Up Baby* (1938) or *The Philadelphia Story* (1940) are remote from the profane, armed, hard-bitten heroines of today's popular films? Whereas Hepburn's staccato banter was pure theater, with no comma misplaced, her sentiments never allowed to slip beneath the mark of the 'lady', today's stars, when not portraying robots or space creatures, talk and behave like teamsters rather than descendants of New England Puritans. And if film reflects its context – as one would suppose based on Merton's thoughts about the sociology of knowledge and mass culture[33] – social relations today call for an analytic apparatus that might hold relatively little in common with one designed to interpret interaction during the third and fourth decades of the century.

This is a contentious set of claims, to be sure. Yet consider, by way of mental experiment, Merton's virtuosic 'Provisional List of Group-Properties' from his book-within-a-book, 'Continuities in the Theory of Reference Groups and Social Structure'.[34] If one studies each of his 26 'properties' – as creative a refinement of **Simmelian** thought as one is likely to find – and then considers contemporary life in its more typical manifestations, something of a gap begins to open between 'that time' and this. Or reconsider, in this context, Merton's (and Alice Rossi's) analysis of *The American Soldier* in 1950,[35] wherein relative deprivation, reference groups' behavior, anticipatory socialization, and related notions are developed, using the Stouffer study as 'data'. As Bierstedt points out in a detailed examination of Merton's arguments,[36] much of this work hinges on the idea that soldiers behave according to certain observable patterns, and that, furthermore, people in society at large conform to group norms, or do not, more or less in continuity with the findings in Stouffer's monumental survey of American troops. Careful reading of the two essays Merton commits to these matters illustrates that normative expectations, and the processes which created them, during and immediately after the Second World War among Americans would appear to differ significantly from those of today. Although I cannot 'prove' this here, in point of fact, the 'new' American military – which, for instance, eschews basic training drills when the temperature exceeds 90 degrees for fear a recruit may suffer discomfort – is so distinct in almost every dimension from the one Stouffer studied that a one-to-one comparison becomes an exercise either in historical imagining or an analytic error, depending on one's point of view. Put still another way, Merton's very language of societal dissection *might* make it harder for him to comprehend thoroughly the depths of *anomia* into which sizeable portions of modern humanity have been cast. Or so it could be argued, given sufficient space, wit, and observable data.

Theory and Research of the Middle Range

Another truism regarding Merton's career and cumulative achievement holds that his brief for 'middle-range' theorizing – in opposition both to Parsons' grandiose schemes as well as to interactional theories of tiny scope – brought his ideas into broad favor with researchers who might otherwise have had little regard for 'pure' theory. Thus, to understand his theories means investigating the 'substantive' studies to which he directly contributed, and also those hundreds more which sought to test his various claims by one means or another. To my knowledge, a systematic study – that is, 'Merton's Influence on Empirical Research' – has not yet been done, although plenty of raw materials exist were someone interested in carrying it out.[37] Yet here, again, the problem would be a superabundance of riches.

It might be argued that as a peer of Merton's, Bierstedt was better positioned than I to evaluate his colleague's ultimate role in the history of social thought. Despite having some harsh things to say about the Mertonian vision of what sociology and social theory ought to be, he concludes his own exposition with two observations that bear repeating, particularly as I cannot express these sentiments any better: 'Ideas are toys for Merton, colored balls to be conjured out of nowhere, thrown in the air, and caught again with a magician's flair and finesse.' Setting aside the mixed image of juggler and magician, this is indeed an essential element of Merton's lasting importance, that he wrote so beguilingly, so convincingly, that his readers were swept away, even sometimes without understanding what exactly it was they were applauding. But more importantly, and again in Bierstedt's words, 'There is, however, a final word for Merton, and that word is quality... He is a serious and thoughtful scholar, a superb sociologist, and one who has illuminated every subject to which he has directed his attention.'[38] In the end it may be this characteristic more than any other – the sheer intelligence and energetic application, over 60 years, of mindfulness to the disentangling of social phenomena – that guarantees Merton's place in the discipline's history. As an exemplar of theoretical brilliance and creative sociological practice, he has had no rival during his lifetime. Perhaps more importantly, the social structure of the special kind that gave rise to him – intensely literate and hopeful, despite its external lack of amenities – is gone, and one must seriously question if, considering these irreversible changes, another of his caliber is likely to appear in the foreseeable future.

9

Simone de Beauvoir

Mary Evans

Driving Impulses

Simone de Beauvoir presents a considerable challenge to anyone attempting to identify the crucial influences in her life and work since in a very important sense they can be summarised by naming Jean-Paul Sartre. This is not, as it might first appear, the suggestion that this brilliant (and productive) woman writer only achieved prominence because of a relationship with a man. This was far from the case (and there is some evidence to lead us to speculate on what de Beauvoir gave to Sartre rather than the reverse) but what we have to acknowledge is the close association (both social and intellectual) between these two figures and the dialogue between them that was so crucial to both. In biographical terms, there is little doubt that Sartre led de Beauvoir away from idealist philosophy and towards existentialism; at the same time de Beauvoir's work was organised around (and here the idea of dialogue is central) the working out, in both fiction and non-fiction, of Sartre's ideas on morality and the limits of personal responsibility. Both individuals, it must be emphasised, have to be located firmly within European modernism. In terms of both philosophy, and politics, de Beauvoir and Sartre entirely endorsed, for most of their adult and working lives, the Enlightenment's expectations of the rule, indeed the possibilities, of the rational. In de Beauvoir's case this discourse made her profoundly sceptical of all religions and of psychoanalysis: the world, as far as she was concerned, could be rationally understood and rationally organised. That emotional life did not always lend itself to such rational principles was a constant theme of de Beauvoir's fiction: from her first published novel *She Came to Stay* she was preoccupied with the problems of subjectivity and the irrational.[1]

For de Beauvoir, these problems were, implicitly, gendered. Thus a consistent theme of her fiction was women's emotional dependence on men, a theme to which she constantly returned and one which she attempted to resolve in terms of the infamous conclusion to *The Second Sex*. In this conclusion de Beauvoir calls on women to adopt male patterns of behaviour and assumptions – an invocation which is, of course, deeply contradictory for a woman who is identified as the most significant feminist figure of the twen-tieth century. Yet that view of de Beauvoir (while rightly acknowledging her intellectual presence) also fails to see that de Beauvoir was discovered by femi-nism rather than de Beauvoir initiating feminism. In the final years of her life, de Beauvoir came to acknowledge the difficulties of assuming universal, and universalistic, truths. Just as Sartre (at about the same time) was discovering the limitations of literature, so de Beauvoir was discovering that the Enlight-enment project of reason and understanding was problematic in terms of both its implicit **Cartesian dualism** and its refusal of the social implications of sexual difference. Nevertheless, it is apparent that de Beauvoir – to the end of her life – resisted the possibilities of the pluralities and diversities of post-modernism. For her, there was a truth and it was identifiable. The emphasis in de Beauvoir's work on specific themes changed throughout her lifetime (women, old age, colonialism were all subjects with which she engaged in her non-fiction), but all of them were approached in terms of the ways in which they could be better understood through de Beauvoir's very precise form of empirical investigation and existential ethics.

Cartesian Dualism

The philosophical idea, deriving from the French philosopher Descartes, that mind and body are separate. Critics feel that such a dualism leads to an overemphasis on the mind, the spirit, ideas, and so on, at the expense of the body and the material world in general, and of the close relation-ship between the two.

In maintaining this position, de Beauvoir put herself in a strikingly different situation from that of her contemporaries in French intellectual life. Just as Jacques Lacan was constructing his theory of sexuality and **Michel Foucault** was contesting the idea of progress and single sources of knowledge and power, de Beauvoir was adamantly refusing the unconscious and main-taining a commitment to hierarchies of knowledge. A later generation of French women writers (among them – Kristeva, Irigaray, Cixous and Wittig) who developed enormously influential ideas about both sexual difference *per se* and sexual difference in language were largely distant, in both political and intellectual terms, from de Beauvoir. De Beauvoir never accepted, for example, the idea that women and men use, and learn, different languages. Yet for all her rejection of the work of these writers de Beauvoir occupied, somewhat paradoxically, a position which was more postmodern than she might have acknowledged. Her most famous work, *The Second Sex*, does argue for the difference (in both social and biological terms) between women and men. Although what de Beauvoir does with this is to suggest (as pointed out above) that women should internalise and assimilate male practices and assumptions, she nevertheless provided a crucial intervention in twentieth-century culture in her identification of the causes and consequences of sexual difference. In that, she can be seen to have provided a starting point for the rereading and reinterpretation of the history of gender relations.

Key Issues

Summary of Key Issues
  (i) Women's Agency
 (ii) Gender Difference
(iii) The Relationship of Women to Knowledge
(iv) Commitment to Social Change and Social Transformation

(See Introduction for an explanation of the ordering of this chapter.)

To identify particular issues in the case of the work of Simone de Beauvoir involves a certain degree of repetition on a theme. The central theme of de Beauvoir's work was that of agency and the discussion of how women could act, in the context of a culture (that of western Europe) which was definitively misogynist. Thus action and agency, in a world which did not expect women to exhibit either of these competencies, are key organising themes for de Beauvoir. At the same time, she was also deeply concerned with the nature and meaning of gender divisions. Her famous remark that 'one is not born, but rather becomes, a woman' has passed into western culture and is always cited as *the* summary of the social constructionist view of gender difference.[2] De Beauvoir does not allow any doubt in her account of what makes a women, 'it is civilization as a whole that produces this creature, intermediate between male and eunuch, which is described as feminine'.[3]

Thus action and agency, and the nature of gender difference are the first two themes for which the work of de Beauvoir is known. At the same time, throughout de Beauvoir's work three other concerns can be located: her discussion of the relationship of women to knowledge (and the accompanying account of western patriarchal culture), the concept of life as a project, and last, but by no means least, a commitment to social change and social transformation which can best be described as rigidly organised around state politics.

Reason, Modernism, Jean-Paul Sartre

What has to be said of all these themes, and indeed of the work of de Beauvoir as a whole, is that she saw the world, and theorised about it, in the light of a belief in reason that was never shattered by events in either her personal or public life. De Beauvoir lived from 1908 to 1986, and as such she remembered (albeit vaguely) the First World War and the humiliation of France at the hands of the Germans. A student and a teacher during the 1920s and 1930s she formed the crucial relationship of her life with Jean-Paul Sartre while both were at the Sorbonne. This couple formed a long and often problematic relationship which lasted until the death of Sartre in 1980.[4] But in the course of that relationship they formed an alliance against the world which was often formidable, in terms of both their ability to exclude other people from their lives and – on a more public and explicit level – to establish political and philosophical positions. They both came late to formal politics: in early maturity their politics had taken the form of resistance to bourgeois convention through their personal behaviour and the development of existential philosophy. But when they did discover the possibilities of national and international politics (a discovery which was largely the result of the Second World War and the occupation of France by the Germans) both became active participants in organised left-wing politics.

These brief remarks can do only brief justice to the lives of two people who have a central place in European culture. Yet what is important about de Beauvoir has to be seen in the context of that culture, and of the changes which were taking place in the twentieth century. De Beauvoir, despite her birth (and education) in the twentieth century remained in many ways a creature of the late nineteenth century and early modernism: her rejection of psychoanalysis, her belief in the individual project of reason and above all her refusal to recognise the often ambiguous boundaries between objectivity and subjectivity all place her in the world-view of early modernism.

Men as the Focus of Attack and the Standard of Achievement

We can see too that the first theme named here as central to de Beauvoir's work (that of women and agency) was understood by de Beauvoir in terms of a society and culture which largely denied the public agency of women. The formal emancipation of women in France occurred later than in Anglo-Saxon countries and de Beauvoir (somewhat inevitably) had few contacts with anything approaching feminism for the greater part of her life. Indeed, to read the first volume of de Beauvoir's autobiography (*Memoirs of a Dutiful Daughter*) is to read of a society which was decidedly non-modern in its attitude to women.[5] De Beauvoir took her inspiration for her future self from British and North American writers: George Eliot's Maggie Tulliver and Louisa Alcott's Jo March were her heroines.

It is true to say of de Beauvoir that although she read the works of women writers such as Eliot and Alcott – who absolutely recognised the extent of patriarchal control in western society – what she did not do was to assume any sense of identity with women in general. Thus what we can observe about de Beauvoir's work is that she was discovered by second-wave feminism rather than having played any key part in its development. *The Second Sex* (which was published in 1949) was a bestseller throughout the West, but de Beauvoir did not then become a spokeswoman for a specifically feminist cause. Indeed, the conclusion to *The Second Sex*, which identifies female agency as only possible through the replication of male patterns of behaviour, was a message of dubious value to feminist concerns. Nevertheless, what de Beauvoir had done was put on (or put back on) the western intellectual and political agenda the question of women, and in particular women's second-class status. For de Beauvoir, the way forward for women is in integration into the public world and the assumption of rigorously independent behaviour. For sociologists, it is essential to point out that de Beauvoir's reference group of men and masculinity was always that of white, middle-class, educated men. She had little to say about the world outside the society where she spent her life. That life was lived, from beginning to end, in Paris and although de Beauvoir travelled extensively (and wrote extensively about her travels) 'the others' – if the rest of the world might be described in this way – did not significantly intrude on her consciousness.

Thus in identifying women as 'the other' in western agency, the defining party in this relationship – men – were both de Beauvoir's focus for attack and her standard of achievement. It is apparent from her account of her own life that she identified closely with her father – and in particular with his anticlericalism and his very publicly lived life. Her mother's pious domesticity held no appeal for de Beauvoir, even though every reader of de Beauvoir's autobiography has encountered de Beauvoir's fierce grief on the death of her mother and her virtual absence of interest in the death of her father. What de Beauvoir loved, and admired, was a certain condition, and a certain set of possibilities of urban masculinity. In this, she internalised many of the characteristics of what Walter Benjamin (and others) have described as the *flâneur*, the person who has the freedom to move about the modern city.[6] But, as Janet Woolf has pointed out, that figure is always male and although modernity and femininity might be closely linked, the public person of the modern city was, throughout the nineteenth and early twentieth century, male.[7] Virginia Woolf, in the essays collected as *The Crowded Dance of Modern Life,* wrote of her love of London and the charm of a city that is built not to last, but to pass.[8] In the same way de Beauvoir was fascinated by the life on the Parisian streets and demanded what was forbidden – access to the streets by a middle-class woman.

Women's Agency and Independence versus Misognyny and the Refusal of Public Space

Through her spectacular and considerable achievements in higher education, de Beauvoir was able to gain for herself the coveted access to the world of the city. She acquired that crucial currency of twentieth-century life – an independent income – and through her efforts was able to live as a formally free person of the urban world. Yet despite these triumphs, what de Beauvoir could not change by her own efforts was the culture in which she lived. That culture still accorded to women not just second-class status but an entirely different status (de Beauvoir, like other adult Frenchwomen could not vote, for example, until after the Second World War). Thus in *The Second Sex* two themes in de Beauvoir's experience came together; the theme of the misogyny of French bourgeois culture and the refusal of this culture of public agency for women. De Beauvoir's first published novel, *She Came to Stay*, concludes with an act of fierce, indeed aggressive, agency; namely, the murder of a female rival by a jealous woman. It is impossible not to notice that two central female characters are fighting over a man and at the same time doing their best to deny their affections for each other. But what is gained in the conclusion is the possibility that women can act, and clearly for de Beauvoir the murderous action was one which made emotional, if not moral, sense.

So when women are given, in an imaginative and fictional sense, the right to act, what is signalled is a way out of the culture which assumes women to be passive. *The Second Sex* cites extraordinary passages of biological essentialism (most notably the descriptions of the 'active' sperm and the 'passive' egg) and with this essentialist account goes a two-pronged attack on its consequences. Her first argument is that women have no history – an idea which would be regarded in many contemporary circles as ludicrous. But at the same time de Beauvoir analyses the consequences of the absence of female power and presence and finds in it much that accounts for what she regards as the foolish femininity of womanhood. Disunited by powerlessness, women have to resort to petty deceit and pretence in order to achieve their ends. Only in this way can some attempt be made to find agency in a society and a culture which is essentially anti-feminine. It is at this point that de Beauvoir introduces her powerful – and influential – attack on western culture. By discussing Montherlant, D.H. Lawrence, Claudel, Breton and Stendhal, de Beauvoir is able to argue that western fiction is – with the exception of Stendhal – deeply anti-woman. This analysis, replicated very effectively by Kate Millett in *Sexual Politics*, remains a passionately argued case, and turns upon the way in which these authors do not and cannot see women as independent beings.[9]

Tensions between de Beauvoir's Enlightenment Modernism and the Perspectives of Feminists and Intellectuals at the End of the Twentieth Century

These remarks have emphasised the importance which de Beauvoir gives to the ideas of autonomy and independence in human existence. They are values which place de Beauvoir within a western tradition of civil emancipation and universal citizenship: the tradition, essentially, of western post-Enlightenment democracies. That de Beauvoir is a child of this tradition is immediately apparent from all her writing: she never wavers in her belief in absolute, universal rights and her travel writing (and some aspects of her political engagement) all demonstrate a consistent belief in the possibility of social engineering. Indeed, if anything these values intensified as de Beauvoir's life went on. In her early maturity she had little interest in formal politics but in her later life she had become an avid interventionist in such areas as the organisation of the family, education and women's rights. But what this shift does is to emphasise some of the disjunction between de Beauvoir and twentieth-century intellectual life in general. For example, while de Beauvoir remained forever a believer in the values of autonomy and independence, second-wave feminism (and to a certain extent environmentally aware communitarian politics) was emphasising the impossibility of organising either personal or social life in this way. Hence one reading of de Beauvoir could be that she was endorsing precisely that ethic of individualism which many social commentators argue is detrimental to the stability of social life. Equally – and this is particularly important in the context of de Beauvoir's association with, and legacy to, feminism – de Beauvoir validated a form of experience, masculinity, which has been deconstructed in the most critical sense by generations of feminist writers. Again, the contrast between Virginia Woolf and de Beauvoir is interesting in that although Woolf belonged to a slightly older generation than de Beauvoir she saw masculinity not as a viable and enviable model but one that ranged from the deeply comic to the positively dangerous.

But what de Beauvoir did give to the twentieth century was a sense of gender as a basic form of social differentiation. This, then, as well as de Beauvoir's arguments about female agency and misogyny, has to be included in any list of other achievements. *The Second Sex*, and much of de Beauvoir's fiction, is organised around the premise that women and men occupy different social and emotional worlds. We have seen that what de Beauvoir wants to achieve is the greater coincidence of female behaviour with male, but however misguided this may be deemed to be, there is no doubt that de Beauvoir's essential premise in emphasising gender difference was emancipatory in terms of its implications for both sexes. De Beauvoir saw, with a perception sharpened both by her experiences as a child and as an adult, the dynamic of mutually destructive dependence in relationships between women and men. Her fiction recorded the jealous women and the hounded men, just as in her own life there was the endless denial of jealousy and grief in her relations with Sartre. But these experiences, both of de Beauvoir herself and other associates, gave to her work on gender difference a passion and an engagement which is seldom matched in more coolly analytical accounts of female subordination or patriarchal discourse. It was well known in Parisian intellectual circles that Michel Foucault could barely tolerate de Beauvoir and her ideas, and this animosity gives some indication of the real difference between de Beauvoir and other, late twentieth century, ideas on gender.[10]

These differences do not originate in diverse accounts of the impact of biology on gender – those 'physical consequences of anatomy' which **Freud** identified. There is a general consensus that gender is learned and constructed in all societies and that the variety of its forms is manifest. It is over the issues of the organisation of sexuality, and particularly of desire, that the problems arise. And it is in this that de Beauvoir's account of sexuality becomes – for some critics – problematic, since what she appears to do is both validate heterosexuality as the definitive form of sexual practice while at the same time constructing male and female within a norm of masculinity. Thus what she does in a sense is offend both feminist (or woman-centred) accounts of sexuality and those of gay men. To de Beauvoir, the work of the 'new' French feminists (Irigaray, Cixous and Wittig in particular) was anathema, since it seemed to challenge one of de Beauvoir's most deeply held (and long argued) positions, namely that women could achieve a condition of existence akin to that of masculinity.[11] To Foucault, the work of de Beauvoir was doubly problematic in that not only did it involve an implicitly emancipatory model of sexuality (which Foucault denied) but it gave a normative priority to heterosexuality. The treatment of lesbians in *The Second Sex* is hardly sympathetic and the fictional presentation of male homosexuality is equally unenthusiastic.

In all, throughout de Beauvoir's account of gender there was a deep ambivalence and a deep paradox. On the one hand, she is the first writer of the twentieth century to confront systematically the issue of the subordination of women. On the other, the rigid dichotomies (indeed the binary oppositions) which she conceptualises between women and men are such as to stand against the main direction of post-Freudian discussions of gender – namely that being male or female is a complex negotiation in which it is impossible to identify any absolute states. Indeed, as Freud was at pains to point out, the belief that we could ever become 'just' men or women was a fiction and a dangerous fantasy. Thus in de Beauvoir's version of masculinity we can read a consistent projection about the immanence, and the transcendence, of masculinity which is never achieved in reality. To put it in terms of de Beauvoir's biography, it is the difference between *assuming* that Sartre did explain the world and *thinking* that Sartre attempted to explain the world. We know, from the careful research which has now been published about the Sartre/de

Beauvoir relationship, that de Beauvoir played a formative part in Sartre's account of existentialism.[12] But what we also know from this same material is that both shared a belief in the same project of explanation: an essentially modern project which took for granted its own range and universality.

Women, Knowledge and Life as a Particular Kind of Project

In terms of de Beauvoir's work as a whole there are numerous debates and discussions still to be held. The range of issues and ideas which de Beauvoir covered was considerable and there remains, despite the extensive secondary material already published, some scope for reinterpretation and re-evaluation. In this context, where constraints of space make impossible a full review of de Beauvoir's work, two issues – in addition to those outlined above – justify attention, since they are closely linked to de Beauvoir's relationship to feminism and to her place within twentieth-century intellectual history. The first of these is de Beauvoir's account of knowledge, and in particular her view of the relationship of women to it. The second is de Beauvoir's assumption of life-as-project: an organising discourse which is profoundly western, and for all of de Beauvoir's rejection of explicitly religious beliefs, equally deeply embedded in the Protestant attitudes and values of northern Europe.

The issue of de Beauvoir and knowledge – or more precisely de Beauvoir *as* woman and knowledge – is one of those questions about de Beauvoir which the woman herself could not have asked, let alone answered. To de Beauvoir, attending school and university in the 1920s and 1930s, there were few questions to be asked about the status, let alone the origin, of knowledge. 'Knowledge' – in the sense of critical, informed inquiry and a body of assessed and agreed understanding about the world – was to be gained and assessed. De Beauvoir, like Sartre, was always critical of much that she was taught, but what was consistent about her attitude to the process of learning was that she did not attempt to theorise from the position which has become known as 'standpoint theory'. This set of ideas – associated with such major figures in the history of science as Sandra Harding and Donna Haraway – argues that any theory must be grounded in the experiences and attitudes of the people producing it.[13] It is an argument which emphasises the different experiences of women and men, just as Patricia Hill Collins has argued that the lived experience of black women leads to a qualitatively different set of ideas, and theorisations, from those of white women.[14] These points are important in the context of that gendering of knowledge which has occurred in the last twenty years but they are not dissimilar to the thesis put forward by Marx in the nineteenth century about the limitations, and the biases, of bourgeois thought.

Harding and Haraway wrote some years after de Beauvoir produced most of her major work but clearly the ideas of Marx were available to de Beauvoir, even if only partially. Nevertheless, what de Beauvoir remained consistently committed to was the view that it was possible to achieve not the plural knowledge of the late twentieth century, but the absolute certainty of early twentieth-century singular knowledge. While authors such as Virginia Woolf acknowledged, and understood, the idea of fundamental differences between masculine and feminine thinking (even while acknowledging that these categories did not necessarily coincide with actually male and female people) de Beauvoir assumed, and went on assuming, that the mind was a gender-free zone. Contemporary scholarship on de Beauvoir has pointed out that her interventions immensely assisted Sartre's discussion of existentialism, in that she persuaded him to locate his theory in reality, but what that scholarship cannot do is associate that intervention with a specifically feminist, or woman-centred, analysis. Despite the fact that de Beauvoir was much concerned to 'test' Sartre's theories in terms of individual experience (*She Came to Stay*, *Pyrrhus and Cinéas* and *The Blood of Others* remain testaments to this project) she nevertheless did not relate this difference in emphasis to differences related to gender.[15] This refusal (or denial if we risk to take the thesis further) was perhaps inevitable, given that de Beauvoir rejected all psychoanalytic interpretations of experience and was never prepared to entertain the possibility that biological difference had an impact on the organisation of an individual's symbolic and emotional world.

In this sense then, de Beauvoir remained (and remains) a figure somewhat at odds with the general shift of contemporary discourses. Woman is for her both a curiously fixed category, and yet at the same time a category of person whose difference from men is best confronted by minimising that difference. Nor for de Beauvoir the woman-centred power or knowledge of such figures as Adrienne Rich, Toni Morrison or Luce Irigaray. De Beauvoir encourages, indeed endorses, the living of life by women on the same lines as men. The project of women must be, for de Beauvoir, the achievement of transcendence, of individuality and of absolute knowledge. Indeed, for both sexes the ideal life is one which is lived in terms of the pursuit of some version of absolute knowledge.

But for all that commitment, one which offered to women the possibility of real intellectual emancipation from the mundane and the parochial, de Beauvoir's thought remained fixed in the oppositions and the rigid dichotomies of the early twentieth century. What is strikingly absent from her non-fiction (and much of her fiction) is a toleration of ambiguity. Even though de Beauvoir wrote a philosophical essay entitled 'Pour Une Morale de l'Ambiguité' the actual possibilities of this state were ones she endlessly resisted.[16] The strength which this gave her work on women was enormous, since for de Beauvoir an absolute category was established and allowed progress to be made in terms of debates on the impact of gender on experience. Yet at the same time the rigidity of the category and the acceptance of woman's experience as inevitably inferior to that of men remains an impossible stumbling block in the reading of de Beauvoir as a guide to a project which is genuinely emancipatory, rather than narrowly located within the confines of the conventional social order of masculinity.

Seeing Things Differently

To a generation of western women, Simone de Beauvoir provided a model of how to live, and how to live differently from many of the expectations of the first half of the twentieth century about women. But in saying this, there is a danger of tacitly accepting and endorsing the idea that there was always one dominant, and enforceable, mode of behaviour for women. There were (and are) clearly normative assumptions about how women should behave, but much of the evidence of feminist history suggests that the history of women is not one of universal, or uniform, powerlessness and oppression. Thus to construct and present de Beauvoir as some kind of torch-bearer for the hitherto unknown emancipation of women is to diminish the work of other women and at the same time to define de Beauvoir in ways that do scant justice to her complexity and contradictions.

I would argue that what de Beauvoir gave to women was far less theoretical and far more symbolic than is generally allowed, or aspired to by de Beauvoir herself. De Beauvoir quite clearly wanted to provide a thesis about the position of women in the world, and set out to demonstrate this in *The Second Sex* through the conventional natural science model of statement, the collection of evidence and conclusion. In doing this, and adopting so closely the model of natural science, de Beauvoir demonstrated many of the disadvantages of that method, not least that the collection of evidence could be closely related to the desired conclusion. In an age which is more sceptical about the method, and the assumptions, of natural science than at the time when de Beauvoir was writing, it is possible to suggest that the actual conclusions of *The Second Sex* (and indeed of de Beauvoir's work as a whole) are less important than the meaning of the project in our understanding about the possibilities, both intellectual and otherwise, of the world. My thesis about de Beauvoir is therefore that she helped to contribute to women's sense of agency in the public world. I would contend that she did so in ways which were deeply traditional (one of de Beauvoir's more problematic statements about the public world and politics was that because her views were so close to those of Sartre she felt no need to express them herself) but nevertheless offered a very powerful opposition to the expectations of womanhood in Europe at the end of the Second World War. These expectations were not, as numerous writers have pointed out, organised around the assumption of sexual equality, least of all in political and intellectual contexts. As Sylvia Plath so verily demonstrated in *The Bell Jar*, the western post-war world was one which wanted its women in the home and sexual difference firmly established.[17] We can now demonstrate that the realities of the post-war world were much more complex than this ideological position suggested, but the point is that there were few generally available critiques of this position in the 1950s: in the homogeneous sexual discourse of the Eisenhower years, *The Second Sex* stands out as a voice of dissent.

Thus after the publication of *The Second Sex* women could look at the history of post-Enlightenment thought about women and identify more than the previous landmarks of *The Vindication of the Rights of Woman* and *The Subjection of Women*.[18] Feminism, until de Beauvoir, had been largely an Anglo-American phenomenon, and so in addition to providing a further 'great book' for feminism, *The Second Sex* gave feminism a dimension which placed it outside the determining concerns of Anglo-American feminism, which were largely those of citizenship and legal emancipation. It is quite clear from *The Second Sex* that de Beauvoir had little or no interest in these issues and her contempt for conventional politics would have made such concerns as an interest in the representation of women in elected assemblies impossible. But this lack of interest was precisely one of the long-term strengths of *The Second Sex*, that it placed the debate about sexual difference on a different level from that of concern about empirical – and ever-changing – reality. Not until the end of her life did de Beauvoir become interested in pragmatic political issues, and even then it was apparent that her interest was fleeting.

De Beauvoir, in summary, gave women an articulate sense of possibility and agency in both intellectual and political life. She was far from the first to claim a space in the public world, and, as I have argued, did so in a way which inherently validated masculine over feminine experience. But she demanded a place for women in post-Enlightenment discourses of power and sexuality and raised, in both her fiction and her non-fiction, issues about the relationship between abstract morality and specific social action which still have to be resolved. Indeed, much of the ground covered by Carol Gilligan in *In a Different Voice* is similar to the debates raised by de Beauvoir – debates about the viability of a morality appropriate for all situations.[19] De Beauvoir belonged to a tradition which maintained that such a morality was possible; a view which few feminists would accept today. Yet even with this variation in position as regards the possibilities for a non-contextual morality, what we cannot ignore, after de Beauvoir and *The Second Sex*, is recognition of the differences between women and men: it was the articulation of the social and symbolic *meaning* of those differences which de Beauvoir provided as her most lasting contribution.

Legacies and Unfinished Business

Any account of feminism includes the work of Simone de Beauvoir. Increasingly, as feminism has an impact on other disciplines and traditions, her work is also included in contexts other than those of feminism. Ironically, as the work of her companion Jean-Paul Sartre appears to belong more and more to the history of philosophy, de Beauvoir's writing appears as central to the ideas and debates of the late twentieth century. Again, there is a paradox here, in that it took some time for de Beauvoir to identify herself as a woman, with women, but in doing so she was able to locate herself within the late twentieth-century shift towards a plurality and diversity of values which gives her work a continuing resonance.

The crucial intellectual legacy of de Beauvoir (rather than her legacy in personal and political terms) is that she opened up the debate on the possibilities of the absolute difference between women and men. De Beauvoir – as already discussed here – took the view that women should seek to become more like men, but this conclusion is, in terms of an intellectual legacy, less significant than the argument about difference. De Beauvoir allowed women to see themselves as different from men, not just different in certain respects or different in certain contexts, but wholly and definitively different. It was (and is) an idea which is enormously radical in its implications, since it makes differences between women and men into the major form of social difference, and places gender difference in a far more significant position than differences of class or race. It is not too much of an exaggeration to say that after de Beauvoir it became extremely difficult for thinking about gender difference to return to its previous position of an explicit bias towards masculinity accompanied by vaguely liberal expectations of equality.

Just what can be done with a position which does robustly assert gender difference has been demonstrated (although far from finally) by feminist writers such as Kate Millett, Adrienne Rich, and – in a later generation and from a different position – Judith Butler.[20] Also de Beauvoir's refusal of motherhood was taken up by Shulamith Firestone in *The Dialectic of Sex* (which is dedicated to Simone de Beauvoir who 'kept her integrity') and de Beauvoir appears as a presence in numerous feminist works.[21] (We might also note here that it is for her contribution to feminism that de Beauvoir has so far been recognised; relatively few accounts discuss her contribution to sociology, philosophy or politics.) But the problem, the crucial problem perhaps, with de Beauvoir is precisely the way in which her work has been, at time, uncritically integrated into contemporary feminism and uncritically discussed in terms of its values and assumptions.

The problem of this legacy – of what de Beauvoir valued and her model of society – is particularly well illustrated in the discussion at the conclusion of *The Dialectic of Sex*. In this conclusion Firestone proposes 'the total integration of women and children into the larger society'; a view entirely similar to de Beauvoir's at the end of *The Second Sex*. But, and it seems to me a very substantial qualification, the nature of that society is left entirely open. Thus what we are left with is a view which is entirely similar to the 'emancipation-through-paid-work' argument of Engels. Women would thus play an enlarged role in a society that would remain essentially the same. This emphasis necessarily detracts attention from the many unsatisfactory dimensions of how women are currently 'integrated' into society. A feminism located in masculine assumptions will by definition be unable to detect many dimensions of women's difference and subordination. Unresolved, in de Beauvoir and in those writers where her influence was strongest, is an understanding of the nature of society, and the values which women are being asked to endorse as an explicit part of membership of this apparent community.

It was a woman (Margaret Thatcher) who denied the existence of society. From the point of view of women (which was hardly that of Mrs Thatcher) this view nevertheless has a certain logic: women in the West have played a relatively limited part in the construction of society if we define it in terms of either its social institutions or its laws. Thus her limited and limiting conception of integration into society remains, I would suggest, crucially important for any reading of de Beauvoir. She allowed women to gain a sense of the historical project of femininity, yet at the same time could not allow that this project had to include an understanding of the way in which women – and feminism – were also part of the historical projects of individualism and personal autonomy that themselves were limiting and shot through with masculine assumptions. Her definition of the boundaries between women and men made possible crucial intellectual advances, yet the failure to name the absence of boundaries between women and hegemonic masculine social values makes it difficult, at times, to distinguish de Beauvoir's work from its context.

Further Reading

Simone de Beauvoir wrote extensively about her own life (the four volumes of her autobiography are: *Memoirs of a Dutiful Daughter*, *The Prime of Life*, *Force of Circumstance* and *All Said and Done*) as well as writing novels (the best known are *She Came to Stay* and *The Mandarins*) and extensive non-fiction (*The Second Sex* and *Old Age* in particular). There is now a considerable secondary literature, including a helpful biography by Deidre Bair *Simone de Beauvoir: A Biography* (London: Cape, 1990).

Other reading includes:

Mary Evans, *Simone de Beauvoir* (London: Sage, 1996).
Jane Heath, *Simone de Beauvoir* (Hemel Hempstead: Harvester Wheatsheaf, 1989).
Toril Moi, *Simone de Beauvoir: The Making of an Intellectual Woman* (Oxford: Blackwell, 1994).
Judith Okley, *Simon de Beauvoir* (London: Virago, 1986).
Signs Special issue on Simone de Beauvoir **18**(1), (1992).

10

Norbert Elias

Jason Hughes

Driving Impulses

Norbert Elias was born into a German Jewish family in Breslau, Germany,[1] in 1897. His most important study entitled *The Civilizing Process* (in its English translation) was first published in Switzerland in 1939. To an outsider, the idea of a German Jew writing on the subject of 'civilization' on the eve of the Second World War may seem more than just a little unusual. Perhaps even more so when one begins to learn of Elias's life history: how, at eighteen, he encountered the carnage of the First World War as a soldier on the Western and Eastern fronts; how he was forced to flee from the Nazis to exile in 1933; how, after seeing his parents for the last time in 1938, his mother was murdered at Auschwitz. However, as one learns more of Elias' life history and his intellectual development, it becomes easier to understand why he chose the topic of civilization to be the central focus of his major work: it exemplified the balance between involvement and detachment which was to become a hallmark of his studies. It is clear that Elias was, in part, driven by the dramatic social changes which were occurring at the time he wrote. Indeed, in the Introduction to *The Civilizing Process,* his 'involvement' with the subject is explicitly stated:

> the issues raised by the book have their origins less in scholarly tradition, in the narrower sense of the word, than in the experiences in whose shadow we all live, experiences of the crisis and transformation of Western civilization as it had existed hitherto, and the simple need to understand what this 'civilization' really amounts to. But I have not been guided in this study by the idea that our civilized mode of behaviour is the most advanced of all humanly possible, nor by the opinion that 'civilization' is the worst form of life and one that is doomed. All that can be seen today is that with gradual civilization a number of specific civilizational difficulties arise. But it cannot be said that we already understand why we actually torment ourselves in this way.[2]

Clearly Elias did not view the process of civilization as 'the progressive triumph of rationality', yet he also resisted the temptation to collapse into a fatalist position; he sustained a high level of 'detachment' from the changes which were unfolding, despite the emotional trauma he was then suffering in relation to these. Elias was much more interested in building an *understanding* of the long-term processes these 'events' were part of, than of servicing more egocentrically emotional, or political, ends. Moreover, in his study of *The Civilizing Process*, Elias aimed to lay the foundations for a *radically processual, relational and developmental sociology*.[3] The study constituted both a synthesis of, and a fundamental break from, the work of Elias' many direct and indirect intellectual influences which included, among others, the sociologists Auguste Comte, Karl Mannheim, **Karl Marx, Georg Simmel,** and **Max Weber;** the psychoanalyst **Sigmund Freud;** the historian Johan Huizinga; and possibly, the philosopher Ernst Cassirer.[4]

As may already be apparent, Elias' preoccupation with the three central foci of his work – relations, process and synthesis – cannot be traced to any single event, or to any single intellectual influence. However, a brief examination of the early stages of Elias' intellectual career will help to serve two interrelated purposes: first, to elucidate the motivation behind his work, and second, to highlight some of the key themes he was to examine in his quest to develop (what has come to be known as) *process sociology*.[5]

In line with his father's wish for him to become a doctor, and in relation to his already deep interest in philosophy, Elias enrolled to read both medicine and philosophy at Breslau University in 1918. After obtaining the equivalent of a British MB degree, Elias dropped medicine, and concentrated his efforts on philosophy. However, Elias continued to draw upon insights gained from his medical background to develop his distinctive sociological position. For example, his dissection work on the musculature of the human face made Elias acutely aware of how laughing and smiling were fundamental indicators of how humanity had evolved as a *social* species.[6] Thus, Elias began to realize, even the most fundamental aspects of human existence should not be taken as 'given', 'essential', 'unchanging', but rather, these should be seen as part of a set of long-term processes. In relation to this understanding, Elias became increasingly unhappy with the dichotomies he so frequently encountered in academic writing, such as those between the 'biological' and the 'social'; the 'mind' and the 'body'; the 'individual' and 'society'. In the course of his study of *The Civilizing Process*, Elias began to develop a sociological understanding of *why* these divisions had become so popular in academic and lay understandings at least since the Renaissance by examining the fundamental interrelationship between 'social' and 'psychological' development (to use Elias' terms *sociogenesis* and *psychogenesis* respectively). In the sections that follow, we shall examine how these insights were developed in Elias' work.

Key Issues

Elias' approach to sociology was not to construct 'logical' arguments to demonstrate the inadequacies of other theories, and the merits of his own work, but rather, to formulate academic problems in such a way as to stimulate readers to be critical of the taken-for-granted assumptions and categories which are often drawn upon when approaching these problems.[7] Indeed, it is very difficult, and highly problematic, to use Elias' work to construct purely 'rational' arguments or *abstract* theories. This is because his work always involved a symbiosis of, or 'two-way traffic' between, 'theory' and 'research'. This, in turn, was related to his effort to move away from the split between 'rationalist' and 'empiricist' academic positions. The five key areas of concern which are discussed below make use of a great deal of 'unfamiliar' terminology, much of which has no direct equivalent in the conventional sociological lexicon. Once again, this relates to Elias' effort to encourage a critical attitude to deeply embedded modes of thinking and conceptualizing on the part of the reader. His aim was to develop alternative sociological concepts which have a higher level of 'cognitive value'. Or, to put the latter statement in another way, to encourage a higher degree of congruence between (what we currently label as) 'theory' and 'research'.

Civilization[8]

One of the most central objectives of Elias' study of *The Civilizing Process* was to move towards a more adequate understanding of how processes of change in the human psychic structure are interrelated with processes of changing social relations. In order to examine these processes, Elias studied long-term shifts in manners and codes of etiquette. He began his analysis by examining the highly influential etiquette manual, *De civilitate morum puerilium* (On civility in children), written by Erasmus in 1530. Elias chose Erasmus precisely because he was standing at a crucial juncture in history: between the Middle Ages and modernity. Erasmus' observations referred both 'backwards' and 'forwards', revealing much not only about conduct which was typical of his time and of 'time gone by', but also about the increasing amount of restraint placed on behaviour. Erasmus thus provided data which indicated the *quite specific direction* (to use one of Elias' favourite phrases) in which codes of etiquette were changing. From this and other similar sources, Elias traced the gradual changes that were occurring in *standards of behavioural expectations* among members of the secular upper classes: this included everything from their 'manners' at the dinner table, to the way they approached and experienced their emotions and bodily functions.

Elias builds a picture of social life in the Middle Ages as characterized by conduct which, by contemporary western standards, would be considered 'distasteful'. For example, it was common for people to urinate and defecate quite publicly. Indeed some medieval texts proposed that 'Before you sit down, make sure your seat has not been fouled.'[9] Similarly, it was normal for people to eat from a common dish, with unwashed hands; to spit on to the floor; or to break wind at the table.[10] In prescribing what one should not do, manners texts also gave a strong indication of what was commonplace. For example, it was recommended that one should not use the tablecloth to blow one's nose.[11] Elias analysed how the restraints on behaviour which we take for granted today began to grow over time. He observes that, gradually, an increasing range and number of aspects of human behaviour came to be regarded as 'distasteful' and pushed *behind the scenes of social life*. Corresponding to this shift, people begin to experience an advancing threshold of repugnance and shame in relation to their bodily functions.

The increasing elaboration of codes of etiquette and manners accompanied a corresponding shift in people's behaviour: for example, defecation, urination and copulation became increasingly conducted in 'private', closed-off places. Thus a defining characteristic of the civilizing process in the West was that people gradually began to exercise higher degrees of self-restraint. This is not to say that one cannot find any evidence of self-restraint among people of the Middle Ages. Indeed, Elias found extreme forms of asceticism and renunciation in certain sectors of medieval society (such as the self-denial of monks). However, these stood in contrast 'to a no less extreme indulgence of pleasure in others, and frequently enough... sudden switches from one attitude to the other in the life of an individual person'.[12] In short, therefore, the western process of civilization has involved a gradual *stabilization* of human behaviour: it has also been characterized by 'diminishing contrasts and increasing varieties'.[13]

Sociogenesis and Psychogenesis: 'The Social Constraint towards Self-constraint'

Having given this brief outline of the process of civilization, one is still left with the question of *why* these changes have occurred, and indeed, are continuing to occur (though not necessarily in the same direction). Elias is able to demonstrate that the changes in behaviour which have occurred as part of the civilizing process cannot adequately be explained in terms of 'health and hygiene', 'material reasons', or 'religion and respect'. Rather, he argues, one needs to examine the immanent dynamics of the changing social relations of which these behavioural changes formed a part. To make this clearer, Elias proposes that we consider the analogy of the different road systems of medieval and contemporary societies. On the roads of medieval societies, Elias writes:

With few exceptions, there is very little traffic; the main danger... is attack from soldiers or thieves. When people look around them, scanning the trees and hills or the road itself, they do so primarily because they must always be prepared for armed attack, and only secondarily because they have to avoid collision. Life on the main roads of this society demands a constant readiness to fight, and free play of the emotions in defence of one's life or possessions from physical attack. Traffic on the main roads of a big city in the complex society of our time demands quite a different moulding of the psychological apparatus. Here the danger of physical attack is [comparatively] minimal. Cars are rushing in all directions; pedestrians and cyclists are trying to thread their way through the *mêlée* of cars; policemen stand at the main crossroads to regulate the traffic with varying success. But this external control is founded on the assumption that every individual is himself [*sic*] regulating his behaviour with the utmost exactitude in accordance with the necessities of this network. The chief danger that people here represent for others results from someone in this bustle *losing* his self-control.[14]

Elias' analogy serves to illustrate how, in medieval western society, the type of personality that flourished was one that was always ready for attack. Threats from violent others and the environment were omnipresent, and thus emotional restraint was of little advantage. Conversely, to be able to engage in wild, unrestrained battle; positively to enjoy the annihilation of anyone or anything hostile; to be able to live out one's feelings and passions, uninhibited by thought for the feelings of others, all would have proven quite positive advantages in the medieval West. However, as monopolies over violence and taxation began to be established, in turn related to processes of state-formation and the lengthening of interdependency chains,[15] so gradually the threat that one person posed to others became 'depersonalized' and more calculable. As societies became more complex, people were compelled to regulate their conduct in an increasingly stable, differentiated, reflexive, and even manner. Everyday life became freer of inse-curities and there were more possibilities for exercising foresight. Indeed, in the contemporary West those who are able to moderate their behaviour and demonstrate foresight are at a distinct advantage. The effort required to behave in a 'civilized' manner becomes so great that there also emerges an almost 'blindly functioning' apparatus of self-control. Social control becomes deeply entrenched in the human psychic structure; it becomes 'absorbed' to such an extent that it functions partly autonomously from one's conscious-ness. It is in this way, Elias argues, that processes of sociogenesis and psychogenesis are fundamentally interrelated.

Homo clausus *versus* Homines aperti: *A Move Away from the Structure–Agency Dilemma?*

Elias argues that his study of civilizing processes throws light on many contemporary debates in sociology. At its current stage of development, sociology is a highly fragmented discipline: it contains a large number of competing paradigms which, in different ways, are divided according to variations of the 'structure–agency' dilemma (as it is contemporarily referred to). Put crudely, some perspectives, such as variants of the structuralist paradigm, focus on 'social structures' and how these are reproduced. This focus often leads to a view of 'individuals' as simply 'driven' by 'external' forces. Others, such as variants of the ethnomethodological and symbolic interactionist paradigms, focus on the 'active' and 'productive' capabilities of the 'individual subject' which, they propose, are largely overlooked by other paradigms. However, this focus often leads to a view of 'individuals' as existing in a vacuum or in isolation from one another. Consequently, it becomes difficult to explain how individuals are compelled to act in one way rather than another. More recently, an increasing number of writers have tried to develop theories which synthesize these polar extremes, perhaps most notably **Anthony Giddens** in his theory of 'structuration'.[16] Yet even these theories often find it difficult to move away from stressing either 'agency' at the expense of 'structure' or vice versa.

By using Elias' sociology, it becomes easier to understand why sociologists seem to be locked into this dilemma. Let us consider once again the long-term changes in the human psychic structure which are embedded in the process of civilization. Elias writes:

> People who ate together in the way customary of the Middle Ages... stood in a different relationship to one another than we do... What was lacking in this... world, or at least had not been developed to the same degree, was the *invisible wall of affects* which seems now to rise between one human body and another, repelling and separating, the wall which is often perceptible today at the mere approach of something that has been in contact with the mouth or hands of someone else, and which manifests itself as embarrassment at the mere sight of many bodily functions of others, and often at their mere mention, or as a feeling of shame when one's own functions are exposed to the gaze of others, and by no means only then.[17]

It is this 'invisible wall of affects' which leads to a common experience among people in the contemporary West. It is manifested in the feeling that it is almost as though there is a 'dividing line' between 'me in here' and 'society out there'.[18] Since academics themselves are not immune from the civilizing process, it is not surprising that this experience of a dividing line is reflected in the concepts, questions and divisions of much contemporary sociology and philosophy. Indeed, Elias is able to demonstrate that the academic splits between 'subjects' and 'objects', 'individual' and 'society', 'ontology' and 'epistemology', and, of course, 'agency' and 'structure' are in fact reifications based in the self-experience of people at a particular stage of their social development. Some of the most fundamental questions asked by philosophers and sociologists can be seen to be related to this particular experience of the 'self'. For example, the theorist might ask 'How can "I" as a single isolated thinking "subject" inside my own shell, know anything of the world "outside"?' Moreover, 'How can "I" know what anyone else (any other "I" equally sealed within its shell) is thinking?' Elias calls this view of human beings as trapped within their containers, *Homo clausus* (or, for want of less sexist language, closed 'man'). Elias proposes that we should move away from this view of humans which is so deeply embedded in our theorizing. Instead, Elias argues, sociologists should aim to view people as *Homines aperti* (open, bonded, pluralities of *interdependent* human beings), as this, in part, will help us to move away from many of the stale debates and dichotomies which currently undermine our understanding.

Power and Interdependence

As will be seen below, Elias' conception of *Homines aperti* is central to his understanding of 'power'. Elias proposes that sociologists should move away from a *Homo clausus* view of power – as a 'thing' we could somehow pick up and hold within our shells – towards a more fundamentally *relational and processual* understanding of power. What we currently label as 'power' is an aspect of relationships. In fact it is an aspect of every human relationship. It is rooted in the fact that people can withhold or monopolize what others need, for example, material resources, food, love or knowledge. Except for the most marginal circumstances, where one party's 'power' is almost that of 'absolute' over the other, we always encounter power relationships, power balances, different or equal 'power ratios'.[19] 'Power' is very rarely, if ever, simply a case of the one-way 'dependence' of one party on another; it almost always refers to people's *interdependence*.[20]

In order to make these points clearer, Elias proposes that we consider the analogy of 'games'. These are greatly simplified analogies, but, Elias argues, because games are themselves social processes, such models are far less dangerous than organic or biological analogies which are frequently used in sociology.[21]

At the most simple level, Elias provides the model of a two-person game; it may help the reader to think of a game of chess. Imagine that player A is a very strong player, and player B is much weaker. The stronger player A can force B to play certain moves, and, in direct relation to this capacity, can very largely steer the course of the game. While A has a high degree of control over B's moves, B is not completely 'powerless'. Just as B must take orientation from A's preceding moves, so must A from B's preceding moves. If B had no strength at all, there could be no game. Thus, Elias concludes from this example, in any game the players always have a degree of control over each other. They are, that is to say, always *interdependent*. However, even when only two players are involved, if their relative strengths become more equal, both players will have correspondingly less chance of controlling each other's moves, or indeed, the overall course of the game. In other words, the players become increasingly dependent on the overall process of the game – its changing course – in determining their moves. Predicting the game even a few moves in advance becomes difficult. Consequently, Elias writes,

> to the extent that the inequality in the strengths of the two players diminishes, there will result from the interweaving of moves of two individual people a game process *which neither of them has planned.*[22]

Elias calls this 'interwoven web' of moves which follows a largely 'blind' course, the game's *figuration*.

Figurations

To clarify the meaning, and also, to stress the significance, of Elias's concept of figurations, consider what happens when more players are introduced into the game models.

As the number of players increases, so the game figurations become a great deal more complex. In the second game model Elias provides, the stronger player plays a number of weaker players simultaneously. While the weaker players do not communicate with one another, the stronger player's capacity to control each game may be undermined by the fact that he or she is having to conduct so many games at once. Clearly, there is a limit to the number of games that one player can effectively participate in simultaneously. Second, if the weaker players unite to form a coalition against the stronger player and they act in unison, their control over the superior player can be enhanced. However, if the coalition becomes beset by internal conflicts and tensions, they might end up at less of an advantage than they had individually.

The next model deals with two groups of almost equal strength. Here it may help the reader to think of a team sport such as football. Just as in the second case of the two-player model, neither party can fully anticipate the other's moves and tactics, and thus neither side can easily control the course of the game. It becomes impossible to understand the moves that each player makes either when considered on their own or when viewed solely in relation to the moves of the other members of their team. To understand each move properly, one must also consider each move in relation to the overall course of the game.

Elias introduces a third group of 'multi-tier' models which involve an even larger number of players. A sporting equivalent is difficult to envisage, since the models are analogies of complex social processes.[23] In relation to these models, Elias writes that, as the number of players in the game increases, so the course of the game becomes more 'opaque' to each 'individual' player. Each single player, no matter how strong, is decreasingly able to control the direction of the game. From the player's perspective, this interweaving 'mesh' of an increasing number of players' actions begins to function 'as though it had a life of its own'. Furthermore, as even more players become involved in the game, the 'individual' players become increasingly aware that they are unable to control and understand it.[24] In the absence of an overall picture of the game, players come under increasing pressure to organize in a different way. They may reorganize to form smaller groups, or begin to configure more complex interdependencies which have a number of different 'tiers' or levels. In the latter case, the moves of the group are increasingly made by people in the 'upper tiers' who have specialized functions, such as leaders, delegates or representatives, those in the lower tiers are also involved in the moves, but more through subsidiary contests with the upper tiers. Elias' models here are intended to elucidate some of the changes which occur as societies become more complex, and 'chains of interdependence' lengthen (the process by which more and more people become interdependent). Of crucial importance is the tendency, which Elias highlights, to view the complex figuration that arises as 'having an existence all of its own'. When considered in conjuction with Elias' understanding of *Homo clausus,* it is no wonder that many concepts of 'social structure' or 'social system' seem to embody a view of 'society' as somehow existing beyond the level of the 'individuals' which constitute it. According to Elias, what these concepts really refer to is a

> basic tissue resulting from many single plans and actions of men (sic) [which] can give rise to changes and patterns that no individual person has planned or created. From this interdependence of people arises an order *sui generis,* an order more compelling and stronger than the will of the individual people composing it. It is this order of interweaving human impulses and strivings, this social order, which determines the course of historical change; it underlies the civilizing process.[25]

Thus the term 'figuration' refers neither to 'metaphysical entities' nor to mere 'amalgamations' of individuals, but rather, to the shifting 'nexus' of interdependencies.

Seeing Things Differently

I first encountered the work of Norbert Elias as an undergraduate at Leicester University. On one day in particular, while smoking a cigarette, I began to think of how interdependent I and the millions of other smokers across the world were with all the people that it would have taken to cultivate the tobacco, and to manufacture and transport the cigarettes I was smoking: people that I had not met, and would probably never meet. I began to observe that it was no accident that my cigarettes contained a quite specific amount of nicotine and tar, and that this was related, at least in part, to a long-term shift in the power relations between governments, tobacco producers, tobacco consumers and the medical profession. Perhaps more interestingly, I began to ask myself why I felt the 'need' to smoke, particularly when thinking or concentrating – was this simply a 'biological urge'? Or were there more 'social' or 'psychological' processes at play? Of course, from a process sociological perspective, I was immediately suspicious of these distinctions.

As part of my doctoral research, I traced the long-term process of tobacco use in the West back to the sixteenth century when tobacco was first introduced into many parts of Europe, and beyond, by examining tobacco use among Native American peoples. I found that among the latter, particularly prior to contact with the West, tobacco was often used in a highly ritualized way. The tobacco cultivated by Native Americans was a great deal stronger than that of contemporary western cigarettes. Indeed, there is a large amount of evidence to suggest that some forms were capable of producing hallucinations.[26] Only the mildest and most palatable varieties of Native American tobacco were initially transferred to the West. Yet even these, by contemporary standards, were extremely strong. Over time, the type of tobacco cultivated and used by western tobacco users became weaker and weaker. The popular medium of tobacco consumption gradually changed from the pipe, to snuff, to cigars, and finally to cigarettes. These first cigarettes contained tobacco which was much milder and more palatable (to western tastes) than that of previous forms of consumption. But these, in turn, also became milder and weaker. Soon afterwards it was possible to buy filter cigarettes, and then, more recently, low tar filter cigarettes. At present in the West, with the advent of 'super' and 'ultra' 'lows', it is possible for smokers to specify to the milligram exactly how much nicotine and tar their cigarette contains.

While the increasing dominance of bio-medical understandings of tobacco use may well have influenced some of these changes, these factors alone cannot be used to explain *all* the changes referred to. Viewed from a process sociological perspective, these changes can be seen to be related to a much broader set of processes. It is almost as if tobacco use itself has undergone a civilizing process: an increasing stabilization of the 'effects' of tobacco using which has involved 'diminishing contrasts and increasing varieties'. Put crudely, there has been a move away from tobacco use to 'lose control' towards an increasing tendency towards the use of tobacco as a means of 'self-control'. One only has to think of some of the popular rationalizations among contemporary western smokers to understand the implications of this process. Many of the smokers I interviewed proposed that smoking helped them to control their 'moods', to relieve 'stress', to relieve 'boredom', to help them control their weight, to help them to 'concentrate'. Consider the contrast between this picture of contemporary western smoking – frequent intakes of relatively weak tobacco largely for 'control reasons' – with the account provided below of tobacco use among the Karuk Native Americans:

> He sucks in... then quickly he shuts his mouth. For a moment he holds the smoke inside his mouth. He wants it to go in. For a moment he remains motionless holding his pipe. He shakes, he feels like he is going to faint, holding his mouth shut. It is as if he could not get enough... He shuts his eyes, he looks kind of sleepy-like. His hand trembles, as he puts the pipe to his mouth again. Then again he smacks in [inhales]. He smokes again like he smoked before. A few or maybe four times he takes the pipe from his mouth. Then, behold, he knows he has smoked up the tobacco, there is no more inside [the pipe]. As he smokes he knows when there are only ashes inside. He just fills up the pipe once, that is enough, one pipeful.[27]

It is clear that a large number of other factors must be considered properly to explain this contrast. However, by using 'process' sociology, one becomes more able to understand the dynamic interplay of 'social', 'cultural', 'psychological', 'biological' and 'pharmacological' processes which give rise to the patterns of tobacco use which are characteristic of the contemporary West.

Legacies and Unfinished Business

Elias' work has been used to research a wide range of fields. For example, process sociology has been used by Eric Dunning to study sport;[28] Johan Goudsblom to study fire;[29] Stephen Mennell to study food;[30] and Cas Wouters, to study processes of 'informalization'.[31] It is important to note, however, that Elias did not see his work as a 'final answer'. Elias was always the first to recognize that his work represented little more than 'Small, hopeful breakthroughs in the process of growing knowledge about ourselves.'[32] Nonetheless, Elias' work has come under attack from a number of writers including: Anton Blok,[33] Edmund Leach,[34] Derek Layder[35] and Benjo Maso.[36] While it is not possible to do justice to these debates here, I would like to focus on a common misunderstanding of Elias' work which is embodied in some of these critiques, and, in relation to this discussion, briefly to mention some of the ways in which his work has been developed by other sociologists.

As Mennell[37] has stated, a common theme in critiques of Elias' work is that changes in the twentieth century – for example, the Nazi period in Germany and the holocaust, and, in a less dramatic way, an increasing permissiveness in the West since the 1960s – would appear to undermine the idea that the West has undergone a 'civilizing process'. On the face of it, such critiques seem to have simply misunderstood Elias' use of the term 'civilization': they do not appear to have recognized the distinction between Elias' technical use of the term, and the value-laden everyday usage. However, these critiques do raise the question of whether developments of more recent years actually constitute a counter-trend to the 'direction' of change observed in *The Civilizing Process*. It is important to note at this point that Elias never saw the process of civilization in the West as a smooth unilinear transition, but rather as a change in a specific direction consisting of 'spurts' and 'counter-spurts'. Moreover, in relation to the holocaust in Nazi Germany, Elias did not propose that violence, killing and torture had ceased to occur in the civilized West, but rather that these had become increasingly monopolized and pushed 'behind the scenes' of everyday life. Indeed, the scale and character of the mass murder of the Jews in Nazi Germany were fundamentally related to processes of civilization. As Mennell observes:

> modern social organization has vastly multiplied the technical capacity to kill. The very long chains of interdependence and 'division of social functions' which play such a part in the civilizing process were also essential to implementing the 'final solution' [in Nazi Germany]. And paradoxically, as Elias argues, 'civilized' controls in turn play their part in making possible those long chains of organized and co-ordinated activities.[38]

In other words, it is quite possible to have 'civilized' forms of violence, torture and murder. In relation to the increase in permissiveness or 'informalization' since the 1960s in the West, it is first important to note that a similar 'wave of informality' also occurred in the 1920s (though perhaps not to the same extent as that of the 1960s and 1970s).[39] Elias was fully aware of these changes when he wrote *The Civilizing Process*. In this connection, Elias gave the example of changes in bathing costumes, particularly those of women, which, at the time he wrote, were becoming increasingly revealing. Only a century previous to this, Elias observed, a woman who wore such a revealing costume publicly would have been socially ostracized.[40] However, rather than representing a counter-trend, these changes could also be understood to be characteristics of a relatively advanced stage of civilization. These developments, Elias wrote, were indicative of 'a society in which a high degree of restraint is taken for granted, and in which women are, like men, absolutely sure that each individual is curbed by self-control and a strict code of etiquette'.[41]

Elias became increasingly interested in processes of informalization in his later work. In 1967, in a joint paper with Dunning, 'The quest for excitement in leisure', Elias and Dunning summarized a number of the changes which were occurring in the 1960s in the West as 'a highly controlled decontrolling of emotional controls'.[42] They argued that developments in the field of leisure – changes in audience participation in sports, changes in film and the arts, changes in music – can all be understood to be complementary to the emotional control and restraint of our ordinary lives. Many of these activities provide the opportunity for *compensatory* 'expressive outbursts', for 'excitement' and 'emotionality'. Yet, nonetheless, these 'are themselves tempered by civilizing restraints'.[43]

Ultimately, it is important that the process of civilization is not viewed as 'inevitable'. Elias did not consider it possible to predict the future on the basis of the very limited amount of knowledge that we have been able to build about ourselves. Indeed, processes of decivilization are equally possible. What Elias hoped was that, through laying down the foundations for a process- and relation-centred sociology, it would be possible for sociologists over time to learn about these processes, by building growing 'islands of certainty in the vast oceans of their ignorance'.[44]

Further Reading

For a general introduction to Elias' work:

S. Mennell, *Norbert Elias: An Introduction* (Oxford: Blackwell, 1989).

Elias' most important work:

N. Elias, *The Civilizing Process* (Oxford: Blackwell combined edition 1994, originally published 1939).

For an explication of key process sociological principles:

N. Elias, *What is Sociology?* (London: Hutchinson [translated in 1978 from the original German publication in 1970]).

Elias on the importance of 'process' for the sociological understanding:

N. Elias, 'The Retreat of Sociologists into the Present', *Theory, Culture and Society*, **4** (1987), 223–47.

Elias on sociological approaches to 'method':

N. Elias, 'Problems of Involvement and Detachment', *British Journal of Sociology*, **7** (1956), 226–52.

A paper on sociogenesis and psychogenesis:

N. Elias, 'Violence and Civilization: the State Monopoly of Physical Violence and its Infringement' in J. Keane, *Civil Society and the State* (London: Verso, 1988), pp. 177–98.

11

Erving Goffman

Robin Williams

Driving Impulses

The complex variety of sociological theories and methods is often reduced to a series of allegedly distinctive 'schools', 'traditions' 'styles' or 'approaches' that together constitute the discipline. Some such categories have been named after individual sociologists sufficiently recognisable through fame or notoriety (for example Marxism, Durkheimianism). A second convention has rested on the invention of new terms signifying the distinctiveness of a particular approach (for example symbolic interactionism, structural functionalism). A third has invoked a geographical or institutional affiliation shared by at least the first generation of those associated with its type of work (for example Chicago School, West Coast School).

Throughout sociology's short and turbulent history, however, there have been scholars who have produced startlingly original and influential work, yet who have both resisted association with any existing configuration and also been unwilling to lend their names or reputations to the establishment of collective enterprises based on their own innovations.

Goffman was one such maverick scholar.[1] He became a professional sociologist shortly after the end of the Second World War in the United States of America at a time when disciplinary expansion encouraged the critical development of the work of the group of founding thinkers discussed in earlier chapters of this book. From his first publication in 1952 to his death in 1983 he pursued a unique and successful programme of empirical research and conceptual development within sociology. The substance of this programme was the close analysis of the 'interaction order' – that part of social life that occurs whenever 'two or more individuals are in one another's response presence'.[2] He aimed to discover the structures and processes (the forms) exhibited in face-to-face interaction – as well as the sources of its orderliness. Goffman wanted to 'make clear what was previously unclear, [to point to] the significance of things which had been regarded as of little or no consequence, and [to disentangle] what was previously an indiscriminate muddle'.[3] He single-handedly initiated and prosecuted an obstinately empirical programme

151

driven by the impulse described above and consisting of the close analysis of what people do when they are in the company of others, and of how those doings are understood by participants. In the course of 25 years' work he explicitly borrowed the insights, findings, concepts and vocabularies of many individuals and groups of researchers (in anthropology, social psychology, ethology, linguistics) to produce his elegant and persuasive microanalysis of a wide range of interactional phenomena. However, the impulses which really drove his work arose from his reading of classical sociological theory, especially the work of **Durkheim** and **Simmel.** He took ideas and interests from both, reshaped them and used them to drive forward his work in ways that were entirely novel. Three of these were particularly important: an interest in the central role of ideals and morality in social life; the attempt to formulate a fully sociological version of the individual person; a concern to develop sociology as an empirical discipline rather than a speculative theoretical enterprise.

Both Durkheim and Simmel stressed the significance of ideals and morality for the organisation of society. In Durkheim's perspective on society as a moral order, the imposition of morality through ritual and routine organisation was treated as a vital element in the determination of individual conduct. Simmel's argument that society was itself a moral ideal, a necessary fiction, was essential to his focus on sociology as the study of social forms. While Goffman borrowed elements from both thinkers, he located the operation of morality and idealisation not in the abstract entity of society, but in our everyday conduct in face-to-face action. The fact that our actions embody ritual concerns, that we orientate to the ideal of 'euphoria' (or 'ease' in interaction) and that a central assumption in our face-to-face dealings is an idealisation of a 'working consensus' are all claims deserving of close attention and analysis.

Neither Durkheim nor Simmel thought that the organisation of society could be explained as the product of individual action, yet both were concerned to understand the nature of the individual person in a way that was consistent with their respective understandings of the primacy of the social. Both developed views of the individual person as a 'social construction'. Durkheim's treatment of 'moral individualism' and Simmel's work on the personality in modernity both offer versions of the human subject as a social product in place of a view that locates the 'individual' and 'society' as opposing entities. Again Goffman's view varies in detail from both Durkheim and Simmel while being closely related to the common intention of them both.

While there are stark contrasts between Durkheim's and Simmel's methodological preferences, Goffman's sociology seems to combine contrary impulses from both of them. Burns correctly argues that Goffman was much influenced by Durkheim's notion of social fact (defined by Durkheim as 'every way of acting, fixed or not, which is general throughout a given society, while existing in its own right, independent of its individual manifestations') even if he restricted his search for such facts within the domain of face-to-face interaction. More obviously Simmel's notion of social forms was immensely useful in Goffman's programme.[4] Common to both classical writers is the view that empirical sociology should be guided by an emphasis on externality and the search for recurrent patterns of action. These two features act as the driving force for Goffman's work too.

Key Issues

Goffman's substantial body of work described and analysed a large variety of actions and events that had previously failed to receive sociological attention. His analyses of this new material remain among the most elegant and exciting examples of writing within the discipline. For example, his essay 'Tie Signs' offers a detailed exposé of the ways that partners in an intimate relationship exhibit public actions that provide – or conceal – evidence of that relationship.[5] Similarly, his essay 'Response Cries' confounds casual reflection by showing how talking to oneself in public can provide evidence of personal competence rather than signify impropriety or carelessness in speech.

In this section I will look at five issues concerning the substance and style of his work, beginning with a discussion of three recurrent substantive issues and concluding with a discussion of two methodological ones.

Structures of Interaction

Although much of our daily lives is spent in face-to-face interaction with other people, we usually take for granted the stability and predictability – the orderliness – of these interactions. While this reliance can sometimes catch us out (interaction can become disordered and unpredictable), these normal stable patterns arise from our orientation to a common set of rules and obligations and also from our common tacit knowledge of how to construct and recognise a range of social actions. These rules, obligations and tacit knowledge both enable and constrain what individuals can accomplish in the course of such interaction. This general approach can be seen in any of Goffman's analyses. An example is his treatment of two recurrent events within the interaction order: 'remedial interchanges' (apologies, requests and accounts); and 'supportive interchanges' (greetings, leavings and so on).[6] Both studies are demonstrations of how such ordinary actions are an essentially collaborative product of individuals who are attentive to rules, obligations and tacit knowledge. However, precisely because such sequences depend on collaborative work he is able to show how what may happen within these interchanges from moment to moment is vulnerable to individual decision making and choice.[7]

The interaction order is an essentially unfinished order. As Burns pointed out, 'individuals are constantly at work not only promoting, reinforcing and repairing the social order, but creating, recreating and arranging it'.[8] If such work was guided by unstated rule obligations and other presuppositions, Goffman argued that it would be possible to provide formulations of such rules following close observation of conduct. There are places in his books where he did just that (for example his formulation of the rule of 'civil inattention' in 'Behaviour in Public Places'; his treatment of the rules of 'involvement' and 'misinvolvement' in several of the essays in 'Interaction Ritual'). But Goffman did not stop at simply stating whatever rule he felt was at work below the surface of a number of instances of social interaction. Having offered a rule for consideration, he usually proceeded by 'uncovering, collecting, collating and interpreting all possible exceptions to a stated rule'.[9] Competent human subjects are expected to be capable of rule interpretation and manipulation, and Goffman was keen to remind his readers of that fact.

Order is not simply the result of people following rules; what rules do is permit people to enact and witness such order. As we think harder about how rules figure in our sense of the orderliness of everyday life we are forced to consider that their application and interpretation require attention to the context in which any action might occur. A second major element in Goffman's treatment of the interaction order lies in his development of a series of concepts to express the complex array of locally relevant contexts within which action may be located. His success in this respect is witnessed by the fact that so much of his conceptual vocabulary has been used by other writers on the same topic.[10]

Structures of the Self

If the interaction order is the ongoing accomplishment of flesh and blood human subjects, how did Goffman think of these subjects and what account does he give of them in his work? His treatment of this issue generated more interest and commentary than any other area of his work. He wanted to provide what he regarded as a distinctly sociological account of the person. In doing this he treated as irrelevant the large variety of ways that people think about their own or other people's 'inner lives'. He was not concerned with individuals in the way that psychologists or novelists are when they attempt to display the full depth of human motivation, feeling, intention, unconsciousness and so on. He was not concerned to describe or theorise the self 'in the round'.[11] To understand the self sociologically it had to be approached as a social institution, and researched by observing and analysing externally observable forms of conduct.

His concern to establish and deploy such a rigorously sociological version of the individual has been the source of a very considerable misunderstanding of his work. He was often assumed to have denied the significance of what we take to be most important about our selves: our undeclared motivations, hidden emotions, private evaluations of our own and other people's conduct and our sense of the meaning of our lives as bound to biography and social location. In fact it would be wrong to say that Goffman believed such matters to be unimportant as such. However his view was that from the standpoint of sociology their significance was to be treated as 'virtual', as available for use rather than unavoidably used: 'My plea... is not that one should not see that it is persons with unique biographies who do the interacting [in social situations] but that one should move on from this warming fact to try to uncover the principled ways in which such personal histories are given place and the framework of normative understanding this implies.'[12]

What was the outline of his sociological perspective on the self? I think that he offers us three versions, the earlier ones in turn being incorporated into the later ones.

The first version (what Manning calls the 'two-selves' version) appears in 'The Presentation of Self in Everyday Life' and in some other essays, especially in 'Where the Action Is' and 'On Face-Work'. Here Goffman describes the self as composed of two separable entities – 'character' and 'performer', but also as the combined entity of 'The self as a performed character...'.[13] The organisation and management of the roles (or characters) assumed by the self-as-performer are his main concern and as Burns has pointed out, his deployment of the vocabulary of drama is well suited to explore the assumptions, advantages and limitations of such a view. However, this version of the self as in contestable command of socially given roles – sometimes only by working hard – gives way to a darker version of the self offered in other books and essays.

This second version is visible in *Asylums* (and in a slightly different form in *Stigma*). In Goffman's own words 'the self arises not merely out of its possessor's interactions with significant others, but also out of the arrangements that are evolved in an organisation for its members'.[14] Here the self is seen as the product of a set of social – especially organisational – circumstances. The image veers towards social determinism except that he drew attention to the ways in which individuals resist, transgress and contest the definitions of themselves embedded and enacted through such organisational arrangements.[15] Battershill comments on such resistances, suggesting that for Goffman 'role transgression is a fundamental social requirement – an agonistic property of society arising from the weight of our manifold attachments and commitments to multi-situated social entities'.[16]

But if the two-selves version overemphasises the scope for the performer and the socially determined version limits the scope for role choice, a third and final version abandons a description of self in terms of differing substances for a more flexible notion of self as social process. In this final version, the self 'is not an entity half-concealed behind events, but a changeable formula for managing oneself during them'.[17] **Giddens** summarises Goffman's final version: 'The self consists in an awareness of identity which simultaneously transcends specific roles and provides an integrating means of relating them to personal biography; and furnishes a set of dispositions for managing the transactions between motives and the expectations "scripted" by particular roles.'[18]

One final feature of Goffman's treatment of the self in sociology deserves mention. Unlike most sociologists before him, he managed to portray the self in interaction as fully embodied. In several papers he described and analysed the way that our bodies are made relevant to interaction. However, the undeniable facts of our physical being are not taken to determine who we are or even how we appear to be. As Burns has written of Goffman's argument, 'What counts in social interaction are the movements and adjustments we constantly make in order to amplify, adapt, refine and reapply the elementary functioning of what physical capabilities we have.'[19] Goffman's view of physicality as a resource rather than a constraint is perhaps best illustrated in his analyses of sex and gender in both 'The Arrangement between the Sexes' and in the illustrated volume *Gender Advertisements*.

Structures of Experience

A third substantive issue became the focus of Goffman's sociology in the latter part of his academic life. I have indicated that the distinctiveness of his approach to face-to-face interaction and to the individual person lay in his commitment to a fully sociological analysis of these matters. The same impulse was at work in his approach to questions of the 'meaning of social action'. The willingness to make such a question central to one's sociology is a distinctive (self-administered) mark of symbolic interactionism, phenomenology and hermeneutics – of the interpretative tradition in general. Goffman was keen to distance himself from that tradition, and he felt that it was possible to treat issues of meaning from within his preferred framework. *Frame Analysis* and his final published paper 'Felicity's Condition' addressed this by considering the question of how 'what behaviour means is displayed and understood in interaction'. In pursuing this concern to look 'at how behaviour is used to display and find meaning' he managed to demystify the issue of meaning and give it a specifically sociological content. He tried to specify what common cognitive materials individuals use to determine the meaning of what they believe to be happening in any particular interaction as well as how they assemble and use such signs and evidences in an attempt to create meanings for others. In *Frame Analysis* Goffman argued that we use a limited number of 'frames' to determine both our sense as observers of what any particular action is and our shaping as participants of our actions as one kind rather than another.[20]

He also sought to show that underlying these strategic concerns with the shaping and interpretation of information and understanding is an even more basic social requirement for our competent participation in the inter-action order. Participants have to show concern with mutual comprehension as a feature of their co-presence, and in this way, a concern with the structure of experience leads us back to a concern with the structures of interaction themselves.

I want now to turn to two final issues in Goffman's distinctive style of sociology. Both are methodological: first, his spirited advocacy of 'naturalistic observations' as the preferred source of basic sociological knowledge; second, his use of metaphor for the development of theoretical understanding in sociology.

Naturalistic Observation and Sociological Description

Even Goffman's most critical detractors grudgingly admit that his observa-tional capacities were extraordinarily acute. Three kinds of observational work recur throughout his work. First, there were traditional ethnographic studies of social settings (for example the hotel, cottages and farm land of the Shet-land island of Unst in his PhD, the wards of St Elizabeth's Hospital in his book *Asylums*). Second, there were systematic naturalistic observations guided by his effort to collect and categorise the empirical variety of a chosen object of study (for example analysis of speech faults in radio broadcasts).[21] Third, there were secondary observations based on the study of a vast array of fictional and factual accounts of many different kinds of action (for example his use of detective and spy fiction in 'Strategic Interaction' and his use of newspaper 'faits divers' in *Frame Analysis*).

In several public presentations, as well as in the prefaces, introductions and conclusions to his books, Goffman exhorted sociologists to cultivate such methods (although he usually stressed the importance of the first two at the expense of the third). Whichever of these three methods Goffman used, however, he never produced traditional ethnographic descriptions aimed at descriptive fidelity in their reportage of the full detail of life in the setting under study. Instead, he produced collections, categorisations and interpreta-tions of a large range of recurrent events and sequences in social life. He often compared this to the practices of specimen or instance collection and cat-egorisation in natural science disciplines – especially botany and biology. In opposition to those who regard such activity as of limited significance, his practice of 'systematics' (as in the natural sciences) was informed by his know-ledge of the importance of a strong empirical basis for disciplinary develop-ment as well as by his disdain for so much of that airy and premature theorising in sociology that he once described as 'two thirds corn flakes, one third taffy'.

Using Metaphors Productively

It would be wrong to approach Goffman as no more than a skilled collector and arranger of sociological exhibits. His interpretative skills were unequalled and his vision of the wider significance of his findings was clear. He also worked hard to write in a way that would persuade his readers to see things his way. The main device he used to accomplish these things was that of metaphor; a number of major and minor metaphors recur throughout his work. The major metaphors of 'theatre', 'ritual', 'game' and 'frame' provided his most robust and extensive devices and while there are many minor metaphors, these four basic ones carried forward the bulk of his work.

His use of his major metaphors followed a common pattern. First he used them to portray interaction fully characterised by the vocabulary of, and understandings available from, the particular metaphor in question. The metaphor of the theatre encourages us to think about how people produce recognisable and convincing performances for others, the team work needed from all those involved in production, the nature of audience participation and so on. Equally, the metaphor of games was used to draw our attention to the complex sequential organisation of events by means of the vocabulary of moves, tactics, strategies, gambits, stakes, players and so on.

But in addition to exploiting this literal use, Goffman probed each metaphor to find its vulnerabilities – to illusion, pretence, deception, fabrication, and finally its exhaustion. Sometimes he examined a single metaphor in isolation; at other times he considered the relationship between several such metaphors.[22]

Goffman's argument was that this reflexive use of metaphors was an essential tool of sociological work. While he sometimes invoked the standard idea that such devices offer simplifications of more complex multi-layered real-world events, his practice was more subtle than this rather clichéd representation suggests. Careful attention to his texts shows (as both Burns and Manning have pointed out) that Goffman's metaphors were not simply 'employed' or 'relied on' in the course of his work. Rather, we should think of them as being 'brought into play'. It is important to understand the difference implied by this distinction – it is most visible in *Frame Analysis*. In this book Goffman directly considered the question of what made his favoured metaphors intelligible in the first place. By asking 'what is it about games that makes them real as games', and 'what is the nature of theatre as a social achievement' his investigations are given an additional reflexive turn. Although in its preface Goffman eschews an over-attentiveness to methodological self-consciousness, the book can be profitably read as an extended methodological self-commentary as well as being a report of his considerations upon the organisation of people's experience of the social.

Seeing Things Differently

In a review of a large range of ethnographic research on social interaction in the public realm, Lyn Lofland drew attention to the many contributions to that research that 'found their initial inspiration in the Goffmanian insight that life in the public realm is both thoroughly social and sociologically interesting'.[23] Most who work in this field accept that one of the main principles relevant for the organisation and analysis of conduct in public is the way that people orientate to the 'rule of civil inattention'. In 'Behaviour in Public Places', Goffman described civil inattention as follows: 'one gives to another enough visual notice to demonstrate that one appreciates that the other is present (and that one admits openly to having seen him), while at the same moment withdrawing one's attention from him so as to express that he does not constitute a target of special curiosity or design'.[24] When following this rule 'persons circumspectly treat each other with polite and glancing concern while each goes about his own separate business'.[25] An orientation to this rule 'makes possible co-presence without co-mingling, awareness without engrossment, courtesy without conversation. It is perhaps, the absolute *sine qua non* of city life.'[26]

There are exceptions to all such rules, these exceptions themselves being socially organised. A public setting that encouraged co-mingling, engrossment and conversation between people previously unacquainted with one another would be one that suspended or varied the operation of the rule of civil inattention. Are there such settings, and what would be the typical patterns of interactions occurring within them in conditions of the suspension of this rule? One set of answers to these questions was supplied by Sherri Cavan's study of behaviour in licensed bars.[27] Cavan's study (and its use of Goffman's original ideas) helps us convert our casual assertions about bars, pubs and other kinds of public licensed premises being places in which people are 'more sociable' into a series of focused researchable sociological issues. The increased possibilities for, and encouragement of, sociability in such settings rest on the assumption that individuals will be more open to encounters with others.[28] Suspending the rule of civil inattention allows those co-present to move from the assumption of openness into the accomplishment of talk or its non-verbal substitute. It should be easy to recognise and understand the significance of Cavan's observation that once the rule is suspended 'not only idle glances at other patrons but also idle glances at features and fixtures of the establishment all convey one's openness. There are no protective goods, no newspapers, letters and books to serve as an alternative form of involvement. If such props are used, they may themselves serve as grounds for initial overtures of sociability.'[29] We can better understand how difficult it is to resist the overtures of sociability from other users of sociability in such places by reference to variations in the operation of civil inattention and their effect on the status of participants. The same variations and effects are also relevant for understanding why the majority of verbal encounters that do occur in such settings remain momentary ones. According to Cavan, mutual openness 'shortens the life span of such interactions'. The same rules that facilitate the opening of encounters make it likely that the conversational content of such encounters will be 'tentative and superficial' and that the interaction will be difficult to maintain.[30] The normal rules that give one person rather than another control over the termination of an interaction are much looser in this context, and this makes it much easier for participants to drift into, out of and away from an encounter. Equally the open status of such conversations makes it more likely that further participants can both enter and appropriate both conversational topic and individual people.

It is difficult to convey the full complexity of the interactional structures that Cavan is able to display in the course of her work. What should be clear, even from this short account, is both the way that her observation of ordinary conduct is informed by Goffman's original vision, and the way that our own sociological understanding can be similarly developed.

Legacies and Unfinished Business

Morality, Self and Interaction

Goffman's work raised issues that lie on the border between sociology and moral philosophy. What moral stance is implied by his vision of human action? Does he license the cynical manipulation of others or is he a critic of the limits of a Machiavellian perspective on the social? Many have argued that Goffman's overall view of the self is distorted by a fascination with appearance and the neglect of deeper issues of morality and motivation.[31] A second group of commentators on Goffman's work have pointed to the emergence of a more complex view of human nature. Burns, Manning, Giddens and others have argued that he was concerned with the polarity of mistrust and trust in social encounters.[32] A third view goes further and seeks to portray Goffman's view of human nature and social order as exemplifying a strong moral commitment quite at odds with previous representations of an amoral voyeur of human conduct.[33]

Further Explorations in the Interaction Order

Goffman's commitment to the close analysis of face-to-face conduct based on a behavioural rather than interpretative programme has been taken up – and subsequently modified – by a new generation of productive scholars. The most powerful of these, describing their work as 'conversation analysis' or 'the analysis of talk-in-interaction', have been critical of both Goffman's methods and some aspects of his overall account of social order, but willing to acknowledge their indebtedness to his original cultivation of a new field of sociological study.[34] Other linguistically orientated researchers outside sociology have also taken forward many of Goffman's original ideas. Recent work in anthropology, discourse analysis and pragmatics have all benefited from his vocabulary and findings.

Situating the Interaction Order

Since Goffman argued that the interaction order was one of several orders of social reality subject to sociological analysis, questions arise about how we should understand the interaction order to be related to the larger social and historical structures in which it is located. And how does the interaction order stand in relation to the biography of individuals and social groups that enliven it? Goffman's own answers continue to provoke commentary and alternative formulations. This is the final piece of unfinished business that I want to discuss in this chapter.

Goffman characterised himself as 'no rampant situationalist'.[35] He argued that it was inappropriate to treat the order of interaction as the creation of co-participants independent of wider historical and social arrangements, asserting that 'the individuals I know don't invent the world of chess when they sit down to play, or the stock market when they buy some shares, or the pedestrian traffic system when they manoeuvre through the streets. Whatever the idiosyncrasies of their own motives and interpretations, they must gear their participation into what is available by way of standard doings and standard reasons for doing these doings.'[36] His characterisation of the relationship between the interaction order and the wider social order on the one hand and to individual biographies on the other hand was in terms of ties of 'loose coupling'.[37]

A number of critics remain unconvinced by Goffman's assertion of the status of the interaction order and unsure about the 'loose coupling' by which he argues it is related to other features of the social. Both of the main alternatives to his views share an attempt to establish a more seamless unity to our view of social life. A first critique suggests that Goffman's claims for the significance of the interaction order were too timid, that he awarded too much importance to 'wider social arrangements' as exemplified by his acceptance of the significance of a micro/macro distinction for sociology. Both Rawls and Burns attack the necessity to recognise claims for the significance of an abstract (for Burns emptily abstract) structural order seen as somehow standing above the interaction order. Burns for example argues that 'social order is always, and essentially locally produced. To try to work out the connections between social interaction and a social order which prevails throughout society is not only impossibly difficult, as it has so far appeared to be, but pointless. For the immediacies and restricted dimensions of everyday interaction and social encounters are neither the elementary constituents of the larger, remote "crystallisations" of social institutions, organisations and the like that Simmel saw in them nor the determinate outcomes of Mandelbaum's "societal facts".[38]

While this first critique collapses all social arrangements into the arrangements of the interaction order, a second critique collapses the interaction order into a larger set of social arrangements. Giddens, for example, is critical of the degree of independence Goffman gives to the interaction order, arguing that a false separation between the interaction and institutional order results in the diminution of the significance of Goffman's work for a unified theory of society.[39]

I am more persuaded by Goffman's own understanding of the matter, particularly because he regarded this understanding of loose coupling as no more than a guide for research. Confidence in seamless webs and unified theories does not sit comfortably alongside Goffman's drive to the close examination of human conduct, his suspicion of grand theory in sociology or his realisation of the necessary arbitrariness of concept formation in the social sciences.

Goffman's work portrayed the details of face-to-face interaction in sharp sociological focus. He demonstrated a remarkable awareness of the possible scope and depth of its investigation while maintaining an awareness of the methodological complexities involved. The range of the concepts and findings he offered, his willingness to think hard about the exceptional as well as the banal, the skill of his literary style, all combine to make his work one of the best introductions to the distinctiveness of the sociological imagination.

Further Reading

T. Burns, *Erving Goffman* (London: Routledge, 1992).
J. Ditton (ed.), *The View from Goffman* (London: Macmillan, 1980).
P. Drew and Anthony Wootton (eds), *Erving Goffman: Exploring the Interaction Order* (Cambridge: Polity Press, 1988).
P. Manning, *Erving Goffman and Modern Sociology* (Cambridge: Polity Press, 1992).
'Erving Goffman's Sociology'. Special Issue of *Human Studies*, 12(1 and 2), (1989).

12

David Lockwood

Nicos Mouzelis

Driving Impulses

David Lockwood began his sociological career at a time when it was **Parsonian** functionalism and its complement – what C.W. Mills called abstracted empiricism – that dominated sociology. Going against the prevailing orthodoxy, Lockwood tried to introduce into the empirically orientated sociological research issues derived from the work of **Karl Marx,** the great absentee from the early post-war sociological canon. His whole *œuvre* can be seen as an imaginative and critical engagement with Marx's thought, his major aim being not a scholastic preoccupation with what the German philosopher 'really said or meant' on various issues, but creatively to use basic Marxist concepts and substantive theories in order to (a) show the inadequacy of Parsonian conceptual tools for understanding the constitution, reproduction and transformation of modern societies; and (b) explore empirically the social structure of modern Britain.

Whether one looks at his theoretical contributions or his empirically orientated analyses of class, the constant, all-pervasive theme of his work is the idea that the type of **Durkheimian** sociology that Parsonian functionalism mainly represents needs to be brought nearer to a Marxist way of conceptualizing the mechanisms of social order and disorder.

Key Issues

White-collar Workers: Becoming Proletarian?

Lockwood's first major empirical contribution, *The Blackcoated Worker,* was in the sphere of white-collar work.[1] He was one of the first social scientists to show in an empirically concrete and at the same time theoretically adequate manner that, as far as the work situation is concerned, white-collar workers in our day are experiencing the type of routinization and bureaucratization of their jobs that blue-collar workers underwent during the emergence and dominance of the modern factory system. In fact the growing importance of the large office, where a great number of employees were brought together under the same roof, had organizational effects similar to those of the factory two centuries ago. It increased the anonymity and impersonality of the employee–employer relationship, while creating favourable conditions for the development of white-collar unions.

From the above point of view Marx was quite correct when he argued that the further development of capitalism would spread the process of proletarianization beyond the factory gates. But if in terms of the work situation there was a certain homogenization between blue- and white-collar workers, in other respects, Lockwood pointed out, the differences between the two social categories were still significant. In terms of market chances, for instance, office workers – due to greater opportunities for promotion as well as to a variety of fringe benefits – still keep an important advantage. This in turn is one of the main reasons why, in terms of status, clerical work still entails higher prestige than manual labour.

The Affluent Worker: Becoming Middle Class?

This type of problematic was further developed by J.H. Goldthorpe *et al.* in the by now classical study of a number of affluent skilled manual workers in Luton.[2] In this context a somewhat similar issue was examined from the blue-collar perspective. Contrary to the *embourgeoisement* thesis,[3] which argued that the affluent working class was increasingly becoming middle class, Lockwood, Goldthorpe and their collaborators posited that such a notion of the assimilation of the working class into the middle class was unduly simplistic. Rather, both groups were changing in such a way that it was a particular kind of convergence rather than assimilation or merger that characterized the overall situation. For if the white-collar worker had moved from non-unionized, personal relationships between employee and employer to one of *instrumental collectivism* (that is, a context where white-collar workers join unions so as to promote their individual interests), the blue-collar worker was reaching the same position by a very different route. From the solidaristic collectivism of the traditional working-class community he or she had come to view the unions in as instrumental/individualistic a manner as his or her white-collar counterpart.

According to Goldthorpe and Lockwood, what is common to both groups is *privatization,* a type of home-centred existence where the joys of consumption or newly acquired gadgets, and of private family life become more important than class struggles and the expression of collective sentiments and interests in the public domain.[4]

> ### The World of the Affluent Worker
>
> The interviews showed that the sample of affluent manual workers shared a predominantly 'instrumental orientation' to their employment, irrespective of differences in skill, occupational status, or the technology with which they were involved. By an instrumental orientation the authors mean that workers were attracted to their jobs because of 'extrinsic', that is, mainly economic, considerations. For example, 87 per cent of skilled men and 82 per cent of those semi-skilled explained their work attachments wholly or partly in terms of the level of pay, degree of security, or extent of the fringe benefits available. Only 29 per cent of the former and 14 per cent of the latter mentioned 'intrinsic' attractions such as job satisfaction. Consistent with this, few participated actively in work-based societies or clubs, and few were members of solidary work groups. Nor did they base their social lives outside the factory on associations with workmates. Home and factory were psychologically and socially isolated from each other. Thus, for example, 76 per cent of skilled men and 66 per cent of the semi-skilled reported they would be 'not much bothered' or 'not bothered at all' if they moved away from their present workmates to another job. (From: G. Marshall, *In Praise of Sociology,* London, Unwin Hyman, 1990, p. 108)

Technology, Workplace, Community, Society: A Holistic Approach

In a further creative engagement with Marxism, Lockwood and Goldthorpe have argued that if one tries to explain the two major features of the convergence trajectory, that is, instrumental collectivism and privatization, neither technology nor the organization of the workplace can provide a satisfactory answer. The workers' instrumental orientation towards their jobs (for example, the fact that they are more interested in higher wages than in work satisfaction and self-fulfilment on the job) was shaped less by factors within the workplace itself and more by broader communal and societal factors.

Contrary to Robert Blauner, therefore, who was trying to establish one-to-one linkages between technology/work conditions and 'alienation' at work,[5] Goldthorpe and Lockwood argued that such rather crude technological determinism was misleading. Although subsequent studies have shown that workers' orientations *are* influenced by both workplace and related conditions,[6] there is no doubt that the empirical studies in Luton have shown the risk inherent in arbitrarily extracting isolated concepts (such as that of Marx's notion of work alienation) from classical theories in order to 'operationalize' them and establish correlations between so-called variables.

What is valuable and enduring in Lockwood's empirical research is that, although he is greatly influenced by Marx's writings, he takes the holistic character of Marxist theory seriously. Unlike Blauner, he does not reduce it to an aggregate of statements and disconnected hypotheses from which the modern researcher picks and chooses at will for purposes of 'operationalization' and empirical testing. In other words, whereas Blauner's excursus into classical theory was rather decorative (in the sense that he could present his research without once referring to Marx's theory of alienation), Lockwood's engagement with Marxism was and is on a more serious and fundamental level.

Social and System Integration

The same can be said of Lockwood's more theoretical writings, where the focus is less on substantive issues and more on the basic conceptual tools that *prepare the ground* for the construction of substantive theories. On this level Lockwood, in order to show the basic differences between Marxism and Parsonian sociology, made the seminal suggestion of distinguishing between social and system integration – a distinction that came to play a leading role in various theoretical debates in the social sciences.[7]

The social/system-integration distinction makes it possible to look at a social system (whether this is a small group, a formal organization, or a whole society) from two analytically distinct but complementary perspectives. The social-integration perspective focuses on *agency*, on the way in which social actors view and relate to each other in specific social contexts. So for Lockwood, social integration refers to 'the orderly or conflictual relationships between actors'; whereas system integration focuses on the compatible or incompatible linkages between the 'parts of the social system'.[8] In this latter case, therefore, the social system and the mechanisms that integrate it are not seen from the 'inside' (not from the actors' point of view), but from the outside, so to speak, from the point of view of the system and its requirements for reproduction/survival. Given this systemic, 'externalist' perspective, the mechanisms leading to integration/disintegration are no longer those of conflict/co-operation, but those of logical compatibility/incompatibility between systemic parts.

Lockwood's Critique of Parsons: An Overemphasis on System Integration

If we look at Parsonian functionalism (which Lockwood identifies with normative functionalism) from the above perspective, systemic parts are seen to be conceptualized in institutional terms. For instance, Parsons subdivides a societal system into four basic institutional subsystems: the adaptation subsystem (which refers to economic institutions), the goal-achievement subsystem (political institutions), the integration subsystem (legal and communal institutions), and the latency subsystem (kinship and religious institutions).[9] (See Chapter 7, above.) Since Parsons overemphasizes system and underemphasizes social integration, his only mechanisms of change are internal to the systsem and refer to incompatibilities between the social system's different subsystems. So for instance in a late-developing country, introducing western technology and modes of management into the economic subsystem (adaptation) might render the values/norms of this subsystem logically incompatible with those still prevalent in the religious or kinship subsystem (latency).

This systemic contradiction or incompatibility between institutional subsystems constitutes the major mechanism of social transformation for Parsonian modernization theorists.[10] For Lockwood, this conceptualization of social change is misleading because of its overemphasis on system integration. Its exclusive focus on systemic incompatibilities between normative orders peripheralizes actors, and prevents one from asking who-questions about social change. For instance, which specific interest groups (entrepreneurs, workers, women, priests, and so on) experience the contradiction between the instrumental rationality of the economic subsystem and the 'expressive' rationality of the religious subsystem, and how do these groups deal with those incompatibilities? Are they aware of them? Do they try to set up formal organizations so as to handle the growing contradictions in one way or another? Such agency questions are peripheral or completely absent from the Parsonian analysis of the modernization process. It is as though a mysterious entity called Society, or Societal System, were handling the contradictions so as to bring about social change in the direction of greater differentiation and higher adaptive capacity.[11]

Advantages of Marx over Parsons

Now, according to Lockwood, if one looks at the conceptual framework underlying Marxist approaches to social change, two basic differences from Parsonian functionalism can be identified.

First, on the level of system integration, systemic parts are not only normative/institutional, but also non-normative/material. For instance, the basic Marxist contradiction between *material base* (forces of production or technology in the broad sense of the term) and *institutional core* (*institutions of private property*) is a type of systemic incompatibility that is not found in Parsons' purely normative/institutional conceptualization of systemic subsystems.

The second major difference between Marx and Parsons is that the former (if one looks at his work as a whole) puts equal emphasis on social and system integration. Unlike Parsons, Marx does ask social-integration, who-questions, such as: what do actors do about growing systemic incompatibilities? Are they aware of the growing contradiction between the increasingly collective character of the forces of production, and the still private character of the institutions regulating the ownership of the means of production? And if so, what are the chances of building up class organizations capable of transforming the prevailing relations of production?

According to Lockwood, regardless of the fact that some of Marx's substantive theories about the development of class consciousness and class struggles in late capitalism were wrong (such as his thesis on the growing pauperization of the proletariat), the basic conceptual framework is pretty sound. It combines in highly ingenious manner the social- with the system-integration perspective. It succeeds in viewing capitalist societies from an agency/internalist as well as a systemic/externalist perspective; both in terms of the strategies and conflicts of the main protagonists, as well as in terms of the basic incompatibilities/contradictions of a mode of production based on the private ownership of the means of production. Marx's theory raised the fundamental question that Parsonian sociology fails to raise: given growing systemic contradictions, what happens on the level of social integration, that is, on the level of actors' consciousness, strategies, struggles? How do their strategies and struggles affect systemic contradictions and vice versa?

It is precisely because it combines system and social integration more effectively that Marxism offers us tools useful for the *explanation* of both stability and change. Parson's underemphasis of social integration, his peripheralization of actors makes them appear as mere puppets of the system's requirements. In consequence, social order and disorder in normative functionalism are, at best, described, but cannot be explained.

The Dynamics of Social Change

Let us now move from Parsons to his major mentor Durkheim who, according to Lockwood, takes social integration rather more seriously. However, here again there is a very interesting contrast between Durkheim's and Marx's attempts to explain social order and disorder.[12]

Durkheim views social structure in status terms. For him, social structure consists of hierarchically organized status groups whose rights and obligations are legally defined and legitimized by the prevailing societal values and norms. This type of distribution of rights and obligations Durkheim calls social classification, and it is social classification that confers cohesion and order on society. As for social disorder, this comes about when this hierarchical structure of normatively regulated groups is undermined by processes Durkheim defines vaguely as 'sudden changes in the economy', 'changes in wealth and power', changes in the ordering of 'men and things', and so on, such changes which (when properly theorized, lead to the Marxist concepts of class structure and class struggles) disrupt the existing system of classification. They bring about 'declassification', a state of affairs characterized by such anomic phenomena as moral deregulation, egoism, social schism, moral polarization and so on.

For Lockwood, therefore, Durkheim's theory of disorder or social change is based on a notion of *discrepancy* between a status hierarchy and a vaguely defined class-power situation – the latter term referring to circumstances where 'life chances are minimally conditioned by legal status defining entitlements', and status hierarchy to circumstances where such entitlements are dominant.[13] This means that status for Durkheim entails a *de jure* distribution of rights and privileges, whereas class entails *de facto* power relationships based on the differential control of situational facilities.

According to Lockwood looking at Marx, there the situation is exactly the reverse: what is central to Durkheim becomes peripheral for Marx, and vice versa. At the centre of the Marxist view of social structure are power rather than status groups, that is, groups struggling over the control of the means of production and over the benefits such control bestows. From this perspective social disorder or social transformation occurs when there is a discrepancy between class and status – status *contra* Durkheim, being defined by Marx only nebulously. For Marx, when power relations between social classes no longer correspond to the distribution of rights and obligations as defined by law, that is, when there is a discrepancy between *de facto* power relations and *de jure* formal arrangements, then we witness processes leading to social change. So while both Marx and Durkheim base their theories of disorder on a discrepancy between status and power relationships, the one considers as the core and conceptualizes carefully what the other considers peripheral and conceptualizes vaguely.

Marx choosing to emphasize power rather than status relations makes sense in view of the fact that his social-action schema is fundamentally utilitarian. And if in classical utilitarianism the ends of action are random, in Marxism they are 'objectively' determined by the prevailing relations of production. For instance, given the fact that the worker in capitalism does not own the means of production, this situation automatically entails 'objective' interest: that is, the overthrow of an exploitative system in which the worker must sell his or her labour power in order to survive, while the capitalist, via labour-market mechanisms, profits from surplus value. Given, moreover, Marx's utilitarian assumption about the economic rationality of actors, the workers will tend to adopt revolutionary, anti-capitalist strategies. If they do not, it is because of false consciousness; because the dominant classes, by means of various ideological mechanisms, prevent them from seeing their situation objectively. According to Lockwood, the introduction of the false-consciousness argument results in Marxists veering between a positivist position (objective class locations more or less automatically bring about certain class practices), and an idealist one (whenever there is a discrepancy between objective interests and class practices, it is due to the adoption of 'false' ideas).

Linking the above considerations with an earlier critique he had developed of certain aspects of historical materialism, Lockwood stresses the fact that the positivist/idealist oscillation in Marxism is due to the fact that it is not possible to identify 'objective interests'. Interests cannot be automatically derived from a given class position; they are constructed by processes that always entail normative considerations. For Lockwood, therefore, Marx's action schema does not seriously take into account that class interests are shaped not only by the relations of production and/or the work situation. In the workers' 'definition of the situation', extra-work and extra-class societal values and norms may, or rather do, play a crucial role.

Another major conclusion Lockwood derives from the Durkheim–Marx comparison is that the tension (or lack of it) between *de facto* power relations and *de jure* status is a fundamental factor for understanding social order and disorder in capitalist societies. In that sense investigations of social change must seriously consider *both* Durkheim's theorization of status hierarchies, and Marx's conceptualization of class/power.

Seeing Things Differently

Lockwood has not tried to construct a meta-theory to bring together the status and power approaches, just as in his earlier work he avoided any theoretical synthesis of the social- and system-integration perspectives. However, what is crucial for empirical research is that his theoretical distinctions do clearly demonstrate the necessity of studying social stability and change in both Durkheimian and Marxist manner, in terms of both status hierarchies and power struggles over the control of scarce resources.

Similarly, his seminal social/system-integration dichotomy encourages the study of changing social systems (micro, meso or macro) from both the systemic/functionalist perspective and that of action/agency. Any one-sided emphasis on system to the exclusion of social integration leads to teleological explanations that portray Society (capital s) as a mysterious entity pulling all the strings behind the actors' backs. As Lockwood has shown, one finds such teleological explanations not only in Parsonian functionalism, but also in those Marxist theorists who underemphasize the voluntaristic dimension of social life (for example the **Althusserian** school).

On the other hand, overemphasis of agency at the expense of systemic considerations – as seen in the various interpretative sociologies that have developed spectacularly in the 1960s and 1970s – takes us from **reification** to **reductionism:** where complex macro-structural developments are reduced to interpretative understandings and actors' face-to-face interactions. Therefore, if an imbalance in favour of system integration leads to mechanistic/deterministic explanations of social order and disorder, an imbalance in favour of social integration leads to social myopia and to the elimination of crucial issues that cannot be fully accounted for by an exclusive focus on actors' orientations and definitions of the social world.[14]

Reification and Reductionism

Reification here refers to the way in which society, which includes people and their actions as part of its reality, can be treated as a thing without people that somehow works entirely by itself and according to goals of its own making. **Reductionism** here refers to the way in which society, which is more than the current actions of people today (it includes, for example, the buildings, roads, information networks, filing cabinets, energy grids, and so on, that were created in the past and are still there today as part of society's functioning), is treated as nothing but (reduced to) the current actions of people today.

Legacies and Unfinished Business

Recent Attempts to Transcend the Social/System-Integration Divide: Elias, Giddens, Bourdieu

I do not think it an exaggeration to claim that the neglect of the social/system-integration *balance* has been at the root of a lot of confusion and numerous false starts and sterile debates in the social sciences. The same can be said about more recent efforts to 'transcend' the social/system-integration divide. So **Elias**' figurational sociology,[15] **Giddens**' structuration theory,[16] or **Bourdieu**'s theory of social practice,[17] are all part of the repeated attempts to go beyond the agency–system or the 'subjectivist'–'objectivist' divide in the social sciences – attempts that have invariably been unsuccessful, however. Their supposed transcendence has always been rhetorical/decorative rather than substantive. They have ostensibly rejected Lockwood's more conventional way of conceptualizing the agency/system distinction, while in fact reintroducing it in a different terminological guise.

Giddens, for instance, rejects functionalism and the agency/system distinction, but brings in both by the back door, so to speak, via his distinction between institutional analysis (which is exactly what Lockwood means by the system-integration approach) and analysis in terms of strategic conduct (Lockwood's social-integration perspective). In similar fashion Bourdieu claims that his habitus concept (see Chapter 16) transcends the objectivist–subjectivist divide, but reinstates exactly the same divide when he talks about objective locations and actors' stances or postures *vis-à-vis* such locations (actors' *prise de position*).[18]

Recent Attempts to Abolish the Social/System-Integration Divide: Foucault, Derrida, Baudrillard

Equally unsuccessful are postmodern/post-structuralist attempts, not to transcend but simply to abolish the agency/system distinction. For postmodernists, proceeding to 'decentre' the subject, or focusing on discourses or practices rather than actors, the agency/system distinction is at best superfluous, and at worst leads to essentialist accounts of the social world.[19] This postmodernist/post-structuralist position, however, makes one view the social world *reductively*, as a chain of discursive practices (**Foucault**), or texts (Derrida) or signifiers (Baudrillard). From this perspective there is no possibility of showing how practices are hierarchized and why, for instance, certain practices have greater transformational impact than others. In view of this limitation there is a tendency in postmodern analyses to explain complex macro phenomena simplistically in terms of signs, symbols or such 'disembodied' notions as desire, power/knowledge and so on.[20]

A Recent Confusion about Social and System Integration: Habermas

If Giddens and Bourdieu have tried to transcend the social- and system-integration distinction, and postmodern theorists to abolish it, **Habermas** accepts its utility but incorporates it with a second distinction that ultimately cancels the heuristic utility of Lockwood's initial formulation.

More specifically, Habermas accepts Lockwood's position that one should look at social systems from both an agency ('internalist' in Habermas' terminology) and a systemic ('externalist') perspective; but in his later work, when Habermas uses the social/system-integration distinction, he conflates the externalist/internalist perspective with that of his system/life-world. For Habermas, in highly differentiated modern societies, *system* refers to the economic and political institutional spheres that are co-ordinated via the systemic media of money and power. *Life-world*, on the other hand (which Habermas identifies with social integration), refers to such institutional spheres as the family, religion, the public domain and so on, which are supposed to be integrated via non-systemic media (that is, via normative and/or communicative modes of co-ordination).[21]

When Habermas conflates Lockwood's *methodological* distinction (agency/internalist – systemic/externalist) with a *substantive* distinction between institutional spheres co-ordinated via systemic and non-systemic media, he creates confusion and counters the heuristic utility of Lockwood's initial distinction. This diverts attention from the obvious fact that one can view all social systems from an internalist and externalist perspective – whether they are embedded in the economic and political spheres (Habermas' system), or in a society's social and cultural institutional spheres.[22]

The Real Weakness in Lockwood's Conception of Social/System-Integration and a Way Forward

The fact that Lockwood's social/system-integration distinction has stood the test of time so well does not, of course, mean it has no weaknesses. I think that the major one lies in the author's attempt to show that contradictions between systemic parts in Marxism are 'qualitatively' (one could say, ontologically) different from systemic contradictions in Parsonian functionalism on a material–normative continuum. To argue, as Lockwood does, that Marxist analysis, unlike normative-functionalist analysis, focuses on contractions between a *material*, non-normative base (forces of production, that is, technology in the broad sense of the term) and a core *institutional* complex (institution of private ownership), implies that technology or certain aspects of the economy are not normatively regulated. This necessarily leads to a type of essentialism that is unacceptable to those who think that the social is symbolically constructed and that institutional spheres (economic, political, religious and so on) entail normative regulation.

A way out of this difficulty is for Lockwood to drop the material/normative or material/institutional distinction because in reality they are always intertwined. Social practices involve both. If we want to investigate the nature of systemic contradictions between the forces of producton and the relations of production then we would do better to accept that both aspects of this systemic incompatibility involve both material and normative, institutional elements. It would be better to work instead a distinction between more and less *durable* institutional arrangements.[23] Marx's contradiction between forces and relations of production can then more fruitfully be conceptualized as a contradiction between more durable, hard-to-change technological structures, and, the more malleable institutions of private ownership of the means of production. Of course, whether the latter are more malleable than the former is an empirical question, and the degree of durability of the forces and of the relations of production can vary from one case to the next. But to replace 'materiality' with 'durability' renders the whole issue less metaphysical, more amenable to empirical research.

To conclude, Lockwood's more substantive writings on the changing class structure of modern societies, his crucial conceptualization of the social/system-integration perspectives, and his more recent theoretical analysis of the Marxist and Durkheimian sociological legacies have generated an important corpus of works attempting to criticize, reformulate or reject the author's basic insights into the mechanisms of social stability and change in modernity. The fact that the debate about the agency/system distinction is still alive, and the fact that, after a rush to transcend or simply reject the subjective/objective divide in the social sciences, this fundamental distinction is still a major organizing principle and a fruitful heuristic device in ongoing research,[24] clearly shows the importance of Lockwood's contribution.

I believe his work will become even more central in the years to come – given the sobering-up process that is gaining strength in both the United Kingdom and the USA. This consists of a growing realization that, instead of trying to transcend or abolish the agency/system divide, it might be more fruitful to try, rather more modestly, to build conceptual bridges facilitating two-way communication between the interpretative and systemic/function-alist sociologies.[25]

Further Reading

J.H. Goldthorpe, D. Lockwood, F. Bechhofer and J. Platt, *The Affluent Worker: Indus-trial Attitudes and Behaviour* (Cambridge: Cambridge University Press, 1968).

D. Lockwood, 'Some Remarks on the Social System', *British Journal of Sociology*, **7**, (1956), 134–46.

D. Lockwood, *The Blackcoated Worker* (London: Allen & Unwin, 1958).

D. Lockwood, 'Social Integration and System Integration', in G.K. Zollschan and W. Hirsch (eds), *Explorations in Social Change* (London: Routledge & Kegan Paul, 1964), pp. 244–57.

D. Lockwood, *Solidarity and Schism: 'The Problem of Disorder' in Durkheimian and Marxist Sociology* (Oxford: Oxford University Press, 1992).

N. Mouzelis, 'Social and System Integration: Habermas' View', *British Journal of Sociology*, **43**(2), (June 1992), 272–7.

13

Harold Garfinkel

John Heritage

Driving Impulses

One of the chief sociological innovations of the post-war era has been the discovery of the world of everyday social life. This discovery was made during a period – the 1950s – in which much sociological analysis was highly abstract and divorced from real events. The sociology of that period was almost entirely concerned with the limits that social organization places on human activities, with no concern at all with how those activities were possible in the first place. Sociologists were content to sketch abstract constraints that 'box in' human action without ever addressing what actually happened in the conduct of action itself. Left out were the details of how people actually reasoned and acted, what they did inside the 'box' of constraint, indeed whether or in what sense there was a 'box' at all.

In this context, two great and original American sociologists offered massive dissent. **Erving Goffman** saw that social interaction is itself a social institution, and one that enables and mediates the operations of all the other institutions in society. Harold Garfinkel went still deeper. He argued that underlying all social institutions – including Goffman's 'interaction order' – is a still more fundamental one. This order he called 'ethnomethodological'. It concerns how persons *make sense* of their circumstances and act on them: how people analyze, understand and act in their social world.

Imagine a simple social setting: for example, a medical consultation in a general practice context. The doctor and patient begin with some conversation about the patient's forthcoming holiday. Then, in response to 'What brings you here today', the patient details some stomach problems he has been experiencing. A five-minute course of questioning ensues, followed by a physical examination and, finally, a diagnosis and a set of treatment recommendations.

Consider some questions which are absolutely central to an analysis of this encounter. How do doctor and patient understand which parts of the conversation are 'social' and which are 'medical'? In what ways and by what means does the patient understand, process and respond to the doctor's questions, and by what means does the doctor grasp the experiences and reasoning behind the patient's answers? How does the doctor reason about the patient's illness, and how is that reasoning expressed in diagnostic questioning? How much of that reasoning does the patient grasp and, more generally, how does the patient make decisions about how to answer the doctor's questions? How does each party grasp the motivations of the other at different moments in the consultation? How do the parties know 'where they are' in the consultation at any point in time? How, in short, do the doctor and patient 'make sense' of one another and their situation, and 'make sense' together? How would you go about answering these questions and analyzing this encounter?

In 1950, when Harold Garfinkel was a student at Harvard University, two main approaches to understanding this interaction were available to him. One approach was to describe the value system underpinning the institution of medicine, and to illustrate the operation of this value system in the behaviors of doctor and patient (**Parsons** 1951). The other was to describe the behaviors of the parties in terms of whether they were orientated to medical tasks or to the management of emotion, using a newly invented coding system called 'interaction process analysis' (Bales 1950). Neither of these approaches has ever offered any significant answers to our questions about sense-making in the doctor–patient encounter. Yet it is obvious that this sense-making process is foundational – for both doctor and patient – in the step-by-step unfolding of the medical encounter itself. For it is the sense-making process that is central to how doctor and patient make decisions about what to do and say next. The process of sense-making and the actions based on it make each specific medical encounter what it is.

Although Parsons and Bales were Garfinkel's teachers at Harvard in 1950, Garfinkel argued against them that what they were missing, sense-making, is the beginning of everything that is possible in the social world. Nothing can happen in society without it. Garfinkel has spent a lifetime working on how human sense-making can be analyzed, and how its input into action and social structure can be grasped. Garfinkel never believed that this business of sense-making was a matter for psychology. On the contrary, he argued that people make *joint* sense of their social world *together*, and that they do so *methodically*, using *social procedures or methods* that they share. Because these methods are shared by the members of specific cultures and subcultures, Garfinkel called them 'ethnomethods'. And he called the sociological study of these ethnomethods 'ethnomethodology'. Ethnomethodology studies how these socially shared methods are used to understand, reason and act in the common-sense world of everyday life.

The underlying ideas with which Garfinkel began his work were conceived in a period of crisis. In the late 1930s, the philosopher Edmund Husserl contrasted the abstract mathematical rationality of science with the ordinary experiences and everyday rationality of what he called the lifeworld. Unconsciously echoing **Weber**, he observed that although modern science is ultimately grounded in this lifeworld of ordinary experience, it has become divorced from it. The result is that science has become an abstract vision of the world stripped of human value and meaning, and useless as a weapon to resist the tide of irrationality that was then engulfing Europe. Shadowed by the Nazi takeover in Germany and stalked by an illness that would be his last, Husserl called this situation *The Crisis of European Sciences*.[1]

Harold Garfinkel came into contact with these and related writings about the lifeworld almost immediately. A student at the University of North Carolina in 1940, and newly in contact with another form of racism – the racial domination of the American South – he used Husserl as part of a scalding analysis of racial factors in North Carolina homicide trials.[2] During this period, he also wrote a short story, 'Color Trouble', which depicted the protest of an African American woman who boarded a bus but then refused to sit at the back.[3] Anticipating by some years the form of Rosa Parks' 1955 protest which ignited the American civil rights movement, the story embodies a vivid sense of the everyday world – Husserl's lifeworld of everyday experience – as the primordial site in which human values are expressed and contested.

After Garfinkel moved to Harvard in 1946 to work with Talcott Parsons (the dominant figure in American sociology during the ensuing 25 years), his concerns with the lifeworld became more theoretically focused. The sociology he encountered there had little interest in the lifeworld of everyday decision-making and action. Instead, it was preoccupied with how persons are motivated to conform with the demands of social structure by the impact of value systems and institutional norms.

Garfinkel vigorously disagreed with this emphasis. He insisted on the fundamental fact that for norms, values and social institutions to exist at all, the parties must somehow know what they are doing and grasp that their understanding is a joint, shared understanding. There is then this primordial social reasoning and shared sense-making that make up the vast majority of our ordinary social experience, and which inform our every move in the world of everyday life. Inspired by this conception, and drawing on Husserl and a sociological follower, Alfred Schutz (1962), for help, Garfinkel sought to develop a sociology of the common-sense world of everyday life. This sociology would focus on how meaning, understanding, knowledge and communication work in the everyday world. It would study how we use social rules and imperfect knowledge bases to achieve ordinary activities and mutual understanding in our daily lives. It would be a sociology focused on practical action, rather than one divorced from it.

Key Issues

Rules and Shared Reasoning

Garfinkel's sociology is based on the idea that common-sense reasoning is *methodical*, that is, based on methods. The methods must be social and shared, otherwise actors would not be able to reason towards the same conclusions, understand one another and act in a co-ordinated fashion. But how to uncover this 'methodology'? To do this, Garfinkel hit on some brilliant quasi-experimental procedures that interfere with the smooth workings of everyday actions.

One of the first of these (Garfinkel 1963) involved violating the rules of a simple game – ticktacktoe (British noughts and crosses). The rules of ticktacktoe do two things. As *rules of action,* they define a domain of possible actions within the field of the game and they specify how those actions should occur. They specify, for example, that the players will take alternate turns, that the moves will consist of making marks within the nine cells available, that once a cell is filled it cannot be altered, that the object of the game is to get three in a row and so on.

But the rules also supply a *method of understanding* the moves in the game, and because everyone who knows how to play knows the rules, the rules supply a shared method for understanding what is going on in any state of the game. For instance, the rules can let you see that in a game that has come to a situation like Figure 13.1,

Figure 13.1   **Figure 13.2**

the person playing 'O' is in a 'fork' and has no chance of winning. Or relatedly, they can be used to see (Figure 13.2) that 'X' has 'two in a row' and is threatening to beat 'O'. They can also be used to see that if you 'miss' seeing that 'two in a row', you are being inattentive. When you are playing with a ten-year-old child, missing 'two in a row' can leave you open to the accusation that you are not playing properly and that 'it's not fair' because 'you're letting me win'.

In his experiment, Garfinkel had student experimenters invite another person to play the game, and suggest that the other person make the first move (Figure 13.3). But when the subject had made that move (most subjects did so because moving first gives you an advantage in ticktacktoe), the experimenter would erase the subject's mark, move it to another cell, and then make the second move (for example Figure 13.4).

Figure 13.3   **Figure 13.4**

In over 250 trials of this procedure, Garfinkel asked the experimenters to determine the nature and strength of the subjects' reactions to what had happened; 95 per cent of the subjects reacted in some way, and over 75 per cent either objected to it strongly or demanded some kind of explanation for it. These people could not make sense of what was going on, but clung to the idea that the experimenter *ought* to be playing ticktacktoe. A small minority, however, laughed at the experimenter, or played along by erasing the experimenter's mark, moving it to another cell and then making a further move of their own. These people had obviously abandoned the idea that they were playing a traditional game of ticktacktoe, and they were able to make sense of what was going on as a joke or a 'new type of game'. Most people did not make sense of the situation in this way, and these people generally had the stronger emotional reactions to the experiment.

Garfinkel interpreted the results of this experiment in the following way. Although anger might be a natural reaction when the subjects saw that the ticktacktoe's *rules of action* had been violated, in fact not everyone became angry. The minority who did not were the ones who could continue to make sense of what was going on. Thus it was the use of ticktacktoe's rules as rules for understanding that was critical in shaping reactions. The persons who hung on to the rules as a means of making sense of the situation were confused and frustrated and angry. Those who abandoned the rules – and saw the situation as a joke or a new game – remained relaxed. In short, it was how the persons succeeded or failed to make sense of the situation, that shaped whether they reacted emotionally or not.

In this simple game situation, it was clear that the participants used the rules as guidelines for action *and* as guidelines for understanding the meaning of what was going on. The rules of ticktacktoe were their 'ethnomethods' for operating in the game situation. These results gave rise to one of Garfinkel's core ideas: *the same set of rules and norms that guide or inform the production of action, also guide or inform reasoning about action.*[4]

This core idea links to a second key concept in Garfinkel's work: the concept of *accountability*. He uses this term in two senses: first, as a synonym for intelligible. In this usage an accountable action is an intelligible action and one which we can therefore name, or describe or, more generally, 'give an account of'. The second sense is the more usual moral one in which we speak of someone being 'accountable for their actions'. These two senses link back to Garfinkel's argument in the ticktacktoe experiment that rules are resources both to guide actions and to make sense of them. The notion of accountability helps to consolidate the idea that reasoning actors use rules to make sense of one another and hold one another to account. The question now becomes: what are these rules like, how do they work, what are their properties, how extensive are they?

Reasoning Using Background Knowledge

If the world was organized like the game of ticktacktoe, then it would be quite a simple matter to analyze how action, meaning and mutual understanding are achieved in everyday life. However, this is not so. There are considerable differences between games and real life. Games have a peculiar time structure, relative to most events of daily life, in that they have a determinate end point. Again, success or failure is defined inside the parameters of the game itself and is not subject to later developments outside the game. Compare this situation with President George Bush and the Gulf War. When American armor rolled across Iraq, Bush was feted as the unchallenged victor of the Gulf War. But in the following year when the US presidential elections were contested, Saddam Hussein's continued domination of Iraq was cited as evidence that Bush's mission had failed, and Bush lost the election. Perhaps most important, the rules of games operate independently of other features of persons – they do not alter if you are playing against a person of the opposite sex, or a movie star or whatever. In real life, by contrast, we have all kinds of *background knowledge* about people and circumstances that we employ and take account of in our dealings with them.

Garfinkel demonstrated the importance of this background knowledge using a simple two-part exercise. Undergraduate students were asked to go home and to observe what was happening under the assumption that they were just lodgers in the house and did not know the people who lived there. They had to do this for between fifteen minutes and an hour. This meant suspending their background knowledge about the identities, personalities and biographies of their own family members. They were asked to write out what they saw and to report on their own feelings while they did this. Here is the kind of thing they wrote:

A short, stout man entered the house, kissed me on the cheek and asked 'How was school?' I answered politely. He walked into the kitchen, kissed the younger of the two women and said hello to the other. The younger woman asked me, 'What do you want for dinner honey?' I answered, 'Nothing.' She shrugged her shoulders and said no more. The older woman shuffled around the kitchen muttering. The man washed his hands, sat down at the table and picked up the paper. He read until the two women had finished putting the food on the table. The three sat down. They exchanged idle chatter about the day's events. The older woman said something in a foreign language which made the others laugh. (Garfinkel 1967a, p. 44)

Garfinkel notes that, once the students had adopted this attitude, they were surprised about how personal people's treatments of each other were. That, within this attitude, family news turned into trivial talk. That people who were criticized were not allowed to stand on their dignity nor to take offence. The students found that hostility and bickering became uncomfortably visible. Most of them said they were glad when the hour was up and they could go back, as they put it, 'to being the real me'. The study highlights the extent to which we all use background knowledge to 'typify' or 'normalize' our view of everyday events. The students suspended their use of these assumptions for just a few minutes and found they were 'seeing' in a dramatically different way that they found uncomfortable and not quite 'real'.

In the second part of this experiment, Garfinkel gave the same instructions only with the addition that the students were not just to look at the scene as lodgers, but to act in that way. Here the consequences were much more dramatic!

Family members were stupefied. They vigorously sought to make the strange actions intelligible and to restore the situation to normal appearances. Reports were filled with accounts of astonishment, bewilderment, shock, anxiety, embarrassment and anger and with charges by various family members that the student was mean, inconsiderate, selfish, nasty or impolite. (Garfinkel 1967a, p. 47)

The family members also worked very hard to try to normalize and make sense of what was going on: the student was working 'too hard' at school, there had been 'another fight' with a fiancée, and so on. However they were infuriated when these explanations were not acknowledged. At all times, family members sought to restore normality by supplying some sort of routine set of background understandings that could 'make sense' of what was going on.

Garfinkel argues that we continually use this kind of background knowledge to understand everything that happens around us. His famous 'breaching experiments' demonstrated this clearly. These experiments involved demanding that people clarify the sense of their ordinary remarks. Here is the kind of thing that happened:

Case 3

On Friday night my husband and I were watching television. My husband remarked that he was tired. I asked 'How are you tired? Physically, mentally or just bored?'

> S: I don't know, I guess physically, mainly.
> E: You mean that your muscles ache or your bones?
> S: I guess so. Don't be so technical.
> (*After more watching*)
> S: All these old movies have the same kind of old iron bedstead in them.
> E: What do you mean? Do you mean all old movies, or some of them, or just the ones you have seen?
> S: What's the matter with you? You know what I mean.
> E: I wish you would be more specific.
> S: You know what I mean! Drop dead! (Garfinkel 1967a, p. 42).

What has happened here? The experimenter (E) has refused to 'make sense' of what the subject (S) says, and has done so in a particular way: by refusing to use her background knowledge of the world to see how the subject's remarks 'make sense'. And when the students repeated this kind of procedure, they found that this refusal had the same effect whenever and with whomever it was used. Experiment after experiment ran off like that, with the subjects reacting with anger and outrage after extremely short periods of time. There is no quicker way, it appears, of provoking moral outrage than by not using background knowledge to make sense of other people's actions. A co-participant can become enraged in seconds – infinitely quicker than becoming angry in an argument about abortion or capital punishment or other issues which you would think have much more potential for conflict.

Let me now summarize Garfinkel's conclusions from all this. They are relatively straightforward. Much of the time we are engaged in achieving mutual understanding by using background knowledge to 'fill in' the meaning of what people say and do. This is a fundamental activity – more fundamental than anything else we do. We absolutely rely on one another's capacities and preparedness to maintain this shared universe. Garfinkel uses the term 'trust' to describe this reliance. Trust involves our expectation that others will work to see the world as we do. Garfinkel argues that, as the term implies, this expectation is a moral one. Making sense is something we morally require of one another.

Producing Sense in Context: The Documentary Method of Interpretation

If sense-making is active and uses background knowledge, how does it work? One of Garfinkel's core ideas in this regard involved a process which, following Mannheim, he called the 'documentary method of interpretation' (Garfinkel 1967a, p. 78). The documentary method, Mannheim said, involves a search for an underlying pattern behind surface appearances. The method basically involves treating actual appearances as 'pointing to' or 'standing on behalf of' a presupposed underlying pattern. In it, you derive an underlying pattern from appearances. But, Garfinkel added, there is an element of circularity in this process of fitting appearances to a pattern because once you have used the appearances to decide what the underlying pattern is, you then use the pattern you have decided on to further interpret the appearances. You can see this process best with gestalt-type figures such as Figure 13.5 (Wittgenstein 1958, p. 194).

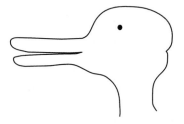

Figure 13.5

Let us assume this figure is a 'duck' and label it accordingly. We have now determined an 'underlying pattern' (the 'duck' pattern) from the appearances of the figure. Notice how this shapes (or reshapes) our view of the individual appearances: those protuberances on the left are the duck's beak, the dot in the middle is the eye, and that bump at the back of his head is an accidental dent – maybe our duck had a narrow escape! But once you construct that same dent as a 'mouth', you begin to see the 'duck' as a 'rabbit' and then you 'see' the protuberances on the left as 'ears' and so on. In each case, we draw on 'background knowledge' about the world in this circular process to fit together 'what we see' with 'what we know'.

Garfinkel argues that this process is continually used in every waking moment to make sense of the world: we recognize dogs, postmen, greetings, social class, bureaucratic red tape, and 'introverted people' using this method. Most of the time, the results of the method are so 'obvious' that we do not notice how we use background knowledge to recognize things. But we become aware of the process when we are faced with ambiguous things. Max Atkinson (1971, p. 181) wrote about a situation in which 'a widow aged 83 was found gassed in the kitchen of her cottage, where she had lived alone since the death of her husband. Rugs and towels had been stuffed under the doors and around the window casements.' As an exercise, try working out the different ways in which your 'background knowledge' of how the world works can make sense of this situation. Use your background knowledge of human motives and physical circumstances to form a picture of how this old person died. Was it suicide, murder or accidental death? What additional information would cause you to rethink and reapply the documentary method of interpretation?

Producing Facts

To see the documentary method of interpretation at work is to realize that every 'fact' in the world has been created using this process. This very much includes the facts that the sciences and the social sciences have to deal with. Garfinkel has illustrated this point with discussions of many issues, including how social scientists make sense of medical records (Garfinkel 1967a, pp. 208–61), how astronomers discover new objects in the sky (Garfinkel *et al.* 1981), and how the police determine whether a dead person committed suicide (Garfinkel 1967b). For example, scientists often have to decide whether an important observation reflects the 'real thing' or is just a product of equipment malfunction. That decision involves making a 'judgment', and that judgment involves using the documentary method of interpretation. The situation is no different for economists evaluating employment data, or medical researchers deciding whether the evidence favors a certain treatment for cancer. Understanding that this is the case does not mean that scientists behave unscientifically and cannot get good results. As we have seen, the documentary method is not something that one can avoid using, and there is plenty of valid science out there.

In some areas though, an understanding of how facts are produced can generate a rethinking of fundamental ideas. I will illustrate this by reference to suicide analysis, which Garfinkel studied. **Durkheim**, the sociological pioneer in the study of suicide, argued that we should ignore subjective opinions and focus on social facts like the suicide rate. Garfinkel argued the reverse: that the suicide statistics are created by policemen who have opinions which, via the documentary method, feed into legal judgments. These judgments, in total, add up to the suicide statistics. The question is how are those judgments made?

Several studies have followed Garfinkel's initiative. They show that the police who investigate cases of death have to coordinate two sorts of facts: the circumstances in which the death took place and the nature of the dead persons themselves (Atkinson 1978; Taylor 1982). The police rank the circumstances of death into sets ranging from almost certain suicide (for example gassing or hanging) to almost certain accidents (for example car crashes). They also rank people into those who are more or less likely to commit suicide: more likely are people who are lonely, or ill, or bereaved, the depressed and people who have had financial disasters. Less likely are people who have 'reasons to live' (for example people with children) or who may be frightened of perdition (for example Catholics). It is rather clear that these assumptions, when fed into actual judgments about suicide, can help account for the distributions of suicides that Durkheim found so important. And other people who share these assumptions and are motivated to manipulate them – the deceased, the family members, coroners and other legal officials – can also strongly impact the suicide statistics (Douglas 1967; Atkinson *et al.* 1975; Day 1987). Understanding that 'facts' are always socially produced, and understanding how they are produced can have a major impact in grasping how everyday judgments affect large-scale societal phenomena.

Producing People and Institutions: Agnes and Gender

Earlier we saw that the notion of accountability helps to consolidate the idea that reasoning actors use rules to make sense of one another and hold one another to account. When you add in background knowledge and the documentary method of interpretation, you get a dynamic view of people and actions operating within a highly complex social framework of accountability. You also get a highly dynamic view of social institutions. Because, via frameworks of accountability, *people's actions reproduce social facts and social institutions.*

Garfinkel demonstrated this in the most vivid way imaginable with the help of a transsexual called 'Agnes' who was born a boy, but who arrived in Los Angeles in search of a sex-change operation (Garfinkel 1967a, pp. 116–85). We normally think that sex and, to a lesser degree, gender are natural attributes 'ordained by nature'. Agnes knew differently. She could manipulate the appearances of sex and gender and, because of her special concerns, she became an intensely astute observer of how we manage to 'do being male' or 'do being female' in society. In the late 1950s, Garfinkel interviewed Agnes extensively about how she managed to bring off her female identity and more generally about 'doing gender' (West and Zimmerman 1987). He found that she had a deep and detailed understanding about how gender shapes both the kinds of actions we can perform, and how we go about doing them and accounting for them. And she understood that to succeed it was vital to have 'female' memories, emotions and reasoning. In her dealings with Garfinkel (and the University of California, Los Angeles medical staff), Agnes always said she was 'naturally' female. She always insisted that she had 'nothing in common' with male homosexuals, transvestites or 'other' transsexuals.

In the end, Agnes got her sex-change operation and sometime later she revealed that she had been taking her mother's birth control pills (which were full of estrogen – a female hormone) since she was twelve. The revelation confirmed just how profoundly Agnes understood the significance of our claims about naturalness when we manage ourselves inside the social institution of gender. She had used that understanding to manipulate Garfinkel and the UCLA doctors into believing in her 'naturalness' as a female. For without convincing them of this, she could not have convinced them to do the sex-change operation.

Sex and gender are things that most people take for granted as natural and 'pre-ordained' – in sociological terms an 'ascribed' characteristic. With Agnes as evidence, Garfinkel was able to show that in fact our sex and gender status is something that we achieve and re-achieve, from moment to moment and day to day across our entire lifetimes. And in this same process, we all dynamically, though often in unwitting fashion, achieve and re-achieve gender as a massive, omnipresent social institution. The paradox that Agnes helps us to see is that while we 'achieve' gender, we view our achievement as an 'ascribed' characteristic – a phenomenon known as 'reification'. Garfinkel's study of Agnes has inspired a great deal of subsequent thinking in this area, and it anticipated by a number of years how 'gender' is conceived in feminist studies (Smith 1987).

Seeing Things Differently

Ethnomethodology's message is: think of the social world as a production, as a 'produced world'. Think of this world as constantly produced and reproduced by sense-makers, who make decisions and act on the basis of the sense they make. Once you start to think this way, everything changes. You can see how the editing in a movie or TV show exploits your own use of the 'documentary method' to build the impression of continuity into observations that would otherwise be 'discontinuous'. You can start to see how your own ideas about people's 'characters' are constructed. You can start to see that science, music and law have their own ethnomethods, and so do police work, economic forecasting and software design.

To give you a straightforward idea of what it means to see the world as 'produced' in this way, I will draw on a study of political speeches done by Atkinson (1984) a few years ago. Atkinson's focus was on how the speeches got applauded. We tend to think of applause as happening at moments when speakers say things the audience agrees with, and as being more likely to happen when the speakers are popular in the first place. Atkinson argued that these things are true, but they are not sufficient to get audience reaction to what a speaker says. Instead, he argued that there is an ethnomethodology of audience reaction. The ethnomethods of applause arise from the situation of each individual in the audience.

Think of yourself as an audience member. You like what you are hearing and you would like to express that feeling by applauding. But that desire is matched by an anxiety: what if you are the only one to start applauding? It would be humiliating to find yourself to be that one person in a 1000-person hall! Each audience member has that dilemma, and audiences will only applaud when speakers 'solve' that dilemma for them. Atkinson showed that politicians solve the dilemma by signalling ahead of time that there will be a place in the speech where it will be 'safe' to applaud. When everyone can anticipate that place, they will be more likely to applaud and, by a kind of self-fulfilling prophecy, everyone will be prepared to risk it. The result is a 'burst' of applause.

How do the signals work? Atkinson showed they are embedded in what the speaker is saying: safe places to applaud work by being emphatic and by being predictable. In particular, two highly predictable kinds of rhetorical statement fit this bill. One kind is the contrastive statement, such as President Kennedy's 'Ask not what your country can do for you. Ask what you can do for your country.' The other kind is the statement formatted in three's, such as Churchill's 'Never in the field of human conflict has so much, been owed by so many to so few.' (Actually this statement uses contrast – between 'many' and 'few' – as well.) Statistical studies of speeches later showed that at least two-thirds of all audience reaction to political speeches is organized by this bit of speech ethnomethodology (Heritage and Greatbatch 1986).

How does this change our perception of speeches and speakers? It does not undermine the idea that audiences applaud things and speakers that they like. But it shows that underlying this there is an ethnomethodological 'mechanics'. No matter how much you admire a person or agree with the point she or he is making, you are unlikely to applaud unless the mechanics are in place. It also turns out that 'charismatic' speakers like John F. Kennedy and Martin Luther King have intricate mastery of these methods (Atkinson 1985). 'Charisma' too is a 'produced' phenomenon.

Ethnomethodology's fundamental reorientation of thought about society is simply this. At the foundation of society is shared sense-making. And there can be no recognizable, shared social world independent of the use of a shared methodology – a shared set of ethnomethods – to achieve it. The production of the entire sensible social world of objects, activities and institutions is based on these ethnomethods.

Legacies and Unfinished Business

Garfinkel is very much alive and still working, so this is an interim view of his legacy. When they first came out, Garfinkel's ideas were treated as peculiar, outrageous or even scandalous. Yet his ideas have permeated almost the whole of sociological theory today. Most theories that make reference to such things as background understandings, taken-for-granted knowledge, practical reasoning, social practices, the production and reproduction of social institutions bear the marks of Garfinkel's influence.

In terms of specific research, ethnomethodology has been particularly successful in areas where more traditional sociology has not done so well – in fields like science, law, music, art and so on. These are all areas of society whose members do use specific 'methodologies' to do their work. Obviously these are highly amenable to ethnomethodological study.

Another area of study where ethnomethodology has established a huge presence is the study of communication in social interaction. This field – known as 'conversation analysis' – represents a fusion between Garfinkel's ideas about the order of sense-making and Goffman's ideas about the 'interaction order'. It is now one of the pre-eminent ways of studying social interaction and language use in the world.

Not surprisingly, ethnomethodology has also established a large presence in the study of artificial intelligence, human–computer interfaces, cyberspace and the application of high technology systems.

Further Reading

A. Cicourel, *The Social Organization of Juvenile Justice* (New York: Wiley, 1968). A classic study of how police beliefs about juvenile offenders are transformed into objective statistics about juvenile offenses and the kind of people who commit them.

P. Drew and J. Heritage (eds), *Talk at Work* (Cambridge: Cambridge University Press, 1992). A set of papers using conversation analysis to study how people work in everyday and professional contexts.

H. Garfinkel, *Studies in Ethnomethodology* (Englewood Cliffs, NJ: Prentice-Hall, 1967). This is a fundamental reference point. The book is complicated to read but, oddly, very clear. Bear in mind when you read it that the author was anthologized in a collection of the best American short stories of 1941: he is not a bad writer!

J. Heritage, *Garfinkel and Ethnomethodology* (Cambridge: Polity Press, 1984). An introduction to Garfinkel's ideas.

M. Lynch, *Scientific Practice and Ordinary Action: Ethnomethodology and Social Studies of Science* (Cambridge: Cambridge University Press, 1996). A very sophisticated account of ethnomethodology in relation to the analysis of science.

M. Pollner, *Mundane Reason* (Cambridge: Cambridge University Press, 1987). A beautifully written analysis of how our sense of reality is methodically sustained.

H. Sacks, *Lectures on Conversation* (Oxford: Blackwell, 1992). The originating ideas behind conversation analysis.

E. Schegloff and H. Sacks, 'Opening up closings', *Semiotica*, **8**, 1973, 289–327. A classic paper in conversation analysis. This gives a good idea of how conversation analysts reason about conversational interaction.

Finally, there are a number of sites on the World Wide Web that are devoted to ethnomethodology. A good starting point is: http://www.pscw.uva.nl/emca/index.htm This site carries a great deal of basic information about all aspects of contemporary work in the field.

14

Louis Althusser

Ted Benton

Driving Impulses

Louis Althusser was a **Marxist** philosopher and social theorist. He was certainly the most influential Marxist thinker of his time, and one of the most influential social theorists working in any tradition. Essays written by him in the 1960s had the greatest and most long-lasting impact. He continued to publish through the 1970s, becoming increasingly explicit in his criticisms of the French Communist Party leadership. Finally the personal turmoil and madness which had been ever present in his life led to tragedy and confinement in a psychiatric institution for much of his last decade.

Althusser was born in Algeria, later (in 1930) moving to France with his parents. According to his autobiography his childhood was very unhappy, tormented by contradictory relationships with his powerful and authoritarian but very distant father, and his sexually repressed and obsessive mother, whose love he experienced as overpowering. Brought up as a Catholic, he spent much of the war in a German prisoner-of-war camp. It was here that he met and was deeply impressed by a fellow prisoner – a Communist named Courrèges. After the war Althusser returned to the Ecole Normale Supérieure in Paris as a student. The French Communists had played a crucial role in the resistance against the Nazis during the war, and were represented in the postwar government. Their influence on French public life, and on intellectuals in particular, was very great. Partly because of his wartime experience, and partly because he had been impressed by Communists he encountered through his involvement in Catholic youth organisations, Althusser joined the Party soon after the war. However, from the beginning he was a dissident within the organisation. As an independent-minded intellectual he found himself in frequent conflict with the Party leadership and the 'official' Party theorists.

The death of Stalin, and the subsequent limited liberalisation which took place in the Soviet Union under Khrushchev in the late 1950s, together with the growing split between the Soviet Union and Communist China had their impact on left-wing circles in France. Small Communist groupings were formed, especially among students, which followed the teachings of Mao

Zedong. The French Communist Party itself, as well as influential intellectuals on the left such as Sartre, Merleau Ponty and Garaudy expressed their moral objection to Stalinism by way of a return to the 'humanist' philosophy of Marx's early writings. In those texts (most especially the famous 'Economic and Philosophical Manuscripts' of 1844) Marx had sketched out a brilliantly original philosophical theory, according to which human history could be seen as a long journey through which the whole species passes through a series of developmental stages on its way to a future in which all individual and collective human potential is fully realised. However, the current phase of history, for Marx, was one in which human potential was stunted and distorted by the prevailing capitalist system. Under this system, workers were 'alienated', or separated from their own autonomous life-activity, because they had to work under the control of the capitalist owners. As a result they could not find fulfilment in work, were set into competitive relationships with other workers, and into class opposition to their employers. All the various dimensions of 'alienation' and opposition produced by capitalist property relations were to be overcome in the future Communist society, which Marx at that time described as 'the riddle of history solved'.

This framework of ideas provided a moral standard by which not only capitalist society could be measured, but also the limitations and 'errors' of the Stalinist type of 'socialism' that had developed in the Soviet Union. Althusser was strongly opposed to this 'humanist' criticism of the Soviet Union and declared himself, scandalously, to be an 'anti-humanist'. This has led to accusations that his work was just a sophisticated justification for Stalinism, and that he did not care about people! In fact, what Althusser wanted was a much more deep-rooted criticism of Stalinism, and an explanation of how the great Soviet attempt at human liberation had ended in oppressive dictatorship. Mere moral condemnation was not enough – the whole terrible process had to be analysed and explained. And, for a Marxist, that meant putting Marxist theory itself to the test of explaining the consequences of the first attempt in history to put it into practice. For Althusser, the problem with the humanist interpretations of Marx was that they implicitly threw out Marx's most important theoretical breakthrough: the establishment of a 'scientific' understanding of historical processes. He thought that Khrushchev's attempt to 'de-Stalinise' the Communist movement had failed, and that moral criticism, while it was certainly justified, could not of itself change anything. Instead, what was needed was a careful recovery and further development of Marx's explanatory approach ('historical materialism'), and of the philosophical work which was necessary to make this recovery possible. Only this return to theory could lead to a renewal of Marxist theory and practice, after decades of distortion by the demands of obedience to the interests of the Soviet state, and unquestioning loyalty to Party bosses. As he later put it in his autobiography: 'only theoretical antihumanism justified genuine, practical humanism' (Althusser 1993, p. 186).

According to Althusser's own account, French culture was very insular during the period when his own ideas were forming. He and his fellow philosophers were rather ignorant of other British and European ways of thinking – even of the work of important non-French Marxists, such as Antonio Gramsci. So, in developing his opposition to the 'humanist' take-over of Marxism, Althusser drew mainly on other influential traditions in French philosophy and social thought. First, his defence of a version of Marxism as a science involved him in a search for a theory of the nature of science: what made science different from everyday thought, or 'ideology'? How do new sciences emerge? How should change in scientific ideas be understood and explained? Althusser's most immediate influence in thinking about these issues was Georges Canguilhem (1988). Canguilhem was a historian and philosopher of science, and belonged to a distinctive French tradition of thinking about science (Alexandre Koyré and Gaston Bachelard were two other famous thinkers in this tradition). Their approach differed from the empiricist philosophy of science which was the dominant view in Britain and America, in that the French based their view of science on careful historical study. This brought into view processes of interaction between science and the wider society, and also suggested that the criteria for what was to count as science changed as science itself changed through time.

But this French school of historians and philosophers of science had concerned themselves mainly with the natural sciences. Althusser was mainly concerned with a defence of Marxism as a social and historical science, and so he had to look for an approach in the human sciences which would provide a viable alternative to the 'humanism' of Sartre, Merleau Ponty and the others. In this he found his main allies in the 'structuralist' approaches which were already doing battle with humanism in psychology, linguistics, anthropology and sociology. **Durkheim**'s instruction to sociologists to 'treat social facts as things', and Ferdinand de Saussure's similar view of language as a social fact, existing independently of the individual purposes of the users of language, were 'founding figures' of structuralism. The anthropologist Claude Lévi-Strauss was perhaps the best-known structuralist among Althusser's contemporaries, but Althusser himself was most influenced by the structuralist interpretation of Freudian psychoanalysis developed by Jacques Lacan. Given Althusser's personal history of recurrent depressions and crises of identity, it is perhaps not surprising that he should have developed a strong theoretical interest in psychoanalysis. Although Althusser repeatedly refused to identify himself as a structuralist, there is no mistaking the influence of structuralist themes in his reconstruction of Marx's historical materialism as a science.

Key Issues

So, armed with historical philosophy of science, and with structuralism as his ally, Althusser set out to 'rescue' the true Marx from the interpretations imposed on his work by 'humanist' philosophers. The results of this work were set out in a series of articles written between 1960 and 1965, and published together as *For Marx,* and in a collaborative work with students (including Rancière and Balibar – who became important thinkers in their own right) called *Reading Capital.* Given that the 'humanists' clearly had a good case for their interpretation of Marx's early works, and especially the brilliant and captivating *Manuscripts* of 1844, Althusser's task was to show that the Marx of 1844 was not yet a Marxist! (even Marx himself, despairing of misinterpretations of his ideas, had insisted *he* was not a Marxist). The essays in *For Marx* are mainly devoted to that task, while *Reading Capital* sets out the basic concepts of 'historical materialism', as derived from the authors' reading and discussion of Marx's later writings.

The Relationship between Marx's Earlier and Later Works

First, then, the account of the relationship between Marx's earlier and later works. Althusser's approach draws upon three key ideas which he takes from Canguilhem and the historical philosophers of science. The first of these is the notion that scientific concepts are not invented one by one, but form a definite interconnected framework, or pattern of thought, each concept getting its meaning from its relationship to the others. This conceptual framework determines what questions or problems can be posed within it, and so, also, excludes the posing of questions which might arise in an alternative framework: it could be compared to the beam of a torch which illuminates everything upon which it falls, but leaves everything else in shadow. This aspect of a science is called its 'problematic'.

The second idea which Althusser uses is that the history of science is discontinuous. That is to say, a new science emerges from previous patterns of non-scientific thinking in its field by establishing a clear conceptual distance from those earlier ideas. The 'ideological' problematics which precede the emergence of a new science are often linked with the wider culture of the society, its 'common sense', or dominant ideology. This means that even after its establishment a new science will continue to be surrounded by ways of thinking which it overthrew as part of the process whereby it came into existence. It follows that scientific problematics are discontinuous with both the patterns of ideas from which they emerged, and with the 'common sense' of the wider culture within which they continue to exist. The history of science is discontinuous in the further respect that, even when it has become established, new problems and solutions are generated which produce subsequent restructurings of the original scientific problematic. Althusser calls the shift from pre-scientific ideologies to the emergent scientific problematic an 'epistemological break'. Third, Althusser follows the historical philosophers of science in recognising that scientific work is not just a matter of gaining new knowledge. For them, ignorance is not just lack of knowledge, but, rather, powerful patterns of erroneous thinking, which are always present, invading and obstructing scientific advance: so science is a struggle to resist and overcome these invading 'epistemological obstacles'.

An example from the natural sciences might help to make it clear how these ideas work. In the late 1830s Charles Darwin was struggling to understand how one living species gives rise to another. His notebooks reveal his realisation that the new ideas he was developing called into question existing religious orthodoxy, as well as the belief that each species remained constant which predominated among the leading scientists of the day. He knew his ideas, which broke with previous assumptions of the special creation of each species and made humans and apes close kin (his 'epistemological break'), would create a scandal. This may be one reason why he waited twenty years before making his scientific breakthrough public. However, after the publication of his *Origin of Species*, his ideas eventually became widely accepted and incorporated into a view of humans (often, in racialist versions, a view of the white European races) as at the apex of the evolutionary process – as if the evolution of life could be told as a story in which the climax is the arrival of humans (or, in the racialist versions, the 'superior' races). These ways of popularising evolutionary biology reasserted human self-importance, implied that progress was written into nature itself, gave some ideologists a scientific backing for their belief in markets and capitalism, and were used to justify the colonisation (even genocide) of non-European peoples.

In fact, however, a close reading of both the notebooks and the *Origin of Species* shows that these uses of Darwin's ideas are quite inconsistent with his scientific 'problematic'. The mechanism of 'natural selection' leads, in his theory, to a gradual change in a species as it adapts, through many generations, to its local environment. On that theory it makes no sense to talk of 'higher' and 'lower' animals, of 'primitive' and 'advanced' forms. As an organism adapted to its environment, a cat-flea is no more nor less 'evolved' than the cat it lives on. In his early notebooks Darwin even compares our treatment of other animals with slavery – to which he was passionately opposed. However, in some later writings, such as his *Descent of Man*, Darwin seems to give in to this misunderstanding of evolution as progressive development, and even to the prevailing views of a hierarchy among the human races. So, evolution as progressive development, beliefs in racial superiority, and human self-importance can be seen as 'epistemological obstacles': Darwin had to struggle against them in order to establish the scientific problematic of evolutionary biology, but they persist as powerful forces in the wider culture, and even go on to 'invade' Darwin's own subsequent writings.

Parallel considerations apply to Marx's work. He had to establish his scientific breakthrough by struggling against the powerful attractions of earlier 'humanist' understandings of history. In Marx's case these pre-scientific ideologies were, most importantly, Hegel's idealist view of history as a 'dialectical' process of self-development of 'absolute spirit', and second, Ludwig Feuerbach's materialist 'inversion' of Hegel's philosophy. In Feuerbach's philosophy, history is understood as, again, a process of self-development, but, now, of the human species itself, not 'absolute spirit'. Althusser reads the early work of Marx as a further development of Feuerbach's 'problematic', which draws upon the economic theories of the time to explain the material basis for human self-alienation, and on the Communist and socialist thought of the time to provide a vision of the future full of self-realisation of humanity. However, because this is merely a development of the Feuerbachian 'problematic', and because this, in turn, had only 'inverted' Hegel's philosophy, the problematic of the early Marx is still trapped within the terms of the idealist philosophy. In short, Marx has to make a break from his own earlier 'problematic', has to struggle against his own former self, in order to establish a genuinely scientific approach to the study of history and society.

This, Althusser claims, started to happen from about 1845 onwards. Of course, such a profound intellectual achievement does not take place all at once, and the actual texts written during the next few years still contain passages which can be read as continuing the 'humanist' and 'historicist' themes of the early writings. This is what fuels the humanist interpretations of Marx against which Althusser is campaigning. There certainly are passages in which Marx seems to be clearly rejecting his early philosophy, as when he denounces philosophers who 'neatly trim the epochs of history' so as to fit them into their theories, and when he insists on the necessity for empirical study for the proper understanding of history. However, Althusser does not rely on the trading of rival quotations. Instead he makes use of the structuralist concept of a 'symptomatic' reading. According to this idea the underlying conceptual structure or 'problematic' is not immediately obvious from the flow of words and sentences in a text. This latter can be compared to the rippling surface of a river, which is not directly determined by the underlying currents of water, but which provides clues to, or 'symptoms' of, them. Althusser's method is to analyse each text, looking for dislocations, contradictions, unresolved tensions and so on, and then to work back to the underlying problematics which generate them.

Anti-historicism

Using this method of symptomatic reading, Althusser is able to confirm the presence of an 'epistemological break' in Marx's thinking, with the emergence of a new and 'scientific' problematic from 1845 onwards. This enables

Althusser to say what Marxism (or 'historical materialism') is *not*, as well as to begin the process of unearthing or recovering what Marxism is. We can begin with what Marxism is now understood *not* to be. For Althusser, of course, the important 'nots' are 'humanism' and 'historicism'. These two 'isms' are closely linked to each other, but it is convenient to consider them separately to begin with. Sometimes the word 'historicism' is used to describe all approaches which emphasise the significance of historical change. However, this is not what Althusser objects to. For him, 'historicism' refers to those accounts of historical change which represent it as a linear series of 'stages' or phases, having a direction, and with an inherent end-point or 'purpose'. This way of thinking about history has many different forms, including Hegel's philosophy of history, Feuerbach's inversion of it, Marx's own early works, and, of course, the humanist interpretations of Marx against which Althusser was arguing. The progressive-evolutionist misinterpretations of Darwin are also examples of it, and it remains deeply engrained in western thinking today, in concepts such as 'modernisation' and 'development'. On Althusser's reading of it, Marx's great breakthrough was to overthrow this way of thinking about history. The faith, often present in the Communist movement, that 'history is on our side', that the eventual victory of the working-class movement was somehow written into the historical process was, in Althusser's view, completely un-Marxist. Historical processes were open-ended. Historical change occurred as a result of the fortuitous coming together – or 'fusion' – of numerous contradictions in society, so that revolutions, far from being inevitable consequences of capitalist 'development', should always be seen as exceptional events. In our own time, 'post-modernist' writers such as Lyotard have proclaimed the end of widespread belief in historical 'meta-narratives' such as Marxism. Ironically, if Althusser's reading is correct, Marx was the first post-modernist!

Anti-humanism

Now to Althusser's criticism of Marxist 'humanism'. One problem here is that it is not always clear what is meant by 'humanism'. There are (at least!) three different things that Althusser might have been objecting to in his 'anti-humanism'. One of these, as we have seen, he explicitly rejects. This is what we might call 'moral humanism': a set of values according to which the primary objects of moral concern are human beings and their welfare. Humanism in this sense is opposed to religious moralities which put duty to God over mere human interests, and to more recent 'ecocentric' value-systems which give equal consideration to human and non-human living creatures. Althusser made it clear that he was not an 'anti-humanist' in this sense. Indeed, as a moral reaction to Stalinist 'errors and crimes' Althusser says humanism has 'a real historical sanction' (Althusser and Balibar 1970, p. 119).

The second possible interpretation is more plausible. In this interpretation, humanism is a philosophical understanding of history as a process which has full development of the human species as its outcome, and which thinks of humans themselves as the agents which bring about their own development – history as human *self*-development. Numerous philosophical views of human 'progress' take this form, and, as we have seen, it is also represented in the philosophies of Feuerbach and the young Marx himself. As Althusser points out, humanism in this sense and historicism constitute different aspects of the same 'problematic'. So, Althusser clearly is against 'humanism' in this sense.

Voluntarism

In the present context (see below) this refers to a view of human actions that tends to overestimate the amount of freedom available to a human actor to do whatever she wants to do. The other side of the same coin is that it also underplays the social influences, pressures and constraints upon the actor and her actions (including the influences of socialisation that will limit quite profoundly even what it will occur to the social actor to 'want' to do). Voluntarism thus entails a view of human agency that is far too free-floating and unsociological.

The third possible meaning of humanism is to describe those approaches which assert the primary role of the conscious agency, or choices of individual human beings (or groups of them) in sociological or historical explanation. This is the form of humanism sometimes called **voluntarism**. It took its most extreme form in Sartre's existentialism, but is still a very widespread approach in mainstream economics, and in 'rational choice' approaches in political science and sociology. The view recently advocated by **Anthony Giddens** of personal identity under conditions of 'reflexive modernisation' as the outcome of a 'project' of self-creation is another example. Althusser's fellow structuralists were strongly opposed to such views. Structuralist approaches are usually committed to a certain view of what an explanation should be like. For them, the surface appearance of things may be misleading as to the real structural causes which underlie them and produce them. Scientific explanation proceeds by a critical analysis of 'appearances' so as to arrive at an adequate account of underlying structures. We have already seen one example of this method in Althusser's practice of 'symptomatic' reading. This method has quite dramatic consequences if we apply it to our own experience and self-understanding. It suggests that we should be sceptical about our own experience of our selves as fully conscious (at least some of the time!) choosers, and in control of our actions, direction in life, and so on. On the structuralist view, the great scientific breakthroughs of the past have all dealt blows to human conceit and self-importance. Copernicus showed that the sun was at the centre of the universe, with the earth as just one of the planets spinning round it. Darwin showed that humans are not results of special creation by God, but just one outcome among millions of the random operation of environmental pressures. Even in the sphere of the human psyche itself, the structuralists recognised **Freud's** concept of the unconscious as a further confirmation of their method. Slips of the tongue, dreams, lapses of memory as well as neurotic and other symptoms of mental illness could all be understood as effects of deep-rooted psychological processes of which the individual remained unaware.

Structuralism, Ideology and Personal Identity

Although Althusser was very wary of identifying himself too closely with structuralism, it was tempting to put Marx's scientific achievements into the same mould. There are many places in Marx's writings where he seems to be arguing that human self-identity and the 'forms of social consciousness' through which people understand and act in the social world are products of their position in the social structure: 'social being determines social consciousness'. Particular types of society give rise to particular patterns of dominant thought, or ideology (for example the link between capitalism and liberal individualism), and a particular position in the class structure will give rise to a particular kind of identity and outlook (for example members of the working class will tend to have socialist ideas, and so on). This kind of approach (which can be traced back to the influence of earlier thinkers, such as Durkheim and his students) further 'decentres' the conscious human subject. Far from being in conscious control of our activity in the social world, we are subject to two levels of influence about which we are unaware – our internal 'unconscious', and the external influence of our social 'conditioning'. Althusser's treatment of this question of the relationship between social structures and the thought and action of individual people was one of the most controversial aspects of his theory, but to see why we have to make a detour into his account of the social structure itself.

Rejection of Economic Determinism

In *Reading Capital,* Althusser and his colleagues provided an analytical account of key concepts in Marx's later view of history and society. The economic structure, or 'mode of production', was analysed as a combination of a set of 'elements' (instruments of labour, the material being worked on, the worker, and, in class societies, owners who do not work) which are bound together by two distinct sorts of relationship – relations necessary to the tasks of production, and ownership relations, through which surplus wealth is acquired by the class of owners. The different types of society that have existed in history, or are found in other parts of the world (ancient, feudal, hunter-gatherer, capitalist, and so on) can be classified in terms of the different ways in which the various elements are combined together. So far, the account is little more than an attempt to make more precise the existing 'orthodox' understanding of Marx's economic thought. However, where the Althusserians parted company with many of their fellow Marxists was in their firm rejection of 'economic determinism'. That is to say, they recognised that whole societies were made up of a number of distinct 'structures' or 'practices', of which the economy was only one. These other practices included ideological, political and 'theoretical' (scientific) practices. Each of these practices has its own reality, its own 'contradictions' (for example conflict between students and university authorities, and ideological struggle conducted by social movements such as the women's movement), and so makes its own distinct contribution to the overall 'flow' of social processes.

Marx himself had drawn an analogy between the relationship of the economy to the legal and political system of a society and the relationship between the 'foundation' and the 'superstructures' of a building. Economic determinist or 'reductionist' versions of Marxism had interpreted this as implying that everything happening 'outside' the economy was a more or less direct consequence, or 'expression', of economic processes. Althusser was critical of the foundation/superstructure analogy, but he also (rightly) points out that it does not imply that nothing important goes on in the superstructures! The real problem was that Marx had not developed an adequate theory of the superstructures to compare with his economic theory. One of the most urgent jobs to be done by contemporary Marxists was to correct this weakness in Marxism by developing theories of ideology and politics. However, Althusser does not revert to a 'pluralist' view of society in which all structures or practices are equal in their contributions to the whole. He retains the view of Marx that economic structures and practices are in some way fundamental – that is, that the 'causal weight' of the economy within the whole society is greater than that of the other social practices. In Althusser's view, implicit in Marx's way of thinking about the internal complexity of whole societies is a novel concept of causality: 'structural causality', according to which the complex whole and the substructures which make it up all influence one another, but some have more influence than others!

Ideological State Apparatuses, Reproductions and Interpellation

Althusser's most systematic treatment of the question of the 'superstructures' came in an essay written soon after the revolutionary events of Paris 1968. In this essay, called 'Ideology and Ideological State Apparatuses' (in Althusser 1971), Althusser shifts from abstract analysis of the structural make-up of society to the question: how is it possible for social structures to persist through time (day to day, year by year, generation by generation)? The key concept Marxists use to think about this process is 'reproduction'. It includes the replacement of elements such as instruments of production as they wear out, and workers as they retire or die, and so on. But it also includes the maintenance of the structures, or persistent patterns of relationships which make up societies. The place of the ideological and political 'superstructures' within whole societies is understood by Althusser by way of this concept of reproduction. The school and the family, for example, play their part in 'reproducing' the labour force, both biologically, and in terms of preparing and distributing people to various positions in society, according to their skills, aptitudes, qualifications, and so on. Also, in the case of class societies (such as capitalism) the prevailing patterns of class domination and subordination, of authority and obedience are also learned as people acquire a certain sense of their own self-identity and place in the wider society.

In developing his account of these processes, Althusser distinguishes between two types of superstructure: the 'Repressive State Apparatuses' (RSAs), such as the police, courts of law, and army, and the 'Ideological State Apparatuses' (ISAs) such as the educational system, trades unions, family, churches, sports clubs and societies, and communications media. The RSAs, as their name implies, function to maintain the social order mainly by the use of coercion (for example the use of police to break strikes, or control demonstrations), while the ISAs function by securing the active consent of the majority to the existing power-relations. Althusser is here following the lead of the Italian Marxist, Antonio Gramsci (1971), in recognising that in most modern western societies the existing system of class domination is 'legitimate'. That is, most people, most of the time, are not in open revolt against the system. The force available to the state is generally kept in reserve, and only used directly when the dominant way of life is challenged by groups such as 'travellers' who can be stigmatised as 'different', or when there is a more powerful threat to the ruling class as in the case of Paris in 1968, or the 1984 miners' strike in Britain. But what Gramsci and Althusser emphasise is that this 'consent' or 'legitimacy' is not spontaneously given by the people. It requires continuous ideological work, conducted under the ideas of the ruling ideology within the institutional framework of the ISAs. As individuals pass from family to school to university or college, as they participate in the rituals of church or sporting associations, watch TV and so on, they acquire a sense of their own personal identity and place in society which at the same time prepares them for a life of (more or less) willing obedience to the requirements and tasks allotted to them.

This process is what Althusser calls 'interpellation': the acquisition by an individual of a sense of who they are, which carries with it a set of ideas about their place in the social world, bound up with the necessary skills and attitudes to fit them for their 'destination' in work, family, leisure and so on.

Now, where Althusser departs from Gramsci and previous Marxists is that he offers this as an account of all ideologies. For him, as for structuralist thinkers, and classical sociologists such as Durkheim, individuals acquire their sense of self and place in society as a result of the effects on them of their participation in pre-existing social structures and practices ('socialisation'). This seems to reduce individuals to the status of mere 'puppets' of the social system, and, deeply problematic for a socialist theorist, seems to rule out the possibility that people might come to understand their own subordination and act to change things. In rejecting the 'voluntarism' of the humanists, Althusser seems to have gone over to the opposite extreme of a 'structuralist' denial of human agency. By contrast, Gramsci had recognised the capacity of oppositional groups in society to challenge the 'hegemony' of the ruling ideas through cultural struggle in favour of an alternative ethical vision and way of life. The great difficulty in Althusser's position is that only the independent development of Marxism as a 'science' can provide an alternative to the dominant ideology. As many of his critics pointed out, this carries with it the implication that intellectuals of the Marxist left, such as Althusser himself, will become a privileged 'priesthood' of the revolutionary movement. Althusser himself saw the force of this criticism, and from the beginning of the 1970s began a series of self-criticisms and revisions to his earlier thought, at the same time becoming ever more critical of the Communist Party leadership. It is not clear how far this later body of writing succeeded in resolving the tensions inherent in the earlier work, and there is little doubt that Althusser left a considerable legacy of 'unfinished business'.

Seeing Things Differently

Looking back over my own long struggle to understand Althusser's ideas, and to define my own in relation to them, I can mention a few things which I most value. One is Althusser's intense 'reflexivity' about the crucial connection in his life between his work as a social theorist and his politics. He always recognised that these two things were different, never bending his theory to political expediency. However, he always remained painfully conscious of the political responsibility of intellectuals who conduct their work in the public sphere. Though he never resolved the tensions inherent in this relationship (as with those which destroyed his personal life) his courage in recognising and struggling with them is one from which we can learn. My engagement with Althusser's work also was genuinely 'liberating' in two further respects – one theoretical, the other political. In the realm of theory, the liberation lay in his challenge to Marxist orthodoxy, and the re-establishment of the materialist approach to history and society as an open and creative research programme. For myself, and many other social theorists of my age group, this made it possible for us to use core insights from the Marxist heritage without being constrained by every dot and comma of Marx's writings. We could address questions (such as ecology, or gender and sexuality) upon which Marx himself was of little direct help, and we could make use of non-Marxist ideas where this was of more help (as, of course, had Marx before us!). The political liberation enabled by Althusser is closely connected. His critique of economic determinism, and recognition of the relatively independent role played by non-economic practices in both maintaining and changing society opened up a new set of possible ways of thinking about how change might occur, and who might bring it about. While Althusser himself never quite broke from the 'orthodox' view of the industrial working class as the agent of revolution, his innovations in Marxist theory allow us to think of the independent role which might be played by social movements responding to 'contradictions' between capitalist development and ecological life-support systems, to gender or racial/ethnic oppression and discrimination, or to cultural exclusion. Althusser's theoretical understanding of the complexity of the whole social structure, and the multiplicity of contradictions and tensions in it provides the theoretical basis for the sort of broad alliance between oppositional movements that Gramsci favoured. In several countries now there are attempts to bring together very diverse campaigns and movements in opposition to the prevailing global concentrations of economic, military and political power (in the UK, for example, 'Green Left Convergence' is one attempt to do this – see Red-Green Study Group 1995). These new alliances include people who have backgrounds in socialist, feminist, green, gay rights, civil liberties, peace and other social movements, as well as people who are coming to active politics for the first time. This sort of grass-roots coalition building is quite a long way from the traditional focus of the orthodox Communist Parties on the industrial working class as the sole, or 'leading' agent of social change. So far as socialists are concerned, Althusser's work was one important way through to this new vision of political activity on the left.

Legacies and Unfinished Business

So, what remains today of the Althusserian project? For at least two decades, Althusser's recasting of Marxism as an open research programme was immensely fruitful. Scholars in many countries, working in numerous disciplinary fields in the humanities and social sciences, took off from Althusser's achievements. Anthropologists such as Emanuel Terray (1972) developed new ways for Marxists to think about non-capitalist societies, while Michel Aglietta (1979), Alain Lipietz (1992) and others made important contributions to the understanding of contemporary economic processes, and Pierre Macherey (1978) drew on Althusser's work in his development of a new theory of 'literary production' (see also Terry Eagleton 1983). As we have seen, Althusser anticipated some themes of post-modernist and post-structuralist thought (Derrida and **Foucault** were both students of Althusser). Althusser's emphasis on the relative autonomy of ideological, or 'cultural' processes made possible approaches to the study of culture which avoided the economic (and sociological) determinism that had marred previous Marxist work. The distinctive approach to cultural studies developed in the Birmingham Centre for Contemporary Cultural Studies, especially during the directorship of **Stuart Hall,** owed much to both Althusser and Gramsci. However, a combination of factors, including the wider crisis of Marxism and the associated turn to the study of language as a self-contained system soon led to the study of 'culture' as something quite removed from social and economic relations – the *absolute* autonomy of the superstructures! Within sociology more narrowly defined, structural Marxism inspired systematic work in the sociology of class: Nicos Poulantzas (1973, 1975) and Eric O. Wright (1978, 1985, 1989); feminist sociology: Michèle Barratt (1980, 1988), Mary McIntosh (1978), Juliet Mitchell (1975); urban sociology: Manuel Castells (1977) and in political and historical sociology: Perry Anderson (1974a, b), Bob Jessop (1982), Poulantzas (1978).

The collapse of the former Soviet 'empire', the conversion of the East Asian 'Communist' regimes to capitalism, and the widespread decline of the western Communist Parties can be seen as the final victory of capitalism and liberal democracy. On this sort of view, we have witnessed the end, not just of Marxism and socialism, but of all serious aspirations for a future beyond global capitalism. However, it is remarkable that Marxist thinkers, though now clearly a minority, retain footholds in most disciplinary fields. There is even evidence of a return of interest in Althusser's own work in the wake of the excesses of post-modernism (for example Elliot 1994, Kaplan and Sprinker 1993 and Resch 1992). Moreover, if we remember that Althusser's revitalisation of Marxism could only take place in opposition to the dogmatism of the French Communist Party leadership, with its loyalty to the Soviet state, then it is at least possible that the demise of state and party might favour a new flowering of creative socialist and even Marxist thought in the new world (dis)order. One thing does seem certain: that the terrible consequences in terms of poverty, unemployment, malnutrition, epidemic disease, social dislocation, and ecological destruction of globalising capitalism continue to intensify. None of the issues which first gave rise to the socialist and Communist movements, and made necessary the critical theoretical work of such thinkers as Marx and Althusser has gone away. It will be depressing indeed if a new generation of sociologists continues to look the other way.

15

Jürgen Habermas

William Outhwaite

Driving Impulses

The most important intellectual source of Habermas' thinking is the broad, flexible and interdisciplinary Marxist tradition which inspired what came to be called the 'Frankfurt School' of Critical Theory, based in the early 1930s and again from 1950 in the Institute for Social Research in Frankfurt. As Habermas showed in detail in his *Theory of Communicative Action,* this tradition draws on both **Marx** and **Max Weber,** on another non-Marxist, Weber's contemporary **Georg Simmel,** and on the father of 'western Marxism', Georg Lukács. In an autobiographical interview, Habermas recalls reading Lukács for the first time with great excitement, but with a sense that his work was no longer directly relevant to post-war societies such as West Germany. His thinking remained shaped, however, by a western Marxist agenda emphasizing the interplay between capitalist exploitation and bureaucratic state rule, and their implications for individual identity and collective political autonomy. More concretely, as a member of what has been called the 'Hitler Youth generation', drawn as a child into complicity with the most appalling regime of modern times, he was horrified both by the crimes of the Third Reich and by the unwillingness of his compatriots to face up to their responsibility for what had happened.

To all this Habermas added a concern with technocracy characteristic of the mid twentieth century. He was concerned to construct a socialist response to the technological determinism deriving from Heidegger (whose failure to confront his complicity with Nazism Habermas found particularly repugnant) and, in post-war Germany, from Arnold Gehlen and Helmut Schelsky. For Habermas, the erosion of political choice by technical means was not inevitable, as some critics of technology had argued, but it was a pervasive feature of modern societies. This anxiety has inspired much of Habermas' work, linking his critical analysis of the decline of the public sphere and the rise of technocratic politics with his critique of positivist social science. And his more positive programme of what he has called a theory of communicative action and the theories of morality, law and democracy which it sustains has again the same double focus on theory and practice. In many ways, indeed, his work has come full circle, working out in detail approaches which were presented in a more intuitive manner in his earlier writing.

Instrumental Reason

The form of reasoning devoted to calculating the best way of getting something, the best way of achieving a goal. The focus is on how to do something, how to achieve some goal, how to acquire some object, rather than, for example, on questions of value and worth or principle. Thus one does not focus on why we should do that thing, why we want to achieve that goal (why it is or should be a valued goal), why it is important to acquire that object. Instrumental reason prioritises calculation, achieving efficiency through the optimum calculation of the best 'means' for an already given end (most often 'given' already by bureaucratic or capitalistic environments whose goals are perceived as imperative and non-negotiable), and there is a tendency in modern societies for a disproportionate amount of our energies to be devoted to this form of reasoning.

Habermas' relationship to Frankfurt critical theory was somewhat indirect in the early stages of his career. Max Horkheimer's interests, like those of Theodor Adorno, had become increasingly philosophical, and their critique of **instrumental reason,** expressed in *Dialectic of Enlightenment* (1947) and subsequent works, increasingly despairing. Habermas felt that a revival of critical theory had once again to engage both with philosophy and with the social and human sciences. He fully shared, however, Adorno and Horkheimer's concern with the way in which enlightenment, in the form of instrumental rationality, turns from a means of liberation into a new source of enslavement. 'Already at that time' [the late 1950s], he has written, 'my problem was a theory of modernity, a theory of the pathology of modernity, from the viewpoint of the realization – the deformed realization – of reason in history.'[1] This involved a working-through of the classics: Marx and Weber, but also Kant, Fichte and Hegel – and of course ancient Greek thought. This theoretical emphasis was, however, constantly combined, as in his early volume of essays on *Theory and Practice,* with a concern for the conditions of rational political discussion in modern technocratic democracies. Only the social sciences, broadly conceived, could provide the means to construct a genuinely contemporary critical theory of advanced capitalism, but their own positivistic deformation was itself part of the problem to be overcome.

Key Issues

Communication in the Public Sphere

The issue of the conditions of communication in the public sphere, the subject of Habermas' first major book, *The Structural Transformation of the Public Sphere* (1962) has remained central to his thinking over the following decades. Habermas' strategy in the book was to relate the concept of public opinion back to its historical roots in the idea of the public sphere or public domain, in which the literate bourgeois (and of course almost exclusively male) public of the eighteenth century in the more advanced European societies took on a political role in the evaluation of contemporary affairs and, in particular, state policy. The 'transformation' of the public sphere begins with the commercialization of the press and leads to a shift from publicity in the sense of openness or transparency to the modern sense of the term in journalism, advertising and politics. The reading public is polarized into active specialists and a merely receptive mass. The same is true of the political process, split between a small number of party activists and a basically inactive mass electorate; public opinion ceases to be a source of critical judgement and checks, and becomes a social psychological variable to be manipulated. The result is a 'gap between the constitutional fiction of public opinion and the social-psychological dissolution of its concept' (p. 244).

In some ways this book recalls Horkheimer and Adorno's *Dialectic of Enlightenment*. Just as, in their argument, the enlightenment critique of tradition and authority ended up creating even more pernicious forms of domination, so, for Habermas, the bourgeois public sphere, concerned with the critical assessment of public policy in rational discussion orientated to a concept of the public interest, turns into what he calls a manipulated public sphere, in which states and corporations use 'publicity' in the modern sense of the word to secure political and financial support. Habermas is, however, somewhat less pessimistic in his conclusions. In an analysis to which he has returned in his most recent work, he envisaged certain counter-tendencies to, and opportunities in, the process he described. First, the development of the liberal constitutional state into a much more pervasive welfare state means that public organizations of all kinds are opened up to scrutiny by a corresponding variety of interest groups which link together members of the public concerned with specific aspects of welfare state provision.

And although the bureaucratization of administration seems, as Max Weber had noted in relation to parliamentary politics, to remove the activity of specialists from rational control, it might be possible, Habermas suggests, to democratize the administrative bodies themselves. In his more recent work on legal and democratic theory, Habermas has returned to this theme, stressing the interplay between law and democratic politics and the relation of both of these to more informal processes of public discussion. Just as important as the formal relations between the legal and political institutions of the constitutional state are the quality and extent of public communication. The public sphere, he writes in *Between Facts and Norms,* should not be seen as an institution or organization, but as 'a network' in which 'flows of communication are filtered and synthesized in such a way that they condense into *public* opinions clustered according to themes' (p. 436). In the modern world, these processes of communication are increasingly mediated, in both senses of the word: they take place both at a distance and increasingly via the mass media. In other words, rational discussion of public issues is not confined to face-to-face encounters in larger or smaller assemblies, taking place in real time. Habermas' early critiques of the restriction of political discussion as a result of technocracy and the 'scientization' of politics feed into a broader critique of scientism discussed in the next section.

Methodology of the Social Sciences

Habermas' work on the methodology of the social sciences is centred on the critique of positivism, understood as involving the abandonment of philosophical reflection on knowledge and a concentration on essentially technical issues – methodology in the narrow sense of the term. Habermas participated in the famous 'positivism dispute' of the 1960s, taking up Adorno's critique of what they both saw as an over-restrictive conception of rationality in the philosophy of Karl Popper and his followers. Habermas' own alternative involved a careful and creative appropriation of models and approaches from a very wide variety of human and social sciences. He focused, in particular, on three major contributions which had become prominent in the 1960s: the 'phenomenological' sociology inspired by Alfred Schutz, Peter Winch's sociological or anthropological extension of Wittgenstein's notion of language-games and Hans-Georg Gadamer's philosophical hermeneutics, which stressed the existential quality of the 'encounter' between reader and text. These, Habermas argued, could be brought into a complementary relation with one another and could then be further complemented by a more materialist reflection on the way in which our understanding of the social world (the common theme of these three currents of thought) is systematically distorted by relations of power and exploitation.

In *Knowledge and Human Interests* (1968), Habermas brilliantly showed how positivism had limited our understanding of the natural and the social world and undermined the possibility of critique; the latter, however, could be reconstructed from the work of Kant, Fichte, Hegel and Marx and shown to inspire, for example, **Freudian** psychoanalytic theory and practice. 'Critical' sciences such as psychoanalysis or the Marxist critique of ideology, governed by an emancipatory interest in overcoming causal obstacles to self-understanding, bridged the gap between the natural or empirical sciences, orientated to the prediction and control of objectified processes and the human sciences, orientated to an expansion of mutual understanding. At this time Habermas engaged in some extended debates with other leading thinkers, notably Gadamer and the system theorist Niklas Luhmann. Against Gadamer, he argued that understanding needed to be supplemented by a materialist critique of power and exploitation, which he justified with an appeal to a notion of social theory contrasted with Luhmann's technocratic conception. In the 1970s, Habermas scaled down some of his claims for emancipatory social science and developed an idea of reconstructive science, seen as a systematic attempt to isolate the conditions and implications of practices such as linguistic communication and moral reasoning.

Crises of State Legitimacy

One of Habermas' best-known books is a short and highly compressed text called *Legitimation Crisis*. Here, and in related essays, published in English under the title *Communication and the Evolution of Society,* he advanced a neo-Marxist theory of historical development and a critique of contemporary advanced or 'late' capitalism. Habermas argued that historical materialist explanations of the development of the productive forces needed to be augmented by an account of the evolution of normative structures, under-stood in a wide sense to include, for example, family forms. In late capit-alism, again, a traditional Marxist account of capitalist crisis which focuses on the economic contradictions of the capitalist system needs to be modified to account for the role of the modern interventionist welfare state and the resultant displacement of crisis tendencies from the economic sphere to the politi-cal and cultural domains. Instead of the economic crises which remain at the root of the problem, what we experience are incoherent state policies leading to what Habermas calls rationality crises which weaken state legiti-macy; these interventions also lead to an erosion of individual motivation and a loss of meaning.

Habermas' subsequent work develops both the historical thesis and the diagnosis of contemporary capitalist crises. *The Theory of Communicative Action* traces the conflict between the rationalization of world-views in early modernity, expressed for example in secularization and formal law and the erosion of appeals to traditional authority. It also focuses on the way in which a newly attained sphere open in principle to rational debate becomes restricted as market and bureaucratic structures come to dominate the modern world. Habermas addresses, in other words, the big question of whether we could have had, or can now have, modernity without the less attractive features of capitalism and the bureaucratic nation-state. More tentatively, in *Between Facts and Norms,* he has begun to reformulate elements of his model of advanced capitalist crisis in the language of his more recent theories.

Theory of Communicative Action

The centrepiece of Habermas' developed theorizing is a theory of communicative action grounded in, but spiralling off from, the analysis of linguistic communication. His basic idea is that any serious use of language to make claims about the world, as opposed, for example, to exclamations or the issuing of orders, presupposes the claims that:

(a) what we say makes sense and is true;
(b) that we are sincere in saying it; and
(c) that we have the right to say it.

These claims can be questioned by our hearers or readers. As Habermas shows with the homely example of a professor asking a seminar participant to fetch a glass of water, even a simple request, understood not as a mere demand but 'as a speech act carried out in an attitude oriented to understanding' raises claims to normative rightness, subjective sincerity and factual practicability which may be questioned. The addressee of the request may reject it as illegitimate ('I'm not your servant'), insincere ('You don't really want one') or mistaken about the facts of the matter (availability of a source of water).

Only a rational agreement which excluded no one and no relevant evidence or argument would provide, in the last resort, a justification of the claims we make and presuppose in our assertions. This idea gives us, Habermas claims, a theory of truth as what we would ultimately come to rationally agree about. Moreover, if he is right that moral judgements also have cognitive content and are not mere expressions of taste or disguised prescriptions, it also provides a theory of morality and of legitimate political authority. Moral norms or political institutions are justified if they are what we would still uphold at the end of an ideal process of argumentation. The latter is of course an idealization; Habermas at one time called it the 'ideal speech situation'. Yet it is presupposed, he argues, by our everyday practice of communication, which is made meaningful by the theoretical prospect of ultimate agreement. This can be seen negatively in our refusal, under certain circumstances, to engage in argument at all: who, except another Nazi, would want to enter an argument with a Nazi about whether the Holocaust was justified?

The analysis of language-use can be expanded into a broader theory of communicative action, defined as action orientated by and towards mutual agreement. In social-theoretical terms, this can be contrasted with the models of instrumental or strategic, self-interested action (*homo economicus*), normatively regulated action (functionalism, for example, **Parsons**) or dramaturgical action (**Goffman, Garfinkel** *et al.*) All of these, Habermas claims, can be shown to be parasitic upon communicative action, which incorporates and goes beyond each of these. The theory of communicative action then underpins a communication theory of morality, law and democracy, and it is these aspects which have dominated Habermas' most recent work.

The Politically Engaged Intellectual

I stressed at the outset of this chapter the practical and historical origins of much of Habermas' thinking, and his recent emphasis on law and democratic theory once again aligns one of the main focuses of his theoretical work with issues of current concern on which he has commented throughout his career. From an early stage, when he worked in part as a journalist, Habermas has actively pursued opportunities to intervene in the public sphere of the Federal Republic and, more recently, what he sees as an emergent globalized public sphere or civil society. These articles and other contributions, republished in successive volumes of 'political writings', stretch, as Robert Holub shows in *Habermas: Critic in the Public Sphere,* from early critiques of the political culture of post-war West Germany through an engagement with the 1968 student movement which was initially sympathetic, became increasingly critical, and finally endorsed the liberalizing long-term role of the movement and its radical democratic ethos. Then, in the late 1980s, Habermas initiated what came to be known as the 'historians' dispute' (*Historikerstreit*) over what he saw as an attempt to rewrite twentieth-century German history in a rosier light to serve the interests of the conservative right. More recently, he has written and commented at length on issues of German reunification and European and global politics.

Habermas stresses the difference between articles and interviews of this kind and his properly theoretical works, but it can be seen that such an engagement is entailed by his theoretical position and that many of his diagnoses of the present are crucially informed by, and in turn inform, his theoretical work. This is not an unmediated fusion of theoretical and practical concerns, but a sustained parallelism with numerous crossover points.

Seeing Things Differently

I have myself been most influenced by his metatheory of the sciences, but the essential point to make about Habermas is the interplay between the various elements of his work. Thus, for example, the thoroughgoing critique of positivism and ethical subjectivism feeds into an approach to legal and democratic theory which transcends conventional separations between, on the one hand, so-called positive law, where what counts is merely that it has been enacted according to due process, and, on the other hand, an individualistic morality. These are in turn internally related, he argues, to representative democracy and public communication. Whether or not Habermas is right that one can formally reconstruct theories of all these domains on the basis of an analysis of the preconditions of communication, the basic notion that communication with others is only meaningful if it is driven by the pursuit of rational agreement, and that such agreement is the only legitimate basis of morality and political authority in the modern world, would be widely shared.

I have always been attracted by Habermas' basic idea that a neo-Marxist theory of the contemporary world must attend to the distinctiveness of advanced capitalism and, in particular, to the state forms with which it coexists, and to the issues of culture and identity to which critical theory has been more sensitive than most other Marxist and non-Marxist traditions in social theory. With the eclipse, in the 1980s and 1990s, of more orthodox variants of Marxism, and a certain fusion of horizons between Marxist and non-Marxist approaches in social theory, Habermas' creative synthesis seems more attractive than ever. It is worth noting also that, although Habermas did not devote much of his published work before 1989 to an analysis of state socialist societies, his approach made possible some of the most creative work in the analysis of these regimes. Thus whereas more orthodox Marxist approaches concentrate on the issue of how state socialist modes of production should be understood, Habermas and others, such as Andrew Arato, using a Habermasian approach, have put these questions in a rather broader framework. Habermas' model of the 'colonization' of the life-world by markets and/or administrative structures can be creatively used in societies where markets are more or less completely replaced by centralized administrative decisions. More particularly, Habermas' model is well placed to analyse both the undermining of free and independent communication in the state socialist dictatorships and the insidious way in which, as he once put it, they simulate or 'sham' communicative relations between 'comrades' in a fantasy world of unaninimity and solidarity.[2] His own work and that of others using a Habermasian approach has also been particularly illuminating in relation to recent discussion of the post-1989 world; thinkers concerned with, for example, the political consequences of globalization for our conceptions of ethics, democracy, citizenship, and (post-) national identity have drawn significantly on Habermas' insights. In particular, Habermas has popularized a concept of 'constitutional patriotism', in which citizens may move beyond the simple loyalties of 'my country, right or wrong' to a more reflective and rational identification with 'their' states.

The rise of social theory since the beginning of the 1970s, and more particularly in the 1990s, as a relatively distinct domain of activity and a source of inspiration to the social sciences as a whole has also been due in considerable part to Habermas' work. He has always been hard to place in disciplinary terms, working on the borders of social theory and philosophy and holding an appointment in both these 'subjects', and always willing to venture into new fields such as the analysis of language or law as required by the development of his own work. In short, he has made it possible both to see the contemporary world differently, and to rethink the relations between theories in the social sciences which are our main resource in understanding this world.

Legacies and Unfinished Business

As noted above, Habermas' work has been influential in a whole range of fields, and has become one of the principal reference points for much discussion both in social theory and, for example, moral philosophy, legal theory and theories of international relations. Historians and theorists of culture have also increasingly been influenced by his conception of the public sphere and other elements of his thought. Critical theory in the broadest sense has been carried on by contemporaries such as Albrecht Wellmer and what may be called a third generation of thinkers including Axel Honneth, Hans Joas, Thomas McCarthy and Seyla Benhabib – all of whom, in different ways, have responded to issues posed by post-structuralist, postmodernist and feminist theory and shown how Habermas' approach can be usefully developed and extended.[3] Habermas' concern with historical sociology and theorizing states and social movements has been carried forward by, for example, Claus Offe and Klaus Eder.[4] Finally, his discourse ethics and his more recent theorizing about law and the state have attracted enormous interest in areas of analytic moral and legal philosophy previously untouched by Habermasian concerns. This is currently the most active area of research and Habermas has himself been working very substantially in this field.

Two other areas of 'unfinished business' are his analysis of the public sphere and of crisis tendencies in contemporary societies, first addressed in his books of 1962 and 1973. He has carried forward this work in his most recent major book, *Between Facts and Norms,* but so far only in outline. In relation to the public sphere, as noted above, he has stressed the interplay of public communication at many different levels and the fact that public spheres in modern societies are increasingly mediated and virtual. What this might mean in practice for a political theory of communicative democracy is an issue which clearly requires further exploration. We also badly need a developed theory of economic, social and political crises in modern societies which Habermas is extremely well placed to provide. At present, there is something of a disjunction between his wide-ranging informal observations on contemporary issues and the more precise and limited focus of some of his theoretical work. Thus, for instance, he is much concerned with the implications of globalization for theories of democracy, but his analysis of the constitutional state is still cast very much in a traditional state framework. These and other issues remain to be addressed in what promises to be an extremely active 'retirement'.

Further Reading

David Held and John Thompson (eds), *Habermas. Critical Debates* (London: Macmillan, 1982).

A. Honneth and H. Joas (eds), *Communicative Action* (Cambridge: Polity Press, 1991).

William Outhwaite (ed.), *The Habermas Reader* (Cambridge: Polity Press, 1994).

William Outhwaite, *Habermas. A Critical Introduction* (Cambridge: Polity Press, 1996).

S.K. White (ed.), *The Cambridge Companion to Habermas* (Cambridge: Cambridge University Press, 1994).

16

Pierre Bourdieu

Loïc Wacquant

Driving Impulses

Born and raised in a remote mountain village of the Pyrénées in southwestern France, Pierre Bourdieu moved to Paris in the early 1950s to study at the prestigious Ecole Normale Supérieure at a time when philosophy was the queen discipline and the obligatory vocation of any aspiring intellectual. There he quickly grew dissatisfied with the 'philosophy of the subject' exemplified by Sartrian existentialism – then the reigning doctrine – and gravitated toward the 'philosophy of the concept' associated with the works of epistemologists Gaston Bachelard, Georges Canguilhem, and Jules Vuillemin, as well as to the phenomenology of Edmund Husserl and Maurice Merleau-Ponty. Shortly after graduation, however, Bourdieu forsook a projected study of affective life mating philosophy, medicine, and biology and, as other illustrious *normaliens* such as **Durkheim** and **Foucault** had done before him, he converted to social science.

This conversion was precipitated by the conjunction of two events. On a personal level, the first-hand encounter with the gruesome realities of colonial rule and war in Algeria (where he had been sent to serve his mandatory stint in the military) prompted Bourdieu to turn to ethnology and sociology in order to make sense of the social cataclysm wrought by the clash between imperial capitalism and native nationalism. Thus his first books, *The Algerians, Work and Workers in Algeria, The Uprooting: The Crisis of Traditional Agriculture in Algeria* (Bourdieu 1958/1962, Bourdieu *et al.* 1963, Bourdieu and Sayad 1964), dissected the organization and culture of the native society and chronicled its violent disruption under the press of wage labor, urbanization, and the so-called pacification policy of the French army, in an effort to illuminate and assist in the painful birth of an independent Algeria. These works of youth bear the hallmark of Bourdieu's writings since: they are the product of an *activist science*, impervious to ideological bias yet attuned to the burning sociopolitical issues of its day and responsive to the ethical dilemmas these entail.

On an intellectual level, Bourdieu's break with philosophy was made possible by the demise of existentialism and the correlative rebirth of the social sciences in France after a half-century of eclipse. Under the broad banner of 'structuralism', the Durkheimian project of a total science of society and culture was being revived and modernized by Georges Dumézil in comparative mythology, Fernand Braudel in history, and Claude Lévi-Strauss in anthropology. It was now possible to fulfil lofty intellectual ambitions and to express progressive political impulses outside of the ambit of the Communist Party, by embracing the freshly reinvigorated empirical disciplines.[1] Thus Bourdieu took to re-establishing the scientific and civic legitimacy of sociology in its motherland where it had been a pariah science since the passing of Durkheim.

In the early 1960s, Bourdieu returned from Algiers to Paris where he was nominated Director of Studies at the Ecole des Hautes Etudes en Sciences Sociales as well as director of its newly formed Center for European Sociology. There he pursued his ethnological work on ritual, kinship, and social change in Kabylia (as recorded in *Outline of a Theory of Practice* and *Algeria 1960,* Bourdieu 1972/1977 and 1976/1977) and took to the sociology of schooling, art, intellectuals, and politics. These domains attracted him because he sensed that, in the prosperous post-war societies of the West, 'cultural capital' – educational credentials and familiarity with bourgeois culture – was becoming a major determinant of life chances and that, under the cloak of individual talent and academic meritocracy, its unequal distribution was helping to conserve social hierarchy. This he demonstrated in *The Inheritors* and *Reproduction in Education, Culture, and Society* (Bourdieu and Passeron 1964/1979 and 1970/1977), two books that impacted the scholarly and policy debate on the school system and established him as the progenitor of 'reproduction theory' (a misleading label, as shall be seen shortly).

During the 1970s, Bourdieu continued to mine a wide array of topics at the intersection of culture, class, and power, to teach at the Ecole, and to lead the research team which edited *Actes de la recherche en sciences sociales*, a journal he founded in 1975 to disseminate the most advanced results of social research and to engage salient social issues from a rigorous scientific standpoint. In 1981, the publication of his major works, *Distinction* and *The Logic of Practice* (Bourdieu 1979/1984 and 1980/1990), earned him the Chair of Sociology at the Collège de France as well as world-wide renown. In the 1980s, the painstaking research conducted over the previous two decades came to fruition in such acclaimed volumes as *Language and Symbolic Power, Homo Academicus, The State Nobility* and *The Rules of Art* (Bourdieu 1990, 1984/1988, 1989/1997, 1992/1997).

Pierre Bourdieu has since extended his inquiries in the sociology of symbolic goods (religion, science, literature, painting, and publishing) and broached onto additional topics: among them, social suffering, masculine domination, the historical genesis of the state, the political construction of the economy, journalism and television, and the institutional means for creating a European social policy. He has also become more visibly active on the French and European political scenes, as new forms of social inequality and conflict linked to the rising hegemony of market ideology spread, challenging the traditional goals and organization of the Left and calling for novel forms of intellectual intervention. This is in keeping with one of the most constant purposes behind Bourdieu's work, namely, to make social science into an effective *countervailing symbolic power* and the midwife of social forces dedicated to social justice and civic morality.

Key Issues

A Science of Practice and a Critique of Domination

With over thirty books and nearly four hundred articles oft couched in a difficult technical idiom, Bourdieu's thought might seem on first sight daunting if not intractable. But beneath the bewildering variety of empirical objects he has tackled lie a small set of theoretical principles, conceptual devices, and scientific-cum-political intentions that give his writings remarkable coherence and continuity. Bourdieu's sprawling *œuvre* is inseparably a *science of human practice* in its most diverse manifestations and a *critique of domination* in both the Kantian and the **Marxian** senses of the term.

Bourdieu's sociology is critical first of inherited categories and accepted ways of thinking and of the subtle forms of rule wielded by technocrats and intellectuals in the name of culture and rationality. Next, it is critical of established patterns of power and privilege as well as of the politics that supports them. Undergirding this double critique is an explanatory account of the manifold processes whereby the social order masks its arbitrariness and perpetuates itself – by extorting from the subordinate practical acceptance of, if not willed consent to, its existing hierarchies. This account of *symbolic violence* – the imposition of systems of meaning that legitimize and thus solidify structures of inequality – simultaneously points to the social conditions under which these hierarchies can be challenged, transformed, nay overturned.

Four notations can help us gain a preliminary feel for Bourdieu's distinctive intellectual project and style. First, his conception of social action, structure, and knowledge is resolutely *antidualistic*. It strives to circumvent or dissolve the oppositions that have defined perennial lines of debate in the social sciences: between subjectivist and objectivist modes of theorizing, between the material and symbolic dimensions of social life, as well as between interpretation and explanation, synchrony and diachrony, and micro and macro levels of analysis.

Second, Bourdieu's scientific thought and practice are genuinely *synthetic* in that they simultaneously straddle disciplinary, theoretical, and methodological divides. Theoretically, they stand at the confluence of intellectual streams that academic traditions have typically construed as discordant or incompatible: Marx and Mauss, Durkheim and **Weber**, but also the diverse philosophies of Cassirer, Bachelard, and Wittgenstein, the phenomenologies of Merleau-Ponty and Schutz, and the theories of language of Saussure, Chomsky, and Austin. Methodologically, Bourdieu's investigations typically combine statistical techniques with direct observation and the exegesis of interaction, discourse, and document.[2]

Third, like Max Weber's, Bourdieu's vision of society is fundamentally *agonistic*: for him, the social universe is the site of endless and pitiless competition, in and through which arise the differences that are the stuff and stake of social existence. Contention, not stasis, is the ubiquitous feature of collective life that his varied inquiries aim at making at once visible and intelligible. Struggle, not 'reproduction', is the master metaphor at the core of his thought.

Lastly and relatedly, Bourdieu's philosophical anthropology rests not on the notion of interest but on that of *recognition* – and its counterpart, misrecognition. Contrary to a common (mis)reading of his work, his is not a utilitarian theory of social action in which individuals consciously strategize to accumulate wealth, status, or power. In line with Blaise Pascal, Bourdieu holds that the ultimate spring of conduct is the thirst for dignity, which society alone can quench. For only by being granted a name, a place, a function, within a group or institution can the individual hope to escape the contingency, finitude, and ultimate absurdity of existence. Human beings become such by submitting to the 'judgement of others, this major principle of uncertainty and insecurity but also, and without contradiction, of certainty, assurance, consecration' (Bourdieu 1997a, p. 280). Social existence thus means difference, and difference implies hierarchy, which in turn sets off the endless dialectic of distinction and pretention, recognition and misrecognition, arbitrariness and necessity.

Constructing the Sociological Object

One of the main difficulties in understanding Bourdieu resides in the fact that the philosophy of science he draws on is equally alien – and opposed – to the two epistemological traditions that have dominated Anglo-American social science and the German *Geisteswissenschaften*, namely, positivism and hermeneutics. This conception of science takes after the works of the French school of 'historical epistemology' led by the philosophers Bachelard and Canguilhem (under whom Bourdieu studied), the mathematician Jean Cavaillès and the intellectual historian Alexandre Koyré.[3]

This school, which anticipated many of the ideas later popularized by Thomas Kuhn's theory of scientific paradigms, conceives truth as 'error rectified' in an endless effort to dissolve the preconceptions born of ordinary and scholarly common sense. Equally distant from theoretical formalism as from empiricist operationalism, it teaches that facts are necessarily suffused with theory, that laws are always but 'momentarily stabilized hypotheses' (in the words of Canguilhem), and that rational knowledge progresses through a polemical process of collective argumentation and mutual control. And it insists that concepts be characterized not by static definitions but by their actual uses, interrelations, and effects in the research enterprise. For science does not mirror the world: it is a material activity of production of 'purified objects' – Bachelard also calls them 'secondary objects', by opposition to the 'primary objects' that populate the realm of everyday experience.

In *The Craft of Sociology*, a primer on sociological epistemology first published in 1968, Bourdieu adapts this 'applied rationalism' to the study of society.[4] He posits that, like any scientific object, sociological facts are not given ready-made in social reality: they must be 'conquered, constructed, and constated' (Bourdieu, Passeron and Chamboredon 1968/1991, p. 24). He reaffirms the 'epistemological hierarchy' that subordinates empirical recording to conceptual construction and pressures conceptual construction to rupture with ordinary perception. Statistical measurement, logical and lexicological critique, and the genealogy of concepts and problematics are three choice instruments for effecting the necessary break with 'spontaneous sociology' and for actualizing the 'principle of non-consciousness', according to which the cause of social phenomena is to be found, not in the consciousness of individuals, but in the system of objective relations in which they are enmeshed.

When it comes to the most decisive operation, the construction of the object, three closely related principles guide Bourdieu. The first may be termed *methodological polytheism*: to deploy whatever procedure of observation and verification is best suited to the question at hand and continually confront the results yielded by different methods. For instance, in *The State Nobility*, Bourdieu combines the results gained by tabular and factorial analyses of survey data, archival accounts of historical trends, nosography, discourse and documentary analysis, field interviews, and ethnographic depiction. A second principle enjoins us to grant *equal epistemic attention to all operations*, from the recollection of sources and the design of questionnaires to the definition of populations, samples, and variables, to coding instructions and the carrying out of interviews, observations, and transcriptions. For every act of research, down to the most mundane and elemental, engages in full the theoretical framework that guides and commands it. This stipulates an organic relation, indeed a veritable fusion, between theory and method.

The third principle followed by Bourdieu is that of *methodological reflexivity*: the relentless self-questioning of method itself in the very movement whereby it is implemented (see in particular Bourdieu 1984/1988, Chapter 1, 'A Book for Burning?'). For, just as the three fundamental moments of social scientific reason, rupture, construction, and verification, cannot be disassociated, the construction of the object is never accomplished at one stroke. Rather, the dialectic of theory and verification is endlessly reiterated at every step along the research journey. It is only by exercising such 'surveillance of the third degree', as Bachelard christened it, that the sociologist can hope to vanquish the manifold obstacles that stand in the way of a science of society.

Overcoming the Antinomy of Objectivism and Subjectivism: Habitus, Capital, Field

Chief among these obstacles is the deep-seated opposition between two apparently antithetical theoretic stances, objectivism and subjectivism, which Bourdieu argues can and must be overcome. *Objectivism* holds that social reality consists of sets of relations and forces that impose themselves upon agents, 'irrespective of their consciousness and will' (to invoke Marx's well-known formula). From this standpoint, sociology must follow the Durkheimian precept and 'treat social facts as things' so as to uncover the objective system of relations that determine the conduct and representations of individuals. *Subjectivism*, on the contrary, takes these individual representations as its basis: with **Blumer** and **Garfinkel,** it asserts that social reality is but the sum total of the innumerable acts of interpretation whereby people jointly construct meaningful lines of (inter)action.

The social world is thus liable to two seemingly antinomic readings: a 'structuralist' one that seeks out invisible relational patterns and a 'constructivist' one that probes the common-sense perceptions of the individual. Bourdieu contends that the opposition between these two approaches is artificial and mutilating. For 'the two moments, objectivist and subjectivist, stand in dialectical relationship'. On the one side, the *social structures* that the sociologist lays bare in the objectivist phase, by pushing aside the subjective representations of the agent, do constrain the latter's practices. But, on the other side, these representations, and the *mental structures* that underpin them, must also be taken into account insofar as they guide the individual and collective struggles through which agents seek to conserve or transform these objective structures. What is more, social structures and mental structures are interlinked by a twofold relationship of mutual constitution and correspondence.

To effect this synthesis of objectivism and subjectivism, social physics and social phenomenology, Bourdieu forges an original conceptual arsenal anchored by the notions of habitus, capital, and field. Habitus designates the system of durable and transposable *dispositions* through which we perceive, judge, and act in the world.[5] These unconscious schemata are acquired through lasting exposure to particular social conditions and conditionings, via the internalization of external constraints and possibilities. This means that they are shared by people subjected to similar experiences even as each person has a unique individual variant of the common matrix (this is why individuals of like nationality, class, gender, and so on, spontaneously feel 'at home' with one other). It implies also that these systems of dispositions are malleable, since they inscribe into the body the evolving influence of the social milieu, but within the limits set by primary (or earlier) experiences as it is habitus itself which at every moment filters such influence. Thus the layering of the schemata that together compose habitus displays varying degrees of integration (subproletarians typically have a disjointed habitus mirroring their irregular conditions of living while persons undergoing great social mobility often possess segmented or conflictive dispositional sets).

As the mediation between past influences and present stimuli, habitus is at once *structured*, by the patterned social forces that produced it, and *structuring*: it gives form and coherence to the various activities of an individual across the separate spheres of life. This is why Bourdieu defines it variously as the 'the product of structure, producer of practice, and reproducer of structure', the 'unchosen principle of all choices', or 'the practice-unifying and practice-generating principle' that permits 'regulated improvisation' and the 'conductorless orchestration' of conduct.

The system of dispositions people acquire depends on the position(s) they occupy in society, that is, on their particular endowment in *capital*. For Bourdieu (1986), a capital is any resource effective in a given social arena that enables one to appropriate the specific profits arising out of participation and contest in it. Capital comes in three principal species: economic (material and financial assets), cultural (scarce symbolic goods, skills, and titles), and social (resources accrued by virtue of membership in a group). A fourth species, symbolic capital, designates the effects of any form of capital when people do not perceive them as such (as when we attribute moral qualities to members of the upper class as a result of their 'donating' time and money to charities). The position of any individual, group, or institution, in social space may thus be charted by two coordinates, the *overall volume and the composition of the capital* they detain. A third coordinate, variation over time of this volume and composition, records their trajectory through social space and provides invaluable clues as to their habitus by revealing the manner and path through which they reached the position they presently occupy.

But in advanced societies, people do not face an undifferentiated social space. The various spheres of life, art, science, religion, the economy, politics, and so on, tend to form distinct microcosms endowed with their own rules, regularities, and forms of authority – what Bourdieu calls fields.[6] A field is, in the first instance, a structured space of positions, *a force field* that imposes its specific determinations upon all those who enter it. Thus she who wants to succeed as a scientist has no choice but to acquire the minimal 'scientific capital' required and to abide by the mores and regulations enforced by the scientific milieu of that time and place. In the second instance, a field is an arena of struggle through which agents and institutions seek to preserve or overturn the existing distribution of capital (manifested, in the scientific field, by the ranking of institutions, disciplines, theories, methods, topics, journals, and so on): it is a *battlefield* wherein the bases of identity and hierarchy are endlessly disputed over.

It follows that fields are historical constellations that arise, grow, change shape, and sometimes wane or perish, over time. In this regard, a third critical property of any field is its *degree of autonomy*, that is, the capacity it has gained, in the course of its development, to insulate itself from external influences and to uphold its own criteria of evaluation over and against those of neighboring or intruding fields (scientific originality versus commercial profit or political rectitude, for instance). Every field is thus the site of an ongoing clash between those who defend autonomous principles of judgement proper to that field and those who seek to introduce heteronomous standards because they need the support of external forces to improve their dominated position in it.

Just as habitus informs practice from within, a field structures action and representation from without: it offers the individual a gamut of possible stances and moves that she can adopt, each with its associated profits, costs, and subsequent potentialities. Also, position in the field inclines agents toward particular patterns of conduct: those who occupy the dominant positions in a field tend to pursue strategies of conservation (of the existing distribution of capital) while those relegated to subordinate locations are more liable to deploy strategies of subversion.

In lieu of the naïve relation between the individual and society, Bourdieu substitutes the *constructed relationship between habitus and field*, that is, between 'history incarnate in bodies' as dispositions and 'history objectified in things' in the form of systems of positions. The crucial part of this equation is the phrase 'relationship between' because neither habitus nor field has the capacity unilaterally to determine social action. It takes the *meeting* of disposition and position, the correspondence (or disjuncture) between mental structures and social structures, to generate practice.[7] This means that, to explain any social event or pattern, one must dissect both the social constitution of the agent and the makeup of the particular social universe within which she operates as well as the particular conditions under which they come to encounter and impinge on each other. Indeed, for the constructivist or 'genetic structuralism' advocated by Bourdieu (1989a, p. 19)

the analysis of objective structures – those of the various fields – is inseparable from the analysis of the genesis within biological individuals of their mental structures which are in part the product of the internalization of these very social structures, and from the analysis of the genesis of these structures themselves.

The concepts of habitus, capital, and field are thus internally linked to one another as each achieves its full analytical potency only in tandem with the others. Together they enable us to elucidate cases of reproduction – when social and mental structures are in agreement and reinforce each other – as well as transformation – when discordances arise between habitus and field – leading to innovation, crisis, and structural change, as evidenced in two of Bourdieu's major books, *Distinction* and *Homo Academicus*.

Taste, Classes, and Classification

In *Distinction* and related studies of cultural practices (notably *Photography: A Middle-Brow Art* and *The Love of Art: European Museums and their Public*), Bourdieu offers a radical 'social critique of the judgement of taste' (the subtitle of the book, in reference to Immanuel Kant's famous critiques of judgement), a graphic account of the workings of culture and power in contemporary society, and a paradigmatic illustration of the uses of the conceptual triad of habitus, capital, and field. He also elaborates a theory of class that fuses the Marxian insistence on economic determination with the Weberian recognition of the distinctiveness of the cultural order and the Durkheimian concern for classification.

First, Bourdieu shows that, far from expressing some unique inner sensibility of the individual, aesthetic judgement is an eminently *social faculty*, resulting from class upbringing and education. To appreciate a painting, a poem, or a symphony presupposes mastery of the specialized symbolic code of which it is a materialization, which in turn requires possession of the proper kind of cultural capital. Mastery of this code can be acquired by osmosis in one's milieu of origin or by explicit teaching. When it comes through native familiarity (as with the children of cultured upper-class families), this trained capacity is experienced as an individual gift, an innate inclination testifying to spiritual worth. The Kantian theory of 'pure aesthetic', which philosophy presents as universal, is but a stylized – and mystifying – account of this particular experience of the 'love of art' that the bourgeoisie owes to its privileged social position and condition.

A second major argument of *Distinction* is that the aesthetic sense exhibited by different groups, and the lifestyles associated with them, define themselves in opposition to one another: *taste is first and foremost the distaste of the tastes of others*. This is because any cultural practice – wearing tweed or jeans, playing golf or soccer, going to museums or to auto shows, listening to jazz or watching sitcoms, and so on – takes its social meaning, and its ability to signify social difference and distance, not from some intrinsic property it has but from its location in a system of like objects and practices. To uncover the social logic of consumption thus requires establishing, not a direct link between a given practice and a particular class category (for example horse-back riding and the gentry), but the structural correspondences that obtain between two constellations of relations, the space of lifestyles and the space of social positions occupied by the different groups.

Bourdieu reveals that this space of social positions is organized by *two cross-cutting principles of differentiation, economic capital and cultural capital*, whose distribution defines the two oppositions that undergird major lines of cleavage and conflict in advanced society.[8] The first, vertical, division pits agents holding large volumes of either capital – the dominant class – against those deprived of both – the dominated class. The second, horizontal, opposition arises among the dominant, between those who possess much economic capital but few cultural assets (business owners and managers, who form the dominant fraction of the dominant class), and those whose capital is pre-eminently cultural (intellectuals and artists, who anchor the dominated fraction of the dominant class). Individuals and families continually strive to maintain or improve their position in social space by pursuing strategies of reconversion whereby they transmute or exchange one species of capital into another. The conversion rate between the various species of capital, set by such institutional mechanisms as the school system, the labor market, and inheritance laws, turns out to be one of the central stakes of social struggles, as each class or class fraction seeks to impose the hierarchy of capital most favorable to its own endowment.

Having mapped out the structure of social space, Bourdieu demonstrates that the *hierarchy of lifestyles is the misrecognized retranslation of the hierarchy of classes*. To each major social position, bourgeois, petty-bourgeois, and popular, corresponds a class habitus undergirding three broad kinds of tastes. The 'sense of distinction' of the bourgeoisie is the manifestation, in the symbolic order, of the latter's distance from material necessity and long-standing monopoly over scarce cultural goods. It accords primacy to form over function, manner over matter, and celebrates the 'pure pleasure' of the mind over the 'coarse pleasure' of the senses. More importantly, bourgeois taste defines itself by negating the 'taste of necessity' of the working classes. The latter may indeed be described as an inversion of the Kantian aesthetic: it subordinates form to function and refuses to autonomize judgement from practical concerns, art from everyday life (for instance, workers use photography to solemnize the high points of collective life and prefer pictures that are faithful renditions of reality over photos that pursue visual effects for their own sake). Caught in the intermediate zones of social space, the petty bourgeoisie displays a taste characterized by 'cultural goodwill': they know what the legitimate symbolic goods are but they do not know how to consume them in the proper manner – with the ease and insouciance that come from familial habituation. They bow before the sanctity of bourgeois culture but, because they do not master its code, they are perpetually at risk of revealing their middling position in the very movement whereby they strive to hide it by aping the practices of those above them in the economic and cultural order.

But Bourdieu does not stop at drawing a map of social positions, tastes, and their relationships. He shows that the *contention between groups in the space of lifestyles is a hidden, yet fundamental, dimension of class struggles*. For to impose one's art of living is to impose at the same time principles of visions of the world that legitimize inequality by making the divisions of social space appear rooted in the inclinations of individuals rather than the underlying distribution of capital. Against Marxist theory, which defines classes exclusively in the economic sphere, by their position in the relations of production, Bourdieu argues that classes arise in the conjunction of shared position in social space and shared dispositions actualized in the sphere of consumption: 'The *representations* that individuals and groups inevitably engage in their practices is part and parcel of their social reality. A class is defined as much by its *perceived being* as by its being' (Bourdieu 1979/1984, p. 564). Insofar as they enter into the very constitution of class, social classifications are instruments of symbolic domination and constitute a central stake in the struggle between classes (and class fractions), as each tries to gain control over the classificatory schemata that command the power to conserve or change reality by preserving or altering the representation of reality (Bourdieu 1985).

The Imperative of Reflexivity

Collective representations thus fulfil political as well as social functions: in addition to permitting the 'logical integration' of society, as Emile Durkheim proposed, classification systems serve to secure and naturalize domination. This puts intellectuals, as professional producers of authoritative visions of the social world, at the epicenter of the games of symbolic power and requires us to pay special attention to their position, strategies, and civic mission.

For Bourdieu, the sociology of intellectuals is not one speciality among others but an indispensable component of the sociological method. To forge a rigorous science of society, we need to know what constraints bear upon sociologists and how the specific interests they pursue as members of the 'dominated fraction of the dominant class' and participants in the 'intellectual field' affect the knowledge they produce. This points to the single most distinctive feature of Bourdieu's social theory, namely, its obsessive insistence on *reflexivity*.[9] Reflexivity refers to the need continually to turn the instruments of social science back upon the sociologist in an effort to better control the distortions introduced in the construction of the object by three factors. The first and most obvious is the personal identity of the researcher: her gender, class, nationality, ethnicity, education, and so on. Her location in the intellectual field, as distinct from social space at large, is the second: it calls for critical dissection of the concepts, methods, and problematics she inherits as well as for vigilance toward the censorship exercised by disciplinary and institutional attachments.

Yet the most insidious source of bias in Bourdieu's (1990) view is the fact that, to study society, the sociologist necessarily assumes a contemplative or scholastic stance that causes her to (mis)construe the social world as an interpretive puzzle to be resolved, rather than a mesh of practical tasks to be accomplished in real time and space – which is what it is for social agents. This 'scholastic fallacy' leads to disfiguring the situational, adaptive, 'fuzzy logic' of practice by confounding it with the abstract logic of intellectual ratiocination. In *Méditations Pascaliennes*, Bourdieu (1997a) argues that this 'scholastic bias' is at the root of grievous errors not only in matters of epistemology but also in aesthetics and ethics. Assuming the point of view of the 'impartial spectator', standing above the world rather than being immersed in it, preoccupied by it (in both senses of the term), creates systematic distortions in our conceptions of knowledge, beauty, and morality that reinforce each other and have every chance of going unnoticed inasmuch as those who produce and consume these conceptions share the same scholastic posture.

Such *epistemic reflexivity* as Bourdieu advocates is diametrically opposed to the kind of narcissistic reflexivity celebrated by some 'postmodern' writers, for which the analytical gaze turns back on to the private person of the analyst. For Bourdieu's goal is to strengthen the claims of a science of society, not to undermine its foundations in a facile celebration of epistemological and political nihilism. This is most evident in his dissection of the structure and functioning of the academic field in *Homo Academicus* (Bourdieu, 1984/1988).

Homo Academicus is the concrete implementation of the imperative of reflexivity. It is, first, an epistemological experiment: it seeks to prove empirically that it is possible to know scientifically the universe within which social science is made, that the sociologist can 'objectivize the point of view of objectivity' without falling into the abyss of relativism. Second, it maps out the contours of the academic field (a subfield within the broader intellectual field) to reveal that the university is the site of struggles whose specific dynamic mirrors the contention between economic capital and cultural capital that traverses the ruling class. Thus, on the side of the 'temporally dominant disciplines', law, medicine, and business, power is rooted principally in 'academic capital', that is, control over positions and material resources, while on the side of the 'temporally dominated' disciplines, anchored by the natural sciences and the humanities, power rests essentially on 'intellectual capital', that is, scientific capacities and achievements as evaluated by peers. The position and trajectory of professors in this dualistic structure determine, through the mediation of habitus, not only their intellectual output and professional strategies, but also their political proclivities.

This became fully visible during the student uprising and social crisis of May 1968, that is, in an entropic conjuncture apparently least favorable to the theory propounded by Bourdieu. Yet it was at this very moment that the behavior and proclamations of the different species of *homo academicus gallicus* turned out to be the most predictable. Bourdieu shows how the 'structural downclassing' and collective maladjustment experienced by a generation of students and professors, resulting in expectations that the university could no longer fulfil, triggered a series of local contestations that abruptly spread from the academic field to the field of cultural production to the political field. The 'rupture of the circle of subjective aspirations and objective chances' caused diverse agents to follow homologous strategies of subversion based on affinities of dispositions and similarities of position in different fields whose evolution thereby became synchronous. Here we discern how the same conceptual framework that served to explore reproduction in inquiries of class and taste can be employed to explain situations of rupture and transformation.[10]

Science, Politics, and the Civic Mission of Intellectuals

Bourdieu insists on putting intellectuals under the sociological microscope for yet another reason. In advanced society, wherein élite schools have replaced the church as the pre-eminent instrument of the legitimation of social hierarchy, reason and science are routinely invoked by rulers to justify their decisions and policies – and this is especially true of social science and its offshoots, public opinion polls, market studies, and advertising. Intellectuals must stand up against such misuses of reason because they have inherited from history a civic mission: to promote the 'corporatism of the universal' (Bourdieu 1989b).

From an analysis of its social genesis from the Enlightenment to the Dreyfus affair, Bourdieu argues that the intellectual is a 'paradoxical, bi-dimensional, being' composed by the *unstable but necessary coupling of autonomy and engagement*: he is invested with a specific authority, granted by virtue of the hard-won independence of the intellectual field from economic and political powers; and he puts this specific authority at the service of the collectivity by investing it in political debates. Contrary to the claims of both positivism and critical theory, the autonomy of science and the engagement of the scientist are not antithetical but complementary; the former is the necessary condition for the latter. It is because she has gained recognition in the struggles of the scientific or artistic field that the intellectual can claim and exercise the right to intervene in the public sphere on matters for which she has competency. What is more, to attain its maximum efficacy, such contributions must take a collective form: for scientific autonomy cannot be secured except by the joint mobilization of all scientists against the intrusion of external powers.

Bourdieu's own political interventions have typically assumed an indirect (or sublimated) form. His major scientific works have repeatedly sought to expand or alter the parameters of public discussion by debunking current social myths – be it school meritocracy, the innateness of taste, or the rationality of technocratic rule – and by spotlighting social facts and trends that belie the official vision of reality. The research undertaking that culminated in the book *The Poverty of Society* is exemplary in this regard. The avowed aim of this thousand-page study of social suffering in contemporary France was not only to demonstrate the potency of a distinctive kind of socioanalysis. It was also to circumvent the censorship of the political field and to compel party leaders and policy makers to acknowledge new forms of inequality and misery rendered invisible by established instruments of collective voice and claims-making.[11]

In recent years, however, Bourdieu has felt the need to intervene directly in the political arena because he holds that we are witnessing a 'conservative revolution of a new type which claims the mantle of progress, reason, and science (in particular economics) to justify restoration and which thereby tries to reject progressive thinking and action on the side of archaism' (Bourdieu 1998). In his eyes, the present *fin-de-siècle* is pregnant with the possibility of immense social regression: 'The peoples of Europe today are facing a turning point in their history because the gains of several centuries of social struggles, of intellectual and political battles for the dignity of workers and citizens, are being directly threatened' by the spread of a market ideology that – like all ruling ideologies – presents itself as the end of ideology, the inevitable endpoint of history.

In accordance with his view of the historic mission of intellectuals, Bourdieu has put his scientific authority at the service of various social movements of the 'non-institutional left', helping to lend public legitimacy and symbolic force to newly formed groups defending the rights of the jobless, the homeless, immigrants, and homosexuals. He famously clashed with Hans Tietmeyer, the President of the German Bundesbank and 'high priest of the rule of markets', to advocate the creation of a 'European welfare state' capable of resisting the onslaught of deregulation and the incipient privatization of social goods. He has also intervened against the persecution of intellectuals in Algeria and elsewhere by spawning the birth of the International Parliament of Writers, and against the tolerance of western states for the banalization of prejudice and discrimination.

Pierre Bourdieu has devoted considerable energy to the creation of institutions of intellectual exchange and mobilization on a transnational scale. In 1989, he launched *Liber: The European Review of Books*, a quarterly published simultaneously in nine European countries and languages, to circumvent national censorship and facilitate the continental circulation of innovative and engaged works in the arts, humanities, and social sciences. In the wake of the December 1995 protest against the downsizing of the French welfare state, he founded the collective 'Raisons d'agir' which brings together researchers, artists, labor officials, journalists, and militants of the unorthodox Left (with branches in different European countries). In 1997, he created a publishing house, Editions Liber, that puts out short books aimed at a wide audience on topics of urgent civic interest – starting with Bourdieu's (1997b) own best-selling analysis of the wilful submission of journalism to political and economic power, *Sur la Télévision*.[12]

In his many interventions before fellow scientists, unionists, social activists of various stripes and in editorial pieces published in the major dailies and weeklies of France, Germany, Italy, or Greece, as well as in his ostensibly scientific works, Bourdieu has doggedly pursued a single aim: to forestall or prevent abuses of power in the name of reason and to disseminate instruments of resistance to symbolic domination. If social science cannot stipulate the political goals and moral standards we should pursue, as Durkheim had hoped, it can and must contribute to the elaboration of 'realistic utopias' suited to guiding collective action and to promoting the institutionalization of justice and freedom. The ultimate purpose of Bourdieu's sociology, then, is nothing other than to foster the blossoming of a new, self-critical, *Aufklärung* fit for the coming millennium.

Further Reading

L. Boltanski, *The Making of a Class: 'Cadres' in French Society* (Cambridge, Cambridge University Press, 1987 [1982]).

A. Boschetti, *The Intellectual Enterprise: Sartre and 'Les temps modernes'* (Evanston: Northwestern University Press, 1988 [1985]).

P. Bourdieu and L. Wacquant, *An Invitation to Reflexive Sociology* (Cambridge, Polity Press, 1992).

R. Brubaker, 'Rethinking Classical Theory: The Sociological Vision of Pierre Bourdieu', *Theory and Society*, **14** (1985), 723–44.

P. Champagne, *Faire l'opinion: le nouvel espace politique* (Paris: Editions de Minuit, 1990).

G. Eyal, I. Szelenyi and E. Townsley, *Making Capitalism without Capitalists* (London, Verso, 1998).

J. Jurt, *Das Literarische Feld. Das Koncept Pierre Bourdieus in Theorie und Praxis* (Darmstadt, Wissenchaftsliche Buchgesellschaft, 1995).

R. Schusterman (ed.), *Philosophers on Pierre Bourdieu* (Oxford, Basil Blackwell, 1997).

J.B. Thompson, 'Symbolic Violence: Language and Power in the Sociology of Pierre Bourdieu,' in *Studies in the Theory of Ideology* (Cambridge, Polity Press, 1984).

L. Wacquant, 'On the Tracks on Symbolic Power: Prefatory Notes to Bourdieu's "State Nobility".' *Theory, Culture and Society*, **10** (1993), 1–17.

17

Nancy J. Chodorow

Karin A. Martin

Driving Impulses

The Reproduction of Mothering (1978), the work for which Nancy Chodorow is best known, seeks to explain not only why women mother, but also how gender is constructed within individuals. That is, why do we feel so deeply that we are girls/women or boys/men? How do these identities take root? And why are these identities, girl and boy, so different? Why do men and women have such different personalities? How is gender both personal and cultural?

These questions, the driving impulses[1] for Chodorow's work, emerged from several social and intellectual influences. *The Reproduction of Mothering* is a product of second-wave feminism, 'grand' theorizing about women's oppression that characterized academic feminist theory of the 1970s, Chodorow's own training in anthropology, psychoanalysis, and sociology, and her experience in a mother–daughter group in graduate school.

In the 1970s feminists were examining, critiquing, and striving to change all aspects of gender inequality in social life. In particular, 1970s feminists much more than feminists who came generations before them, claimed that personal, private life – marriage, love, families, sex – was political, just as public life – voting, work, education – was. Hence the famous slogan of second-wave feminism, 'the personal is political'. This claim that personal life was important to gender politics shaped many feminist theorists of the day and led to an examination of all aspects of personal life. Chodorow, herself, participated in a mother–daughter group that considered the implications of women's parenting. For Chodorow the claim that the personal was political also supported her interest in psychoanalytic theory (see below), a theory of the most personal aspects of the self – emotions, the unconscious, fantasy – and also of the development of sex and gender within family relations.

Chodorow's theorizing was also influenced by the types of questions academic second-wave feminists were asking. Many feminists in the academy were writing 'grand theory'. They searched for a single explanation that would account for all of gender inequality. Many of these theorists were anthropologists (Michelle Rosaldo, Sherry Ortner, Gayle Rubin) who were trying to understand what they perceived to be women's universal oppression around the globe. Data from around the world seemed to suggest that women everywhere were oppressed. Such a large, grand scale observation, called for grand theory, a theory that could explain women's oppression everywhere and could explain it with a single cause. Chodorow trained as an anthropologist as an undergraduate, asked questions about gender and searched for a single cause to explain gender inequality in this academic context.

The profound influence of psychoanalytic theory on Chodorow's thinking often seems unusual to feminist thinkers. What, many feminists ask, can we learn about women and gender from a theory that dreamed up penis envy, that said early childhood sexual abuse was fantasy, that claimed women who did not have vaginal orgasms were frigid and immature? Looking beyond and between these issues, Chodorow found much that was useful in psychoanalytic theory and in fact describes herself as 'passionately "hooked on"' psychoanalytic theory.[2] There were many aspects of psychoanalysis that Chodorow found appealing and useful for feminist theorizing. Psychoanalysis brings to the study of gender relations the understanding that 'the social and political organization of gender does not exist apart from the fact that we are all sexed and gendered in the first place… '[3] Chodorow argues that psychoanalysis, unlike many sociological theories, has always theorized about gender and sexuality, however distortedly, and if we want to understand how people become gendered and how they develop sexual identities, psychoanalysis is the best place to start. Psychoanalysis, she suggests, reveals that the social location of gender is partly in the self and partly in social relationships, that the social and psychological are intertwined. With regard to mothering, a psychoanalytic perspective suggests that mothering is not only social and cultural but also a psychological stance toward the world. Finally, Chodorow suggests that psychoanalytic theory is the only theory that provides any insight into how people give cultural phenomena, like gender, deep personal and emotional meaning.

Thus, studying psychoanalysis during second-wave feminism led Chodorow to a career of trying to understand the personal and cultural constructions of gender identity, sexuality, and mothering and the relationship between psychoanalysis and feminism.

Key Issues

Chodorow's theory asks a key sociological question: (1) *Why do women mother?* In answering this question she answers many other questions as well. Her theory offers explanation of (2) how we acquire gender identities and gendered personalities, (3) how we acquire sexual identity (especially heterosexuality) or object choice, (4) adult love relationships and the reproduction of mothering and (5) why change in gender norms and structures is difficult but possible.

The Significance of the Question: Why do Women Mother?

In asking this question Chodorow problematizes the one aspect of being a woman that seems most natural, biological, and innate. Some critics have suggested that there is no need to even ask the question, 'why do women mother?' These critics often argue that women mother because it is a biological fact. Women bear children and nurse them, and therefore it makes sense that they mother. Chodorow, however, suggests that this is an inadequate explanation. There is no logical reason that because women bear the baby and often nurse it that they should be the ones to do all of the caretaking, every minute of the day. In fact, in many societies women who are not biologically a child's mother are the ones who care for it. Similarly, there is no biological reason that fathers are incapable of caring for children. Finally, biological factors can explain little about the quality and emotional meaning of mothering or of the mother–child relationship.

Many sociological thinkers have attempted to critique Chodorow's explanation for why women mother by suggesting that there are many alternative explanations. Some theorize that women mother because of socialization. These thinkers claim that women are taught from the time they are children that they will grow up to care for children. As girls they are given dolls to play with and learn the mothering role. Others claim that women mother for economic reasons. In order to survive in our society as a woman, such theorists argue, one must take up the position of wife and mother which gives women their only real access to men's economic resources. Chodorow argues that these explanations are only part of the answer to why women mother. What they cannot explain she argues is why women *want* to mother. Why do women get gratification from mothering? Why do they enjoy it? Mothering, according to Chodorow, is not just an activity that is forced on women but one in which most women desire to participate. Another problem with these previous sociological explanations for why women mother is that they define mothering as a behavior or set of behaviors. Chodorow suggests that mothering is much more than that. It is a stance in the world, empathy, a relation to an infant or child. When we define mothering this way, a much deeper, more complex explanation of women's mothering is required. Chodorow turns to psychoanalytic theory for this explanation and ultimately argues that women get this desire and ability to mother through having been mothered by women themselves.

Because Chodorow is working from a psychoanalytic account and such accounts are often developmental, the best way to understand her theory is to learn the developmental story that she tells. Bear in mind, however, that this story of intrapsychic, relational family dynamics takes place within a larger social structure where there is a gendered division of labor in which women care for infants and small children. Chodorow is not explaining the origin of this division of labor but its reproduction.

Psychoanalytic developmental stories about gender, usually cast in terms of the oedipal conflict, seek to explain how people achieve gender identity – one's sense of self as a girl or boy – and how they achieve sexual identity or object choice – do you desire men or women? Chodorow also sets out to answer these questions, but does so quite differently from **Freud** and others, as she is a different kind of psychoanalytic theorist from those with whom most of us are familiar. Chodorow is an object relations theorist. Unlike traditional Freudians who think people seek to gratify drives, object relations theorists think people seek relations with 'objects'. Objects in object relations theory refer to people. Object relations theorists privilege the preoedipal period of development (as opposed to Freud's privileging of the oedipal) and object relations theorists focus on the mother as the key figure in children's development (as opposed to Freud's focus on the father). The developmental story for both girls and boys has the same beginning, both boys and girls begin life attached to their mothers.

The Development of Gender Identities and Gendered Personalities

When they are born, both girls and boys experience a oneness or symbiosis with the mother. As an infant suckling at the mother's breast, being held and cuddled by her, and simply doing what babies do, the child cannot distinguish between mother and self. To the infant it is as if the two are physically and psychologically one. However, as both boys and girls begin to separate from their mothers and establish selves, their experience of the preoedipal phase (approximately 0–3 years) changes because mothers mother girls and boys very differently. Through mothering a girl child a mother re-experiences herself both as mothered child and as her mother. She feels 'like' her daughter and encourages closeness and connection with her daughter. This preoedipal mother–daughter relationship continues to include many of the early mother–child issues – boundary confusion, dependence, individuation. From this relationship with mother, girls establish their gender identity. Gender identity is not difficult for girls to establish as it is built on their sense of oneness with their mothers. From the beginning girls are attached, dependent, and connected to their mothers and the mother confirms that the girl is like her. Later this relationship may become difficult, ambivalent, boundary confused as a girl tries to separate from her mother, but it is this relationship that establishes a girl's gender identity. Through her connection or what psychoanalysts would call her 'identification' with her mother, the daughter establishes a deep, unconscious, fixed sense about herself as a girl. She comes to feel deeply that she is a girl/woman. From their relationships with their mothers girls also develop personalities that are boundary permeable, connected, relational, dependent.

Like girls, boys experience a symbiosis or feeling of oneness with the mother at birth. However, boys have a more difficult time establishing gender identity. Boys must shift their identificatory love from their mother. As boys develop, mothers encourage separation of sons and convey to boys that they are different from her. It is not that mothers love sons any less than they love daughters, but that they experience the mothering of boy children differently and treat sons differently from the way they do daughters. These differences, according to Chodorow, are subtle differences of 'nuance, tone, quality'.[4] That is, boys cannot identify with their mothers in order to establish their sense of themselves as boys, as masculine. However, because there is (usually) no father parenting (or mothering) in the same way that the mother is, no real, concrete, available masculine person for him to identify with, he forms a masculine gender identity based on being not mother, not feminine, not woman. A boy must repudiate all that is feminine. His masculine identity is based on being not a girl/woman and is filled in with cultural stories about symbols of masculinity, for example, superheroes. Another outcome of this developmental route is that masculine identity is a fragile identity. Because masculine identity is based on being 'not mother, not feminine', men constantly seek to reconstruct and reconfirm their masculinity through repudiating that which is feminine. This psychological story underlies men's derogation of women. Masculinity is not all that is produced at this developmental moment. Through this process, boys also come to develop personalities that are more autonomous, independent, and boundary heightened than women's.

The Development of Sexual Object Choice/Sexual Identity

While boys have a more difficult time establishing their gender identity, according to Chodorow, the establishment of sexual identity for boys is easier developmentally. Because all children are originally 'matrisexual', that is erotically connected to their mothers, boys maintain this connection throughout their development, much in the same way that girls maintain their identifications with their mothers. Thus, in the course of oedipal development boys eventually shift their object choice from mother specifically to women in general and become adults with heterosexual sexual identities.

However, how heterosexual sexual identity is developed for the girl is more complex in Chodorow's theory. Chodorow argues that as girls develop, their bonds with their mothers become fraught with ambivalence, boundary confusion, an unclear sense of what is 'me' and 'not me'. These feelings cause tension and anxiety and eventually cause the girl to shift her erotic ties to the father as a means of helping her to separate from her mother and easing the tension of the mother–daughter relationship. What Chodorow does not explain is exactly what changes so dramatically at this point that a girl can no longer bear this relationship with her mother without shifting some of her ties, and specifically her sexual ties, to the father (and eventually to men in general). Some critics argue this explanation about girls' heterosexuality ignores structures such as compulsory heterosexuality that shape women's heterosexual object choice.[5]

Heterosexual Knots and the Reproduction of Mothering

As adults these gendered psychological family dramas continue to shape lives. The interplay of gendered personalities and heterosexuality complicate adult love relationships. Men and women become tied in 'heterosexual knots', according to Chodorow. Men and women experience adult love relationships differently because of the way their identities are constructed in early childhood. Through sex with a woman an adult man can find the connection, oneness, and dependence that he had only as a very small child with his mother. However, 'women have a richer, ongoing inner world to fall back on, and… the men in their lives do not represent the intensity and exclusivity that women represent to men'.[6] Women recreate the connection they felt with their mothers in many parts of their lives, including within friendships with other women. Thus, ultimately 'men do not become as emotionally important to women as women do to men'.[7] These differences lead to many of the difficulties we see and experience in contemporary intimate adult heterosexual relationships.

Finally, as adults women also seek to recreate their relationships with their mothers through having children of their own. Women want to (become) mother(s) in order to re-experience the relationship they had with their own mother. Through mothering a child, a woman recreates her deepest feelings of connection and dependency. Thus, the gender division of labor is reproduced as women come to want to mother. In short, Chodorow theorizes that women mother because women mother.

Social Change

One of the things that Chodorow's theory explains is that gender is rooted within our psyches. It is not simply an external social relation. Because gender is anchored deeply within us, it is extremely difficult to change. Chodorow suggests that social change will come partly from a change in parenting structures. If men and women both cared for children in a daily, emotional, immediate way throughout childhood, then these dynamics would be reshaped. Boys and girls would have equal opportunity to identify with both parents, and this would eliminate many gender differences in personality and would at least lessen men's denigration of women and the feminine.

Some critics have challenged Chodorow on this point of change. How, they ask, can men ever parent when Chodorow describes their adult personalities as independent, disconnected, and arelational? Men, it seems, do not have the ability to mother. However, Chodorow responds to such criticisms with a reminder that men do have 'the foundations of parental (maternal) capacities and desires for primary relationships, but these have been repressed in their development'.[8] Because all people begin their relationships connected to mothers, all have some sense of these capacities. Thus, Chodorow argues that such parenting qualities are available within men. If men could use these capacities to share equally in child care, then social change would be possible.

Seeing Things Differently

Chodorow's work can be used to understand a wide range of social phenomena from mother–daughter relationships and adult heterosexual relationships to the construction of masculinity in organizations like fraternities and the military. I find most compelling the way that Chodorow's theory helps us to understand the derisiveness and derogation that men direct at women in our society. According to Chodorow, such sentiments derive from a sense of masculinity that is based on being not like mother, not like women. Remember, masculinity is constructed psychologically as the opposite of femininity. And, according to Chodorow and other psychoanalysts, such a construction of masculinity is never complete. It must be constantly worked on and reconstructed. Such a view of masculinity is useful for understanding a variety of institutional constructions of masculine identity in contemporary society.

In her book, *Gender Differences at Work*, Christine Williams draws from Chodorow's work to explain just such an institutional construction of masculinity. Williams examines the construction of masculinity (and femininity) by Marines. She finds that much of the misogyny in the Marines and the purpose it serves can be explained by Chodorow's theory. 'Psychoanalysis is uniquely able to supply us with insight into the unconscious and often irrational interests served by certain socially institutionalized practices. In the case of the military, it provides us with an explanation for what is at stake in preserving masculinity...'[9] Let us examine the Marines and Williams' analysis of them more closely.

Even before the moment that recruits arrive at boot camp the understood purpose of Marine training is that it will 'make a man out of them'. Such sentiments will often have been seen in advertisements recruiting the men into the military. For example, an ad for the Army National Guard said 'kiss your momma goodbye'. Boot camp, according to Williams, 'has been culturally defined as an activity only masculine males can accomplish. It unambiguously fulfills men's largely unconscious desires to prove once and for all that they are masculine.'[10] Throughout the training new male recruits are demeaned by others as 'girls', and they march to misogynist chants ('I don't know but I've been told, Eskimo pussy is mighty cold').[11] Men also demean women through their display of pornography in their barracks and in the slang they use to refer to women. Williams, following Chodorow, suggests that such behavior derives from the psychological construction of masculinity where women mother and boys must give up feminine identification in favor of a masculinity that is defined only as the opposite of feminine. Military training draws on this psychological construction of masculinity.

Williams finds that this construction of masculinity with its contempt for femininity is institutionalized in the military.[12] She argues that the military has invested much effort in constructing differences between men and women. Men are Marines; women are Women Marines. Despite much evidence that women are capable of achieving the same standards as men in military training, the military continues to segregate basic training. Similarly, the military constructs gender differences, constructs masculinity as the opposite of femininity, by institutionalizing gender appearance and behavior. Williams finds that Women Marines are required to wear make-up, to take etiquette classes, to wear skirts (unless it is below freezing). Williams suggests that it is 'ironic that the branch of the military most closely associated with masculinity seems most concerned with preserving women's femininity'.[13] Williams suggests that the Marines' resistance to gender integration and their institutional construction of gender difference are products of the threat to men's masculinity when women enter a previously all-male institution. Williams suggests that more than economic interests are at stake because economic interests cannot explain the stridency and irrationality that accompany the Marines' talk about women in the military. Chodorow's theory allows us to explain such stridency, along with the general construction of gender difference in the Marines as motivated by the fragile, early childhood construction of masculinity as that which is not feminine or female.

Legacies and Unfinished Business

Chodorow's theory has been extended by a number of sociological thinkers. Carol Gilligan's famous work about moral reasoning, *In a Different Voice,* has its foundation in Chodorow's theory. Gilligan argues and tries to demonstrate empirically that men and women differ in how they make moral decisions. Men make moral decisions based on the ethic of justice (abstract moral principles) and women based on the ethic of care (relational dynamics and the implications of decisions). Drawing on Chodorow, Gilligan suggests that these differences in moral reasoning are a result of women's mothering and the different gender personalities that develop from this structure.

Jessica Benjamin's work also extends Chodorow's thinking about what happens to gender psychodynamically when women mother. In particular, she asks what happens to women's desire? A question that she says drops out of Chodorow's theory which depicts women as relational and caring but without any sexuality. Benjamin claims that desire is a component of personality that is quite important in traditional psychoanalytic accounts of personality and should be returned to feminist object relations accounts.

Chodorow's theory has also been critiqued somewhat for a specific set of issues concerning generalizability. Because Chodorow relies on psychoanalytic case studies and theory to develop her explanation for women's mothering, many critics have asked, to whom does this theory apply? To only nuclear families? To only white families? Can we generalize from case studies of middle-class western European clinical patients of previous generations to contemporary, nonclinical populations that are diverse not only in class and race but also culture and society? After all, Chodorow is trying to explain a universal phenomenon (women's mothering). These questions were asked of much of the grand theorizing feminist thinking produced in the 1970s. Chodorow responds to such criticism in a variety of ways in the collection of her work *Feminism and Psychoanalysis*. She argues in part that there is more variation than her early account may have suggested, yet insists that psychoanalysis is still a useful tool for understanding the personal construction of gender. After all 'people everywhere form a psyche, self, and identity'.[14] Similarly, like many psychoanalysts she argues that clinical data is not problematic for generalizing to nonclinical populations because 'pathology reflects normal tendencies and becomes useful sociological evidence when a number of clinical cases reveal systematic, patterned responses...'[15]

Perhaps in response to her critics but also because she is now a practicing psychoanalyst, Chodorow has begun theorizing differences in individuals' constructions of gender and of love and how these individual constructions are shaped by cultural constructions of gender and love. Men and women love, she argues, 'in as many different ways as there are men and women'.[16] Since *The Reproduction of Mothering*, Chodorow has further developed an understanding of unconscious gender identity by documenting that gender is both a cultural and personal construction. According to Chodorow, all people have the ability to shape cultural experiences and cultural meanings emotionally and unconsciously. She writes, 'I do not mean only that people create individualized cultural and linguistic versions of meaning by drawing upon cultural or linguistic categories at hand. Rather, perception and meaning are psychologically created. As psychoanalysis documents, people use available cultural meanings and images, but they experience them emotionally and through fantasy, as well as in particular interpersonal contexts.'[17] I suspect Chodorow's work will continue to pursue ways of understanding the importance of personal, and personal gendered, meaning in people's lives.

Further Reading

J. Benjamin, *The Bonds of Love* (New York: Pantheon, 1988).

N. Chodorow, 'Gender as a Personal and Cultural Construction', *Signs*, Spring (1995), 516–44.

C. Gilligan, *In a Different Voice* (Cambridge, MA: Harvard University Press, 1982).

V. Goldner, 'Toward a Critical Relational Theory of Gender', *Psychoanalytic Dialogues*, 1(1991), 249–72.

E. Person, 'Sexuality as the Main Stay of Identity', *Signs* (1981).

C. Williams, *Gender Differences at Work* (Berkeley, CA: University of California Press, 1989).

18

Arlie Russell Hochschild

Simon J. Williams

What is emotional labour, what do we do when we manage emotion, and what are the costs and benefits of doing so in public and private life? These and many other pertinent sociological questions have been centrally addressed by Arlie Russell Hochschild over the years in her pioneering work on the commercialisation of human feeling and the gender division of emotional labour. In doing so, she has effectively pioneered a whole new way of seeing the world, one which not only places human feeling at the heart of the sociological enterprise, but also provides a profound critique of the problems of authenticity and estrangement in late-twentieth-century capitalist society. It is to these central, albeit neglected, sociological issues that this chapter is devoted.

Driving Impulses

Like all key thinkers, the inspiration for Hochschild's work comes from a complex fusion of personal biography, intellectual exposure and scholarly apprenticeship. In her particular case this stemmed – as she duly acknowledges in the preface to *The Managed Heart*[1] – from the time her parents joined the US Foreign Service. At the tender age of eleven, Hochschild found herself plunged into a world of diplomatic smiles and strategic emotional exchanges. Afterwards, she would listen attentively to her parents interpreting these gestures: gestures conveying information not simply from person to person, but from nation to nation, state to state.

As a graduate student at Berkeley some years later, Hochschild found herself captivated by another intellectual source, namely, the sociological writings of C. Wright Mills, especially his chapter in *White Collar* entitled 'The Great Salesroom'.[2] Mills' sociological deliberations on the self-estrangement of goods sellers in advanced capitalist society caused her to reflect on whether this particular type of labour might, in fact, be part of a distinctly patterned, yet invisible, emotional system – one comprised of individual acts of 'emotional work', 'feeling rules' and a great variety of embodied exchanges between people in private and public life.[3] These questions soon led Hochschild to **Erving Goffman's**[4] work on the insincere art of impression management and the vicissitudes of self-presentation in everyday life. This, coupled with Freud's insights into the 'signal function' of human emotions,[5] prompted her to explore the idea that emotion functions as a messenger from the self; an agent that gives us an instant report on the connection between what we are seeing and what we expect to see, telling us in the process, what we feel ready to do about it.[6]

These ideas were developing when Hochschild went out into the field, in the late 1970s and early 1980s, in order to try and 'get behind' the eyes of flight attendants and bill collectors, as each moved through their work-a-day world. The more she saw and listened, the more she came to appreciate the dilemmas of emotion management in advanced capitalist society and the loss of authenticity this involves. It is to a fuller exposition of these central sociological themes, and the insights they afford concerning the place of emotions in contemporary social life, that we now turn in the next section of this chapter.

Key Issues

Straddling the Biology–Society Divide

A defining hallmark of Hochschild's work on emotions is the manner in which she is able to straddle, in a way that so many sociological accounts in the past have failed to do, the biology–society divide. In contrast to 'organismic' or 'social constructionist' models of emotions – models which prioritise the biological and the social respectively – Hochschild adopts instead an approach which sits in the analytical space between these two extremes.[7] For Hochschild, emotion is unique among the senses, being related not only to *action* but also to *cognition*. Emotions emerge when bodily sensations are joined with what we see or imagine – forged on the template of prior expectations – and it is on this basis that we discover our own particular view of the world and our readiness to act within it.[8]

In taking this interactional stance, Hochschild joins three intellectual currents. First, drawing on Dewey,[9] Gerth and Mills,[10] and Goffman[11] within the interactionist tradition, she explores what gets 'done' to emotions and how feelings are permeable to what gets done to them. Second, from Darwin,[12] within the organismic tradition, she is able to posit a sense of what is there, impermeable, to be 'done to' (that is, a biologically given sense, which in turn, is related to an orientation to action). Finally, through **Freud's**[13] work on the 'signal' function of anxiety, she is able to complete the circle working backwards from the organismic to the interactionist tradition, by tracing the way in which social factors influence what we expect and thus what these feelings actually 'signify'.[14]

In advancing this model, Hochschild's interactionist approach to emotions is a lesson to us all on the role of the biological in social explanation. For far too long now, any mention of biology has raised the spectre, in sociological minds, of crude or vulgar 'reductionism'. Yet as Hochschild rightly argues, while a sociology of emotions clearly needs to 'go beyond' the biological, this does not necessarily mean 'leaving it out altogether'. Reciprocally, incorporating the biological into social explanation does not, in fact, necessitate an overly deterministic role for the latter. Indeed, while any adequate inquiry into the sociology of emotions must confront the 'limits of the social', it nonetheless remains the case that human biology, far from being fixed and immutable, displays a high degree of plasticity in relation to broader sociocultural influences. Seen in these terms, feelings are not stored 'inside' us, as the organismic theorists would have it. Rather, in a more sophisticated interactionist model, the management of feeling may contribute to the very creation of it. In this way, Hochschild builds up a subtle and sophisticated view of human emotions, thereby effectively side-stepping the either (biology) or (society) debates of the past.

Feeling Rules and Emotion Management

Leading directly on from this first point is a second core feature of Hochschild's work, namely her ability to shuttle back and forth, in fruitful ways, between the private realm of 'personal troubles' and broader 'public issues' of social structure. In this respect Hochschild's work is an illustration, *par excellence,* of what C. Wright Mills has elsewhere termed *The Sociological Imagination.*[15]

Through the concept of 'emotion management', Hochschild is able to inspect the relationship between emotional experience, feeling rules and ideology. As she explains, feeling rules are the side of ideology which deals with emotions: standards which determine what is 'rightly owed and owing in the currency of feeling'.[16] Emotion management, in contrast, is the type of work it takes to cope with these feeling rules. From this perspective, acts of emotion management are not simply private acts, rather they are used in exchanges under the 'guidance' of public feeling rules. Feeling rules, in effect, give 'social pattern' to our acts of emotion management; patterns which may be more or less equal, depending on the distribution of power and authority within any given society.

What happens then when there is a *transmutation* of the private ways we use feelings for commercial purposes? Answers to this question, for Hochschild, run very deep indeed, providing as they do a stunning indictment of the 'managed heart' in advanced capitalist societies. These issues, as Hochschild shows, are clearly illustrated in her empirical sociological study of flight attendants. While all of us must confront the requirements of emotional labour in some shape, sense or form, the dilemmas of the flight attendant are particularly acute in this respect. Forced to wear their 'company hearts' on their sleeve and to publicly peddle the corporate image through a pretty, continually smiling, face; *'the emotional style of offering the service becomes part of the service itself*.[17] Drawing on Goffman's earlier work on the vicissitudes of impression management, Hochschild makes a useful distinction here between what she terms 'surface' and 'deep' acting. In surface acting, we try to change how we outwardly appear through the manipulation of our body language. Deep acting, in contrast, requires a taking over of the 'levers of feeling production' in order to actually alter what we feel (for example, the suppression of anger and its replacement with sympathy). It is this latter strategy of deep acting which concerns Hochschild most. To 'work on' a feeling or emotion, as she explains, is the same as to 'manage' an emotion or to do 'deep acting'. Emotion work can be done by the 'self upon the self', by the 'self upon others' or by 'others upon oneself'.[18] Whatever the result, it is the *effort* rather than the *outcome*, and the *context* within which this occurs, which matters. Emotion management, in short, may be an honourable theatrical art or a perilous capitalist enterprise.

In particular, Hochschild identifies three specific stances which workers may take toward their work, each with its own sort of risk. In the first, the worker identifies too wholeheartedly with the job, unable to develop appropriate depersonalising strategies, and therefore is more likely to suffer stress and burnout. In the second, the worker clearly distinguishes between herself and her job and is less likely to suffer burnout. She may, however, blame herself for making this very distinction and denigrate herself as 'just an actor, not sincere'. In the third strategy, the worker distinguishes herself, like the second, from the act, but does not blame herself for doing so and sees the job as positively requiring the capacity to act. For this actor, however, there is, as Hochschild stresses, some risk of estrangement from acting altogether, and indeed some cynicism about it: 'We're just illusion makers.'[19]

If in the first stance, the worker is too much present in the role, then in the third, the problem is wholly reversed. In all three, however, the essential dilemma remains, namely, 'how to adjust one's self to the role in a way that allows some flow of self into the role but minimizes the stress the role puts on the self'.[20] In each, this problem is aggravated by the lack of control the worker exerts over the conditions of work itself. As Hochschild explains, the less the influence the worker has, the more likely it is that one of two things will happen: 'Either she will over-extend herself and burn out, or she will remove herself from the job and feel bad about it.'[21]

In highlighting these emotional dilemmas of the 'managed heart', Hochschild's study points to the more general sociological point that human feeling, in advanced capitalist society, has become increasingly 'commoditised', thereby linking the public and private worlds through the domain of emotions. As she states:

When deep gestures of exchange enter the market sector and are bought and sold as an aspect of labour power, feelings are commoditized. When the manager gives the company his [sic] enthusiastic faith, when the airline stewardess gives her passengers her psyched-up but quasi-genuine reassuring warmth, what is sold as an aspect of labour power is deep acting.[22]

Gender and Class Patterns to Emotion Work

Underpinning these issues is a third key characteristic of Hochschild's work, namely her central preoccupation with issues of gender and class. In general, as she argues, lower-class and working-class people tend to work more with *things*, and middle-class and upper-class people tend to work more with *people*. This division, in turn, is overlaid by the fact that more women than men deal with people as a job – males, for example, comprise only 15 per cent of flight attendants. Thus there are both gender- and class-related patterns to the civic and commercial use of human feelings; public patterns with private emotional costs.

This intersection of gender, class and emotions is, perhaps, most fully brought out in Hochschild's other major book, *The Second Shift*;[23] an empirical study of working parents and the so-called 'revolution' at home. A deeply personal, compassionate view of couples struggling to find the time and energy for jobs, children and marriage, Hochschild identifies what she sees to be a major division in gender ideology between a 'traditional ideal' of caring and another more 'egalitarian ideal'. Indeed, as she shows, a split between these two ideals seemed to run not only between social classes, but also between partners within marriages and between 'two contending voices inside the same conscience'.[24]

At the time of Hochschild's first interviews, only 18 per cent of wives were married to men who shared the second shift. Most of the rest, for a variety of reasons, did not press their husbands to change. Given these tensions and dilemmas, women usually pursued several strategies over time; first being a 'supermom', then cutting back on her hours at home, precipitating a crisis, and then either cutting back on her hours at work or further limiting her work time at home. In doing so, wives often needed to do a great deal of emotion work in order constantly to sustain the ideology or myth that the relationship was indeed 'a good one'. Within these strategies, resentment and cynicism frequently resurfaced in different areas of the relationship; emotional costs borne by husbands as well as wives.

In highlighting these gender-related issues, Hochschild is able to show how the revolution at home has influenced women faster than it has influenced men. The unevenness of this revolution has thus driven a wedge, at the present time, between husbands and wives; the home, in effect, becomes the 'shock absorber' of contradictory pressures from the outside world. Seen in these terms, women's emotion work – whether cast in terms of 'denial' or 'intuitive genius' – is often all that stands between the 'stalled (feminist) revolution on the one hand, and (a deluge of) broken marriages on the other'.[25]

Methodology and the Study of Emotions

Perhaps the fourth salient feature of Hochschild's work concerns her methodological stance on the study of emotions in social life. Within the sociology of emotions, debates continue to rage over positivism versus anti-positivism, quantitative versus qualitative methods, prediction versus description, and managing versus accounting for emotions.[26] While some sociologists, emulating the model of the natural sciences, see emotions as more or less objective phenomena which lend themselves to measurement, prediction and control, others in contrast, stress the more subjective aspects of emotions, including forms of emotional feeling, identity and selfhood. Kemper,[27] for example, in a positivist vein, argues that social structures (power and status) give rise to specific emotions – at least modally – and that a sociology of emotions must incorporate the physiological underpinnings of emotional response. In contrast, writers such as Denzin[28] assert a vigorous anti-positivist stance, resisting efforts to quantify emotions and focusing instead on self-feeling as an ongoing structure of lived experience, including the phenomenal body and the inner moral meaning of this feeling for the self which feels the feeling.

Enough has already been said here to place Hochschild's work firmly within this latter, more qualitative or 'naturalistic', tradition of sociological research. While meta-emotional concepts such as emotion management techniques may indeed lend themselves to basic frequency counts according to factors such as class and gender,[29] Hochschild's commitment is, first and foremost, to a qualitative, anti-positivist, view of the (emotional) world. This is clearly evident, not simply in her interactional theory of emotions (described above), but also in her preferred choice of methods with which to study these issues empirically. *The Managed Heart*, for example, combines a variety of qualitative methods including observation, interviews, attendance at training sessions and so on, using flight attendants and bill collectors – 'the toe and heel of capitalism' – to illustrate two extremes of occupational demand on feeling. Similarly, *The Second Shift* involved intensive interviews with fifty couples, together with observational work in a dozen homes, using couples such as Nancy and Evan Holt, Ann and Robert Myerson, Barbara and John Livingstone, to bring the study 'to life' in an emotionally illuminating way. In doing so, Hochschild offers us deep insights into the rich, complex and contradictory nature of emotional life and gender relations in late-twentieth-century society; insights lost to large-scale surveys, and other forms of quantitative assessment.

The Search for Authenticity

A fifth characteristic of Hochschild's work, one which underpins many of the previous themes and issues, is her moral stance and humanistic concern for the fate of emotions in contemporary social life. This is perhaps most clearly evident in her concern with problems of 'authenticity' and 'estrangement' in advanced capitalist society. *The Managed Heart*, for example, is replete with references to the 'human costs' of emotional labour, from 'burnout' to feeling 'phony', 'cynicism' to 'emotional deadness', 'guilt' to self-'blame'; costs which could, she suggests, be reduced if workers felt a greater sense of control over the conditions of their working lives.

As Hochschild observes, the more our activities as individual emotion managers are managed by organisations, the more we tend to celebrate the life of 'unmanaged feeling'.[30] In this way, Hochschild, in true Goffmanesque style, champions the little ways in which the self resists the institutional pull of commoditised emotional exchange, from the circumvention of feeling rules to the wider cultural concern with so-called 'spontaneous', 'natural' or 'authentic' feeling – a development manifest in the growing popularisation of 'psy' therapies which add a new 'introspective twist' to the self-help movement begun in the last century.[31]

Yet it is precisely here, as Hochschild points out, that a central paradox emerges, namely that the more we attempt to 'get in touch with' or 'recover' our 'true feelings', the more we make feeling itself subject to command, manipulation and various forms of management.[32] In this respect, Hochschild's concern with issues of authenticity – including the inauthenticity of the search for authenticity itself – ultimately translates into a Rousseauesque concern with the Noble Savage. What, in this day and age, makes Rousseau's Noble Savage seem so noble, Hochschild argues, was his ability to feel what he felt spontaneously, unfettered by any (conventionalised or commercialised) feeling rules. He did not, in other words, 'let himself feel good', 'get in touch' with, or 'into', his emotions. Rather, what distinguishes him from his latter-day pop therapy admirers is the utter absence of any calculation, will or conscious ratiocination:[33] a truly spontaneous form of spontaneity, a deeply authentic form of authenticity, which Hochschild, like Rousseau himself, (romantically?) longs for. Seen in these terms, Hochschild's work provides a profound Rousseauesque critique of the human condition in late-twentieth-century capitalist society; one which calls not simply for a practical politics of worker control, but an existential reclaiming of authentic self-feeling and a championing of the 'unmanaged heart'.

Seeing Things Differently

As I have already suggested, one of the major strengths of Hochschild's work lies in her ability to transcend many traditional boundaries and divisions within the social sciences. In this respect, like the sociology of emotions itself, her work has relevance to a broad range of issues, from organisational theory[34] through to recent work on gender and intimacy.[35] However, perhaps the area where her work has had the most personal impact on me is in the area of health and illness.

Hochschild's perspective on emotion management has been readily translated into studies of the emotional division of labour in health care. Such investigations range from studies of the 'sentimental order' of the technologised hospital right through to those of the detechnologised hospice,[36] and constitute a rich new seam of research within the sociology of health and illness. Most importantly for me, however, alongside critical explorations of the emotional sides of health and illness,[37] including the experience of pain and suffering,[38] it has opened up a whole new way of viewing social inequalities in health and the social causes of disease.

How, for example, does society affect the health of its members? How do the social and economic conditions in which you find yourself affect the likelihood of your suffering from mental and physical illness? What role do emotions play in the social patterning of disease? Following Freund's[39] pioneering work in this area – one which builds on the sociological insights of Goffman and Hochschild – it is possible to explore these questions more fully through a critical exploration of the interrelationship between social status, social control, emotion work and bodily states, including those that may contribute to health and disease.

For Freund, differing modes of emotional being are, in effect, different ways of feeling empowered or disempowered. These feelings of empowerment or disempowerment are, in turn, very much linked to people's material and social conditions of existence. Having one's feelings ignored or, perhaps even worse, termed irrational – what Hochschild[40] terms the absence of 'status-shields' to protect the self – is so fundamental that it is analogous to people questioning your very sense experience ('you must have imagined it'). Less powerful people, face a 'structurally in-built handicap' here. Their confidence is undermined from the start when it comes to trying to manage social and emotional information and this handicap may, in turn, contribute to 'dramaturgical stress', existential fear and neuro-physiological perturbation. Emotional being, social agency and structural context, are therefore inextricably related, and it is this cluster which physically and emotionally seeps into the body in a range of different ways.

Somatic

Pertaining to the cells and tissues of the body as opposed to the (reproductive) germ line. The stress of the emotion work required of a working-class woman in her daily life, for example, could lead to an over-production of adrenalin that could, in turn, lead – slowly but surely – to damaging changes in the cells of the body. Such somatic mutations are not passed on to children as somatic cells are non-reproductive.

In particular, Freund argues that social relationships may engender a form of 'schizokinesis' in which a split arises between what is consciously shown and experienced, as opposed to what occurs **somatically**. It is clear that emotional and other kinds of distress alter physiological reactivity. Stress can cause neurohormonally related functions such as blood pressure to markedly increase even while this is not consciously experienced. Here Freund poses two extremely pertinent sociological questions: first, just how 'deep' can the social construction of feelings go? and second, do certain forms of emotion work leave their scars on an 'unconsciously knowing body'? The answer to the first question seems to be 'very deep indeed': society affects physiological reactivity deep within the recesses of the human body. In answering the second question Freund's concept of schizokinesis certainly implies that the conscious mind can be damagingly unaware of the body's response. Freund notes that our position in a social hierarchy, especially if it is a less powerful one, can be a strong factor in the shaping of our emotions. There is a tendency to internalise the emotional definitions that others impose on what we are or 'should' be. The physiological aspects of such processes are of interest to those studying emotions. However, these physical aspects may also be seen as examples of ways in which social controls are sedimented and fixed in the psycho-soma of the person. Physiological aspects of social activity can also act as a form of feedback that colours the tone of existence. This feedback can *indirectly* serve social control functions. For instance, conditions that create depression construct an emotional mode of being where the motivation to resist is blunted.[41]

The argument here is for a subtle and sophisticated form of 'socialised' (that is, externally 'pliable') biology rather than a reductionist socio-biology; one which accords emotional modes of being a central role in linking the health and illness of the embodied social agent to the wider structures of power and domination, civilisation and control in society. In these and many other ways, the sociology of health and illness is proving a particularly fertile terrain upon which to fashion these newly evolving debates about emotions in social life.

Legacies and Unfinished Business

Legacies are often talked about posthumously. In Hochschild's particular case, however, they are thankfully both active and ongoing. Perhaps Hochschild's major contribution in this respect has been the manner in which, through her pioneering sociological work on the 'fate' of emotions in contemporary society, she has enabled us to 'see' the world differently; a view as relevant to sociological practitioners themselves, as emotionally embodied agents, as it is to those they seek to study. Seen in this new, corporeally expressive light, it is emotions which inform our particular view of the world, emotions which suffuse our sense of selfhood and identity, emotions which provide the 'social glue' that binds members of society together, emotions which underpin our (intimate) embodied relations with others, emotions which are bought and sold in the capitalist marketplace, and emotions which provide the effervescent basis for social conflict and change. Intellectually as well as socially, economically as well as politically, culturally as well as therapeutically, emotions are now big business. In this sense, Hochschild's work both resonates with and reinforces the reflexive spirit of an emotion-conscious age; one involving an ever-increasing search for authenticity, spontaneity and so-called 'natural' expression.

Despite these important legacies, however, Hochschild's work is not without its critics. Not only is her analysis disappointing from a comparative-historical perspective – one which reveals that 'emotion management' has, in fact, been going on for millennia – it is also limited in focusing simply on contemporary commercial constraints and operating with a problematic private/public distinction. As Wouters states, from an **Eliasian** perspective:

> Developments in standards of behaviour and feeling do not stop at the borders of either public or private life; to live up to them signifies overall demands on emotion economy, an overall pattern of self-regulation, a sort of 'overall design of emotion management'. Hochschild only deals with the process of commercialisation in this century. In the more remote past she apparently visualizes a more ideal society. But such an ideal society never existed. Emotion management was never a private act, nor were rules for feeling ever only privately negotiated.[42]

Over the last hundred years, emotional exchange has become more varied and more open to idiosyncratic nuances. What Wouters refers to as a process of *informalization* can, therefore, be interpreted as a 'reversal' of a long-term trend, while at the same time being a 'continuation' as far as demands on affect economy and the management of drives and emotions are concerned. From this viewpoint, only stronger, more even, all-rounded self-restraints, allow for a greater sensitivity and flexibility of social conduct.[43] These observations highlight the importance of time to any adequate sociological account of emotions – the topic of Hochschild's most recent book which explores the 'shifting emotional magnets' undergirding home and the workplace.[44]

Duncombe and Marsden[45] also raise some important points regarding Hochschild's emotion management perspective, drawing upon their own recent empirical work on intimate heterosexual relationships in support of their claims. As they suggest, too little research has been done to date on how individuals actually *feel* about the emotion work they do: whether, for example, they see it as burdensome and alienating, or positive and rewarding. It is also important, as their own research shows, to explore more fully variations *among* as well as between men and women in how they actually *do* emotion work. Perhaps the key issue, however, concerns the need to distinguish more clearly between so-called 'real' underlying feelings – which Hochschild continues to describe as 'authentic' – and individuals' *sense* of authenticity in relation to the core self and identity they have developed through their earlier experiences. Lacking any independent guide to truly 'authentic' emotional behaviour, we have to accept, as Duncombe and Marsden rightly argue, that some individuals derive their sense of authenticity from 'core selves' and 'core identities' which various social, cultural and psychoanalytic commentators might wish to criticise as deeply 'inauthentic'.

Discussion of these issues of time and gender, in turn, lead us to another key issue concerning the 'fate' of human emotions in the newly emerging digital world of cyberspace and virtual reality. Here, in this 'non-place' of electronic bulletin boards (BBS), virtual conferences, virtual communities and virtual experiences, issues of social reflexivity, it is claimed, take on critical new dimensions as alternative forms of social interaction, emotions, trust and (cyber)sexual intimacy begin to open up – the harbinger of **Giddens**'[46] 'pure relationship' perhaps? While, as I have argued elsewhere,[47] much of this to-date is rhetoric rather than 'reality', the growing imbrication of humans and machines, and the ever-increasing (electronic) mediation emotional experience, does, nonetheless, open up the possibility of having to critically rethink a number of existing sociological concepts, including the 'framing' of 'reality', the nature of self-identity, and the relationship between 'emotion work', 'feeling rules', 'deep' and 'surface' acting within the (virtual) future.

All in all, this suggests an exciting and challenging future for the sociology of emotions, keying in as it does to a number of critical issues and debates within sociological theory and contemporary culture – from the problem of human embodiment to the challenge of postmodernism, and from the salience of the 'psy' complex to the vicissitudes of cybersex. Perhaps, like Hochschild herself, exposure to these sociological issues will help readers to 'see things differently' and to interpret, in a new emotional light, the smiles and expressive gestures they now see around them at eye level.

Acknowledgements

Thanks to Gill Bendelow for introducing me to the world of the '(un)managed heart'.

Further Reading

G. Bendelow and S.J. Williams (eds), *Emotions in Social Life: Critical Themes and Contemporary Issues* (London: Routledge, 1998). A useful collection of original essays on the sociology of emotions, including chapters by Hochschild, Denzin, Duncombe and Marsden, Freund, Williams and Bendelow, and Wouters.

N.K. Denzin, *On Understanding Emotion* (San Francisco: Jossey-Bass, 1984). A classic text, which explores, from an existential-phenomenological perspective, the lived relationship between emotions, the body and the self.

A.R. Hochschild, *The Managed Heart: The Commercialization of Human Feeling* (California: University of California Press, 1983). A shorter version of her emotion management perspective can be found in A.R. Hochschild, 'Emotion Work, Feeling Rules and Social Structure', *American Journal of Sociology*, **85**, (1979) 551–75.

A.R. Hochschild (with A. Machung), *The Second Shift: Working Parents and the Revolution at Home* (London: Piatkus, 1990/[1989]).

P. Stearns, *American Cool: Constructing a Twentieth Century American Style* (New York: New York University Press, 1994). For an interesting account of the historical and cultural construction of emotions, juxtaposing the Victorian era with contemporary America.

19

Michel Foucault

Lawrence Barth

Driving Impulses: The Enthusiasm for Experiment

What strikes one most immediately about the work of Michel Foucault is its intellectual breadth, and indeed more than one commentator paid tribute to his curiosity. The broad sweep of his work interests the sociological audience first because of the persistence with which it crosses the themes, both central and minor, of sociological teaching. From his early books on the history of madness to his last works on sexual experience among the ancient Greeks, Foucault pursued a continuous critical reflection upon 'the human subject'. His examination of the emergence of modern medical reason speaks to medical sociology; his analysis of western punitive reason touches criminology and the study of deviance; his discussion of deep shifts in the rationality of the human sciences goes to the heart of sociological thought. Yet, it is clearly not within sociology – neither in its accumulated knowledge nor with its point of view – that his writings would find their coherence, and in fact, Foucault was famous for finding no home among any of the established scholarly disciplines.[1]

Interestingly, this is the second reason Foucault has appealed to many within sociology: as with other human sciences there is a certain value placed upon both interdisciplinary work and a self-critical awareness of the discipline's limits. Foucault's writings provide a distinct and challenging perspective on the relations between power, subjectivity, and the human sciences, and while his work is noticeably unique, it can be understood as a creative response to certain intellectual legacies and political problems. Foucault was very much in the tradition of those annoyed and troubled by contemporary liberal society, but who have been horrified by the excesses of certain historical attempts to escape it: the Nazi slaughter of Jews because of 'who they are'; the Stalinist mass imprisonment and execution of dissenters on the grounds of a government's claim to 'know the truth'. These dangers – the will to define one's nature or identity, and the sovereign claim over one's life on the basis of truth – Foucault noticed running throughout modern society, and of course, it is easy to notice a connection between the human sciences and both of these dangers.

This did not lead Foucault to renounce rationality and the human sciences, but to analyze them with an eye toward holding these dangers in check. This places Foucault in a long philosophical tradition, for the elaboration of universal limits that reason itself must observe can be found in the eighteenth-century writings of Immanuel Kant.[2] It is respect for these limits that gave the human sciences their sense of being well founded, even reliable for the purposes of government. Obviously, this combination of power and know-ledge has brought western society a long way, and now our dangers appear to be different from those which troubled the eighteenth century. Foucault, like a number of others in France at the end of World War Two, sought a philo-sophical countertradition critical of our faith in the foundational subject of knowledge, and potentially more sensitive to particular connections between reason and domination. Reading Friedrich Nietzsche in the 1950s had a profound and lasting impact on Foucault's work in this respect, for it was Nietzsche's **genealogical** writings which showed that even our morality had a particular history, one moreover which bore the traces of an ongoing contest of wills.[3]

Genealogy

By 'genealogy' Foucault refers to an attitude based on a rejection of an immanent direction to history and society. Following Nietzsche it places much emphasis on the struggle for power by different forces and on the lack of a necessary order inherent in this. The methodological conse-quence of this attitude is that the historian should try to uncover the contingent and violent course that society has historically taken. Geneal-ogists do not look for grand evolutionary laws or deep meanings that can provide a key to the direction of history because they do not think that such an overarching direction exists. Instead, they trace developments from 'the surfaces of events, the small details, minor shifts, and subtle contours' (Dreyfus and Rabinow 1982, p. 108). By uncovering and tracing the power shifts and plays of domination inscribed in societal regimes genealogists seek to 'shatter their aura of legitimacy' (McNay 1992, p. 14).

The philosophical trajectory we have traced here bears a similarity to that which influenced both **Max Weber** and the early Frankfurt School writers, Theodor Adorno and Max Horkheimer (see Chapter 15, **Habermas**). Unfor-tunately, Foucault felt, their work was little known in mid-century France. However, the Nietzschean critique of reason did appear in France in the form of a history of science. Foucault's analytical methods, the particular practical aspects of his research, owe a great deal to this tradition, and particularly to the work of Georges Canguilhem and Gaston Bachelard (see Chapter 14, **Althusser**). Here, one might find an important source of Foucault's attention to detail, to the specific techniques by which knowledge of the human is gained, and to the certain effects the deployment of that knowledge would lead. The level and detail of his analyses suggest an important difference between Foucault's sense of our present dangers and that which one can find in Weber or the Frankfurt School: our fate is given less in the great shifts of western rationality than in the many and various practices by which we become both subjects and objects of the human sciences. It was for this reason that Foucault could give his intellectual attention to the many minor struggles he witnessed: they testified to a continuing enthusiasm for experimentation and contest. It should be noted that it is this ethos of practical experimentation which Foucault's writings can help one bring to criminology, law, or social work.

Rather than distill from Foucault a few generalizations about certain socio-theoretical categories, like power, truth, or the subject, we might remain closer to the spirit of Foucault's work by considering some topics which captured his analytical attention. The five central issues which follow, *discipline, sexuality, the dangerous individual, ethics,* and the *genealogy of the present,* represent *different kinds* of issues Foucault analyzed, and we have in these five respectively, a set of practices, an experience, a fear, the relationship with oneself, and a question, one he felt a philosopher must ask today. In each case, we can see something of what Foucault learned about the formation of the human subject at the intersection of knowledge and power.

Key Issues: Critiques of the Subject

Discipline

Western culture tends generally to value the humanity of each and every individual, even those judged to be criminal or deviant. One aspect of this humanity within ourselves is one's capacity for moral reform, for self-diagnosis and improvement. Our societal norms encourage us to measure and adjust our conduct; our prisons, in principle, insist upon it. In *Discipline and Punish,* Foucault analyzed our pervasive and reasoned compulsion to normalize individuals, to punish and reform deviance.[5] The book opens with a historical alteration in our rationality and practices of punishment around the turn of the nineteenth century, an event which also displays certain connections we continue to make today between imprisonment as our mode of punishment, the human sciences as our source of individual standards, and the constant improvement of our individual capacities as a political goal. To highlight that historical alteration, Foucault juxtaposes an account of a mid-eighteenth-century torture and execution and an early-nineteenth-century prisoners' timetable. In the eighty years separating the two, imprisonment had become the nearly universal mode of punishing criminals, and the disciplinary techniques it rested upon would also define the new humanist terrain upon which punishment, norms, and politics would intersect.

The change was not on account of the value we place upon the human individual; rather, discipline made that value practicable and politically useful. Discipline refers to a series of techniques or arts for the observation, measurement, training, and direction of individuals. Foucault found that these were already widely practiced in the military, in schools and monasteries: places in which one's actions come under the direction of another's will. The practical knowledge of human capacities and reformability which was compiled in this sort of institution clearly displays a link between the human sciences and domination. Nevertheless, the point that Foucault emphasizes throughout is that discipline works upon one's actions, engages one's will to perform. The tortured body of the condemned is replaced in the nineteenth century by the trained and mobilized body of the disciplines. It is this which makes discipline distinctly well suited not only to the reform of criminals, but also to the education of students, the management of workers, or the training of the modern army: it is the kind of power which 'makes' the necessary individuals who will populate the western nation-states in the nineteenth and twentieth centuries.

Foucault was interested not only in analyzing the problems of our contemporary prison system, but also in the practical genealogy of the moral individual upon which the rationality of prisons is based. What his historical investigation reveals is a disciplinary power which is diffused throughout society, and may even be said to work in specific institutions because of this wider generalization and acceptance. Our reliance upon and belief in norms circulates through our language and politics; deviations draw public attention and arouse concern. Nevertheless, disciplinary practices operate only in relation to a specific program and goal, only on the basis of a certain knowledge and authority, only in a well-defined setting on a limited number of people.[6] Foucault's emphasis upon the **panopticon** – its finite architecture, its organization of the activity and observation of the few – alerts the reader to this essential point. One might say that the power *to* discipline depends upon the limited authority of a certain practical expertise; the power *of* discipline refers to our generalized concern to measure and adjust our conduct in relation to norms. It would be a mistake to understand Foucault as suggesting that western society is governed like a prison. Because of the power of discipline, our society is precisely unlike the prison.

Panopticon

Jeremy Bentham's idea of the panopticon had a great influence on the new technology of power brought into the nineteenth-century prison. Panopticon means 'all-seeing' and involved a tower situated in the middle of a courtyard from the top of which the prison guards could look down into the prisoner's cells and observe them twenty-four hours a day. The prisoners were aware that their 'correct behaviour' was being monitored. Even if the guards were not observing them the prisoners did not know this because the guards could not be seen from the cells. Psychologically the prisoners were under constant surveillance, and were aware that the guards had the power to issue punishments and rewards.

Sexuality

During the 1960s and early 1970s, the time just prior to Foucault's writing of *The History of Sexuality*, there was a tendency to imagine a general prohibition and silence concerning our sexuality. There was talk of the importance of sexual liberation; connections were drawn to the workers' struggle and the women's movement; political programs traced its linkages to social revolution. It seemed curious to Foucault that an experience which had clearly not been denied us, which was the topic of such pervasive and endless discussion, should be imagined as having been repressed and censored. This seemed more the result of our misconception of power, and he proposed an alternative series of questions. How have we been led to speak endlessly of sex? Why has sexuality been so intensely pursued by western governance? Why has sex been the object of such scrutiny, the key to so many types and disorders of the personality, the occasion of so many therapies? How have we been led to experience our sexuality as the private experience of the individual, an inner truth which one must master or express? The history of sexuality suggested to Foucault that it could be mapped at the intersection of a vast array of western techniques by which we know and govern ourselves. Not surprisingly, given this scope, when *The History of Sexuality* was published, it was presented as the introduction to a projected six-volume study.[7]

In spite of the vastness of the topic, there are three important themes which can be distilled from *The History of Sexuality*. First, we learn that relations of power have affected even what we take to be our innermost experience of ourselves, our 'secret' desires. However, contrary to the repressive hypothesis, the character of this effect is not that of a prohibition, but that of a mobilization, an incitement, and an organization of our sexual experience. Foucault concedes that since the seventeenth century there has been a screening and control of statements about sex, a new decorum and propriety. However, he also discovered a massive proliferation of public discourses concerning sex: 'an institutional incitement to speak about it, and to do so more and more; a determination on the part of the agencies of power to hear it spoken about, and to cause *it* to speak'.[8] The effects of this public discourse are to multiply individual sexualities, perversions, and aberrations, to charge parents, educators, doctors and others with a vigilance toward the 'hidden' sexual practices of children, students, and patients, in short, to saturate social space, by the nineteenth century, with the powers and pleasures of sexuality.

As a second theme, Foucault traces the multitudinous practices of confession by which we have been obliged to render our desires in speech and subject ourselves to interpretation. Beginning with the early Christian monastery, and progressively dispersed throughout law, psychiatry, medicine, pedagogy, family relationships, and so on, 'it is in the confession that truth and sex are joined, through the obligatory and exhaustive expression of an individual secret'.[9] Our twentieth-century calls for self-expression, liberation, or fulfillment are no doubt variations on the imperative to subject ourselves to the disclosure of our inner truths. However, this endless interpretation of ourselves as subjects of desire, as though our individual truth originated in this inner nature, occludes the extent to which the very practices of self-interpretation and self-disclosure have a political history.

Finally, then, it is through a certain political history that Foucault accounts for the highly charged network of relations which enlivens and orders our western sexual experience. Beginning in the eighteenth century, 'governments perceived that they were not dealing simply with subjects, or even with a "people", but with a "population", with its specific phenomena and its peculiar variables: birth and death rates, life expectancy, fertility', and so on.[10] In this way one may understand the importance sex has assumed in western culture over the last three centuries, for it was 'at the pivot of the two axes along which developed the entire political technology of *life*', namely, the disciplines of the body, and the regulation of populations.[11]

The Dangerous Individual

A court case in 1975 involving a serial rapist caught Foucault's attention.[12] It seems the defendant refused to speak prior to his sentencing, refused to give an account of himself. This troubled the judge, and moved a juror to blurt out to the defendant the imperative of revealing himself. Foucault wants us to notice that the law falters before punishing those whose inner truth we do not know. It is not enough to know the crime that has been committed, for it is the criminal rather than his action which is punished. The functioning of the law is linked to the question, 'Who are you?' But, surrounding this question there is a fear, now generalized in our social perceptions: that of the dangerous individual. Drawing together a number of themes from his work throughout the 1960s and 1970s, Foucault presents an analysis of these connections, and points to a danger which he considers still more troubling:

that of a society which links together the power to punish, a public concern with social dangers, and the various institutions arrayed to probe and define one's individual truth.[13] He asks, does this 'not give society rights over the individual based on what he is?... on what he is by nature?'[14]

Foucault's analysis follows a subtle and complex interweaving of psychiatry and penal law during the nineteenth century, through which the former could lend its expertise in determining the motivation and responsibility of those accused before the law, and which also served the purposes of psychiatry, striving at that time to consolidate and justify its function of controlling the dangers hidden in human behavior.[15] It is important to notice that, in spite of psychiatry's usefulness to the criminal justice system, our legal codes did not fundamentally change; they did not relinquish to the human sciences the power to judge or assess guilt. Nevertheless, Foucault asks, is not the criminal court under a certain pressure to consider the dangerousness of an individual?

The problem of the dangerous individual arose, not within, but at the margins of, this nineteenth-century interaction of law and psychiatry, that is, at the limits of their respective capabilities. Certain cases involving violence with neither reason nor definitive signs of madness exposed the juridical difficulty of assessing one's responsibility and reformability, and hence the appropriate punishment. On the other hand, as criminal cases threatening society they posed a question of dangerous behaviors which psychiatry might name, but was powerless to control. As one can see, a solution would lie with a psychiatric science 'advanced' enough to make a definitive *judgement* separating the responsible from the insane in each case. Just such a science, however, might heighten pressure on the criminal system to consider in *its* judgement, not only guilt or innocence, but the dangerousness of an individual. While law resisted the formal pressures which came from psychiatry, Foucault points to a series of other changes in law, society, and the human sciences toward the end of the nineteenth century which served to expand and intensify this pressure, creating a public obsession with the danger of criminality.

In this context, Foucault mentions but does not elaborate, 'the intensive development of the police network, which led to a new mapping and closer surveillance of urban space'.[16] In this new field of urban dangers, did not sociology find one of its important functions, namely to assist in the adjudication of responsibilities and dangers? And this leads to a question a sociologist might often ask today: when sociology pursues the truth of a group, a community, or a culture within the city, when they assign responsibility for its dangers, or even defend it against the judgements of power on the basis of that truth, is the sociologist also enlivening a terrain obsessed with the fear of the dangerous individual?

Ethics

Running throughout Foucault's work, through his analyses of discipline, sexuality, and the many interactions of law and medicine, is the understanding that we are subjects who may resist power, may refuse to confess an inner truth, indeed, may make a difference. Of course, this would depend upon the subject having certain inner resources, the capacity for a relationship with oneself in excess of that drawn from us by power. It is this relationship with oneself that Foucault calls ethics; it makes possible the cultivation of one's life as distinctive. Foucault explored the question of ethics by analyzing the problems one's sexual conduct posed for the ancient Greeks.[17] Their writings on the topic indicated four kinds of relationship – that with one's body, with one's wife, with boys, and with truth – in which one's sexual practices occasioned consideration, reflection, and debate. Interestingly, however, in none of these relationships did the sexual practices of Greek men meet with a prohibition imposed by power or a moral code. Nevertheless, their writings discussed and prescribed the cultivation of oneself in such a way as to meet the moral concerns and problems which arose around their sexual practices.

So, when Foucault asked how sexual behavior came to be conceived as a domain of moral experience – and this was the central problem addressed in his last two books – his questions were directed to these practical matters of one's relationship with oneself, such that one could experience moral choices and actions as one's own. Between a moral code, handed down over time, and a moral action, there are many different ways of conducting oneself. These differences depend upon, for example, what aspect of oneself is to be, say, promoted, restrained, or shaped; or upon the exercises that will make one capable of complying; or upon the goal promised by a life of compliance. By focusing his analysis at this level of the relationship to oneself, Foucault noticed something he considered very important: although we share with the ancient Greeks certain moral themes – the importance of conjugal fidelity, prohibition of incest, recommendations against excess – the Greeks practiced and experienced a very different sexual life.

Furthermore, precisely because their sexual ethics emerged around issues which were neither prohibited by moral precept nor governed by law, they demonstrate a historical example of practices of freedom. For the Greeks, acts associated with intense pleasure were meant to be regulated, not by universal legislation or morality, but by a cultivated personal art which involved both one's judgement and one's knowledge, and which entailed one's dominion over oneself.[18] Also, this cultivation of oneself was not in opposition to an active or political life, nor was it connected either to an individualism or to a positive valuation of private life, of family or domesticity.[19]

It is important to note that Foucault's writings do not present a nostalgia for the Greeks and their sexual practices. In interviews, he repeated often that it cannot be a question of returning to an ancient experience, and for that matter, he did not find the Greeks admirable. What one learns from these writings is that it has been possible to experiment upon, consider, reflect upon one's relationship to the self without the imposition of law or recourse to a universal morality. Another caution is also in order here, for in our western enthusiasm for freedom one is liable to forget those other dimensions of Foucault's work, those through which he describes precisely the normalization and regulation of the free. One should remember that Foucault undertook his research in relation to a specific political problem in the present – that of the mobilization and regulation of sexual practices – just as the Greeks had conducted their own reflections.

The Genealogy of the Present

We can see from these examples that Foucault's writings draw upon issues both near at hand and from the occasionally quite distant past. It is in the particular way that a question of the present is defined and then illuminated by the materials of the past that we can see the distinctive manner in which Foucault's historical analyses, his politics, and his intellectual ethics link together. The present-day contestations he noticed around prison reform, in the experience of our sexuality, or in a courtroom story, drew Foucault's attention because collectively these and others indicated a certain alteration in our history, a new challenge to the ways in which power makes individuals into subjects. Importantly, it is the fact of contestation itself which highlights a problem for our contemporary thought, for it demonstrates the will to make a difference. This is the impulse which drives both the philosophical question of the present and the practical critique of our subjectivity.[20]

Additionally, Foucault felt that this impulse was experienced today in terms of specific problems and goals, that these contests were directed toward the achievement of immediate ends, rather than toward broad social transformation. They were contests around the particular and local status of the subject. Nevertheless, the three great modes of social critique, namely Marxism, feminism, and psychoanalysis, had shown themselves to be less than attentive to the particularity of these local contests, leaving the *practical* critique of our subjectivity at an impasse. It was this present impasse in the intellectual practice of critique which compelled Foucault to reflect upon the particular philosophical terrain which linked critique to universal foundations and an ideal of total transformation.

Again, it is Kant whom Foucault takes as the originator of this way of thinking about the present, when the former characterized the Enlightenment – his present – as the 'way out' of people's self-imposed acceptance of another's authority: 'both as a process in which men participate collectively and as an act of courage to be accomplished personally'.[21] Kant is here formulating the question of the present as one which includes another within its frame: who are we today, such that we might fulfill this present promise? Foucault could recognize his own project in this aspect of Kant's critique of the present. Unfortunately, he would have to avoid its further ties to 'programmes for a new man', which link the practice of critique both to universal knowlege of the human subject and to ideals of total transformation. In place of Kant's universal foundations for the human sciences, Foucault proposes we ask different questions: 'in what is given to us as universal, necessary, obligatory, what place is occupied by whatever is singular, contingent, and the product of arbitrary constraints?'[22] Foucault's realignment of critique is directed against both our present normalization of the human subject and the traditions of total critique connected to it.

Foucault's research on madness, medical reason, discipline, and sexuality collectively presented examples of a form of critique which assessed the costs of our practical knowledge of the human subject, and yet which also avoided treating that knowledge as false, ideological, or repressive of the 'true' human subject. These studies of the practical elaborations of western knowledge about ourselves forced one to reflect upon those critical understandings of power which rendered it alternately as that which repressed or falsified the true human subject. One of Foucault's gifts to sociological study is the recognition that it will always be a mistake to isolate the theory of what power is from the analysis of how it works.[23] What is at stake in the historical analyses Foucault pursued is the extent to which a different thought and a different conduct might be introduced into the present, that is, the extent to which the growth of our human capabilities can 'be disconnected from the intensification of power relations'.[24] The signs around us today suggest that this requires a rather different critique of the subject than that which Kant employed to challenge monarchy.

Seeing Things Differently

Foucault's research into ethical practices among the ancient Greeks revealed the constitution of a domain of moral experience which could be referred neither to a fundamental human nature nor to the imposition of law or a moral code. This made it possible to construe 'personal life' as having a history, but one nevertheless different from those which derive from prevailing conceptions of the private self. Against a libertarian perspective which conceives one's private life as a domain of moral autonomy, Foucault was able to present the cultivation of one's ethical self as the practical response to particular problems in the domain of experience. Against certain versions of feminism which understand the private sphere as both false and repressive, Foucault described an ethics which was both a practice of freedom and a cultivated relationship with knowledge. Understood as a domain of experience and conduct, the question of the subject could be opened to genealogical research which avoids the absolute polarization of public and private life, and yet without collapsing the distinction into a ruse of power. One of the most important effects of Foucault's research into the constitution of the moral subject has emerged in a reconceptualization of the family in its relation to both public and private life.

Jacques Donzelot's *The Policing of Families* is perhaps the earliest and one of the most important books to have taken up Foucault's lead and investigated the network of relations by which the family became linked over the course of the nineteenth century to the development of liberal governance.[25] Of course, from the liberal point of view, the family is by nature an enclosed and private domain of sentiment, care, and nurture. The impulse toward these affective family relationships is taken to reside within the timelessness of one's soul or inner self. Instead, Donzelot is able to show how the family was reconstructed during the early nineteenth century as an intimate environment emphasizing the bonds of marriage and the parental care of children. Furthermore, these family relationships were overseen and evaluated by an extensive 'tutelary complex' involving educators, doctors, psychiatrists, social workers, and philanthropists. Rather than supposing the 'private' family to have succumbed to such intrusions by the state, the autonomy of the family was promoted as an instrument in relation to the wider mobilization and normalization of social life.

This latter point must be further emphasized, for a number of critical perspectives on the family imagine it to be simply or primarily a domain subject to the repressions and oppressions of patriarchy or capitalism. Donzelot agrees that the nineteenth-century mobilization of the family involves both a differentiation of gender roles within the family, and a differential deployment of the tutelary complex in relation to class. However, his version of the family's role in the socialization process does not conform to an understanding of the family as essentially constraining the potentials of one's personal life. Instead, Donzelot tells us, 'It could even be said that this familial mechanism is effective only to the extent that the family does not reproduce the established order, to the extent that its juridical rigidity or the imposition of state norms do not freeze the aspirations it entertains, the interplay of internal and external pressures and pulls that make of it a locus of possible or imagined transformations.'[26] The family, then, describes a domain of personal and social relationships organized to provide a certain dynamism within liberal governance. Within liberalism, that is, the family becomes the practical and privileged domain not only of moral regulation, but also for the pursuit of that personal growth, freedom, and fulfillment so valuable for capitalism.

Donzelot's account of the nineteenth-century family has been further developed for the twentieth century in Nikolas Rose's *Governing the Soul,* in which he traces a virtual explosion of psychological knowledge and its implantation within the networks governing the conduct of our personal lives.[27] One of the key pursuits of psychological research has been the development of visible, normative standards for the evaluation of child development. These standards were widely disseminated among all who were in a position of responsibility or authority toward children, such as teachers, health workers, parents, and so on. The result was a kind of continuous and intensified reflection on the care of children: 'In the space between the behaviours of actual children and the ideals of the norm, new desires and expectations, and new fears and anxieties could be inspired in parents, new administrative and reformatory aspirations awakened in professionals.'[28]

These and other similar developments in psychological knowledge encouraged the design and implementation of governmental programs directed toward the scrutiny, evaluation, and reform of the family. Importantly, however, the outcome of this extensive deployment of new rationalities of conduct was not the erosion of family autonomy, but its reaffirmation; nor was it the repression of the field of personal desires, but their intensification. 'The modern private family remains intensively governed, it is linked in so many ways with social, economic, and political objectives. But government here acts not through mechanisms of social control and subordination of the will, but through the promotion of subjectivities, the construction of pleasures and ambitions, and the activation of guilt, anxiety, envy, and disappointment.'[29] Since the nineteenth century, one's ethical and personal life, tightly bound to family relationships, has become the instrument and target of an ever-changing and proliferating set of governmental practices: not a repression, but an expanding incitement to be better than we are.

Legacies and Unfinished Business: Governmentality and Conflict

As Gilles Deleuze has suggested, 'the study of the variations in the process of subjectification seems to be one of the fundamental tasks which Foucault left to those who would follow him'.[30] One must agree with Deleuze's further point that this sketches a particularly 'fecund' area of research extending well beyond the analytical histories of private life discussed above. The terrain upon which Foucault came to place this question of the subject was that of governmental rationality, for which he often used the neologism, 'governmentality'. The term refers to the particular arts or rationalities by which people might be led to conduct themselves toward positive political goals, such as prosperity, vitality, security, and so on. Governmentality presents itself to genealogical analysis as a domain of reasoned practices, as we have seen in the foregoing examples of research into the government of the family. Nevertheless, Foucault's governmentality studies represent a certain shift in his work which he never fully elaborated, but which we may situate in relation to three points of reference: a problem, an emphasis, and a question.[31]

In a lecture at the beginning of 1976, Foucault indicated he felt his research to be at something of an impasse.[32] Between the normalization of individuals – those practices associated with discipline and confession – and the sovereign law of states, Foucault discerned an absolute opposition, in the sense that the former designates the measured differentiation of each individual and the latter describes the uniform imposition of laws upon all. No doubt there was an interrelation, but a gap had opened in Foucault's terrain of analysis. Further illuminating this problem was Foucault's sense that the conceptual opposition between the individual and the state which he had sought to avoid had returned within his own work, along with a model of power understood as struggle and submission, which he had also come to question. However, the change of emphasis in Foucault's work toward ethics, subjectification, and the practices of freedom both helped to define the problem and suggest a way forward.

This change of emphasis directs one's analytical attention to a field of governmental practices for the shaping of conduct, in relation to which the normalizing objectification of the individual represents only one axis. Government consists of the various instruments and rationalities assembled to link the power of the state, the regulation of populations, and a 'pastoral' power which addressed itself to the conduct of those who recognized themselves as subjects.[33] This raises the genealogical question of an art of government directed toward the conduct of each and all, in their individuality and uniformity, and which furthermore emphasizes the freedom of the subject as a central part of that art. In his courses and a number of lectures, Foucault sketched the outlines of such a genealogy, although this was never developed in book form.[34]

Foucault's governmentality studies have obviously presented a rich legacy for further research, as indicated by the ever-increasing number of books and articles which have taken these lectures as their point of departure.[35] Common to most of this recent research is an intention to flesh out Foucault's bare but suggestive outlines of a liberal art of government, and in particular to clarify the changes in our twentieth-century rationalities and practices of government which are manifested in the particular problems one faces today. The key question confronting the future of this research concerns the extent to which it will introduce creative responses to those areas of social life characterized by conflict and opposition, and here we might think especially of the problem of racism.

As a prelude to considering this issue of racism, we might remind ourselves that Foucault's analyses were conducted in relation to certain contemporary conflicts, for example, those which surround the pursuit of gay life. However, Foucault rejected the polarization of conflict around homosexuality as that which pitted the power of the state or society against the desires of an identifiable group of individuals. For reasons that should now be clear, he rejected both the notion of a 'global' homophobic power and the need to confess one's identity in the pursuit of rights. In an interview, Foucault pointed to the example of legal rights protecting homosexual practices, but without cultivating any broader acceptability and choice in one's wider relationships and sexual practices.[36] It is not just a question of gay rights, but a question of accepting differences and experimentation in the practice of a life.

Similarly, the problem of racism is almost uniformly presented in terms of domination, segregation, and 'othering', but might we not recognize here the continuation of those global and binarizing conceptions of power Foucault hoped to avoid? Ann Laura Stoler's recent book, *Race and the Education of Desire,* has gathered together Foucault's fragmentary and brief insights on the question of racism, and pressed them into a fruitful dialogue with postcolonial understandings.[37] Significantly, Stoler resituates Foucault's statements on to a geographical terrain with which he was relatively unfamiliar, namely the global terrain of colonial empire. The lesson here is that the spaces upon which genealogical questions are deployed will influence the power relations one may trace, as Foucault had already discovered in his interrogations of the prison, the clinic, and the asylum. In carefully attending to the spaces in which racist discourses array themselves we may learn more about the many 'singular, contingent, and arbitrary' uses to which they are put. The capacity of future research to insert a certain possibility of difference into this polarized field will no doubt help sociologists assess the legacy of Foucault for their work.

Further Reading

M. Foucault, 'Governmentality' in G. Burchell, C. Gordon and P. Miller (eds), *The Foucault Effect: Studies in Governmentality* (London: Harvester Wheatsheaf, 1991), pp. 87–104.

M Foucault, 'Afterword: The Subject and Power' in H. Dreyfus and P. Rabinow, *Michel Foucault: Beyond Structuralism and Hermeneutics* (Chicago: University of Chicago Press, 1982) pp. 208–26.

M. Foucault, *The History of Sexuality: An Introduction* (Harmondsworth: Penguin, 1978).

M. Foucault, *Discipline and Punish: The Birth of the Prison* (Cambridge: Polity Press, 1992).

M. Foucault, *Politics, Philosophy, Culture; Interviews and Other Writings, 1977–1984*, L. Kritzman (ed.), (New York: Routledge, 1988).

M. Foucault, 'What Is Enlightenment?' in P. Rabinow (ed.), *The Foucault Reader.* (New York: Pantheon Books, 1984), pp. 32–50.

20

Stuart Hall

Michèle Barrett

Key sociologist? Stuart Hall certainly is a key figure in contemporary sociology, but he was not trained in the discipline and his preoccupations are very different from those of mainstream sociology. Much of his work has been directed towards the development of 'cultural studies', which is now (largely through his efforts) widely recognized as an independent discipline. It is a sign of the current pluralism within sociology, and an indicator of the inter-disciplinarity of the subject in its present form in Britain, that Hall is such an influential figure.

Stuart Hall was born and raised in Jamaica; in 1951 he came to study English at Oxford. At Oxford he was identified with the politics of the West Indies, and of colonialism in general; also with the development of the 'new left' in Britain. In 1956 he abandoned the thesis he was writing on Henry James – a figure he was interested in as the last novelist before the dissolution of the 'narrative "I"' in the modernist literary revolution. Why in 1956? Because that was the year Soviet tanks rolled into Hungary, provoking anger and dissent among his colleagues and friends.

Stuart Hall married (the historian Catherine Hall) and settled in Britain. The 1950s were a formative period for him: they marked a complete break with traditionalist notions of culture and literature and his move towards a view of culture that binds it indissolubly to politics. The exploration of culture and power, much of it filtered through the lens of a socialism that rejected Stalinism, that turned to **Marx** only in a spirit of criticism and contestation, was to exercise him for many years.

He is best known for his work at the Centre for Contemporary Cultural Studies in Birmingham, indeed for many people Stuart Hall *was* CCCS, which in turn now is an international phenomenon called 'British Cultural Studies'. This period (1964–79) saw an incredible production of work, much of it collectively produced by staff and students at the Centre, on issues of theory, popular culture, class and resistance. The fluency of that output was disrupted, no doubt beneficially but also traumatically, by the challenges of feminist and black students, both of whom insisted on a different agenda of work.

In 1979 Stuart Hall moved to the Open University, with the project of making the ideas of cultural studies, and its radical politics, meaningful to a much wider range of students. He turned out to be a natural TV communicator. From this time his writing became more 'teacherly' – he typically now addresses his readers as 'you'. At the OU he has revolutionized the sociology curriculum twice over: by junking the 'founding fathers' and reconceptualizing the core mainstream of the subject in terms of the historical rise and decline of western modernity, and by introducing major courses in cultural studies, whose focus is representation, **signification,** identity and **cultural difference.** His time at the OU saw – outside the academic world – the establishment of a reputation as a political analyst of great perception, which was triggered by his prescient insights into the phenomenon of 'Thatcherism'.

Signification

A term used by structuralists and post-structuralists to refer to the way in which meanings are created by a double action. This double action involves, first, written or spoken words, or images – an advertisement, fashionable clothes, or whatever – that provide us with a kind of raw material for our senses. Second, we now have to interpret or understand this raw material – these script marks, sounds, arrangements of colours and shades – as *meaning* something. Usually we do this automatically, routinely, without giving it a second thought, with the meanings appearing as natural and inevitable. The meanings seem to press themselves on us, and they seem to be stuck with superglue to the raw material of these words, these sounds and these images. The term signification tells us that the bond between raw material (the 'signifier') and meaning (the 'signified') is much weaker than it seems, and that they are pasted together in different ways at different times by different societies, cultures and sub-cultures. Signification, thus, draws our attention to the *cultural process* by which the lines on a page, sounds in the air, a certain length and cut of cloth, become meaningful in very precise ways to people within particular social contexts.

Cultural Difference

Cultural difference is related to signification. It refers to the way that in particular societies and cultures, at particular times, some groups of people come to be seen as 'different'. The Nazis, to take an extreme example, singled out Jews, Gypsies and gays as 'different' in a radically discriminatory and negative manner. Post-structuralist thought highlights the many ways in which groups can be picked out, and 'signified' as different – it shows the cultural processes at work – and, in a definitely positive manner, it wishes to safeguard the rights of people to be 'different'. The main indicators of difference discussed in this literature tend to be those associated with differences of gender, ethnicity, race, age, religion, class, sexual orientation and language. The emphasis on such cultural differences often goes along with a political commitment to a radical pluralism.

In recent years, he has returned to the themes of colonialism and identity that preoccupied him earlier, this new work enriched through what he might describe as a 'necessary detour' through the study of class, power and culture. He has been able to settle personal accounts between Jamaica and England, and to explore the more general construction of what he has coined 'the West and the rest'. Migration is not only his own experience, it is *the* significant experience of the twentieth century. Thus Stuart Hall's identity as a 'diasporic intellectual' stands in for a more general experience in the postmodern, decolonizing world. His interest in identity is rooted in a passionate, if melancholy, sense of the structural power of social relations. Colonial culture can and does destroy you subjectively, he says, in an interview that is the nearest we have to an autobiography.[1] There is no separation between power, culture and the self.

Key Issues

Cultural Circuitry

It would be a mistake to push the electrical metaphor too far, since this is a model with some dud connections and fuses that can blow at any time. The central idea is that there is a circuit that is completed between the production and consumption of culture. The function of the circuit metaphor is to emphasize that, for cultural meaning to be established, it has to be received as well as sent. The question is not only what meaning did the producer intend to convey, but what meaning actually was conveyed? In other words, the audience is not a passive recipient but an active participant in the creation of meaning. The classic statement of this argument is found in one of Stuart Hall's most cited and reprinted papers, entitled 'Encoding/Decoding'.[2]

Hall argues that if we are interested in televisual meaning, for instance, we should not be working with a simple model of a message and an audience. Meanings are more complexly 'coded', through conventions which may be arbitrary – just as language codes are arbitrary rather than derived from their referents – but nonetheless powerful. We may not notice these codes in situations where we are decoding them automatically – we can say that in these cases they have become 'naturalized'. Hall is using here the basic principle of Saussurean linguistics – that signification works through a set of conventions causing signifiers (sounds or images) to indicate the concepts that are being signified. He indicates that a second basic argument from semiotics – that we should distinguish between literal (denotative) and associational (connotative) meaning – is more complex. Simple denotative meaning is possible in the abstract, but in practice is normally compounded with associations. Furthermore, these connotative codes are not equal, they often form part of a much wider cultural meaning and they relate to ranked hierarchies of understanding: the way that 'our society' sees things has power.

This is the context in which a television programme is produced. There are institutional relations at play in its production, there is a technical infrastructure, and there are frameworks of knowledge in which it takes place. None of these are necessarily determining, but they set the boundaries on the meanings that can be produced, or encoded into the broadcast. All the factors affecting the moment of encoding can be seen to be related to power, what Hall calls power 'in dominance' (that is, not comprehensive and inclusive, but exerting a push in one direction), and this leads to the encoding of what Hall terms a 'preferred reading' of the meaning. But the preferred reading is only one possible way of understanding the broadcast – Hall suggests we might have an 'oppositional' reading in which we reject its message, or a 'negotiated' one in which we only accept it in part. We might accept the general argument, but see how it affects particular groups differently. To take a simple example, a news item reporting a government decision to ban the export of land mines. It might be framed as 'the government today took a moral stand on the export of land mines that kill innocent children', or it might be framed as 'the government today put British industry in jeopardy by banning the production of land mines'. Depending on our views, we will 'read' the meaning with agreement or disagreement. We can take the dominant or preferred reading, accepting the item within the frame of what it takes for granted. Or we can oppose it, recognizing and rejecting its assumptions about what is right. Or we might say, well that is a good thing for children in Angola but a bad thing for my uncle who earns a living from making the mines (a 'negotiated' response).

The point is that a meaning has been encoded into the terms in which the item is framed – it is constructed as a discourse with assumptions about what is important and right. The paper has been so influential because it offers a more complex model of meaning than that of a simple message and a passive audience. It presents meaning in terms of an ineradicable link between cultural production and consumption. It constructs meaning as a two-way process and in this it is more similar to a 'hermeneutic' approach that focuses on understanding, than to any of the models characterizing sociology of the media. Most importantly, it locates meaning within a context of power and domination. It holds in suspension questions about the technical and aesthetic properties of cultural works, locating them in reference to an analysis of ideology and cultural hegemony. Finally, the case of television broadcasting is an example of Hall's general focus on popular culture – a choice that rejects traditional distinctions between 'high' art and 'mass' culture. In all these respects, 'Encoding/Decoding' can be read not only as an argument about interpreting television: it is also an indicator of the defining elements of the approach that has become 'cultural studies'.

The encoding/decoding model was put forward as a political one in two senses. The model inscribes power at the heart of the media, emphasizing the degree to which media output is formed within the institutions and discourses of power. It was also a political intervention in the field of media studies, which Hall regarded as dominated by a bland positivism typified by the approach of the Mass Communications Centre at Leicester. In a subsequent interview, he candidly described the motivation for the paper in unusually militaristic terms: 'Who I had in my sights was the Centre for Mass Communications Research, that was who I was trying to blow out of the water.'[3]

Stuart Hall's idea of a cultural circuit has taken hold as a better paradigm for cultural studies than the model previously dominant in media studies, which had tended to separate the message from the audience and studied them independently. Of course, the circuit itself can be conceived in different ways, and in Hall's own work we can find different ways of distinguishing the elements of it. The earlier work invokes Marxist categories of production and consumption, later formulations tend towards including regulation and identity; the key point is that the underlying dynamic model of a circuit remains a constant in Hall's way of approaching culture.

Hall's new paradigm solved more than the methodological problems of media studies. It also radically resolved a theoretical stalemate in the field known as 'sociology of art and literature'. This sub-field of sociology had been dominated by an approach that we might call 'reductionist' or 'reflectionist': influenced by the work of Marxists such as Lukács, it tended to interpret art as the expression of changing historical class forces. As we shall see later, the fundamental problem was that of 'determination'. This problem was posed in terms of explaining art as the superstructural reflection of more important factors – themselves understood rather narrowly as the economics of class relations. Sociology of art and literature was primarily concerned with explicating the 'class content' of the classical canon of western culture and its rigid formulations were beginning to disintegrate as the cultural studies approach came along.

Hall's emphasis on the circular character of cultural processes in society was thus well placed, and well timed, to offer an alternative to both the mechanistic descriptiveness of media studies and the narrow reflectionism of sociology of art and literature. It is no exaggeration to conclude that cultural studies as a discipline – now far more influential than sociology's attempts to study either art or the media – was definitively established in the encoding/decoding model.

Cultural Politics: Thatcherism and After

Stuart Hall's insistence on power as a central element of culture is complemented by his insistence on culture as a crucial element of power. Indeed, this has proved particularly indigestible to those on the left who see power as essentially driven by economic interests, and who persist in the view that cultural processes are somehow superficial in comparison with these 'structural' determinants. Stuart Hall has annoyed many of them by claiming that the study of cultural meaning is not a leisure activity, but the bread and butter of sociological work.

This theme in his work could be described, in the manner of a musical attribution, as 'Antonio Gramsci [*arr*. S. Hall]'. The Marxist tradition is classically divided between those who take an economic determinist position and those who see cultural and ideological practice as important in determining (rather than simply reflecting) political change. Gramscian Marxism, perhaps the most obvious and abiding theoretical influence on Hall's work, offers the strongest statement of the 'culturalist' position in this debate. It is, however, a debate of much more general significance than an internecine struggle within Marxist theory: contemporary sociology's unease about the place of cultural and media studies reflects a widespread disagreement within social and political analysis. This is why what is called the **linguistic turn**, the 'cultural turn', and the emphasis on 'discourse' in post-structuralist thought, has provoked such controversy in disciplines ranging from anthropology to urban studies. Philosophical materialism – the idea that material being is theoretically more important than culture or consciousness – is not simply a doctrine that underpins classical Marxism, it is a founding assumption of the social sciences.

Linguistic Turn

This refers to the widespread influence on philosophy, the humanities and the social sciences of structuralism and post-structuralism's insights into the processes of 'signification' (see above). It attempts to capture the significantly increased emphasis that these disciplines consequently placed upon the role played by language in the construction of social meanings and practices, cultural differences, and also upon scholarly attempts to 'represent' the world and what goes on in it.

The orientation and insights of Gramsci's work can be traced throughout Hall's writing. He has himself documented the ways in which his thinking on race – about which Gramsci did not write – has been influenced by his reading of Gramsci.[4] It is, however, in Hall's analysis of Thatcherism that we find the most effective application of Gramscian ideas to a new political situation in Britain. In January 1979, before the election which was to be the start of eighteen years of Conservative government, Hall published an analysis of 'The Great Moving Right Show' in the magazine *Marxism Today*. The article laid out the terms of his position on Thatcherism, and its wider political implications, particularly for the cherished assumptions – or the rigid and irrelevant certainties – of a puzzled and rudderless left.

Hall argued that Mrs Thatcher's political programme represented more than the usual pendulum swing between Labour and Conservative popularity – it was a decisive and irreversible shift to the right. He characteristically began by insisting that it was a fundamental mistake to see and discount these changes as mere ideology: reversing the usual chain of determinism he made the claim that 'the ideology of the radical right is less an "expression" of economic recession than the recession's condition of existence'. So the first move against the *doxa* of the left was to make the contentious theoretical point that Mrs Thatcher's political and economic programme was based on, drew its strength from, an ideological force – not vice versa.

To understand what was happening, Hall invoked the ideas of Gramsci. Considering that in the years to follow, Hall has often been accused of pessimism, it is perhaps appropriate that he cited Gramsci's slogan: 'pessimism of the intelligence, optimism of the will'. He argued that the crisis was an *organic* one, not merely *conjunctural*; it was *formative* of a new *historic bloc* which was emerging to construct a new *settlement*. The Thatcher programme had succeeded in translating a theoretical *ideology* into a popular *idiom*, with a language of *moralism*. Hall summarized the programme as a rich mix, combining 'the resonant themes of organic Toryism – nation, family, duty, authority, standards, traditionalism – with the aggressive themes of a revived neo-liberalism – self-interest, competitive individualism, anti-statism'. These elements were the building blocks of a new *hegemonic* project – the key feature of Hall's analysis. Gramsci's concept of hegemony (the securing of consent) allows us to see Thatcherism for what it was, a project to change the way in which people live out social and political conflict. In this, the popular appeal of an authoritarian language was crucial. Hall concludes that only by understanding the deep nature of the shift towards *authoritarianism* at a *popular* level, could the left begin to think about challenging the Thatcher project.

The history of British politics since 1979 has borne out Hall's analysis. The reluctance of the left to accept the seriousness of the popular shift rightwards played a large part in the successive failures of any Labour electoral challenge to Conservative government. The currently successful Blair project of what we might call 'free-market Christian populism' is only explicable, only conceivable, as a successor to the hegemonic penetration of Thatcherism. It relies explicitly on *common sense* and the mobilization of popular sentiment. Stuart Hall's timely and incisive dissection of the politics of Thatcherism was contentious for the left, mainly because it assigned such an important political role to ideology – which traditionally the left had been rather dismissive of. That events should have proved him right has certainly strengthened Hall's own standing and reputation as a political commentator. Perhaps more importantly, it has brought us a new understanding of politics – not so much a rational choice between clearly defined programmes but an attempt to capture people's lived experience and how they make sense of it.

Colonialism and Cultural Difference

Stuart Hall's recent work has revolved around three interlocked themes: colonialism and its role in the formation of modern western society; the question of identity in a social world characterized by migration and diaspora; and the issue of 'race' in cultural representation. These three themes can be separated out in his work, but it is more useful to consider them in conjunction with each other.

This new work differs from the Thatcherism project, where Hall spoke as a freelance intellectual, in its being firmly related to a teaching project. At the Open University Stuart Hall pioneered a new definition of the sociology core curriculum, focusing on the questions of what makes modern societies 'modern', and where are they going; he has complemented this by developing a group of courses on 'media, culture and identities'. These courses may be directed to students, but they carry the unmistakeable imprint of Hall's current theoretical priorities. Although this recent work still bears traces of the Gramscian Marxism that was so explicit in his earlier work, it is centred on some much newer theoretical debates: **Foucault,** psychoanalysis, poststructuralism and postmodernism. Before considering the implications of this change of emphasis in Hall's theoretical approach, I want to illustrate these new themes in his work.

We can best explore his approach to colonialism by starting with 'the West and the rest', a formulation that has already become standard phraseology. Hall reads the history of colonialism as not only about the impact of imperialism on colonized peoples, but as an account that shows how the emerging character of western modernity was constituted through its difference from the colonial 'other'. He uses Foucault's concept of discourse, and its illustration in Said's account of 'orientalism', to analyse this process.

Hall's own account examines representations by Europeans of their encounters with indigenous peoples, drawing out their failure to recognize human difference, the explicit sexual fantasies, their constructions of barbarism, cannibalism and so on. The European discourse was predicated on power – they 'had outsailed, outshot and outwitted peoples who had no wish to be "explored", no need to be "discovered" and no desire to be "exploited"...'. This power influenced what they saw, how they saw it, and what they did not see.[5]

Hall concludes that these representations of the barbarous 'other' played not just an important part, but an essential part, in the definition of the West as 'developed, industrialized, urbanized, capitalist, secular, and modern'. The West would have been unable to define itself as enlightened *without* such an 'other', whose function was to represent the opposite of what 'the West' stood for. Stuart Hall has subsequently expressed this in a specific theoretical vocabulary. Colonization does not signify simply imperial conquest, it refers to the process that 'constituted the "outer face", the constitutive outside' of western modernity.[6]

Alongside this analysis of colonialism, Stuart Hall has been developing an account of identity in the contemporary world which – whether or not we use the vexed descriptor of 'post-colonial' – is dominated by the effects of migration and the dispersal of peoples. Migration, he has argued, is the typical twentieth-century, indeed postmodern, experience, and it leads to a relative destabilization of the self. Diasporic cultures produce an acute awareness of cultural difference and have fostered the development of 'hybridity' – a key term in postmodern debates about identity and culture. Hall's approach to identity uses a historical, sociological, understanding of the global context in which we fashion our identities, and is critical of the claims that national identities are – ever were – unified and integrated. The idea of a national culture, he suggests, is a *discursive device* that enables us to represent as a unified entity that which is in reality fragmented and differentiated – rather as Lacanian psychoanalysis sees the self to be 'misrecognized' as whole.[7] Hall's work on identity draws more explicitly on psychoanalytic ideas than this parenthetical reference to Lacan would suggest. In a recent essay on this question he argues that the insights of **Freud** and others on *identification* should not be imported wholesale into thinking on cultural identity, which would lead to psychoanalytic reductionism, but nevertheless can help us to theorize identity in terms which are 'strategic' and 'positional' rather than essentialist.[8]

There is another important current in Hall's thinking on identity, and this is Foucault's work on the technology of the self. Although he is critical of the place of the body as a kind of residual 'transcendental signifier' in Foucault's work (and in that of those influenced by his approach), Hall is nonetheless engaged by Foucault's attempts to describe *performative* practices of self-production. In Hall's most recent discussions of these questions, he looks to Judith Butler's work as a source of productive exploration of the tension between Foucauldian and psychoanalytic accounts of the self.

If all this takes us to the heart of the contemporary 'post-structuralist' theory of the subject, Stuart Hall has simultaneously been examining the more concrete question of race and ethnic identity in the here and now. His paper entitled 'New Ethnicities' can be singled out as marking – both noting and contributing to – a decisive shift on this issue. Hall argues that the category of 'the black subject' can no longer serve as a basis for identity politics: there is no guarantee, from nature or from experience, to justify it. There is hence emerging a new politics of the representation of ethnic difference, operating within the hybrid modalities of diaspora experience. In the British context, where white Englishness has dominated national identity, there are newly contested meanings around what it means to be black British.[9]

Hall's recent work on identity in relation to race and ethnicity is inflected by his personal interest in the cultural output of black film-makers and photographers, with whose projects he has for some time been associated. It is, then, not surprising that he has recently brought together several of his theoretical and political concerns in an analysis of what he terms a 'racialized regime of representation'. The focus here is on the politics of representation, and Hall examines some difficult images in the sorry parade of racial stereotyping as well as casting light on the visual staging of racial difference.[10] Hall's analysis of the 'spectacle of the other' reminds us again of the importance of one of the moments in the cultural circuit – representation – with which he has always been concerned.

Seeing Things Differently

One of Stuart Hall's recent books gives the following as a description of the author: 'His work has had a profound influence on cultural studies and on the rethinking of the sociological understanding of contemporary societies.' This is an understatement. Stuart Hall has had more than a profound influence on cultural studies, he virtually *is* cultural studies. As well as his intellectual influence, which has brought a 'political' version of cultural studies to the fore around the world, he has done more than anyone to establish cultural studies as an academic discipline in Britain. Cultural studies has tended to operate in academia as a satellite of either English literature or sociology, with the attendant disadvantages of each, but has now been accepted (for example for purposes of research assessment) as an independent discipline. This obviously brings its own problems, in terms of the institutionalization of disciplinary assumptions and histories, but is nonetheless worth noting.

Hall's influence on sociology is more complex, as his work both contributes to and has to be seen in the context of what is known as the 'cultural turn'. This 'turn' has both theoretical and empirical aspects. It reflects an awareness that the study of culture has been marginalized, and that classical sociological orthodoxies such as those canonized in the 'founding fathers' Marx, **Weber** and **Durkheim** gave us an inadequate account of it. There has been a long-running attempt to right this theoretical wrong. In this, Hall's theoretical polemic has been an important voice. Morley and Chen summarize his position in an epigrammatic way: 'culture thus lies *beneath* the "bottom line" of economics'.[11]

The 'cultural turn' has another dimension too, a more historically specific one. This is the recognition that, in the late twentieth century, technological and social changes have made the media and culture more important, more necessary, for sociologists to study. As I have already indicated, Stuart Hall has made a specific and important contribution to this, in his insistence that new patterns of migration and diaspora-ization, and the development of global information and media systems, have effects on cultural difference and cultural identity.

One could also add that Stuart Hall's work does, literally rather than metaphorically, cause us to 'see' things differently. The study of representation is his first and last love, the element of the cultural circuit that most engages him personally. It is no coincidence that he is best known from 'being on television', is most recognized visually as a communicator, and is most successful at offering a new way of looking at what is on the screen.

Legacies and Unfinished Business

This heading has an obituary ring to it, which is scarcely appropriate in the case of someone who is still thinking, writing, responding, changing their ideas. It does, however, give the opportunity to comment on some general issues in relation to Hall's work. One such comment concerns disciplinary boundaries. As I have characterized 'cultural studies', it has a distinctive focus on popular culture. Stuart Hall, having been trained in 'Eng Lit', has to all appearances abandoned a detailed dialogue with the analysis of non-popular culture. As a young man he made a television programme on Blake, but these concerns are now in the archive. Yet his own participation in contemporary cultural production, with the films of Isaac Julien and Mark Nash for instance, shows an enthusiasm for a style of cinema and photography that is not obviously 'popular' – it is rather *avant-garde* as an art form. It would be interesting to hear what he has to say about the interface between cultural studies and the study of non-popular culture.

More importantly, reviewing Hall's work over time raises the question of the theoretical vocabularies he deploys and their objectives. It is striking to compare the earlier, Marxist vocabulary with the concepts he uses in his recent work. From the 1970s to the mid-1980s the terminology is Marxist. He now, however, explains his ideas in terms such as *binary oppositions, the constitutive outside, difference, différance, discursive techniques, enunciative strategies, identification, irreducibility, iteration, suture* – all terms drawn from Derrida, Foucault and Lacan. Does this mean that he has rejected the Marxist paradigm and moved wholesale into a 'post-structuralist' theoretical position?

The answer is not the simple one that those who police and politicize theoretical work incline to. Certainly, this change of terminology is important, in that it signals a new set of preoccupations – particularly with the question of identity – and Hall's insistence that new concepts are needed to explore them. Stuart Hall's current appropriation of psychoanalytic and Foucauldian vocabularies is a deliberate use of perspectives that, respectively, compete with and dismiss Marxism as an interpretation of the social subject. In that sense, his work can now be described as 'post-Marxist'. Yet, important continuities remain, and they are instructive in the polarized debate that now exists in relation to the political implications of post-structuralist theory.

In the first place, Stuart Hall works at a higher level than those who simply learn a new (fashionable) vocabulary in order to participate in the current conversation, junking the old because they cannot see how to reconcile the two. His latest writings show that he is not willing to let go of 'articulation' as an organizing concept. Similarly, notions of 'over-determination' and 'interpellation' (see **Althusser**, Chapter 14) – as well as references back to Gramsci – continue to make themselves heard in a new context. Stuart Hall has not become a convert to 'textualism' or what is disparagingly called 'idealism': he continues to insist that representation must be thought within the cultural circuit – and this includes production. He is opposed to what he calls the 'playful' variant of deconstruction, which dissolves power in its description of difference. (For the very sectarian, I might also point out that the position from which he is publicly critical of the project of 'Blairism' is a staunchly socialist one.)

Hall's recent work has certainly constituted its object of study in very different terms from his earlier work, but it retains his characteristic purpose and methodology. Let me give an example. Hall writes that 'we cannot afford to forget the over-determining effects of the colonial moment, the "work" which its binaries were constantly required to do to *re-present* the proliferation of cultural difference and forms of life, which were always there, within the sutured and over-determined "unity" of that simplifying, over-arching binary, "the West and the rest"'.[12] The logical structure of this argument is recognizable from Hall's insistence in the 1970s that we pay attention to the *work* that the superstructures were doing for capital. Western modernity has replaced capitalism as the object of study, but the techniques of discursive analysis are deployed (rather as the concept of hegemony was employed) to insist on the historic articulation of discourse and power.

Another way of looking at this is to argue, as many people have, that the labels 'post-Marxist' and 'post-structuralist' tell us more about the process through which these positions have emerged than they signal a definitive break. Let us give Stuart Hall the last word on this: 'So "post" means, for me, going on thinking on the ground of a set of established problems, a problematic. It doesn't mean deserting that terrain but rather, using it as one's reference point.'[13]

Further Reading

'Culture and power: Stuart Hall Interviewed by Peter Osborne and Lynne Segal' in *Radical Philosophy*, **86**, (Nov/Dec 1997), 24–42.

S. Hall, 'When Was The Post-Colonial? Thinking At The Limit' in *The Post-colonial Question*, Iain Chambers and Lidia Curti (eds), (London: Routledge, 1996), 242–60.

S. Hall, 'Who Needs "Identity"'? in *Questions of Cultural Identity*, S. Hall and P. du Gay (eds) (London: Sage, 1996).

S. Hall (ed.), *Representation: Cultural Representations and Signifying Practices* (London: Sage, 1997).

S. Hall and B. Gieben (eds), *Formations of Modernity* (Cambridge: Polity/OU Press, 1992).

S. Hall and M. Jacques (eds), *The Politics of Thatcherism* (London: Lawrence & Wishart, 1983).

S. Hall, D. Held and T. McGrew (eds), *Modernity and its Futures* (Cambridge: Polity/OU Press, 1992).

D. Morley and K.-H. Chen (eds) *S. Hall: Critical Dialogues in Cultural Studies*, (London: Routledge, 1996).

21

Anthony Giddens

Ira J. Cohen

Driving Impulses

As if by intuition, Anthony Giddens has always gravitated to the intersecting strengths of theoretical positions. As early as *Capitalism and Social Theory* which helped bring **Marx** into the sociological mainstream in 1971, Giddens proposed that for all of their differences Marx, **Durkheim**, and **Weber** address a common agenda of problems in the analysis of modern society.[1] More recently, as centrifugal forces have carried bits and pieces of Marx, Durkheim, and Weber (and others) to far-flung extremes, Giddens has managed to write with theoretical originality as he pulls ideas out of distant orbits back to intellectual common ground. In *Beyond Left and Right*, he enlists philosophic conservatism in support of what is generally regarded as a left-wing ideological agenda.[2] In *Modernity and Self-identity*, he tempers post-modernist pessimism and cynicism with sociological realism by transposing apparently intractable philosophical dilemmas from philosophy and the arts to problems actors deal with pragmatically in their everyday lives.[3]

A theorist like Giddens who writes with a distinctive sensibility can easily assume the role of the fox, Isaiah Berlin's master metaphor for social thinkers who canvas many unrelated, and even contradictory themes.[4] Stylistically, Giddens' writings appear very fox-like indeed. He shifts in and out of topics quite abruptly, as if to linger over the details of his thoughts might entrap him in a theoretical system of his own design. Yet, while he avoids the systemic trap, two very unfox-like projects provide a good deal of consistency in his work:

1. his theory of modernity to which I have already referred, and
2. structuration theory, a set of basic concepts regarding the constitution of social life, which requires additional commentary here.[5]

Although the name structuration theory may appear to imply an explanatory model, it qualifies as a theory only in the heuristic sense of the term. That is, it provides abstract insights into the generic characteristics of society, but explicitly excludes any explanatory or descriptive 'application' to substantive problems or historically or culturally specific events. What purpose does an abstract and generic heuristic theory serve? Just as music theorists must know the generic principles of music composition before studying any particular musical genre, so social theorists must have some idea of the generic principles of the constitution of society before social life in any historical period makes sense. Structuration theory sets out a conception of the basic possibilities or potentials of social life.[6] Substantive analyses informed by structuration theory always refer to historically delimited settings, for example, particular epochs in specific cultures.

Characteristically, Giddens originates structuration theory between two positions other theorists regard as antitheses: theories of collectivities on the one hand and theories of the individual on the other. He finds common ground between them by developing structuration theory from one simple idea: everything in social life, from encompassing world-systems to an individual's state of mind originates in social *praxis* (that is, the skilful performance of conduct and interaction.) Giddens' confidence in the centrality of praxis derives from **Harold Garfinkel** and **Erving Goffman**'s remarkably subtle examinations of interaction in everyday life. Giddens seems less aware of some remarkable parallels between his thought and early-twentieth-century American pragmatic philosophy, particularly John Dewey's writings on human conduct.[7] But, unlike Dewey, Giddens frames his thinking in terms of sociological problems rather than philosophical disputes. This sociological basis also distinguishes Giddens from many European theorists who try to solve philosophical problems by sociological means.[8]

Giddens clearly has a lot riding on the significance of social praxis. But why should praxis make a difference to sociological thought? Consider what would happen to contemporary social life if we subtract just two mundane practices: the use of financial credit and telling time. Although both practices may fade into the background in everyday life, public life as we know it (and much of our private life as well) would be impossible in their absence. Individuals almost immediately would be bewildered to the point of anomie. It can be surprisingly difficult for newcomers to think of practices as the most important constituents of social life. Most of us are disposed to think that individuals and social groups exhaust the possibilities. As will be evident below, much of Giddens' originality stems from reconceiving collectivities and individuals in a novel, praxiological light.

Exaggerations are conceits that magnify the power of a theorist's sociological vision. But Giddens, as I have said, writes with an aversion to ideas carried to extremes. His emphasis on praxis reinforces this aversion. To take praxis seriously one must accept two ideas beyond the basic insight that social life at large is produced through social practices:

1. that social practices are mutable, that is, they develop and change in different ways in different historical periods, and
2. that the manifold consequences of social practices can never be fully plotted or controlled in advance.

To be sure, Giddens knows that conduct often is reproduced in highly routinized forms. But he also knows that perversity in praxis is a part of social life, that is, every practice includes some opportunity for innovation and every occasion of praxis has some potential to yield surprising results.

Given the mutability and perversity of praxis, it is out of the question for Giddens to insist upon the centrality of one mode of conduct (for example, Marx on labor), or to envision an inevitable destination for history (for example, communism, organic solidarity), or to claim that insidious practices or structures thoroughly dominate our lives (for example, Weber on the 'iron cage', **Foucault** on power/knowledge, **Bourdieu** on the *habitus* and cultural fields). As a result, social life appears far 'messier' in Giddens' writings than in many theoretical works.

Key Issues

What is a Collectivity?

A simple question with no easy answer. In fact, there is no such thing as an abstract collectivity, only particular kinds of groups such as the Roman empire, medieval towns, or the modern state. In structuration theory, Giddens outlines the generic qualities of collectivities by rephrasing the question. Instead of asking: what is a collectivity? Giddens asks: how are collectivities formed and structured through social praxis? The shift in question permits him to avoid misleading metaphors of biological organisms and analogies to material things that permit many collectivists (for example, Durkheim) to suggest that social groups are entities *sui generis* with properties of their own. If we look past misleading figures of speech, this proposition is difficult to defend. Social groups lack genetic codes that standardize biological relations between organs, and they lack chemical bonds that fix the physical properties of material things. What makes 'thing-like' images of collectivities plausible is that, considered over long periods of time, most groups exhibit two characteristic features:

1. enduring patterns of positions and relationships
2. characteristic structural features (for example moral codes, types of domination, class structures).

Giddens' intention is to account for these long-lasting characteristics of groups in praxiological terms without backsliding into the language of things. He proceeds on two tracks, dealing separately with relational patterns of groups on the one hand and structural features of groups on the other.[9]

Consider, first, relational patterns. The illusory image of collectivities as objects actually obscures an observable material basis for collectivities, the performance of practices by embodied actors, that is, actors physically located in a particular material setting during a particular period of time. Now the fact that human conduct and interaction require space and time may seem more interesting to geographers than social theorists. But Giddens builds a fresh connection between geography and social theory that leads to new vistas on collectivities here.[10]

Giddens' basic image of collective life begins with the following image: actors repeating routines and rituals (reproduced practices) across time and space over and over so that the pattern itself becomes a taken-for-granted feature of social life.[11] Social rounds in a peasant farming village provide a simple, but useful example. Each day begins with routine family activity as people arise in their dwellings. During their daily rounds, they disperse and congregate in order to perform everyday activities in fields, markets, neighbors' dwellings and so on, until, at the day's end, family members reconvene for dinner and domestic affairs. The relational pattern of the village thus takes shape in the recurrent patterns of convergence and divergence through time and space, that is, across settings of conduct throughout the day. In reality, of course, these simple social rounds are complicated by weekly market days and sabbaths, seasonal holidays, and nonroutine events such as disasters or wars. Complications multiply further in large, modern groups employing technology that extends group connections (the term relations now seems too robust) across vast stretches of space and time.

One more point epitomizes Giddens' sense of the 'messiness' of social life. He cautions against thinking of group boundaries as demarcations between internally coherent and self-contained entities. In fact, the intensity and duration of relations and connections across time and space can establish all kinds of boundaries in any given case.[12]

Consider now structural properties, Giddens' second aspect of collectivities. If social groups consist of relations reproduced across time and space, then the properties of social groups never exist altogether at the same time. Empirical sociologists deal with this problem by inferring collective features of groups from statistics and other data collected across time and space but analyzed as if all observations were taken simultaneously. Giddens does something similar to conceive structural properties of collectivities in structuration theory.

The term 'structure', as it is typically used, is misleading here. Social groups are *structured* by commonly reproduced practices. To grasp the point, consider how a single practice is structured, for example the practice in modern business firms of hiring less qualified men in preference to more qualified women. What does the term 'structured' mean here? It means preferential hiring practices are chronically reproduced. Many thousands of personnel officers perform this practice (in a variety of specific ways) over and over in the course of doing business in various firms every year. As a result, the practice comes to seem a permanent feature of business firms. And this sense of *reproduced permanence* is what the adjectives 'structured' or 'structural' imply in structuration theory.[13]

Now, consider the broader structuring (or 'structuration') of gender relations in business firms. Here we find not only preferential hiring practices, but preferential practices in pay, promotion, and job evaluation, exclusionary practices of male bonding, chronic forms of sexual harassment, and more. These practices never occur all at once, and any given practice may be performed in some firms more often than others. But when all of these reproduced practices are considered at large, the structured subordination of women to men is an unmistakable property of business firms.

The example deceives by its simplicity. Complexities abound in structural analysis. But one essential caveat must be registered here. Just as all social practices are subject to historical change, so are all structural properties of groups. The structural subordination of women undoubtedly looked fixed for all time to a woman attempting a business career in a modern firm *circa* 1955. Today the permanence of the subordination of women in business firms looks less certain. The future remains to be seen.

The Consciousness of the Acting Subject

For Giddens, the most basic quality of the social actor is neither motivation (as in **Freud**), nor meaning (as in Weber and Geertz), nor interests (as in theories of rational choice). Giddens' unorthodox image of the individual begins with the postulate that she *knows how to act.* From this insight Giddens infers a hierarchy of menial activity with *discursive consciousness* at the top, *practical consciousness* in the middle, and *the unconscious* at the bottom. This hierarchy comprises the centerpiece of his theory of the acting subject.

Practical consciousness bears particularly important theoretical weight because this level refers to knowledge of how to act. Knowledge of how to act is nonverbal, tacit knowledge, which means we learn much of it without didactic instruction, and we take it for granted most of the time. All of this is not as mysterious as it sounds. For example, we all know how to say hello to close friends and we know when and where to say hello too. Most of us say hello without giving these skills (the 'know-how') a second thought. Each day, we perform a myriad of other practices, some quite subtle, others more obvious, without conscious reflection. We perform so many, in fact, that our practical consciousness is almost always engaged. But the secret of practical consciousness is that it works best when we fail to notice it at all.

What, then, of fully conscious thought? For Giddens, we enter a state of discursive consciousness,[14] that is, a state of awareness of our own thoughts, when for any reason, a situation arises where we lack the taken-for-granted ability to go on. Examples range from illness or disaster that dramatically disrupt day-to-day routines, to more structured problems such as puzzle-solving or artistic creation that require a synthesis of fully conscious thought and taken-for-granted skills. Of course, actors often conduct themselves for extended periods while relying exclusively on practical consciousness. Insofar as they do, they may give no attention whatsoever to their own motivation or to the meaning of their conduct. Hence meaning and motivation in the fully conscious sense of these terms appear more episodic in Giddens' structuration theory than in many other theories of the actor.

Now, it may seem that Giddens has trapped himself into saying that unreflective conduct lacks any motivation at all. But, in a move of importance both for structuration theory and for his theory of modernity, Giddens actually claims that human conduct is always subject to a very powerful unconscious motivation, the need to maintain *ontological security*. Ontological security refers to a comfortable mental state in which actors engage in taken-for-granted activities in familiar surroundings and in the company of unthreatening others. It is, in brief, a state of mind fostered whenever actors take for granted that they know how to go on without any disruption. Should an actor altogether lose the ability to go on, as might occur in the aftermath of a socially paralyzing earthquake or a physically paralyzing injury, she would feel helpless, anxious and intensely anomic until she works out a comfortable *modus vivendi* again. But disasters are not the only threat to ontological security. Indeed, disruptions of ontological security are a chronic feature in Giddens' substantive investigations of modernity.

Modernity and Social Change

The term 'modernity' has been synonymous with social change for several centuries. But in the period Giddens terms 'late modernity' (from 1900 and primarily since World War II), the pace of change has intensified, its scale has expanded, and its life-altering consequences have reached into even the most intimate details of everyday life. Mainstream authors suggest a widespread public ambivalence (hope/fear, excitement/bewilderment) about the life-altering consequences of modernity.[15] Giddens concurs, finding challenging opportunities on the flip side of modern dilemmas. Above all he resists the temptation to exaggerate alienation, or succumb to despair.

Someday, someone will write a master theory of modernity, something like a *Das Kapital* for the twenty-first century. Nothing like this has surfaced in Giddens' writings to date. Instead, all of his writings implicitly respond to one big question: how are the life-altering consequences of modernity implicated in the local details of everyday life? Praxis, the hub of structuration theory, operates at the center of his thought here again. Giddens outlines the extraordinary scale and intensity of modern change with reference to two historically unique modes of praxis, reflexivity and technologically mediated relations that enable markets, bureaucracies, and cultural media to stretch across the globe and back again into our local workplaces, homes, and everyday lives.[16]

Reflexivity refers to practices guided by observation and thought (that is discursive consciousness). Pragmatic problem solving in all historical settings is reflexive in this sense. But reflexivity takes on an unprecedented life-altering momentum in modernity as methodically gathered information facilitates systematic planning and organization on previously unimaginable scales. Reflexive practices abound everywhere we turn: in accounting procedures and investment planning, bureaucratic management, architectural and industrial design, military operations, medical practices, the list goes on and on. Computerized information processing produces quantum leaps in the tempo of reflexivity, but the origins of reflexivity antedate the computer by several hundred years.

Why does reflexivity continue to grow? Competition and domination in many forms undoubtedly play a part. Once someone introduces reflexive practices, it is very difficult for anyone to revert to traditional ways. But Giddens stresses this 'genie-out-of-the-bottle' effect from another point of view. Just as social life appears too 'messy' to permit overly coherent social theories, so it also appears too 'messy' to allow reflexively drafted plans to succeed very often without unintended, perverse effects. The pollution of the environment by well-planned industrial organizations is an archetypical example, so are iatrogenic diseases that turn up in even the most well-run hospitals. To mitigate unwanted side-effects of any kind, we need new reflexive planning and organization. And to mitigate the next round of side-effects that inevitably will ensue, we need more reflexivity again. And so it goes on what Giddens terms the 'juggernaut' of modernity.[17]

Turning now to social relations at a distance: capitalist enterprises, diplomatic missions, and military expeditions established long-distance lines of connection well before the advent of modernity.[18] However, long delays occasioned by slow means of transport severely limited the effectiveness of these connections. Since time and space figure prominently in structuration theory, Giddens is intellectually well positioned to appreciate the enormous difference instantaneous electronic communication, and rapid transshipment have made to the globalization of many fundamental processes in social life. Every facet of everyday life, from a prosaic tuna sandwich, to the newspaper article we read with our lunch, to the pop song playing on the radio as we eat was produced somewhere far away from where we dine.

Empowerment and Risk in Post-traditional Society

Why should ambivalence be such a common reaction to modernity? Giddens conceives the root of this ambivalence as a counterpoint between empowerment and risk.[19] On one side of the issue, modern forms of reflexivity empower social actors by undermining taken-for-granted authority and practice. New forms of knowledge enable actors to challenge taken-for-granted forms of authority everywhere from the family, to the professions, to the state. Actors now, not only have the right to decide on everything from their medical treatment to their cultural lifestyle, in many cases they are compelled to choose. As recently as the 1950s, many people in modern societies remained tradition-bound 'locals' in many respects. Today, almost everyone exercises a range of 'cosmopolitan' freedoms.

But, on the other side of the issue, this empowering reflexively produces its own set of uncomfortable side-effects. Recall here that Giddens postulates a basic human need for ontological security, a sense of well-being grounded in a taken-for-granted competence in negotiating familiar ways of life. But the life-altering dynamics of modernity challenge our competence and disturb our well-being too often to permit us to take much for granted for very long. The recurrent need to make informed decisions about uncertain events opens up everywhere from career-paths, to retirement planning, to the choices parents make for their kids. Trust, which is an integral feature of ontological security, cannot be taken for granted when so many weighty decisions need to be made. We confront too many situations where we risk unhappy outcomes to simply assume that what we have done in the past will work out for the best here and now once again.

Giddens' emphasis on unavoidable risk and insecure trust has the important effect I mentioned earlier of transposing the philosophical agenda of postmodernism into everyday life.[20] Giddens observes that philosophical doubts about truth and ethics that startle postmodernists are nothing new. The same doubts motivated the early modern philosophers, for example Descartes, Hume, Kant, none of whom would have bothered to write philosophy if they took truth and ethics for granted. But philosophical doubt took quite some time to migrate into daily routines. Only for the past 50 years have sociological conditions replaced trust with doubt as a widespread problem in everyday life. Of course, everyday people cope with their doubts in practice not principle, and in the process temper *angst* which predominates in many postmodern philosophies, with hope, which is a philosophically underrated resource in everyday life.

The Politics of Modernity

Discussions of empowerment often imply that politics is a zero-sum game (that is power-holders dominate subordinates) or else presume the potential for unrealistic degrees of empowered freedom. Before turning to the politics of modernity, it is worthwhile to have in mind Giddens' most fundamental insight into power relations in structuration theory. Although domination (and hence subordination) are inescapable facts of social life, power relations between the more and less powerful always involve a mix of autonomy and dependence. But the powerful also depend upon less powerful others to carry out certain practices (which, in given situations, may range from hard labor to simply staying out of the way). To whatever extent the powerful depend upon the less powerful, this dependence can be skilfully exploited as leverage by subordinates to open up some areas of autonomy for themselves. Strikes, violent and nonviolent civil disobedience, boycotts, and strategic voting in elections are all useful tactics of the less powerful in what Giddens terms the dialectic of control.[21]

In relation to modernity, Giddens defines two broad sets of power relations and, in effect, two separate dialectics of control. Inevitably, but uncharacteristically, Giddens takes a partisan stand when normative political issues are at stake. His analyses of both sets of power relations implicitly begin from the standpoint of those with less power rather than those with more.

Does this partisanship imply that Giddens has a left-wing bias in ideological terms? Yes and no. Yes, if left wing means a partisanship for those engaged in what he terms 'emancipatory politics', that is, struggles for freedom from poverty and deprivation, political oppression, and social exclusion.[22] But even this partisanship is unusual in that Giddens finds fault with the unintended side-effects of left-wing programs in the past such as state welfare policies that trap the needy in cycles of poverty. Here Giddens points out the reasonable side of right-wing criticism of social democratic policy, albeit he does so pragmatically with the problems of the needy in mind.

But the more original aspect of Giddens' politics of modernity refers to 'life-politics', that is, the politics of how we should live our lives in a world of reflexivity and globalization where traditions have given way, and the awareness of risk continually disturbs our ontological security. Life-politics encompasses personal struggles to achieve satisfying and secure lifestyles and relationships, as well as ecological, feminist, and other movements that seek new ways of life in a post-traditional world.

Giddens' commentaries on life-politics crystallize a growing sense in the post-Marxist era that the nature of radical politics has changed. But Giddens, in a characteristically unorthodox move, enlists a durable strand of conservative political thought in service to life-politics. As opposed to conventional left-wing thinkers who rarely hesitate to propose social change, many conservative political philosophers respect the security and community fostered by tradition. The challenge to radical politics from Giddens' point of view, is to restore traditions that nurture the 'good life' without sacrificing the reflexive empowerment that fuels life-politics from the start.

Seeing Things Differently

As befits a sociologist who seeks theoretical common ground rather than radical extremes, Giddens almost never tries to falsify familiar points of view. His objectives are more subtle: both in structuration theory, and, especially, in his investigations into modernity, Giddens directs us to the unseen structuring of the familiar without losing sight of what we have noticed in the past. Giddens forfeits some of the 'shock of the new' that theorists like Marx, Foucault, and Bourdieu employ to persuade us that we misrecognize our social world. But finding the unnoticed without denying the familiar ultimately is a more demanding task.

Space permits only a brief demonstration of seeing the unnoticed in the familiar here. Recently I have been thinking about solitude in modernity and in the process I have been observing what people do during rush hours while alone in their cars. One thing I have noticed is a good deal of personal grooming: women applying make-up, men combing their hair and so on. As recently as 1970, the practice was unconventional if not slightly bizarre. Today, auto makers have installed grooming mirrors on sun visors to meet a growing demand. Now, these drivers obviously are concerned with presentation of self. But the fact that they are grooming themselves in their cars indicates that some of the most deep-seated aspects of modernity have silently infiltrated their solitude as they drive.

Consider the broader structuration of highway grooming. First of all, it is primarily practised by commuters. Commuting, in turn, hinges on the separation of home and workplace, and the accelerating tempo of transportation that is part of the modern attempt to overcome constraints of time and space. But, like all other aspects of modernity, the attempt to overcome constraints of time and space produces perverse effects. Specifically, as more and more drivers clog the roads during rush hours, commuters must be on their way as quickly as possible if they are to arrive at work or home on time. Hence, the driver with one hand on the steering wheel and the other on the lipstick or comb engages in practices invisibly structured by the complex time–space dynamics of modernity that dislodge grooming practices from the privacy of the bathroom to the front seat of the car.

Legacies and Unfinished Business

In 1976, Giddens published his first book on structuration theory.[23] That work, and subsequent works theoretically established praxis as the common ground where the actions of the individual merge with the structuration of social order. Two world-class sociologists who have embedded much of their best work in deeply theoretical empirical studies, namely **Norbert Elias** and Pierre Bourdieu, should be credited, along with Giddens, for launching what has turned out to be a consequential movement in sociology (and other disciplines).[24] The 'new institutionalism' in the study of complex organizations, 'practice theory' in anthropology, William Sewell Jr's transposition of structuration theory into historical sociology, and Rob Stones' new work bringing structuration theory to bear on theoretical methods illustrate the growing role of praxiological reconstructions in sociology and other disciplines today.[25]

And yet, Giddens is no exception to the perversity of praxis: which is to say that in the process of making a substantial difference to the development of social theory, Giddens, no less than any other theorist, generates implicit restrictions as a by-product of his thought. Space permits only brief mention of one restriction here.[26]

Giddens' aversion to exaggeration, his unwillingness to engage philosophical questions by sociological means and his centripetal impulse to draw disparate ideas back to common ground keep his sociological compass pointed toward social life. The same features of his thought also keep his moral compass pointed toward the 'is' more than the 'ought' in normative terms; that is, toward problems that disrupt, or threaten to disrupt, the security and satisfaction people experience in their everyday lives.[27] To be quite clear, as is evident in his analyses of 'emancipatory politics' and 'life-politics' in modernity, Giddens has no problem picking up moral themes as defined by everyday actors on their own behalf. Nor does he have any problems picking up latent tensions and seen but unnoticed dilemmas that may emerge as problems somewhere down the road. But Giddens installs no moral bearings in the fundamental conception of praxis in structuration theory, nor in his analyses of the consequences of modernity. All of this works reasonably well in an era such as our own where political movements and public policies are open to academic debate, journalistic scrutiny, and some degree of political pressure from 'below' as well as 'above'. But in societies where values are less subject to debate (for example, the USA in the 1950s) or where politics and moral discourse about values such as justice, freedom, or democracy are altogether suppressed as is true in most authoritarian regimes, a more normative theory is needed. Inevitably, normative theories exaggerate some aspects of social life they seek to condemn or praise. And for these purposes, Giddens' theories do not work very well.

So, like all theories, the value of Giddens' theories depends upon the context in which they appear.[28] In my view, writing as an American in 1997, social theory appears to be concluding a thirty-year cycle in which some of the brightest sociological minds have invested great dedication, enthusiasm, and insight in developing various denominations of normative theory. This does not seem to me to have been an era in which conflicts over values have remained latent or suppressed. If I am right about this, then perhaps the moment has arrived to stand back from debates about what 'ought' to be and pragmatically assay people's private lives and their public situations in terms of their own hopes and fears. To do this we need a lucid understanding of both the seen and the unnoticed dimensions of the social world we all help to produce every day. And to this end Giddens provides sociological theories for our times.

Further Reading

C.G.A. Bryant and D. Jary, 'Coming to Terms with Anthony Giddens' in idem, *Giddens' Theory of Structuration: A Critical Appreciation* (London: Routledge, 1991) pp. 1–32.

I.J. Cohen, *Structuration Theory: Anthony Giddens and the Constitution of Everyday Life* (London: Macmillan, 1989).

I.J. Cohen, 'Structuration Theory and Social Order: Five Issues in Brief' in J. Clark, C. Modgil, S. Modgil, *Anthony Giddens: Consensus and Controversy* (London: Falmer Press, 1990) Chapter 4. Reprinted in C.G.A. Bryant and D. Jary, *Anthony Giddens: Critical Assessment* (London: Routledge, 1996) selection 40.

I. Craib, *Anthony Giddens* (London: Routledge, 1992).

A. Giddens, *The Constitution of Society: Outline of the Theory of Structuration* (Cambridge: Polity Press, 1984).

A. Giddens, *The Consequences of Modernity* (Cambridge: Polity Press, 1990).

Conclusion

Tolerance, Plurality and Creative Synthesis in Sociological Thought

Rob Stones

In this conclusion I want to briefly pursue further some of the themes of the introduction in the light of the twenty-one chapters on the twenty-one key thinkers that have followed. My base point is that these chapters tell us clearly that 'the stuff we need to know about society' – to stay with the language of the introduction – is rich, complex and diverse. The more one looks at the plural and varied insights offered by thinkers as insightful and as different as **Weber** (Chapter 2), **de Beauvoir** (Chapter 9), **Garfinkel** (Chapter 13) and **Foucault** (Chapter 19), to name just four, the more one realises that there is much to know about society that cannot be contained in news sound bites, chat shows and indignant emotional remonstrations about the topical issues of the moment. The more one should realise, also, that all that is worth knowing about society will not be contained in the writings of just one, two, three or even four major thinkers or schools of thought.

As mentioned in the introduction, most of the theoretical positions contained in this book have developed out of a spectrum of concerns with a rich and varied range of quite disparate questions and problematics. Very rarely do theorists share an identical focus. Usually a light is being shone on a different, albeit often neighbouring, piece of social life. The perspective of the torch holder is at least slightly different and the part of society being singled out by the light is also slightly different. The nearest we come to an identical focus is in those cases, such as with **Marx** (Chapter 1) and **Althusser** (Chapter 14), or with de Beauvoir (Chapter 9) and her late-twentieth-century critics, where the later theorist(s) directly engages with the problematic of the previous tradition. But even in the latter cases there will be differences of focus as well as the points of direct confrontation and critique, and it is important for us to distinguish the one from the other, carefully and methodically. It is important not to fall into the trap of assuming *a* *priori* that there is nothing but direct confrontation and critique between the theories. There is room for a plurality of torch holders, and for a plurality of areas of interest. It is possible to illuminate one area without needing to darken another. The more lights we have – the more plural, creative, rigorous and systematic that sociological thought is able to be – then, to switch metaphors, the more extensive will be our inventory of the social stuff we need to know.

The sociological enterprise should be – and at its best it manages to be – characterised by a spirit of openness and the sense of a collective enterprise. Many of the key thinkers influenced each other, the ones that continue to work continue to be influenced by those who long ago stopped working. Contemporary thinkers are also influenced by other contemporary thinkers, even while they continue to be influenced by those long dead. There is an ongoing learning process and exchange of ideas between the living and the living and between the living and the dead. The sociological debate is centred on the evolving sociological canon but the borders of this canon are malleable, historically evolving and forever contestable. The influences on this canon are, as they should be, wide indeed – philosophy, biology,[2] psychology, history, politics, culture, literature, the list is long.

On the basis of this tolerance towards a plurality of different theoretical perspectives how do we begin to think through the relationship between them? How do we maintain our inventory of resources in such a way that the stuff we need to know is cross-indexed and mutually informing and not just parcelled up into useful and interesting but completely discrete packages? In other words, how can we *combine* theories? There is not just one answer to this question of synthesis, and many have already been given by the contributors to the volume in their discussion of particular theorists. We have seen, for example, how **Habermas** (Chapter 15) has combined Weber with Marx, and drew also from figures as diverse as Adorno, **Freud** (Chapter 4), Winch, Wittgenstein, Schutz, Gadamer and Luhmann; and, at the other end of the spectrum we saw how even the arch anti-synthesiser[2] **Blumer** (Chapter 6) combined the writings of G.H. Mead on the self with the influence of Robert E. Park and the Chicago School of Sociology. And we had already highlighted in the introduction, using the examples of **Hochschild** (Chapter 18) and **Hall** (Chapter 20), how theorists can combine influences from sociology with those from a range of different disciplines. Thus, the particular answer that I want to suggest here to the question of how one might combine theories is quite clearly just one choice from among several, and I do not in any way want to insist that it is necessarily either the best way or the only way that one should ever go. On the contrary, I offer it as just one example of a potentially fruitful way of proceeding, of beginning to think further about the relationship between theories.

Combining Theories: Step One – Micro, Meso, Macro

This route requires a number of steps and has the virtue of being quite simple to relate to the wide-ranging work of the key thinkers, and to provide a template for exercises in creative synthesis, drawing imaginatively on the work of the different theorists covered here. The *first step* involves the classic distinction between the micro, the meso and the macro levels of sociological analysis (a focus on either small, medium or large-scale phenomena). In his chapter on Garfinkel, John Heritage argues that the discovery of the microsociological world was one of the chief sociological discoveries of the post-war era. And he cites Garfinkel and **Goffman** (Chapter 11) as two 'great and original American sociologists' in this mould who offered 'massive dissent' to those grand masters of sociological theory who tended to theorise social constraints on human action, boxing them in, without ever addressing what happened on the ground as people actually reasoned and acted, asking what they did inside the 'box' of constraint or how they built the 'box'.[3] **Parsons** (Chapter 7) was the most recent in the line of theorists who were thought to focus too much on the macro and meso levels of value systems and normative structures, and not enough on the microsociology of mutual understandings, inferences and reasonings of people in particular contexts, about how people carried out, and made sense of each other within, actual interactions. When measured against the foci of Garfinkel and Goffman it would not be difficult to see that Marx and **Durkheim** (Chapter 3), for example, also tended towards the meso and the macro at the expense of the micro.

Robert Merton (Chapter 8), in turn, has a reputation as one of the great meso (via his emphasis on the 'middle-range') theorists. But in following Heritage – as we must surely do – in acknowledging the power of the insights of microsociology we would hardly want to dismiss the insights of the macro and meso theorists in the same breath. To see the importance of the work of Garfinkel and Goffman, or of Blumer and Hochschild among others, surely does not mean that we cannot also see the importance of Marx's insights into the nature and dynamics of capitalism, or of Durkheim's exploration of the continuing significance of ritual in modern societies characterised by organic solidarity, or of Parsons' appreciation of the potential for friction between, for example, the values and norms of a technologically advanced economy and those of the religious subsystem of that society. We need to find ways of appreciating the different levels of analysis for what they are, and of looking for ways of combining their different emphases when this would help us to answer a question or to shed light on a social phenomenon.

Combining Theories: Step Two – Widespread Practices and System Linkages

This brings us to the *second step* involved in combining theories. This second step itself requires a distinction between:

(i) the identification of *widespread practices* within, say, modern and late modern societies, and
(ii) the identification of the linkages between the different institutional 'parts' of the social system that have produced these widespread practices.

Widespread Practices

Widespread practices can include: voting practices, forms of punishment, the workings of bureaucracies, or regimes of military training, to take just a few from countless possible examples. These are all practices that are going on in many different places at the same time within a society and within different societies. They are widespread and more or less simultaneous. Widespread practices are usually widespread because they are ordered, routine, disciplined. There will typically be social pressures, inducements and a range of structurings that contribute to the day-by-day, or year-by-year, undertaking of these practices. Most key thinkers have particular widespread practices that are a distinctive part of their theoretical provenance. The widespread practices that they focus upon provide a distinguishing mark by which one characteristically identifies that theorist. Studies of such phenomena could focus upon, for example, the habituality of routines (**Bourdieu**, Chapter 16; **Giddens**, Chapter 21), the regularity of the forms of discipline and regulation (Foucault), the evidence for embedded norms, consistently and persistently adhered to (Parsons), the widespread occurrence of the same *a priori* forms of interaction that have a profound effect on the content of that interaction (**Simmel**, Chapter 5), the structured economic preconditions (Marx; Althusser, Habermas), or the near uniformity of gender preconceptions (de Beauvoir; **Chodorow**, Chapter 17; Hochschild) involved.

It is possible to look at these widespread practices at any of the micro, meso or macro levels. That is, one could look at a few local (micro) practices, at a greater number of those practices spread over a larger geographical region (meso) or at a very large number of them spread out over an even greater geographical expanse (macro). Thus a macro analysis of some of the widespread practices discussed in Karin Martin's chapter on Chodorow could, for example, focus on the *similarities* between many different local or micro instances of widespread practices. It could look at the similarities between the displays of misogyny and psychological constructions of masculinity in the many different boot camps for the training of Marines in America, or between American boot camps and those in other countries. It would be a macro analysis because it would focus upon what is common to all (or many) of the widespread practices. It would be looking at macro, large-scale, phenomena. A meso analysis might focus upon a smaller number of boot camps, at just the ones in a certain region of the country or those organised by particular branches. It would limit the analysis in scope and, all things being equal, would be able to pay closer attention to the detail of what was going on, provide more detail about the widespread practices of Marine training. Perhaps it could give much more detail about the specific rules about gender appearance and behaviour – about the letter and practice of the requirement that 'women Marines' wear make-up, about the content of the etiquette classes they have to attend.

At any one of these levels theorists – as in Martin's and Chodorow's case – tend to be partial and limited, naturally focusing on their preferred patch of light, creatively indulging their own distinctive obsessions. It is on the basis of this insight that we can begin to see the virtues and the potential for an open-minded orientation to the sociological enterprise that seeks also, when appropriate, to combine theoretical approaches, to look carefully at the way that particular practices are combined with – articulate with – other social practices such as, for example, those related to economic considerations. In the case of military training there will clearly be certain macro, meso and micro economic preconditions for these 'superstructural' practices (to use Marxist terminology), even while these economic factors 'cannot explain the stridency and irrationality that accompany the Marines' talk about women in the military'.[4] Chodorow's own combination of sociological and psychological processes could be employed at the micro level to go even further into the detail of gender difference and look at the empirical evidence within particular boot camps for Chodorow's suggestion that one of the reasons for the widespread difficulties in heterosexual relations is that women have a richer inner world to fall back upon than men, entailing that the men in their lives are not as emotionally important to them as women are to men. In all these cases we are taking widespread practices as our focus, as our point of interest.

Systemic Linkages

It is clear just from these few remarks that one does not get very far into the work of a sociological theorist before one sees that what might seem to be fairly descriptive tasks of identification of particular practices at particular levels of the micro, meso or macro, are bound up very tightly with *explanations* of what has caused these social practices to come about. Such explanations will almost invariably involve an encounter with the ways in which different social practices (widespread or otherwise) are linked to each other. The work of many theorists who look at large social systems – such as Marx, or Weber, or Habermas, for example – is focused at one and the same time on widespread practices *and* on the way in which these practices are linked together causally, on the way in which the continued existence of one set of widespread practices relies on a working interdependence with other widespread practices.

In **David Lockwood**'s (Chapter 12) terms they are all concerned with issues of system integration. The different 'parts' – sets of institutional practices – of the system that are integrated in these processes refer to the many sets of preconditions that combine to create the context for any practice, any action, that a person or a collective agent – such as a cabinet, a multinational company, or an environmental pressure group – may perform. A concern with system integration in a very static, descriptive sense might involve looking at the distribution of warheads or at the number and spatial distribution of retail outlets, warehouses and delivery trucks, and, more dynamically, it could involve investigating routine systems of command – routine in the sense that the systems will be 'rationalised' in Weber's sense, ready to go at a moment's notice, according to certain preordained bureaucratic rules, administered by trained and skilled technicians. We are looking at system linkages here in terms of their ordered, disciplined, and routinised 'system-ness'. Other examples one could think of would be: in static, descriptive terms, the spatial distribution and number of multinational companies and their component units in western Europe or the Pacific Rim; or, more dynamically, the ways in which the different parts (units) of particular industrial or service organisations (whether it be IBM, Disney or McDonald's) are internally integrated into an interconnecting, working system. Such systems themselves have subsystems with their own internal connections, like the social system of the Sociology Department at the Flinders University of South Australia described by Bob Holton (Parsons, Chapter 7) which has a range of subsystems performing interlinking tasks of policy setting, the formation of values, the provision of resources and the overall integration of the department (Parsons' AGIL functions). One can easily see the connection in Holton's example between policy decision (G) and the provision of resources (A) as the department considers the pros and cons of devoting more time to teaching first-year and less to upper-year topics.

We also see in the same chapter on Parsons how widespread functions (practices) of normative system integration (I) – such as those carried out by English common law in the seventeenth century – were connected to processes of technological change and industrialisation.[5] Althusser's work is also clearly concerned with system integration as he strives to adequately conceptualise how widespread political practices are linked to widespread economic practices. He does this primarily at a fairly abstract macro (and meso) level. And, of course, one can look at how particular widespread practices – such as the treatment of labour as a commodity (Marx) – are produced by a number of systemic linkages that combine to sustain them, to keep them in place. There are so many systemic connections relevant to the reproduction of this aspect of society, so many systemic linkages that articulate with each other in sustaining it. There are, of course, the relations between the propertied and the propertyless (and the other components of the capitalist mode of production outlined by Marx – Chapter 1), but also there are the systemic effects of the practices of politicians, the military and the state in general in capitalist societies, the activities of the international financial system, the education system and its relationship to employment practices, the long-term historical civilising processes that inhibit the expression of dissatisfaction with a society (**Elias**, Chapter 10), the systems of regulation and surveillance that produce identities and bodies that are, more or less, docile and regimented (Foucault), and the many bureaucratic systems through which, and by which, all the above are administered (Weber), to name but just a few.

A further example of two related sets of widespread practices can highlight the way in which they are often not historically (*causally*) separable even while they clearly have their own identifiable *existence*[6] as separate widespread practices with their own *sui generis*[7] reality. The two sets of widespread practices involve, firstly, Parsons' emphasis on the growing *specificity* of social interactions and functions in modern societies – so a dentist looks at your teeth and your teeth alone – (in contrast to the diffuseness of practices in traditional societies), and second, Simmel's insight that we have more and more to do with strangers in the modern metropolis. In short, by looking at these two perspectives in combination with each other we can investigate creatively the relationship between the widespread *specificity* of modern practices and the widespread incidence and character of our encounters with strangers. The elective affinity and suggestion of a connection between them prompt us to think about the nature of modernity in a manner that suggests a larger, more macro, engagement with issues of causality, an engagement that, as we shall see, draws us towards other theorists which, in turn, suggest yet further affinities and connections that lure us and alert us, in a virtual siren call, to the attractions and advantages of combining theoretical perspectives.

Both Parsons and Simmel are making points about the nature of modern societies, the nature of modernity. They are both talking about aspects of the social that are macro – that are pervasive characteristics of modernity – but each instance of 'specificity', each encounter with a stranger, actually occurs one by one in many, many local places. In other words, they are widespread practices that have macro and micro dimensions to them. Taken individually, looked at separately, they are micro manifestations of a macro phenomenon. When we start to look at what is happening here in terms of causality then it is very soon apparent that such macro phenomena are socially produced by large historical and social changes such as the move from the countryside to the towns and cities; the growth of the nuclear family and of solitary living arrangements; the use of money as an impersonalising means of exchange that has no interest in distinctions of character and biography between its millions of users (Simmel); the growth of the division and interdependence of social tasks such that we continually rely on millions of other people to carry on doing their jobs if we are to continue living the lives that we live (Durkheim); the growth of the division of labour such that we have specialist jobs and professions whose job it is to administer to just one part of our lives (our health, our electricity supply, our local taxes, our supermarket purchases, our hair, our pensions and life insurance, our childcare needs, our furniture purchases, or our burial, cremation or memorial requirements). Indeed, more and more of our 'social' interactions are completely faceless, from an ATM or 'hole in the wall' cash till, right through to the shopping or holiday arrangements transacted by telephone, fax or through the world wide web.

These dimensions of the larger social context dovetail smoothly with Weber's emphasis on the disenchantment of the world and the rationalisation of life that has us sitting in padded offices filled with white noise as we respond to impersonal targets, quotas and productivity metrics in a world in which institutions work increasingly by way of algorithmic monologues and 'commodities speak in place of people'.[8] And it is clear that there are also affinities here with one of the central messages of the German social theorist and philosopher Jürgen Habermas who tells us that the logics and rationalities of modern capitalist economies and modern bureaucracies are such that the mind-sets of calculation, treating people as things, thinking of goals and targets – thinking of profits, of efficiency, of engineering the urban landscape, of engineering the rural landscape, of engineering the human body and all aspects of the natural world, thinking of how to calculate and manage levels of consumption or savings, or of how to get other people, strangers, to do things for us, specific things, in the pursuit of our goals – are forever increasing in their scope, their reach respecting no limits. According to Habermas we are losing many of our distinctive capacities as human beings as what he calls our 'life-world' is being slowly but surely strangled ('colonised' and 'impoverished', to use his terminology). Our ability to engage in social practices that involve communication and solidarity with each other, that involve these things even at the expense of our individualistic, blinkered, goals and targets, is being eroded by the form that the major 'parts' of society are taking. For Habermas these major 'parts' are constituted primarily by the economic and administrative systems, respectively. The economic system crushes the energy and capabilities of people's life-worlds in the ways it moulds, pushes, pulls, influences and makes demands on them in their social roles as 'employees' and 'consumers', and the administrative system does the same in the way it subdues and tames people into becoming passive objects, either as 'citizens' who offer mass loyalty in return for political decisions from up on high or as 'clients' who – if they are lucky – offer up taxes in return for state services and welfare.

Combining Theories: Step Three – Social Praxis

System Integration and Social Praxis

Nicos Mouzelis makes much of the way that David Lockwood distinguishes system integration from something he calls 'social integration'. While system integration refers to the connections between the different 'parts' of the social system, social integration refers to whether individuals or groups are in conflict with each other or whether they co-operate harmoniously with each other. The distinction between social and system integration can be seen as a distinction between people and parts.[9] If we look at two presidents arguing with each other then we are focusing upon social integration, and, conversely, if we look at the geographical distribution of warheads and the logistical system of command that could organise their launch then we are looking at system integration. If social integration is specifically about whether or not people get on or do not get on with each other, then it can be seen as a sub-category of the more encompassing category of *social praxis,* of what social actors do. One of the things they do is to get on with each other, another is to not get on with each other. These are important dimensions of social life – we can think of class struggle or class harmony, of social order or disorder, of reformism or revolution – but there are many other dimensions to the things that people do, collectively or individually, besides whether they do those things co-operatively or conflictually.

Social Praxis as Habits and Skills

Thus – and this is the *third step* in thinking about the combination of theories – it is probably more fruitful to think of *system* integration as relating to the 'parts' of society and *social praxis* as relating to the 'people' acting in particular contexts provided by these parts. *Social* integration will refer to just one dimension of such acting. In his chapter on Giddens, Ira J. Cohen explains the importance of the notion of social praxis – the skilful performance of conduct and interaction – for examining all the things that people do, their social practices *in situ*, and he points to the significant role played in the development of the notion of praxis by Garfinkel and Goffman's 'remarkably subtle examination of interaction in everyday life'.[10] Most of the crystallised social influences that inhabit and guide individual social actors as they go about their social practices are, to use an expression coined by Garfinkel, 'seen but not noticed' by the people who are thus inhabited and influenced. That is to say, most of the ways in which we learn to behave and to feel, are not learned through formal teaching, they are learned simply by growing up as a member of a particular society – or sub-group – that just does things this way. We learn by imitation, by osmosis. Norbert Elias leaves us in no doubt that it is because we live in a particular society at a particular time that we do not routinely pass wind or burp at the dining table – at least in the large middle chunk of our lives. Even when we are taught according to explicit instructions, from table manners to driving lessons, it is not long before we have so fully assimilated the lessons that they are second nature to us, we no longer think about what we are doing, we just do it. We see ourselves and our dining companions using a knife and fork and not passing wind but it would not be true to say that we positively notice this.

Most of the things that society teaches us to do are things that we come to do routinely, habitually, without an explicit thought. We quite literally come to embody many of them. Just as a ball player has a sense of where the other players are on the park, and knows which line her body should take without a second's pause for reflection, so, when a middle-class cosmopolitan American does notice the skills involved in the accomplishment of eating, it is an unfamiliar and unexpected aesthetic feast for his eyes to witness the harmony of body and elements as his friend executes that curve from plate to mouth, the teeth closing down beneath pouting lips as in one unbroken movement he slides the egg plant and capsicum off the gleaming copper fork which is returned with awesome dexterity to a seemingly choreographed space about two inches above the plate, wrist resting with poise on the edge of the table. In the conceptual language used by Pierre Bourdieu there is a match here, a perfect effortless union, between the *habitus* of acquired and routinely embodied social skills, on the one hand, and the implicit expectations of the social *field* of relations, on the other.

Innovation, Surprise and Structured Incompetence in Social Praxis

This emphasis on the reproduction of conduct in highly routinised forms is clearly noted by Cohen in his account of Giddens' insistence on the significance of praxis. However, just as central to the latter's work is the 'perversity of praxis', the fact that praxis by its very nature entails contingency, 'every practice includes some opportunity for innovation and every occasion of praxis has some potential to yield surprising results'.[11] There is a great deal involved in the process by which tasks are successfully or unsuccessfully carried out and this fact, as Cohen point out, sounds a powerful warning bell to overly deterministic, narrow or teleological conceptions of society.[12] There are many things that can go wrong when one is relying on learned skills, background knowledges and assumptions of 'how to' do things, mutual understandings and one's ability to accurately interpret messages. For its successful accomplishment praxis requires the necessary structural conditions of action, and it relies on its perpetrators having the appropriate pre-reflexive 'routine' abilities inscribed in their appropriate bodies, it often also depends on accurate knowledgeabilities of probable punishments and rewards for compliance and non-compliance with the rules (knowledgeabilities, in other words, of power and norms), it needs to avoid mistakes – slips of tongue and hand, and in Bourdieu's terms, misfits between *habitus* and the field of relations in which a social practice is required.

The possibility for error, for making a hash of it, and for the stress and emotional tension that come with a heightened awareness of this possibility can be seen if we imagine – or, quite likely, recall – a situation in which one's ordinary taken-for-granted *habitus* of eating skills is confronted with an unfamiliar field of social relations. Forgiving the exaggeration and the improbability (not to mention my own cultural ignorance) in the name of graphic illustration imagine a home-grown, small town mid-Western farmer of the 1970s, reared in splendid isolation on potatoes, two veg and beef steak. With a desperate eye on branching out with a trading contract he acquires an invitation to dine at the Chinese Embassy in Washington where, dressed up to the nines, he encounters chopsticks instead of the familiar knife and fork, rice instead of potatoes, pancake rolls instead of goodness knows what, dishes and sauces seemingly scattered at random across a revolving table, other guests dipping in with their chopsticks, possibly at random, possibly in some unfathomable sequence, new dishes arriving from all directions. Should he pop the lettuce leaves into the bowl of cold tea before drinking it? He will need to draw unstintingly on his inner resources to get through the evening, but most importantly he will have to be consciously and explicitly thinking about what to do and how to do it all night long, and even with all this effort he is very likely to do things the wrong way either because he does not know what the right way is, or because although he believes he knows what the right way is he cannot seem to get his body into line with it. Misfits between a person's routinely stored *habitus* and a social field of relations in which that personal *habitus* is out of its depth, or just ill-suited, are the food and drink (indeed) of much comedy, but they can also tap into a range of darker emotions from humiliation and shame to anger and rage.

Social Praxis as the Consolidation of Public and Private Meanings

Another dimension of social praxis – beyond conflict and co-operation, beyond routines and contingency, and beyond competency and incompetency – in which symbols and language take on and consolidate meanings that are more than individual, that have a social resonance and degree of permanence, has been clarified by a number of the key thinkers in this volume. In their different but overlapping ways Georg Simmel, Herbert Blumer (think of the name of the school with which he is associated, '*symbolic* interactionism'), and Norbert Elias (see Chapter 10, the sections on 'process sociology' and 'dyads and triads') all – in their subtly different ways – see the process by which individuals interact with other individuals, and then with other individuals in pairs, threes, then groups, then larger groups and even larger groups, as one which in itself changes the quality and character of that individual, her character and her behaviour, as well as giving groups and societal forms themselves their own distinctive characteristics that are not the characteristics of individuals on their own. The meanings of symbols are at one and the same time attenuated and consolidated as they become more and more supra-individual. They are attenuated in the process of interaction and negotiation with others who recognise and use the symbols in slightly different ways in different types of groups. As Whitney Pope reminds us in his crystal-clear chapter on Durkheim (Chapter 3), symbols are also consolidated as women and men, girls and boys, look for each other and assemble together, pouring their emotions and their meanings into symbols, sacred and profane, visual and linguistic. The mention of Durkheim – arguably the first structuralist – draws to mind a point already made in the introduction (see above) about the opportunities that exist for combinations of insights between theories of 'praxis' and the work of structuralists and post-structuralists such as Hall and Foucault who, likewise, emphasise the powerful socialising qualities of language and the symbolic.

It is important also to note that the relationship between sociology and psychology with respect to language and the symbolic is a subtle one that has to be handled with some skill. The conscious and unconscious (Freud) ways in which individuals respond to events in their lives will, of course, bear the mark of individuality. Each individual is unique in this sense – notwithstanding the normalising impulses of disciplinary regimes – and their psychological processes will be complex and, at least to a degree, be special to them. They cannot be read off from their class position or from their sex, gender, ethnicity or nationality, or from the fact that they are openly singing nationalistic songs, cheering their local team, or gathering together to mourn for a public figure or to demonstrate against the government of the day, whether it be in Belgrade, Prague, Washington or Tehran. In entering into the public rituals of singing, cheering, weeping or demonstrating with passion, resignation or principle, individuals may well also be – almost inevitably will also be – singing, cheering, weeping and demonstrating the very private individual hymns, longings and losses, actual and metaphysical, that this ritual occasion allows them to express. We might like to think that we know everything about someone's inner life from a few external indicators, but we do not. Here, we begin to reach the limits of sociology, or, at least, to reach the point at which sociology must combine with psychology. Just as the creation of sacred symbols gives a more enduring basis to social sentiments, Ian Craib's chapter on Sigmund Freud implies strongly that it is equally true to say that the symbols would not be invested with as much sacrality or relative social permanence without the profound idiosyncratic impulses derived from individual biographies.

On the other hand, a substantial weight of the form and the content of a person's inner life will indeed be markedly affected by the sociological context of that person's life. This could be by such simple and varied influences as the current dominant ideas on how to care for babies and children, current educational practices, the subtle and not so subtle differences between the way in which boys are treated from that in which girls are treated (cf. Chodorow), and the prescribed ways in which one can and cannot express emotion, in public and in private, at work and in leisure, and on and off the playing field. Social structuring can be found deep within even the most seemingly idiosyncratic and personalised actions. It is not, in the end, spontaneous individualism that creates the tutored professional 'genuine' smile and patience of the Delta Airlines air hostess but a tightly structured social organisation (cf. Hochschild). The routine internalisation of a social sub-group's rules of the game by most of its members goes deep indeed as Simon Williams makes clear in his discussion of the impact of social rules on the health and illness of the people who are caught up in them (Chapter 18, Hochschild). The emotional investment in such social rules is often hidden by the routine, habitual internalisation of particular genres of rules by 'insider' participants, together with an often implicit understanding of what these are on the part of 'outsiders' – the wider public. The rules themselves, and hence the emotional commitment invested in them, are often only brought to the surface when one of the participants suddenly breaches those rules. Hence, the social impact of the inappropriate anger of Mike Tyson as he bit off his opponent's ear in the boxing ring when etiquette ruled that he was supposed to use his hands, and not his teeth, to beat the shit out of his opponent (cf. Elias, section on the 'civilising process').

Sociological Thought as 'The Stuff We Need To Know'

We can return, in the light of praxis, to the theme of social constraints and possibilities. We can note that when we have particular principles, morals or passions about the kind of society we want, or about what should be done in relation to a particular issue, the sociological world-view tells us that we first have to consider whether we think that the parts of the social system that stand in our way, that are inimical to a better society, will be susceptible to our touch. Most sociologists of the parts, from Weber to Habermas to Giddens give the distinct impression that 'modernity is a juggernaut', the systems that treat us as things to be turned to their ends, and which induce us to treat others as things, will not allow us to treat *them* as things that we can turn to *our* ends. The degree of hope and optimism that remains must lie in the fact that not all systems are equally resilient and obdurate. Sociological discipline can help us to see which parts will be amenable to the wishes of which people, and conversely, which social structures will block and constrain those desires of agency. One of the major implications of Lockwood's insights is that social struggles will come home empty-handed if the relevant parts of the social system are not ripe for the picking. While we have seen that the 'parts' of society relate to the many sets of preconditions that combine to create the context for the actions and struggles of people and collectivities, there is another closely related but still distinct way in which it is important to view the parts. This is in terms of their role in determining *the degree to which the actions of the people* – individual or collective – can make a difference to social outcomes. It is about the ways in which the parts themselves can be changed, more or less. It is also, crucially, about the extent to which the parts of society change in ways that people control. Putting it the other way around, and in the form of a direct question, one can simply ask: how far is society out of control? In trying to face up to this question it is vital that we understand straight away that systemic *consequences* of all kinds cannot be reducible to the wishes or intentions of individuals or collective agents (cf. Merton, Chapter 8; Giddens, Chapter 21). The picture is complex here, but sociology does provide tools for beginning to unravel the complexity.

The distinction between the levels of micro, meso and macro within the analysis of system connections can allow us to begin to trace the consequences of social actions by means of thinking in terms of a hierarchy of social actors.[13] The actions of mega or macro actors – those at the top of an institutional hierarchy – will affect many, many people, many, many parts of the social system; the actions of meso actors will affect fewer people and parts of the system; and the actions of micro actors will affect very few people and very few, if any, aspects of the system. If I spend a few dollars then I will have very little effect on the state of the national economy, but if a government department spends a billion or two then the effect on the system and the people within it will be significant. If a corner shop decides to end its discriminatory employment practices then this may affect several people through the years, but if a large national company does the same then this will have an effect on tens of thousands of people. We can see the connections here between one point of decision-making within a system and other points within that system; we could trace the linkages between a policy decision and larger deposits in many banks and financial institutions which then loan more to many people in many different branches in many different towns on the basis of those greater deposits; we could follow the connections between the policy decision taken at the headquarters of the large national company and the employment criteria used by its many regional branches. In terms of their geographical reach these would be macro system linkages.

The systemic outcomes or consequences of macro, meso and micro decisions and practices have a cumulative effect on society. These cumulative outcomes emerge from many structured interactions and, it must be stressed, they are partly intended, and partly a surprise. These social outcomes often have discernible trends but if there is an overall strategy to be discerned in such trends then it will be, as Foucault puts it, 'a strategy without a strategist', a strategy without a master villain or an arch heroine. The vast majority of social consequences are in large part the unintended result of many systemic chains of effect, of subsystems sustaining each other and articulating with each other to produce outcomes. It is hardly surprising that major contemporary theorists, including Anthony Giddens, have begun to characterise late modernity in terms of 'unavoidable risk and insecure trust'.[14] The consequences of a number of interlocking actions, what is left behind as the result of many co-ordinated and uncoordinated actions by many people and collective actors, can be thought of as 'emergent properties'. They provide the social conditions in which the next round of actions take place. They provide, in the language of Giddens' structuration theory, the context of constraints, possibilities, enablements and moulding influences. The parts of these partly out-of-control systems are made up of meaning and culture, but also of such things as institutions, means of communication, transport and production, sources of energy, raw materials in general, human bodies, time and space, and nature and biology themselves as preconditions for the existence of society.

The thinkers represented in this book – with their many perspectives on many widespread practices, with their accounts of causation and system connections, with the possibilities they open up to us for combining and articulating theoretical insights – provide us with the resources we need to consider closely the question of social possibilities. They provide the resources that we can use in order to think adequately and responsibly about the societies we live in, about the social issues which affect every one of us and which we usually have an opinion about. Sociological thought of the highest order can enable us to work hard at those opinions. We can work out which systemic parts of society would be positively resistant to action and which parts would be more amenable to the 'will' of social actors. We have the resources to ask about the extent to which particular social actors can direct particular societies in particular ways – to what extent is it possible to resist the seeming imperatives of the capitalistic and bureaucratic *systems*? Even with the resources it is still the case that every specific question will require much hard thought, imagination, creativity, rigour and discipline. There is no royal road to good social thought. Nothing can change that. But I hope that this book has managed to convey a sense of the sociological possibilities open for anyone who is willing to put in that hard work, hard thought, and hard imagination. I hope that the book – this collection of fine, hard worked, hard thought, creatively imagined contributions about outstanding thinkers – has infected readers with the enthusiasm for sociology that the key thinkers deserve as their legacy, and that – most importantly – it has persuaded readers that sociological thought provides us with the stuff we need to know to enable us to think in a grown-up way about society.

Notes

Introduction

1. For a recent collection that takes the 'school' route see the excellent volume edited by Bryan Turner, *The Blackwell Companion to Social Theory* (Oxford: Blackwell, 1996).

Chapter 1

1. G. Lichtheim, 'Historical and Dialectical Materialism', in *Dictionary of History of Ideas*, vol. 2 (New York: Charles Scribner's Sons, 1973). G. Therborn, *Science, Class and Society: On the Formation of Sociology and Historical Materialism* (London: New Left Books, 1976).
2. Karl Marx, 'Preface' (to *A Contribution to the Critique of Political Economy*), (1859).
3. Karl Marx, Letter to Weydemeyer, 5 March, 1852.
4. Eduard Bernstein (1961), *Evolutionary Socialism: A Criticism and Affirmation* (New York: Schocken; originally published in German, 1899).
5. Ernest Mandel (1975) *Late Capitalism* (London: New Left Books; first published in German, 1972). Daniel Bell (1973) *The Coming of the Post-industrial Society* (London: Heinemann).
6. Bell, *The Coming of the Post-industrial Society*.
7. Marx did not simply extrapolate from trends in England; he used them to illustrate claims grounded in a more fundamental theoretical critique of capitalism.

Chapter 2

1. Max Weber, '"Objectivity" in Social Science and Social Policy,' in E. Shils and H. Finch (eds), *The Methodology of the Social Sciences* (New York: Free Press, 1949), pp. 68, 103.
2. 'The Social Psychology of the World Religions,' in H. Gerth and C.W. Mills (eds) *From Max Weber: Essays in Sociology* (New York: Oxford, 1946), p. 270.
3. *The Protestant Ethic and the Spirit of Capitalism*, tr. T. Parsons (New York: Scribner's, 1958), p. 194.
4. Ibid., p. 17.

5. Ibid., p. 26.
6. Ibid., pp. 180–1.
7. 'Politics as a Vocation' and 'Science as a Vocation', in *From Max Weber: Essays in Sociology*, pp. 120–9, 153.
8. 'Science as a Vocation', p. 138.
9. '"Objectivity" in Social Science and Social Policy', p. 57 (translation modified).
10. 'Science as a Vocation', pp. 148, 155.
11. '"Objectivity" in Social Science and Social Policy', p. 84; a more literal translation would read, 'For scientific truth is only what *wants* to be valid for all who *want* the truth.'
12. 'On Liberty' in J. Gray (ed.), *On Liberty and Other Essays* (Oxford: Oxford University Press, 1991), p. 65.
13. G. Roth and C. Wittich (ed.) *Economy and Society: An Outline of Interpretative Sociology* (New York: Bedminister, 1968) vol. 1, p. 244; Weber's original title for this unfinished work read literally, 'The Economy and the Social Orders and Powers,' and it was intended as a contribution to the *Handbook of Social Economics* for which he served as chief editor.
14. *Noise: The Political Economy of Music*, tr. B. Massumi (Minneapolis: University of Minnesota Press, 1985), pp. 3, 111; with a foreword by F. Jameson that acknowledges Weber's contribution.
15. See Peter B. Evans, Dietrich Rueschemeyer and Theda Skocpol (eds) *Bringing the State Back In* (Cambridge University Press, 1985); and Walter W. Powell and Paul J. DiMaggio (eds) *The New Institutionalism in Organizational Analysis* (Chicago: University of Chicago Press, 1991).
16. For an exception and perhaps a harbinger of a new approach to Weber, see Neil J. Smelser and Richard Swedberg, 'The Sociological Perspective on the Economy,' in Smelser and Swedberg (ed.) *Handbook of Economic Sociology* (Princeton: Princeton University Press, 1994), pp. 3–26.
17. Robert M. Solow, 'How Did Economics Get That Way and What Did It Get?' *Daedalus* **126** (Winter 1997): 54.
18. Weber's untitled study, published posthumously in 1921, was translated as *The Rational and Social Foundations of Music*, tr. Martindale *et al.* (Carbondale: Southern Illinois University Press, 1958).
19. The outstanding exception is the untranslated study of Christoph Braun, *Max Webers 'Musiksoziologie'* (Laaber: Laaber-Vrlag, 1992).
20. For interesting examples see the *Methodology of the Social Sciences*, pp. 27–33.

Chapter 3

1. *The New Encyclopedia Britannica*, 15th edn, vol. 29 (Chicago: Encyclopedia Britannica), p. 987.
2. S. Lukes, *Emile Durkheim* (New York: Harper & Row, 1972), p. 93.
3. Ibid., p. 80.
4. E. Durkheim, *Moral Education* (New York: Free Press, 1961), p. 101.
5. R.K. Merton, *Social Theory and Social Structure*, rev. and enl. edn (Glencoe, IL: Free Press, 1957), pp. 131–60.

6. E. Goffman, *Interaction Ritual* (Garden City, NY: Anchor Books, 1967), pp. 47–95.
7. R. Collins and M. Makowsky, *The Discovery of Society*, 5th edn (New York: McGraw-Hill), pp. 272–9. R. Collins, 'The Durkheimian Tradition in Conflict Sociology', Chapter 5 in J.C. Alexander (ed.) *Durkheimian Sociology* (Cambridge: Cambridge University Press, 1988), pp. 107–28.

Chapter 5

1. G. Simmel, *Les Problèmes de la philosophie de l'histoire* (1907) (Paris: PUF, 1984), pp. 99, 100.
2. G. Simmel, Uber sociale Differenzierung, in *Gesamtausgabe*, vol. 2 (Suhrkamp: Frankfurt am Main, 1989), p. 117.
3. G. Simmel, *Soziologie*, Untersuchungen über die Formen der Vergesellschaftung, in *Gesamtausgabe*, vol. 2 (Suhrkamp: Frankfurt am Main, 1992), p. 436.
4. Ibid., p. 7.
5. Célestin Bouglé, 'Review of *Soziologie*', *L'Année Sociologique*, vol. xi, 1906–09, p. 18.
6. G. Simmel, *Soziologie*, p. 11. This aspect of socialisation, that of groups, of collectivities has been particularly stressed by Michel Maffesoli cf. notably *Au creux des apparences*, Paris, Plon, 1990.
7. G. Simmel, Secret et société secrète, *Circé*, Saulxures, 1992, p. 63.
8. Ibid., 1992, p. 23. To look at the relations between these concepts of frontiers, indiscretion and the construction of the other, cf. Exkurs über die soziale Begrenzung in *Soziologie*, pp. 698–702.
9. *Soziologie*, p. 44.
10. Ibid., p. 35.

Chapter 6

1. Quoted from Paul Colomy and J. David Brown (1995), p. 20 (see Bibliography).
2. A wonderful account of this which bridges Blumer and Becker is to be found in David Matza's *Becoming Deviant* (Englewood Cliffs: Prentice-Hall, 1969).
3. Commented upon by Lonnie Athen as he describes 'Blumer's Advance Social Psychology Course' in *Studies in Symbolic Interaction* 14 (1993), 156.
4. This debate can be found embodied in the controversy over the publication of J. David Lewis and Richard L. Smith's 'American Sociology: Mead', *Chicago Sociology and Symbolic Interactionism* (Chicago: University of Chicago Press). The debates are found in Plummer, 1(III) (1991) pp. 227–326.
5. Elsewhere he suggests three basic postulates: 'that human beings act toward things on the basis of the meanings that the things have for them'; 'that the meaning of such things is derived from... the social interaction that one has with one's fellows'; and 'these meanings are handled in, and modified through, an interpretative process used by the person' (Blumer 1969, p. 2) (see Bibliography). These are a rather limited and possibly even trivial set of postulates –

although as he points out, such a view is 'ignored or played down in practically all contemporary social science' (p. 2).

6. For discussions of pragmatism, see Plummer (1997), **2**.
7. The central location of this discussion is Blumer (1969), Chapter 1.
8. In this he followed Mead and Dewey: For Dewey, 'Every generation has to accomplish democracy over and over again. (Dewey 1946, p. 31) 'The very idea of democracy... has to be constantly discovered, and rediscovered, remade and reorganized...' (p. 47).
9. This quote is from Blumer (1958), reprinted in Lyman and Vidich (1988, p. 206). The section which follows is culled from quotes on Blumer's writings on race prejudice and I have tried to piece together a kind of systematic statement. See pp. 183–233 of Lyman and Vidich (1988) for the original statements.
10. See the last key statement in Blumer and Duster (1980, p. 235).
11. This is not Blumer's example, but mine. I write this at a time when there is a growing concern with 'Islamophobia' in the UK. The point is the groups keep changing. The Runnymede Trust has just announced a research project into this newly named phenomenon.
12. A word needs to be said about his style. In reading Blumer, one is immediately struck by the almost total lack of referencing. These days sociology books are cluttered with references, quotes from others, long bibliographies. All of these are absent from Blumer. He hardly ever does any of the above. Nobody is cited; there are no references; and no bibliographies. It is not that there are not many allusions to the works of others – only that they are never named. Most of his essays – and that is what they are – read like thoughtful self-reflections. His standard mould is to rally against several dominant views of the world, and then to proceed to evolve his own painstaking account of it.
13. See, for instance, the journal, *Symbolic Interaction*; the year book, *Studies in Symbolic Interaction*; and the organisation, The Society for the Study of Symbolic Interaction. Details are provided in Plummer (1991).

Chapter 7

1. A brief but useful biographical sketch of Parsons is available in P. Hamilton, 'Systems Theory', in B.S. Turner (ed.) *The Blackwell Companion to Social Theory* (Oxford: Blackwell, 1996), pp. 151–9.
2. This cross-disciplinary engagement is reflected in T. Parsons, *The Structure of Social Action* (New York: McGraw-Hill, 1937), and T. Parsons and N. Smelser, *Economy and Society* (London: Routledge, 1956).
3. *Structure*, passim.
4. Ibid., pp. 64–9.
5. T. Parsons, *The Social System* (Chicago: Free Press, 1951).
6. T. Parsons, 'Evolutionary Universals in Society', *American Sociological Review*, **29**(3) (1964), 339–57.
7. *The Social System*, pp. 58–67.
8. T. Parsons, *The System of Modern Societies* (Englewood Cliffs: Prentice-Hall, 1971).

9. T. Parsons, 'The Professions and the Social Structure', *Social Forces* 17 (1939), 457–67 and T. Parsons, 'Illness and the Role of the Physician: a Sociological Perspective', *American Journal of Orthopsychiatry* 21 (1951), 452–60.

10. These issues are discussed in T. Parsons, 'Some Comments on the Sociology of Karl Marx' in T. Parsons, *Sociological Theory and Modern Society* (New York: Free Press, 1967).

11. *The Social System*, pp. 428–54.

12. M. Weber, *The Protestant Ethic and the Spirit of Capitalism* (trans. M. Weber), (London: Allen & Unwin, 1930).

13. J. Habermas, *Legitimation Crisis* (Boston: Beacon Press, 1979) and J. Habermas, *The Theory of Communicative Action*, vol. 1 (London: Heinemann, 1984).

14. N. Chodorow, *The Reproduction of Mothering* (Berkeley: University of California Press, 1978).

15. See, for example: C. Wright Mills, *The Sociological Imagination* (Harmondsworth: Penguin, 1959), especially Chapter 2; A. Giddens, 'Power in the Recent Writings of Talcott Parsons', *Sociology*, 2 (1968), 257–72; F. Parkin, *Marxism and Class Theory* (London: Tavistock, 1979).

16. Symptomised by A. Gouldner, *The Coming Crisis of Western Sociology* (London: Heinemann, 1971).

17. Key works include: J.C. Alexander, *Theoretical Logic in Sociology, the Modern Reconstruction of Classical Thought: Talcott Parsons*, vol. 4 (London: Routledge, 1984) and R.J. Holton and B.S. Turner, *Talcott Parsons on Economy and Society* (London: Routledge, 1986).

18. *Talcott Parsons on Economy and Society*, pp. 88–90.

Chapter 8

1. Ruth W. Schultz, 'The Improbable Adventures of an American Scholar: Robert K. Merton', *The American Sociologist* 26(1) (Fall 1995), 68–77, at 69 (reprinted from *Temple Review* 47(1) [Spring 1995]). For a partial list of books and articles that focus on Merton's ideas, see the bibliography in Robert K. Merton, *On Social Structure and Science*, P. Sztompka (ed.) (Chicago: University of Chicago Press, 1996), pp. 361–8.

2. I. Bernard Cohen (ed.), *Puritanism and the Rise of Modern Science: The Merton Thesis* (New Brunswick, NJ: Rutgers University Press, 1990); see especially pp. 89–111 where Cohen lists works that analyze Merton's ideas.

3. David L. Sills and Robert K. Merton (eds), *The Macmillan Book of Social Science Quotations* (also published as vol. 19 of the *International Encylopedia of the Social Sciences*) (New York: Macmillan, 1991), p. 160; the quotation originally appeared in 1949 in 'Manifest and Latent Functions', one of Merton's most famous essays. Inasmuch as this quotation is one of only four which Merton (presumably) selected for inclusion in this summary volume of significant remarks from the history of all the social sciences, I am assuming from this that he puts significant store by it, and have quoted it with this self-estimate in mind.

4. Robert K. Merton, *Social Theory and Social Structure*, enl. edn (New York: Free Press, 1968), pp. 69–70; reprinted in *On Social Structure and Science*, pp. 57–8.

5. *On Social Structure and Science*, p. 1. It may be that Sztompka compiled this list of neologisms and conceptual distinctions after seeing Merton's own, which in part reproduces but also supplements Sztompka's; see Robert K. Merton, *Social Research and the Practicing Professions*, Aaron Rosenblatt and Thomas Gieryn (eds) (Cambridge, MA: Abt Books, 1982), p. 102.

6. Robert K. Merton, 'The Unanticipated Consequences of Purposive Social Action', *American Sociological Review*, I (1936), 894–904. In the vast majority of contemporary references to Merton's idea, particularly in the popular press, the phrase is changed to 'unintended consequences of social action', which somewhat alters the original meaning, carrying still further the denaturing process of 'obliteration'. Interestingly, compare Weber's more cumbersome exposition of a related process: 'The final result of political action often, no, even regularly, stands in completely inadequate and often even paradoxical relation to its original meaning. This is fundamental to all history'; in Hans Gerth and C. Wright Mills (eds), *From Max Weber* (New York: Oxford University Press, 1946), p. 117.

7. Robert K. Merton, 'Social Structure and Anomie,' *American Sociological Review*, III (1938), 672–82. The record of reprintings was compiled by Mary Wilson Miles as part of 'The Writings of Robert K. Merton,' in Lewis A. Coser (ed.), *The Idea of Social Structure: Papers in Honor of Robert K. Merton* (New York: Harcourt Brace Jovanovich, 1975), pp. 500–1.

8. Robert K. Merton, 'Bureaucratic Structure and Personality,' *Social Forces* XVIII (1939), 560–8. The reprint record is in Coser (ed.), *The Idea of Social Structure*, pp. 501–2. Writings of this sort, which turned out to be his *métier*, he recently defined as 'highly condensed paradigmatic essays, typically running to few more than a dozen-or-so pages'; 'A Life of Learning (1994)', in Merton, *On Social Structure and Science*, p. 357.

9. Robert K. Merton, 'Science, Technology and Society in Seventeenth Century England'. Published in *OSIRIS: Studies on the History and Philosophy of Science, and on the History of Learning and Culture*, 4(2); George Sarton (ed.) (Bruges, Belgium: St Catherine Press, 1938), pp. 362–632. Reprinted with 'Preface: 1970' (New York: Howard Fertig, 1970; New York: Harper & Row, Torchbook edn, 1970). Arranging for the publication of Merton's dissertation in this privileged venue was Sarton's 'threshold gift' to Merton, as the latter, borrowing from Lewis Hyde, eventually termed this magnanimous act; see Merton, 'A Life of Learning (1994)', p. 352.

10. I pick these symbolically loaded dates because of Talcott Parsons' *Structure of Social Action* (New York: McGraw-Hill, 1937) at one end, and Alvin Gouldner's *The Coming Crisis of Western Sociology* (New York: Basic Books, 1970) – largely a repudiation of Parsons' version of theorizing – on the other. Undergraduate enrolment in sociology courses in the US also peaked just after 1970, as did the number of 'majors', thus ending a steady increase in student interest that had been growing since the end of the Second World War.

11. James S. Coleman, 'Robert K. Merton as a Teacher,' in Jon Clark, Celia Modgil, and Sohan Modgil (eds), *Robert K. Merton: Consensus and Controversy* (London: Falmer Press, 1990), p. 29.

12. Robert K. Merton, *On the Shoulders of Giants: A Shandean Postscript*, vicennial edition with a new Preface by the author (New York: Harcourt Brace Jovanovich, 1985); there is also a 'Post-Italianate Edition' (Chicago: University of Chicago

Press, 1993). Of the many commentaries this unique book has inspired, one of the most memorable is Stephen Jay Gould's 'Polished Pebbles, Pretty Shells: An Appreciation of OTSOG,' in Clark *et al.* (eds), *Robert K. Merton*, pp. 35–47.

13. Kenneth M. Setton, 'Foreword to the Torchbook Edition', in Henry Osborn Taylor, *The Emergence of Christian Culture in the West* (originally, *The Classical Heritage of the Middle Ages*) (New York: Harper and Brothers, 1958), p. vii.

14. Robert K. Merton, 'On the History and Systematics of Sociological Theory', in his *Social Theory and Social Structure*, enl. edn (New York: Free Press, 1968), pp. 5–6. Earlier editions had appeared in 1949 and 1957; the quoted passage itself was added to the 1968 edition.

15. An instance of this hermeneutic tangle was recorded in a journal I once edited, *History of Sociology*, when a scholar who has since become a well-known theorist attacked Merton's putative position regarding the history of social thought, and I, as editor, was called upon to 'assemble' Merton's response (with his collaboration) based on his already published statements; see Steven Seidman, 'Classics and Contemporaries: The History and Systematics of Sociology Revisited' and the response, 'The Historicist/Presentist Dilemma: A Composite Imputation and a Foreknowing Response', Drawn by the Editor from Writings of R.K. Merton, both in *History of Sociology* 6(1) (Fall 1985), 121–36, 137–52. I should note here that Merton and I have been corresponding regularly for the last dozen years or more, and that he has generously sent me a large amount of material from his private archives, including books, offprints, preprints, historically interesting letters from himself to other theorists, and the like. I elected not to draw from this store of printed goods for reasons of privacy, and because I wanted my interpretation of Merton's importance to rely on easily accessible material rather than on the dozens of letters which have passed between us. Using that material, with his permission, awaits another opportunity, and would require much more space than is available here.

16. Robert K. Merton, 'A Life of Learning (1994)', The Charles Homer Haskins Lecture, delivered in Philadelphia (April, 1994), and published in Merton, *On Social Structure and Science*, pp. 343–7.

17. Gerald D. Suttles, *The Social Order of the Slum: Ethnicity and Territory in the Inner City* (Chicago: University of Chicago Press, 1968), a study of Chicago slums in the 1960s, and thus a far cry from the culturally promising Jewish 'slum' of Merton's youth.

18. Merton, 'A Life of Learning (1994)', p. 349.

19. Ibid., p. 350.

20. It could be argued that the British sociology of science was inaugurated by J.D. Bernal's *The Social Function of Science* (London: J. Routledge and Sons, 1939; New York: Macmillan, 1939), although Bernal's politicized view of the task was distinct from Merton's more dispassionate (Sartonian) approach; see Merton's generous and wise review of Bernal in *American Journal of Sociology* XLVI (1941), 622–3 (one of the few publications which identifies him with Tulane University).

21. Because Merton himself never leaves literary reference unexplored, and for those who no longer consider seventeenth-century French drama a necessary part of their evening reading, the famous exchange comes in Act IV, Scene 6 of Molière's 'The Cit Turned Gentleman' (*Le Bourgeois Gentilhomme*): Philosophy-Master: Is it verse that you would write to her? Jordan: No, no, none of your verse. P.M.: You

would only have prose? Jordan: No, I would neither have verse nor prose. P.M.: It must be one or t'other. Jordan: Why so? P.M.: Because, sir, there's nothing to express one's self by, but prose, or verse. Jordan: And when one talks, what may that be then? P.M.: Prose. Jordan: How? When I say, Nicola, bring me my slippers, and give me my nightcap, is that prose? P.M.: Yes, sir. Jordan: On my conscience, I have spoken prose above these forty years, without knowing anything of the matter; and I have all the obligations in the world to you, for informing me of this. (Molière, *Comédies*, vol. 2, no trans. named [Everyman's Library, No. 831, Poetry and Drama] (London: J.M. Dent and Sons, 1929), p. 234.

22. One wonders how many owners of cars who sport this slogan on their bumpers know anything of the book it parodies, *I'm OK, You're OK* by Thomas Anthony Harris, with the subtitle, *A Practical Guide to Transactional Analysis* (New York: Harper & Row, 1969). Despite its glib title, the book was widely discussed with some seriousness when it first appeared. The utterly predictable pattern within mass culture of devolution, from academic thoughtfulness to light repartee, is also something Merton has probably reflected upon regarding his own work. That this particular use of 'dysfunction' is psychological in nature and not sociologically informed, as was Merton's, may suggest that it was his own widely broadcast redefinition of the term (itself borrowed from medicine and biology) that made it available for psychologistic parlance. It is possible, however, that the psychologistic trivialization came more from the tradition of medical writing than from sociology. For clarifying details of Merton's own use, see his 'Social Dysfunction' in *On Social Structure and Science*, pp. 96–100, especially note 1.

23. Robert Bierstedt, *American Sociological Theory: A Critical History* (New York: Academic Press, 1981); see my review, *American Journal of Sociology* **XCI** (March 1986), 1229–31.

24. Robert Bierstedt, 'Merton's Systematic Theory,' in Clark *et al.* (eds), *Robert K. Merton*, pp. 67–74, 76–7.

25. Bierstedt, *American Sociological Theory*, p. 486.

26. Piotr Sztompka, 'R.K. Merton's Theoretical System: An Overview' in Clark *et al.* (eds), *Robert K. Merton*, pp. 53–64, 75–6; see also Charles Crothers, *Robert K. Merton*, Key Sociologists Series (London: Tavistock Publishers, 1987), pp. 64–118. Other leading Mertonians who would likely find Bierstedt's opinion contrary to observable scholarly data might include Arthur Stinchcombe, Raymond Boudon, Aage Sorenson, and Neil Smelser, whose particular elaborations of Merton's work I cannot pursue here. None of these, however, seem to have given quite so much attention to Merton *qua* writer as has Bierstedt, which is why I call upon his testimony more often than would otherwise be justifiable.

27. Ezra Pound, *A Lume Spento and Other Early Poems* (New York: New Directions, 1965), from the 'Foreword 1965'.

28. Merton, *Social Theory and Social Structure* (1968 edition), p. 74; emphases in original.

29. For a new sociological meditation on what postmodernity means for social theorists, see Charles Lemert, *The Postmodern Is Not What You Think* (Malden, MA: Blackwell Publishers, 1997), especially pp. 19–68, 132–64.

30. Robert K. Merton, *Science, Technology and Society in Seventeenth Century England*, *OSIRIS* vol. 4, Part 2 (1938), p. 495; rep. edn, Harper & Row (Torchbook), 1970, p. 136.
31. Ibid., (1970 edn), p. xvii.
32. Robert K. Merton, *Sociological Ambivalence and Other Essays* (New York: Free Press, 1976), p. 7.
33. Merton, *Social Theory and Social Structure* (1968 edn), pp. 493–582.
34. Ibid., pp. 364–80.
35. Ibid., pp. 279–334.
36. Bierstedt, *American Sociological Theory*, pp. 470–83.
37. Both Lewis Coser's *The Idea of Social Structure* and Jon Clark *et al.* (eds), *Robert K. Merton* have extensive bibliographies toward this end, to which could be added Piotr Sztompka's *Robert K. Merton: An Intellectual Profile* (New York: St Martin's Press, 1986), pp. 304–14.
38. Bierstedt, *American Sociological Theory*, pp. 486, 489.

Chapter 9

1. *She Came to Stay* was first published in 1943 as *L' Invitée* (Paris: Gallimard).
2. Simone de Beauvoir, *The Second Sex* (Toronto: Bantam Books, 1964) p. 249.
3. Ibid., p. 249.
4. De Beauvoir and Sartre had an extensive correspondence, some of which is published. See Simone de Beauvoir, *Letters to Sartre* (New York: Arcade, 1991) and Jean-Paul Sartre, *Witness to My Life* (London: Hamish Hamilton, 1992).
5. Simone de Beauvoir, *Memoirs of a Dutiful Daughter* (Harmondsworth: Penguin, 1983).
6. Walter Benjamin, *Charles Baudelaire: A Lyric Poet in the Era of High Capitalism* (London: New Left Books, 1973).
7. Janet Woolf, 'The Invisible Flaneuse', in Janet Woolf, *Feminine Sentences* (Cambridge: Polity, 1990) pp. 34–50.
8. Virginia Woolf, *The Crowded Dance of Modern Life* (London: Penguin, 1993).
9. Kate Millett, *Sexual Politics* (London: Virago, 1977).
10. This relationship is discussed by David Macey in *The Lives of Michel Foucault* (London: Vintage, 1994), pp. 413–14.
11. The 'new' French feminism (which is of course now well established) is well presented in Elaine Marks and Isabelle de Courtivron (eds), *New French Feminisms* (Brighton: Harvester, 1981).
12. This account of the relationship between the work of Sartre and that of de Beauvoir is best represented in: Toril Moi, *Simone de Beauvoir* (Oxford: Blackwell, 1994) and Kate Fullbrook and Edward Fullbrook, *Simone de Beauvoir and Jean-Paul Sartre: The Remaking of a Twentieth Century Legend* (London: Wheatsheaf/Harvester, 1993).
13. For Donna Haraway, see *Primate Visions: Gender, Race and Nature in the World of Modern Science* (New York: Routledge, 1989) and Sandra Harding, *The Science Question in Feminism* (Ithaca: Cornell University Press, 1986).

14. See Patricia Hill Collins, 'The Social Construction of Black Feminist Thought', *Signs* **14**(4) (1989), 745–73.
15. *Purrhus and Cinéas* was first published in 1944 (Paris, Gallimard) and *The Blood of Others* in 1945, as *Le Sang des Autres* (Paris, Gallimard).
16. Simone de Beauvoir, *Memoirs of a Dutiful Daughter* (Harmondsworth: Penguin, 1987).
17. Sylvia Plath, *The Bell Jar* (London: Faber, 1963).
18. John Stuart Mill, *On the Subjection of Women* (London: Dent, 1970) and Mary Wollstonecraft, *A Vindication of the Rights of Woman* (London: Dent, 1970).
19. Carol Gilligan, *In a Different Voice* (Cambridge: Harvard University Press, 1982).
20. Adrienne Rich, *Of Women Born* (London: Virago).
21. Shulamith Firestone, *The Dialectic of Sex* (New York: Bantam Books, 1970).

Chapter 10

1. Breslau was later to become the city of Wroclaw in Poland. However, when Elias lived there it was 'entirely German'. S. Mennell, *Norbert Elias: An Introduction* (Oxford: Blackwell, 1989), p. 5.
2. N. Elias, *The Civilizing Process* (Oxford: Blackwell [combined edition 1994, originally published 1939]), p. xvi.
3. I owe much to Professor Eric Dunning for this interpretation of Elias' work.
4. There is considerable controversy over the extent to which Cassirer influenced Elias' work. For a comprehensive account of the debate see *Theory Culture and Society* **12**(3) August, 1995.
5. It also came to be known as 'figurational' sociology, but Elias preferred the term 'process sociology' as it had more everyday currency.
6. Mennell, *Norbert Elias*, p. 7.
7. R. Kilminster, 'Introduction to Elias', *Theory, Culture and Society* **4** (1987), 213–22.
8. It is important to note that Elias begins his discussion in *The Civilizing Process* by examining the long-term social processes in which the term came to gain its 'progressive' overtones. Elias wanted clearly to distinguish his use of the term as a technical concept from the popular usage which often embodies evolutionary, colonial, racist, and derogatory sentiments. Moreover, Elias is able to show how Britain and France fought against Germany in the First World War in the name of civilization.
9. Elias, *The Civilizing Process*, p. 105.
10. Ibid., pp. 68–105.
11. Ibid., p. 118.
12. Ibid., p. 451.
13. Ibid., p. 460.
14. Ibid., p. 446.
15. The process by which more and more people become 'interdependent', this concept is explained below in relation to power.
16. A. Giddens, *The Constitution of Society* (Cambridge: Polity Press, 1984).
17. Elias, *The Civilizing Process*, pp. 55–6.

18. N. Elias, *What is Sociology?* (London: Hutchinson [translated in 1978 from the original German publication in 1970]), p. 119.

19. 'Knowledge and Power: an Interview by Peter Ludes', in Nico Stehr and Volker Meja (eds), *Society and Knowledge* (London: Transaction Books, 1984), pp. 252–91.

20. To provide an example of the 'marginal circumstances' referred to above, consider the case of an unwanted new-born baby in a medieval society.

21. Perhaps the chief danger with the analogy with games is their dependence on 'rules'. Elias does not want to give the impression that rules are essential to all of social life. He thus provides the model of the 'Primal Contest' to demonstrate how games without rules can, nonetheless, settle into a relatively stable pattern. Elias, *What is Sociology?*, pp. 73–80.

22. Ibid., p. 82.

23. Mennell, *Norbert Elias*, p. 261.

24. Elias, *What is Sociology?*, p. 85.

25. Elias, *The Civilizing Process*, p. 444.

26. J. Goodman, *Tobacco in History* (London: Routledge, 1993), p. 25.

27. J. Harrington, 'Tobacco Smoking among the Karuk Indians of California', Smithsonian Institute Bureau of American Ethnology, *Bulletin* **94** (1932), 193–4.

28. N. Elias and E. Dunning, *Quest for Excitement: Sport and Leisure in the Civilizing Process* (Oxford: Blackwell, 1986).

29. J. Goudsblom, *Fire and Civilization* (London: Penguin, 1992).

30. S. Mennell, *All Manners of Food: Eating and Taste in England and France from the Middle Ages to the Present* (London: Blackwell, 1985).

31. C. Wouters, 'Informalization and the Civilizing Process' in P.R. Gleichmann, J. Goudsblom and H. Korte (eds), *Human Figurations: Essays for Norbert Elias* (Amsterdam: Stichting Amsterdams Sociologisch Tijdschrift, 1977), pp. 437–53.

32. E. Dunning and C. Rojek (eds), *Sport and Leisure in the Civilizing Process: Critique and Counter Critique* (Basingstoke: Macmillan, 1992).

33. A. Blok, 'Primitief en geciviliseerd', *Sociologisch Gids* **29**(3–4) (1982), 197–209.

34. E. Leach, 'Violence', *London Review of Books*, October (1986).

35. D. Layder, 'Social Reality as Figuration: a Critique of Elias's Conception of Sociological Analysis', *Sociology* **20**(3) (1986), 367–86.

36. B. Maso, 'Riddereer en riddermoed – ontwikkelingen van de aanvalslust in de late middeleeuwen' (Knightly honour and knightly courage: on changes in fighting spirit in the late Middle Ages), *Sociologische Gids* **29**(3–4) (1982), 296–325.

37. Mennell, *Norbert Elias*.

38. Ibid., p. 248.

39. Ibid., p. 241.

40. Ibid., p. 242.

41. Elias, *The Civilizing Process*, p. 187, cited in Mennell, *Norbert Elias*, p. 242.

42. Elias and Dunning, *Quest for Excitement*, p. 44 in Mennell, *Norbert Elias*, p. 242.

43. Elias and Dunning, *Quest for Excitement,* p. 66.

44. Dunning and Rojek, *Sport and Leisure in the Civilizing Process*, p. 248.

Chapter 11

1. Goffman's distaste for treating sociology as a set of schools or perspectives is brought out very clearly in his comments on Denzin and Keller's review of 'Frame Analysis'. See 'Reply to Denzin and Keller', *Contemporary Sociology – An International Journal of Reviews* **10**(1981), 60–8.
2. See Erving Goffman, 'The Interaction Order', *American Sociological Review* **48** (1983), 3.
3. T. Burns, *Erving Goffman* (London: Routledge, 1992), p. 6.
4. Goffman's PhD thesis begins with a long quotation from Simmel in which Simmel refers to 'an immeasurable number of less conspicuous forms of relationship and kinds of interaction' that should be of interest to sociologists alongside our interest in 'large social formations'. Simmel goes on to write, 'That people look at one another and are jealous of one another; that they exchange letters or dine together, that irrespective of all tangible interests they strike one another as pleasant and unpleasant; that gratitude for altruistic acts makes for inseparable union; that one asks another man after a certain street, and that people dress and adorn themselves for one another – the whole gamut of relations that play from one person to another and that may be momentary or permanent, conscious or unconscious, ephemeral or of grave consequence (and from which these illustrations are quite casually chosen), all these incessantly tie men together. Here are the interactions among the atoms of society. They account for all the toughness and elasticity, all the colour and consistency of social life that is so striking and yet so mysterious', G. Simmel, *The Sociology of Georg Simmel* (Glencoe, IL: Free Press, 1960), p. 10.
5. See Chapter 5 of E. Goffman, *Relations in Public* (Harmondsworth: Penguin Books, 1972).
6. See Chapters 3 and 4 of Goffman, *Relations in Public*.
7. A more general account of this may be found in the essay 'Replies and Responses' in E. Goffman, *Forms of Talk* (Oxford: Blackwell, 1981).
8. See Burns, *Erving Goffman*, p. 82.
9. P. Manning, *Erving Goffman and Modern Sociology* (Cambridge: Polity Press, 1992).
10. I have provided an account of this vocabulary elsewhere. See R. Williams, 'Goffman's sociology of talk' in J. Ditton (ed.), *The View from Goffman* (London: Macmillan, 1980).
11. See R.J. Anderson, J.A. Hughes, and W.W. Sharrock, *The Sociology Game: An Introduction to Sociological Reasoning* (London: Longman, 1985).
12. Goffman, 'Reply to Denzin and Keller', p. 62.
13. 'In this report, the individual was divided by implication into two basic parts: he was viewed as a performer, a harried fabricator of impressions involved in the all-too-human task of staging a performance; he was viewed as a character, a figure, typically a fine one, whose spirit, strength and other fine qualities the performance was intended to evoke. The attributes of a performer and the attributes of a character are of a different order, quite basically so, yet both sets have their meaning in terms of the show that must go on', E. Goffman, *Asylums: Essays on*

the Social Situation of Mental Hospital Patients and Other Inmates (Harmondsworth: Penguin, 1961), p. 244.

14. Ibid.
15. See 'The Underlife of a Public Institution' in Goffman, *Asylums*, pp. 157–280.
16. C. Battershill, 'Erving Goffman as a Precursor to Post-modern Sociology', in S. H. Riggins (ed.), *Beyond Goffman: Studies on Communication, Institution and Social Interaction* (New York: Mouton de Gruyter, 1990), pp. 163–86.
17. Ibid., pp. 163–86.
18. A. Giddens, 'Erving Goffman as a Systematic Social Theorist', in A. Giddens (ed.), *Social Theory and Modern Sociology* (Cambridge: Polity Press, 1987), p. 18.
19. Burns, *Erving Goffman*, p. 24.
20. See especially Chapters 2–4 of *Frame Analysis: An Essay on the Organisation of Experience* (New York: Harper & Row, 1974).
21. 'Radio Talk: The Ways of our Errors' in Goffman, *Forms of Talk*, pp. 197–330.
22. Manning has noted the way that the metaphors of games and rituals are put against one another such that 'Games emphasise information, fatefulness, manipulation and so on, while ritual emphasises morality, concern, co-operation' in Manning, *Erving Goffman and Modern Sociology*, p. 36.
23. L.H. Lofland, 'Social Life in the Public Realm: a Review', *Journal of Contemporary Ethnography* 17 (1989), 459.
24. Goffman, *Relations in Public* and *Behaviour in Public Places: Notes on the Social Organisation of Gatherings* (Glencoe: Free Press, 1963), p. 84.
25. Goffman, *Relations in Public*, p. 86.
26. Lofland, 'Social life in the public realm', p. 462.
27. See S. Cavan, *Liquor License* (Chicago: Aldine, 1966). While Cavan's study is now more than 30 years old and was limited to bars in the United States of America, her observations and analyses of the dynamics of interaction in such settings continue to offer important insights into what happens in similar places here and now.
28. This can, of course become a problem for those who want to use such settings while remaining closed to the overtures of others. Many potential solo users find the work of resisting the overtures of others to be too burdensome to allow them to remain comfortable.
29. Cavan, *Liquor License*, p. 50.
30. This does not mean of course that a good deal of interactional work cannot be accomplished during such superficial conversational topic exploration.
31. For example: A. MacIntyre, 'The Self as a Work of Art', *New Statesman*, March (1969) and *After Virtue* (London: Duckworth, 1981); T.G. Miller, 'Goffman, Social Acting, and Moral Behavior', *Journal for the Theory of Social Behaviour* 14 (1984), 141–63; A. Ryan, 'Maximising, Minimising, Moralising', in C. Hookway and P. Pettit (eds), *Action and Interpretation* (Cambridge: Cambridge University Press, 1978), pp. 65–81; R. Sennett, *The Fall of Public Man* (Cambridge: Cambridge University Press, 1977).
32. See Manning, *Erving Goffman and Modern Sociology*, p. 39; Giddens, 'Erving Goffman as a systematic social theorist', pp. 109–39.
33. See P. Creelan, 'The Degradation of the Sacred: Approaches of Cooley and Goffman', *Symbolic Interaction* 10 (1987), 29–56.

34. See for example: H. Sacks, *Lectures on Conversation* (Cambridge: Blackwell, 1992); H. Sacks, E.A. Schegloff and G. Jefferson, 'A Simplest Systematics for the Organisation of Turn-taking in Conversation', *Language* **50** (1974), 696–735; E.A. Schegloff, 'The Routine as Achievement', *Human Studies* **9** (1986), 111–51; E.A. Schegloff, 'Between Micro and Macro: Contexts and Other Connections', *The Micro-Macro Link*, J.C. Alexander (ed.), (Berkeley: California University Press, 1987), pp. 207–34; E.A. Schegloff, 'Goffman and the Analysis of Conversation', *E. Goffman: Exploring the Interaction Order*, P. Drew and T. Wootton (eds), (Cambridge: Polity Press, 1988), pp. 89–135; E.A. Schegloff, 'Reflections on Talk and Social Structure', *Talk and Social Structure: Studies in Ethnomethodology and Conversation Analysis*, D. Boden and D.H. Zimmerman (eds), (Cambridge: Polity Press, 1991), pp. 44–70.
35. In Goffman, 'Reply to Denzin and Keller', p. 4.
36. Goffman, 'The Interaction Order', p. 4.
37. 'In general then, (and qualifications apart) what one finds in modern societies at least is a non-exclusive linkage – a 'loose coupling' – between interactional practices and social structures, a collapsing of strata and structures into broader categories, the categories themselves not corresponding one-to-one to anything in the structural world, a gearing as it were of various structures into interactional cogs. Or, if you will, a set of transformation rules, or a membrane selecting how various externally relevant social distinctions will be managed within the interaction', Goffman, 'The Interaction Order', p. 11.
38. Burns, *Erving Goffman*, p. 376.
39. See Giddens, 'Erving Goffman as a systematic social theorist', pp. 109–39.

Chapter 12

1. D. Lockwood, *The Blackcoated Worker* (London: Allen & Unwin, 1958).
2. J.H. Goldthorpe, D. Lockwood, F. Bechhofer and J. Platt, *The Affluent Worker: Industrial Attitudes and Behaviour* (Cambridge: Cambridge University Press, 1968).
3. See F. Zweig, *The Worker in an Affluent Society* (London: Heinemann, 1961).
4. See Goldthorpe *et al.*, *The Affluent Worker*; *The Affluent Worker in the Class Structure* (Cambridge: Cambridge University Press, 1969).
5. R. Blauner, *Alienation and Freedom* (Chicago: University of Chicago Press, 1964).
6. D. Wedderburn and R. Crompton, *Workers' Attitudes and Technology* (Cambridge: Cambridge University Press, 1972).
7. D. Lockwood, 'Social Integration and System Integration', in G.K. Zollschan and W. Hirsch (eds), *Explorations in Social Change* (London: Routledge & Kegan Paul, 1964), pp. 244–57; T. Parsons, *The System of Modern Societies* (Englewood Cliffs, NJ: Prentice-Hall, 1971).
8. Ibid., p. 244.
9. See T. Parsons and E.S. Shils (eds), *Toward a General Theory of Action* (New York: Harper & Row, 1951); Parsons, *The System of Modern Societies*.

10. For an exposition and early critique of Parsonian-based modernization theories see H. Bernstein, 'Modernisation Theory and the Sociological Study of Development', *Journal of Development Studies* **VII** (1971).

11. See on this point N. Mouzelis, *Modern Greece: Facets of Underdevelopment* (London: Macmillan, 1978), Ch. 2.

12. D. Lockwood, *Solidarity and Schism: 'The Problem of Disorder' in Durkheimian and Marxist Sociology* (Oxford: Oxford University Press, 1992).

13. Ibid., p. 178.

14. For a further development of these points and their linkages with the social/system-integration distinction see N. Mouzelis, *Back to Sociological Theory* (London: Macmillan, 1990), Chs 3–7; N. Mouzelis, *Sociological Theory: What Went Wrong? Diagnosis and Remedies* (London: Routledge, 1995), Ch. 5.

15. See N. Elias, *What is Sociology?* (London: Hutchison, 1978).

16. A. Giddens, *The Constitution of Society* (Cambridge: Polity Press, 1984).

17. P. Bourdieu, *Outline of a Theory of Action* (Cambridge: Cambridge University Press, 1977).

18. See Mouzelis, *Sociological Theory*, Ch. 6. It might be useful to note here that Giddens has not only unnecessarily substituted the distinction between institutional analysis and analysis in terms of strategic conduct for the social- and system-integration distinction; he has also used the social/system-integration dichotomy as a substitute for the micro–macro-integration dichotomy, so making the confusion even worse. See on this point N. Mouzelis, 'Restructuring Structuration Theory', *Sociological Review* **37**(4) (1989), 617–35.

19. See for instance E. Laclau and C. Mouffe, *Hegemony and Social Strategy: Towards a Radical Democratic Politics* (London: Verso, 1985); E. Laclau, *New Reflections on the Revolution of our Time* (London: Verso, 1990).

20. For a critique of post-structuralism along such lines see N. Mouzelis, *Sociological Theory*, Ch. 3.

21. J. Habermas, *The Theory of Communicative Action*, vol. II, *Lifeworld and System* (Cambridge: Polity Press, 1987).

22. See N. Mouzelis, 'Social and System Integration: Habermas' View', *British Journal of Sociology* **43**(2) (June, 1992), 272–7.

23. See N. Mouzelis, 'Social and System Integration: Lockwood, Giddens, Habermas', *Sociology, Sociological Review* (May, 1997). See also my earlier critique of Lockwood's social/system-integration distinction, 'System and Social Integration: a Reconsideration of a Fundamental Distinction', *British Journal of Sociology* (December, 1974).

24. For an application of the social/system-integration distinction to the analysis of political transformations in nineteenth and early twentieth-century Greece, see N. Mouzelis, *Post-Marxist Alternatives* (London: Macmillan, 1990), Ch. 4.

25. See on this point D. Layder, 'Contemporary Sociological Theory', *Sociology* **30**(3) (August, 1996).

Chapter 13

1. The title of Husserl's book was: *The Crisis of European Sciences and Transcendantal Phenomenology*.
2. This study, written in 1942, was published after Garfinkel's service in World War II (Garfinkel 1949).
3. The story was anthologized in a collection of the best American short stories of 1941 (Garfinkel 1940).
4. As Garfinkel would later put it (in more complex prose), a 'central recommendation is that the activities whereby members produce and manage settings of organized everyday affairs are identical with members' procedures for making those settings "account-able"'.

Chapter 15

1. Jürgen Habermas, *Autonomy and Solidarity*, Peter Dews (ed.), (London: Verso, 2nd edn, 1992), p. 97.
2. See, in particular, Andrew Arato's contribution, 'Critical Theory and Authoritarian State Socialism', in David Held and John Thompson (eds), *Habermas. Critical Debates* (London: Macmillan, 1982), pp. 196–218 and Habermas, 'A Reply to my Critics', pp. 219–83 in the same volume. In my own occasional discussions of these issues I have found this approach particularly useful; see, for example, 'Steering the Public Sphere. Communication Policy in State Socialism and After', in B. Einhorn, M. Kaldor and Z. Kavan (eds), *Citizenship and Democratic Control* (Edward Elgar, 1996), pp. 159–72.
3. See, in particular, Seyla Benhabib, *Critique, Norm and Utopia* (New York: Columbia University Press, 1980); Axel Honneth, *Critique of Power* (Cambridge, MA: MIT Press, 1992, first published in 1985); Axel Honneth, *The Struggle for Recognition* (Cambridge: Polity Press, 1994).
4. Klaus Eder, *The New Politics of Class. Social Movements and Cultural Dynamics in Advanced Societies* (London: Sage, 1993); Claus Offe, *Contradictions of the Welfare State* (London, Hutchinson, 1984); Claus Offe, *Disorganized Capitalism* (Cambridge, Polity Press, 1985).

Chapter 16

1. Bourdieu (1980/1990, p. 8) recalls that the work of Lévi-Strauss 'imposed upon a whole generation a new manner of conceiving of intellectual activity' that held out the hope of 'reconciling theoretical with practical intentions, the scientific vocation with the ethical or political vocation'.
2. Unlike most scholars of like stature, Pierre Bourdieu has continued to conduct much of the primary data collection and analysis for his research himself. No doubt this constant contact with the mundane practicalities of the research routine has helped shelter him from the conceptual reification and desiccation that often affect the work of social theorists.

3. Michel Foucault's work is also rooted in, and an extension of, this school of 'historicist rationalism'. Many of the affinities or convergences between Bourdieu and Foucault can be traced back to this common epistemological mooring.

4. This is particularly visible in the selection of texts in the philosophy of science that make up the second part of the book and illustrate its core propositions: of the 45 selections, five are by Bachelard and four by Canguilhem (as against six by Durkheim, three by Weber, and two by Marx).

5. Habitus is an old philosophical concept, used intermittently by Aristotle (under the term *hexis*), Hegel, Weber, Durkheim, Mauss and Husserl, among others. Bourdieu retrieved it in a 1967 analysis of the thought of art historian Erwin Panofsky and has refined it since, both empirically and theoretically, in each of his major works. His most sophisticated explication of the concept is in *Méditations Pascaliennes* (Bourdieu 1997a: especially pp. 158–93 and 247–79).

6. The concept of field (*champ*) was coined by Bourdieu in the mid-1960s for purposes of empirical inquiry into the historical genesis and transformation of the worlds of art and literature. It has since been extensively modified and elaborated, by Bourdieu and his associates, in the course of studies of the intellectual, philosophical, scientific, religious, academic, poetic, publishing, political, juridical, economic, sporting, bureaucratic, and journalistic fields. The most accessible and compact sources on the uses and effects of the concept is in the collection of essays entitled *The Field of Cultural Production* (Bourdieu 1993: especially Part II, 'Flaubert and the French Literary Field').

7. The two most common misinterpretations of Bourdieu's theory of practice are those that omit either term of the equation (and thus their varied relationship): the 'structuralist' misreading overlooks habitus and deducts conduct mechanically from social structure while the 'utilitarian' misreading misses field and condemns itself to construe action as the pursuit of the agent's interest.

8. While Bourdieu's demonstration is carried out with French materials, his theoretical claims apply to all differentiated societies. For pointers on how to extract general propositions from Bourdieu's specific findings on France and to adapt his models to other countries and epochs, see 'A Japanese Reading of Distinction' (Bourdieu 1995) and the preface to the English translation of *The State Nobility*.

9. This insistence finds a paradigmatic (and dramatic) illustration in Bourdieu's inaugural lecture at the Collège de France. In this 'Lecture on the Lecture', the freshly consecrated professor dissects 'the act of delegation whereby the new master is authorised to speak with authority' so as to emphasize this fundamental property of sociology as he conceives it: 'Every proposition that this science formulates can and must apply to the subject who produces it' (Bourdieu 1982/1991: 8).

10. The theory of 'symbolic revolution' adumbrated in the closing chapter of *Homo Academicus* is fully developed in *The Rules of Art* (Bourdieu 1992/1997), which contains both an account of the historical invention of the institution of modern literature and a sociological theory of intellectual innovation that does away with the charismatic notion of 'genius' by elucidating it.

11. The book had an impact unmatched by any social science book in recent memory: it sold over 100,000 copies in three months and stood atop the best-seller list for months; it was extensively discussed in political circles and popular magazines alike (conservative Prime Minister Balladur publicly ordered his

cabinet members to read it); it has been adapted for the stage and is widely used by schoolteachers, social workers and grassroots activists.

12. Bourdieu has also sought to make his own theories more accessible to a broad educated public in several collections of lectures and talks, notably *Sociology in Question, In Other Words,* and *Practical Reasons* (Bourdieu 1980/1993, 1987/1991, 1994/1998).

Chapter 17

1. Throughout the writing of this chapter I could not help but think of the Freudian connotations of the sub-heading 'driving impulses', that we were asked to use to introduce the influences of the sociological thinkers. Driving impulses, as you will see, are as absent from object relations theory as they are present in traditional Freudian drive theory.
2. N. Chodorow, *Feminism and Psychoanalysis* (New Haven: Yale University Press, 1989), p. 8.
3. Ibid., p. 167.
4. N. Chodorow, *The Reproduction of Mothering* (Berkeley, CA: University of California Press, 1978), p. 99.
5. In her more recent work, Chodorow (1994) has taken up issues of sexuality again. In particular she investigates why psychoanalysis has so many theories about homosexuality but so few about heterosexuality. She argues that like all sexuality, heterosexuality is a 'compromise formation' or a symptom.
6. Chodorow, *The Reproduction of Mothering*, p. 198.
7. Ibid.
8. N. Chodorow, 'Reply by Nancy Chodorow', *Signs* Spring (1981), 512.
9. C. Williams, *Gender Differences at Work* (Berkeley, CA: University of California Press (1989), p. 64.
10. Ibid., p. 66.
11. Ibid., p. 66.
12. Ibid., p. 67.
13. Ibid., p. 64.
14. Chodorow, *Feminism and Psychoanalysi,* p. 4.
15. Chodorow, 'Reply by Nancy Chodorow', p. 504.
16. Chodorow, 'Individuality and Difference in How Men and Women Love,' *Femininities, Masculinities and Sexualities: Freud and Beyond* (Lexington, KY: University of Kentucky Press, 1990), pp. 70–92.
17. Chodorow, 'Gender as a Personal and Cultural Construction,' *Signs* Spring (1995), pp. 517.

Chapter 18

1. A.R. Hochschild, *The Managed Heart: The Commercialization of Human Feeling* (Berkeley, CA: University of California Press, 1983).
2. C. Wright Mills, *White Collar* (New York: Oxford University Press, 1956).

3. Hochschild, *The Managed Heart*, pp. ix–x.
4. E. Goffman, *The Presentation of Self in Everyday Life* (New York: Doubleday Anchor, 1959).
5. S. Freud, 'The Ego and the Id', in S. Freud, *On Metapsychology* (Harmondsworth: Penguin, 1923/1982), pp. 357–66.
6. Hochschild, *The Managed Heart*, p. x.
7. For a detailed account of this perspective see Appendix A in Hochschild, *The Managed Heart*.
8. Ibid., p. 17.
9. J. Dewey, *Human Nature and Conduct: An Introduction to Social Psychology* (New York: Holt, 1922).
10. H. Gerth, and C. Wright Mills, *Character and Social Structure: The Psychology of Social Institutions* (New York: Harcourt, Brace and World, 1964).
11. Goffman, *The Presentation of Self in Everyday Life*.
12. C. Darwin, *The Expression of Emotion in Man and Animals* (New York: Philosophical Library, 1955).
13. Freud, 'The Ego and the Id'.
14. Hochschild, *The Managed Heart*, p. 222.
15. C. Wright Mills, *The Sociological Imagination* (New York: Oxford University Press, 1959).
16. Hochschild, *The Managed Heart*, p. 18.
17. Ibid., p. 5.
18. A.R. Hochschild, "Emotion Work, Feeling Rules and Social Structure', *American Journal of Sociology* **85** (1979), 561–2.
19. Hochschild, *The Managed Heart*, p. 187.
20. Ibid., p. 188.
21. Ibid., p. 189.
22. Hochschild, 'Emotion Work', p. 569.
23. A.R. Hochschild with A. Machung, *The Second Shift: Working Parents and the Revolution at Home* (London: Piatkus, 1990/[1989]).
24. Ibid., pp. 188–9.
25. Ibid., pp. 46.
26. T.J. Kemper, 'Themes and Variations in the Sociology of Emotions', in T.J. Kemper (ed.), *Research Agendas in the Sociology of Emotions* (New York: State University of New York Press, 1990).
27. T.J. Kemper, 'Social Relations and Emotions: a Structural Approach', in Kemper (ed.), *Research Agendas in the Sociology of Emotions*, intro.
28. N.K. Denzin, *On Understanding Emotion* (San Francisco: Jossey-Bass, 1984). See also N.K. Denzin, 'On Understanding Emotion: the Interpretive–Cultural Agenda, in Kemper (ed.), *Research Agendas in the Sociology of Emotions*, pp. 73–85.
29. P.A. Thoits, 'Emotional Deviance: Research Agendas', in Kemper (ed.), *Research Agendas in the Sociology of Emotions*, pp. 135–52.
30. Hochschild, *The Managed Heart*, p. 190.
31. Ibid., pp. 192–3.
32. Ibid., p. 193.
33. Ibid., pp. 192–4.
34. S. Fineman, *Emotions and Organisations* (London: Sage, 1993).

35. J. Duncombe and D. Marsden, 'Love and Intimacy: the Gender Division of Emotion Work', *Sociology* **27**(2) (1993), 221–41. See also: J. Duncombe and D. Marsden, '"Stepford Wives" and "Hollow Men": Doing Emotion Work, Doing Gender and "Authenticity" in Intimate Heterosexual Relationships', in G. Bendelow and S.J. Williams (eds), *Emotions in Social Life: Critical Themes and Contemporary Issues* (London: Routledge, 1998), pp. 211–27.

36. See for example, N. James, 'Emotional Labour: Skill and Work in the Social Regulation of Feelings, *Sociological Review* **37**(1) (1989), 15–42; N. James, 'Care=Organisation+Physical Labour+Emotional Labour, *Sociology of Health and Illness* **14**(4) (1992), 488–509; V. James and J. Gabe (eds), *Health and the Sociology of Emotions* (Oxford: Blackwell, 1996); J. Lawler, *Behind the Screens: Nursing, Somology and the Problem of the Body* (Melbourne/Edinburgh: Churchill Livingstone, 1991); P. Smith, *The Emotional Division of Labour in Nursing* (Basingstoke: Macmillan Educational Books, 1992).

37. S.J. Williams and G. Bendelow, 'Emotions, Health and Illness: the "Missing Link" in Medical Sociology?', in James and Gabe (eds), *Health and the Sociology of Emotions*, pp. 25–54.

38. S.J. Williams and G. Bendelow, 'Transcending the Dualisms: Towards a Sociology of Pain', *Sociology of Health and Illness*, **17**(2) (1995), 139–165; G. Bendelow and S.J. Williams, 'Pain and the Mind–Body Dualism: a Sociological Approach, *Body and Society* **1**(2) (1995), 82–103, and G. Bendelow, 'Pain Perceptions, Gender and Emotion', *Sociology of Health and Illness* **15**(3) (1993), 273–94.

39. P. Freund, 'The Expressive Body: a Common ground for the Sociology of Emotions and Health and Illness, *Sociology of Health and Illness* **12**(4) (1990), 452–77; P. Freund, 'Social Performances and Their Discontents: Reflections on the Biosocial Psychology of Role-playing, in G. Bendelow and S.J. Williams (eds), *Emotions in Social Life: Critical Themes and Contemporary Issues* (London: Routledge, 1997), pp. 268–94.

40. Hochschild, *The Managed Heart*, pp. 174–81.

41. Freund, 'The Expressive Body', p. 470.

42. C. Wouters, 'The Sociology of Emotions and Flight Attendants: Hochschild's "Managed Heart"', *Theory, Culture and Society* **6**(1) (1989), 104–5.

43. Ibid., pp. 105–6. See also A.R. Hochschild, 'Reply to Cas Wouter's Review Essay on the "Managed Heart"', *Theory, Culture and Society* **6**(3) (1989), 439–45, and C. Wouters, 'Response to Hochschild's Reply', *Theory, Culture and Society* **6**(3) (1989), 447–50.

44. A.R. Hochschild, *The Time Bind: When Work Becomes Home and Home Becomes Work* (New York: Metropolitan Press, 1997). For other historical studies of emotions and time, see: N. Elias, *The Civilizing Process,* vols I and II (Oxford: Basil Blackwell, 1978, 1982); N. Elias, 'On Human Beings and Their Emotions: a Process-sociological Essay, in M. Featherstone, M. Hepworth and B.S. Turner (eds), *The Body: Social Process and Cultural Theory* (London: Sage, 1991), pp. 103–25; P. Stearns, *American Cool: Constructing a Twentieth Century American Style* (New York: New York University Press, 1994), and C.Z. Stearns and P. Stearns, *Emotions and Social Change* (New York: Holmes and Meier, 1988).

45. Duncombe and Marsden, '"Stepford Wives" and "Hollow Men"'.

46. A. Giddens, *The Transformation of Intimacy* (Cambridge: Polity Press, 1992).

47. S.J. Williams, 'Emotions, Cyberspace and the "Virtual" Body: a Critical Appraisal', in G. Bendelow and S.J. Williams (eds), *Emotions in Social Life* (London: Routledge, 1998), pp. 120–32.

Chapter 19

1. Foucault's Chair at the College de France was given the special title of Chair in the History of Systems of Thought. Foucault's major books are listed in the Bibliography. In addition, the following books are particularly useful introductions: J. Rajchman, *Michel Foucault and the Freedom of Philosophy* (New York: Columbia University Press, 1985); B. Smart, *Michel Foucault* (Chichester: Ellis Horwood Ltd., 1985); and A. Sheridan, *Michel Foucault: The Will to Truth* (London: Routledge, 1990).

2. M. Foucault, *The Order of Things: An Archaeology of the Human Sciences* (New York: Vintage Books, 1973).

3. For the influence of Nietzsche on Foucault's thought students may refer to M. Foucault, *Language, Counter-memory, Practice*, D. Bouchard (ed.) (Ithaca: Cornell University Press, 1977); M. Mahon, *Foucault's Nietzschean Genealogy: Truth, Power, and the Subject* (Albany: State University of New York Press, 1992); or D. Owen, *Maturity and Modernity: Nietzsche, Weber, Foucault, and the Ambivalence of Reason* (London: Routledge, 1994).

4. For the influences of Canguilhem and Bachelard on Foucault, see G. Gutting, *Michel Foucault's Archaeology of Scientific Reason* (Cambridge: Cambridge University Press, 1989).

5. M. Foucault, *Discipline and Punish: The Birth of the Prison* (New York: Vintage Books, 1979).

6. These points are well captured in G. Deleuze, *Foucault* (Minneapolis: University of Minnesota Press, 1988); and T. Dumm, *Michel Foucault and the Politics of Freedom* (Thousand Oaks: Sage, 1996).

7. M. Foucault, *The History of Sexuality*: vol. 1: *An Introduction* (New York: Vintage Books, 1980). The following five volumes did not appear as projected, and for reasons that we will explore below, Foucault directed his research into the experience of sexuality toward the ancient Greeks. M. Foucault, *The Use of Pleasure* (New York: Pantheon Books, 1985); M. Foucault, *The Care of the Self* (New York: Pantheon Books, 1986).

8. M. Foucault, *The History of Sexuality*: vol. 1: *An Introduction*, p. 18.

9. Ibid., p. 61.

10. Ibid., p. 25.

11. Ibid., p. 145 (emphasis added).

12. M. Foucault, 'The Dangerous Individual', in L. Kritzman (ed.), *Politics, Philosophy, Culture: Interviews and Other Writings, 1977–1984,* (New York: Routledge, 1988).

13. In addition to the themes we have covered here, namely discipline and sexuality, Foucault was also weaving in his work on those practices through which madness was separated from reason, and on transformations in the medicalization of

society. See M. Foucault, *Madness and Civilization: A History of Insanity in the Age of Reason* (London: Tavistock, 1967); and M. Foucault, *The Birth of the Clinic* (London: Tavistock, 1973).

14. M. Foucault, 'The Dangerous Individual', p. 150.
15. Ibid., p. 135.
16. Ibid., p. 142.
17. M. Foucault, *The Use of Pleasure* and *The Care of the Self*.
18. M. Foucault, *The Use of Pleasure*, p. 91.
19. M. Foucault, *The Care of the Self*, p. 86–9; p. 42.
20. The issues in this section may be pursued more closely in the following essays: M. Foucault, 'Afterword: The Subject and Power', in H. Dreyfus and P. Rabinow (eds), *Michel Foucault: Beyond Structuralism and Hermeneutics* (Chicago: University of Chicago Press, 1982); 'Kant on Enlightenment and Revolution', *Economy and Society* 15(1) (1986), 88–96; and 'What Is Enlightenment', in P. Rabinow (ed.), *The Foucault Reader* (New York: Pantheon Books, 1984).
21. M. Foucault, 'What Is Enlightenment?', pp. 34, 35.
22. Ibid., p. 45.
23. For a particularly useful elaboration of Foucault's approach to power, see J. Ransom, *Foucault's Discipline: The Politics of Subjectivity* (Durham: Duke University Press, 1997).
24. M. Foucault, 'What Is Enlightenment?', p. 48.
25. J. Donzelot, *The Policing of Families* (Baltimore: The Johns Hopkins University Press, 1979).
26. Ibid., p. 94.
27. N. Rose, *Governing the Soul: The Shaping of the Private Self* (London: Routledge, 1989).
28. Ibid., pp. 149–50.
29. Ibid., p. 208.
30. G. Deleuze, 'What Is a Dispositif?', T. Armstrong (trans.) *Michel Foucault: Philosopher* (London: Harvester Wheatsheaf, 1992), p. 162.
31. These themes may be followed in M. Foucault, 'Politics and Reason', in L. Kritzman (ed.), *Politics, Philosophy, Culture: Interviews and Other Writings, 1977–1984* (New York: Routledge, 1988); and 'Governmentality' in G. Burchell, C. Gordon, and P. Miller (eds), *The Foucault Effect: Studies in Governmentality* (London: Harvester Wheatsheaf, 1991), pp. 87–104.
32. M. Foucault, 'Two Lectures', in C. Gordon (ed.), *Power/Knowledge: Selected Interviews and Other Writings, 1972–1977* (New York: Pantheon Books, 1980).
33. Especially useful for clarifying the connection between subjectification and governmentality is G. Burchell, 'Peculiar Interests: Civil Society and Governing the "System of Natural Liberty"' in Burchell, Gordon and Miller (eds), *The Foucault Effect*, pp. 119–50.
34. For Foucault's course summaries and other materials, see M. Foucault, *Ethics: Subjectivity and Truth*, P. Rabinow (ed.) (New York: The New Press, 1997).
35. See Burchell, Gordon and Miller (eds) *The Foucault Effect* and A. Barry, T. Osborne, and N. Rose, *Foucault and Political Reason: Liberalism, Neo-liberalism and Rationalities of Government* (London: UCL Press, 1996); M. Dean, *The Constitution of Poverty: Toward a Genealogy of Liberal Governance* (London: Routledge, 1991).

36. M. Foucault, 'Sexual Choice, Sexual Act: Foucault and Homosexuality', in L. Kritzman (ed.), *Politics, Philosophy, Culture: Interviews and Other Writings, 1977–1984* (New York: Routledge, 1988), pp. 286–303.
37. A. Stoler, *Race and the Education of Desire* (Durham: Duke University Press, 1995).

Chapter 20

1. 'The Formation of a Diasporic Intellectual: an Interview with Stuart Hall by Kuan-Hsing Chen', in *Stuart Hall: Critical Dialogues in Cultural Studies*, David Morley and Kuan-Hsing Chen (eds) (London: Routledge, 1996), pp. 484–503.
2. 'Encoding/Decoding' first published in 1977 (CCCS Working Papers in Cultural Studies); reprinted in S. Hall (ed.), *Culture, Media, Language* (London: Unwin Hyman, 1990); in S. During (ed.), *The Cultural Studies Reader* (London: Routledge, 1993), pp. 90–103.
3. 'Reflections upon the Encoding/Decoding Model: an Interview with Stuart Hall' in Jon Cruz and Justin Lewis (eds), *Viewing, Reading, Listening: Audiences and Cultural Reception* (Boulder: Westview Press, 1993), pp. 253–74.
4. 'Gramsci's Relevance for the Study of Race and Ethnicity', in Morley and Chen (eds), pp. 411–40.
5. 'The West and the Rest: Discourse and Power' in Stuart Hall and Bram Gieben (eds), *Formations of Modernity* (Polity/OU Press, 1992), p. 294.
6. 'When Was "the Post-colonial"? Thinking at the Limits', in Iain Chambers and Lidia Curti (eds), *The Post-colonial Question* (Routledge, 1996), pp. 242–60.
7. 'The Question of Cultural Identity' in Stuart Hall, David Held and Tony McGrew (eds), *Modernity and its Futures* (Polity/OU Press, 1992), p. 297.
8. 'Who Needs Identity?' in Stuart Hall and Paul du Gay (eds), *Questions of Cultural Identity* (London: Sage, 1996).
9. 'New Ethnicities' in Morley and Chen (eds), pp. 441–9.
10. 'The Spectacle of the "Other"', in Stuart Hall (ed.), *Representation: Cultural Representations and Signifying Practices* (London: Sage, 1997).
11. Morley and Chen (eds), p. 16.
12. 'When Was the Post-colonial?', p. 249.
13. 'On Postmodernism and Articulation' (an interview with Lawrence Grossberg) in Morley and Chen (eds), p. 149.

Chapter 21

1. A. Giddens, *Capitalism and Modern Social Theory: An Analysis of the Writings of Marx, Durkheim and Max Weber* (Cambridge: Cambridge University Press, 1971), p. 224 *passim*.
2. A. Giddens, *Beyond Left and Right: The Future of Radical Politics* (Cambridge: Polity Press, 1994), see especially Chapter 1.

3. A. Giddens, *Modernity and Self-identity: Self and Society in the Late Modern Age* (Cambridge: Polity Press, 1991). See also A. Giddens, *The Consequences of Modernity* (Cambridge: Polity Press, 1990), p. 150.

4. Isaiah Berlin, *The Hedgehog and the Fox: An Essay on Tolstoy's View of History* (London: Wiedenfeld & Nicolson, 1953), pp. 1–2. In social theory Berlin's sensibility of the fox corresponds in salient respects to what Robert Merton terms 'sociological ambivalence'. Insofar as Giddens consistently works at two projects of his own, he is not sociologically ambivalent in Merton's sense of the term. See R. Merton (with Elinor Barber), 'Sociological Ambivalence' in idem. *Sociological Ambivalence and Other Essays* (New York: Free Press, 1976 [1963]), Ch. 1.

5. Giddens' most extensive exposition of structuration theory appears in *The Constitution of Society: Outline of the Theory of Structuration* (Cambridge: Polity Press, 1984).

6. For a technical discussion of the 'ontology of potentials' in structuration theory see I.J. Cohen, *Structuration Theory. Anthony Giddens and the Constitution of Social Life* (London: Macmillan/New York: St Martin's Press, 1989), pp. 12–18 *passim*.

7. For some brief comparisons between Giddens and Dewey on social practices see I.J. Cohen, 'Theories of Action and Praxis', in B.S. Turner (ed.), *The Blackwell Companion to Social Theory* (Oxford: Basil Blackwell, 1996), pp. 131, 134–5.

8. Giddens has maintained a distinction between philosophy and social theory from the beginning of his career. See *Capitalism and Social Theory*, p. x. A. Giddens, 'The Social Sciences and Philosophy – Trends in Recent Social Theory' in idem. *Social Theory and Modern Sociology* (Cambridge: Polity Press, 1987), p. 72 *passim*.

9. For a somewhat more extensive summary of these issues see I.J. Cohen, 'Structuration and Social Order: Five Issues in Brief' in J. Clark, C. Modgil, S. Modgil, *Anthony Giddens: Consensus and Controversy* (London: Falmer Press, 1990), Ch. 4. Reprinted in C.G.A. Bryant and D. Jary, *Anthony Giddens: Critical Assessments* (London: Routledge, 1996), selection 40.

10. See Giddens, *The Constitution of Society*, Ch. 3. Giddens acknowledges important debts to Torsten Hägerstrand, Derek Gregory, Nigel Thrift and other innovators in time-geography.

11. As I stress below, this image of repetitive routines in no way denies the potential for change that remains open in every instance of praxis.

12. Giddens converges with network analysis on the uneven strength and weakness of boundaries. For extensive commentary on the foundations of network analysis and other morphological theories from a structurational point of view see Cohen, *Structuration Theory*, Ch. 2.

13. I omit a discussion of Giddens' technical concept of the *duality* of structure here. I also omit Giddens' template of structural properties. Interested readers should consult A. Giddens, *Central Problems in Social Theory: Action, Structure and Contradiction in Social Analysis* (London: Macmillan, 1979), Chs 1, 3; idem, *The Constitution of Society*, pp. 16–34.

14. The adjective 'discursive' implies that our fully conscious thoughts are structured by the patterns of language (both grammar and semantics) we commonly employ. The philosophical precedents for this position begin with various American pragmatists and the later philosophy of Ludwig Wittgenstein.

15. See Roger Rosenblatt, 'No Escaping Modern Times', *U.S. News and World Report* October 2, 1989, pp. 10–11 for an exceptional example of commentary on modernity in the popular press. Rosenblatt may have been influenced by Marshall

Berman's evocative literary study of ambivalence toward modernity in *All That is Solid Melts into Air: The Experience of Modernity* (New York: Simon & Schuster, 1982), see especially Ch. 1. I have found Rosenblatt's brief but elegant essay exceptionally useful in teaching courses on modernity.

16. In *Consequences of Modernity*, Giddens outlines his basic views on reflexivity in modernity. He carries these themes forward in *Modernity and Self-identity* and *Beyond Left and Right*. For his most recent account, this time in relation to the problem of culture, see 'Living in a Post-traditional Society' in U. Beck, A. Giddens and S. Lash, *Reflexive Modernization: Politics, Tradition, and Aesthetics in the Modern Social Order* (Cambridge: Polity Press, 1994), Ch. 2; reprinted in A. Giddens, *In Defence of Sociology* (Cambridge: Polity Press, 1996), Ch. 1.

17. On Giddens' image of the juggernaut see *The Consequences of Modernity*, Ch. 5.

18. See A. Giddens, *A Contemporary Critique of Historical Materialism:* vol. 1: *Power, Property and the State* (London: Macmillan, 1981), Ch. 4; idem, *The National-State and Violence* (London: Macmillan, 1985), Ch. 7 *passim*.

19. On risk and empowerment see *Consequences of Modernity* and *Modernity and Self-identity*.

20. See citations at note 3 above.

21. On the dialectic of control and Giddens' theory of power in structuration theory which is developed in bits and pieces throughout many of his works see Cohen, *Structuration Theory*, Ch. 5.

22. On emancipatory and life politics see *Beyond Left and Right*. For a briefer statement see *Modernity and Self-identity*, Ch. 7.

23. A. Giddens, *New Rules of Sociological Method: A Positive Critique of Interpretive Sociologies* (London: Hutchinson, 1976).

24. For commentary and bibliography on Elias see S. Mennell, *Norbert Elias: Civilization and the Human Self-image* (Oxford: Basil Blackwell, 1989). For commentary and bibliography on (and by) Bourdieu see P. Bourdieu and L.J.D. Wacquant, *An Invitation to Reflexive Sociology* (Chicago: University of Chicago Press, 1992).

25. On the 'new institutionalism' see W.W. Powell and P.J. DiMaggio, 'Introduction' in idem. *The New Institutionalism in Organizational Analysis* (Chicago: University of Chicago Press, 1991), pp. 1–38. On 'practice theory' in anthropology see P.B. Roscoe, 'Practice and Centralisation: A New Approach to Political Evolution', *Current Anthropology* **13**(2) (April 1993), 111–40. William Sewell Jr's historical sociological work appears in his essay 'A Theory of Structure: Duality, Agency, and Transformation: Dialectic, and History', *American Journal of Sociology* **98**(1) (July 1992), 1–29. Rob Stones' recent book on theoretical method is *Sociological Reasoning: Towards a Past-modern Sociology* (London: Macmillan, 1996).

26. In a more extensive account I would include a critique of what I judge to be Giddens' excessive reliance on ontological security as the basis of consciousness. This is one of the few reductionist tendencies in Giddens' work, but its consequences color a great deal of his thought, including his normative limitations which I briefly summarize below. I hope to write more on this theme in future works.

27. To be clear, I make no claim here that Giddens is 'objective' or 'value-free'. In fact, whenever Giddens or any other sociologist exposes any unfamiliar aspect of everyday life, that revelation challenges ordinary moral interpretations of everyday

life, albeit to a greater extent in some cases than in others. My main point here is that Giddens does not make a normative vision or an ethical principle the keystone of his thought.

28. See Giddens' defense of his normative position in 'A Reply to My Critics' in D. Held and J.B. Thompson, *Social Theory of Modern Societies: Anthony Giddens and His Critics* (Cambridge: Cambridge University Press, 1989), pp. 288–93.

Conclusion

1. While the relationship between biology and sociology is broached in Simon Williams' chapter on Hochschild this particular connection is perhaps less evident from the chapters in this volume than the others in this list. This no doubt reflects the relative neglect of biology in twentieth-century sociological theory. For a necessary corrective to, and an argument for an end to, this neglect see Ted Benton, 'Biology and Social Science: Why the Return of the Repressed Should be Given a (Cautious) Welcome', *Sociology* **25**(1) (1991), 1–29; and T. Benton, 'Biology and Social Theory in the Environmental Debate', in M. Redclift and T. Benton (eds), *Social Theory and the Global Environment* (London: Routledge, 1994).
2. Plummer, Chapter 6.
3. Heritage, Chapter 13.
4. Martin, Chapter 17.
5. Holton, Chapter 7.
6. See R. Bhaskar, *A Realist Theory of Science* (Hassocks: Harvester Press, 1978), pp. 163–85; A. Sayer, *Method in Social Science* (London: Hutchinson, 1984), pp. 108–11, and R. Stones, *Sociological Reasoning* (London: Macmillan, 1996), pp. 30–2.
7. See Pope, Chapter 3, on Durkheim and emergent reality, pp. 47–8.
8. Scaff, Chapter 2.
9. The simplified shorthand of 'parts' and 'people' to refer to 'system integration' and 'social integration' is drawn from Margaret Archer, *Realist Social Theory: The Morphogenetic Approach* (Cambridge: Cambridge University Press, 1996).
10. Cohen, Chapter 21.
11. Ibid.
12. Ibid.
13. These points draw from Nicos Mouzelis, *Back to Sociological Theory: The Construction of Social Orders* (London: Macmillan, 1991); and *Sociological Theory: What Went Wrong?* (London: Routledge, 1995).
14. Also see Ulrich Beck, *The Risk Society: Towards a New Modernity* (London: Sage, 1992).

Bibliography

Abbott, A. and Gaziano, E. 'Transition and Tradition: Departmental Faculty in the Era of the Second Chicago School' in G.A. Fine (ed.) *A Second Chicago School? The Development of a Postwar American Sociology*, Chicago: University of Chicago Press, 1995, pp. 221–72.

Adorno, T., Frankel-Brunswik, E., Levinson, D. and Sanford, R. *The Authoritarian Personality*, New York: Harper, 1950.

Aglietta, M. *A Theory of Capitalist Regulation*, London: New Left Books, 1979.

Alexander, J.C. *Theoretical Logic in Sociology, the Modern Reconstruction of Classical Thought: Talcott Parsons*. vol. 4, London: Routledge, 1984.

Althusser, L. *For Marx*, London: New Left Books, 1969.

Althusser, L. *Lenin and Philosophy and Other Essays*, London: New Left Books, 1971.

Althusser, L. *Essays in Self-Criticism*, London: New Left Books, 1976.

Althusser, L. *Philosophy and the Spontaneous Philosophy of the Scientists and Other Essays*, London: Verso, 1990.

Althusser, L. *The Future Lasts a Long Time*, London: Chatto & Windus, 1993.

Althusser, L. and Balibar, E. *Reading Capital*, London: New Left Books, 1970.

Anderson, P. *Lineages of the Absolutist State*, London: New Left Books, 1974a.

Anderson, P. *Passages from Antiquity to Feudalism*, London: New Left Books, 1974b.

Anderson, P. *Considerations on Western Marxism*, London: New Left Books, 1976.

Anderson, R.J., Hughes, J.A. and Sharrock, W.W. *The Sociology Game: An Introduction to Sociological Reasoning*, London: Longman, 1985.

Archer, M. *Realist Social Theory: The Morphogenetic Approach*, Cambridge: Cambridge University Press, 1996.

Armstrong, T. (trans.) *Michel Foucault: Philosopher*, London: Harvester Wheatsheaf, 1992.

Atkinson, J. Maxwell *Discovering Suicide: Studies in the Social Organization of Sudden Death*, London: Macmillan, 1978.

Atkinson, J. Maxwell *Our Masters' Voices: The Language and Body Language of Politics*, London: Methuen, 1984.

Atkinson, J. Maxwell 'Refusing invited applause: preliminary observations from a case study of charismatic oratory', in Teun van Dijk (ed.) *Handbook of Discourse Analysis*: vol. 3: *Discourse and Dialogue*, London: Academic Press, 1985.

Atkinson, J. Maxwell 'Societal reactions to suicide: the role of coroners' definitions', in S. Cohen (ed.) *Images of Deviance*, Harmondsworth: Penguin, 1971.

Atkinson, M.W., Kessel, N. and Dalgaard, J. 'The comparability of suicide rates,' *British Journal of Psychiatry* (1975) 127.

Attali, J. *Noise: The Political Economy of Music* (trans. B. Massumi), Minneapolis: University of Minnesota Press, 1985.

Avineri, S. *The Social and Political Thought of Karl Marx*, Cambridge: Cambridge University Press, 1968.

Bair, D. *Simone de Beauvoir: A Biography*, London: Cape, 1990.

Bales, R.F. *Interaction Process Analysis: A Method for the Study of Small Groups*, Reading MA: Addison Wesley, 1950.

Barratt, M. *Women's Oppression Today*, London: Verso, 1980 and 1988.

Barry, A., Osborne, T. and Rose, N. *Foucault and Political Reason: Liberalism, Neo-liberalism and Rationalities of Government*, London: UCL Press, 1996.

Battershill, C. 'Erving Goffman as a precursor to post-modern sociology', in S.H. Riggins (ed.) *Beyond Goffman: Studies on Communication, Institution and Social Interaction*, New York: Mouton de Gruyter, 1990, pp. 163–86.

Beck, U. *The Risk Society: Towards a New Modernity*, London: Sage, 1992.

Becker, H.S. *Outsiders: Studies in the Sociology of Deviance*, Illinois: Free Press, 1963.

Becker, H.S. *Doing Things Together*, Chicago: Aldine, 1986.

Becker, H.S. 'Herbert Blumer's conceptual impact', *Symbolic Interaction* **11**(1) (1988), 13–21.

Bell, D. *The Coming of Post-industrial Society*, London: Heinemann, 1973.

Bendelow, G. 'Pain perceptions, gender and emotion', *Sociology of Health and Illness* **15**(3) (1993), 273–94.

Bendelow, G. and Williams, S. 'Transcending the dualisms: towards a sociology of pain', *Sociology of Health and Illness* **17**(2) (1995), 139–65.

Bendelow, G. and Williams, S.J. 'Pain and the mind–body dualism: a sociological approach', *Body and Society* **1**(2) (1995), 82–103.

Bendelow, G. and Williams, S.J. (eds) *Emotions in Social Life: Critical Themes and Contemporary Issues*, London: Routledge, 1997.

Benjamin, J. *The Bonds of Love*, New York: Pantheon, 1988.

Benjamin, W. *Charles Baudelaire, A Lyric Poet in the Era of High Capitalism*, London: New Left Books, 1973.

Benton, T. 'Biology and social science: why the return of the repressed should be given a (cautious) welcome', *Sociology* **25**(1) (1991), 1–29.

Benton, T. *The Rise and Fall of Structural Marxism*, London/Basingstoke: Macmillan, 1984.

Benton, T. 'Biology and social theory in the environmental debate', in M. Redclift and T. Benton (eds) *Social Theory and the Global Environment*, London: Routledge, 1994, pp. 28–50.

Berlin, I. *The Hedgehog and the Fox: An Essay on Tolstoy's View of History*, London: Wiedenfeld & Nicolson, 1953.

Berman, M. *All That is Solid Melts into Air: The Experience of Modernity*, New York: Simon & Schuster, 1982.

Bernal, J.D. *The Social Function of Science*, London: J. Routledge and Sons, 1939; New York: Macmillan, 1939.

Bernstein, E. *Evolutionary Socialism: A Criticism and Affirmation*, New York: Schocken, 1961; originally published in German in 1899.

Bernstein, H. 'Modernisation theory and the sociological study of development', *Journal of Development Studies* **VII**, (1971).

Bhaskar, R. *A Realist Theory of Science*, Hassocks: Harvester Press, 1978.

Bierstedt, Robert 'Merton's Systematic Theory' in J. Clark, C. Modgil, and S. Modgil (eds), *Robert K. Merton: Consensus and Controversy*, London, Falmer Press, 1990.

Bierstedt, R. *American Sociological Theory: A Critical History*, New York: Academic Press, 1981.

Blauner, R. *Alienation and Freedom*, Chicago: University of Chicago Press, 1964.

Blok, A. 'Primitief en geciviliseerd', *Sociologisch Gids* **29**(3–4) (1982), 197–209.

Blumer, H. *Movies and Conduct*, New York: Macmillan, 1933.

Blumer, H. 'Society as symbolic interaction' in A. Rose (ed.) *Human Behavior and Social Processes*, Boston: Houghton Mifflin, 1962.

Blumer, H. 'Sociological implications of the thought of George Herbert Mead', *American Journal of Sociology* **LXXI** (March 1966), 535–44.

Blumer, H. *Symbolic Interactionism: Perspective and Method*, Englewood Cliffs, NJ: Prentice-Hall, 1969.

Blumer, H. *The Critique of the Polish Peasant*, rev. edn., New Jersey: Transaction Books, 1979a.

Blumer, H. 'George Herbert Mead', in B. Rhea (ed.) *The Future of the Sociological Classics*, London: Allen & Unwin, 1979b.

Blumer, H. *Industrialization as an Agent of Social Change: A Critical Analysis*, ed. with an introduction by D.R. Maines and T.J. Morrione, New York: Aldine de Gruyter, 1990.

Blumer, H. and Duster, T. 'Theories of race and social action', in *Sociological Theories: Race and Colonialism*, Paris: UNESCO, 1980, pp. 211–38.

Bocock, R. *Freud and Modern Society*, Walton-on-Thames, Surrey: Nelson, 1976.

Bouglé, C. 'Review of *Soziologie*', *L'Année Sociologique*, vol. xi, 1906–09.

Bourdieu, P. *The Algerians*, Boston: Beacon Press, 1958/1962.

Bourdieu, P. (with A. Darbel, J.P. Rivet and C. Seibel) *Travail et Travailleurs en Alégérie,* Paris and The Hague: Mouton, 1963.

Bourdieu, P. (with Adbelmalek Sayad) *Le Déracinement. La Crise de l'Agriculture Traditionnelle en Algérie*, Paris: Editions de Minuit, 1964.

Bourdieu, P. (with Jean-Claude Passeron) *The Inheritors: Students and their Culture*, Chicago: The University of Chicago Press, 1964/1979.

Bourdieu, P. (with Jean-Claude Passeron and Jean-Claude Chamboredon) *The Craft of Sociology: Epistemological Preliminaries*, New York and Berlin: Aldine de Gruyter, 1968/1991.

Bourdieu, P. *Outline of a Theory of Practice*, Cambridge: Cambridge University Press, 1972/1977.

Bourdieu, P. *Algeria 1960*, Cambridge: Cambridge University Press, 1976/1977.

Bourdieu, P. *Outline of a Theory of Action*, Cambridge: Cambridge University Press, 1977.

Bourdieu, P. *Distinction: A Social Critique of the Judgement of Taste*, London: Routledge, 1979/1984.

Bourdieu, P. (with Jean-Claude Passeron) *Reproduction in Education, Culture, and Society*, London: Sage, 1980/1977.

Bourdieu, P. *The Logic of Practice*, Cambridge: Polity Press, 1980/1990.

Bourdieu, P. *Sociology in Question*, trans. Richard Nice. London and Newbury Park: Sage, 1980/1993.

Bourdieu, P. *Leçon sur la leçon*, Paris: Editions de Minuit (reprinted as closing chapter in 1987/1991), 1982/1991.

Bourdieu, P. *Homo Academicus*, Cambridge: Polity Press, 1984/1988.

Bourdieu, P. 'Social space and the genesis of groups', *Theory and Society* **14**(6) (November 1985), 723–44.

Bourdieu, P. 'The forms of capital', in J.G. Richarson (ed.) *Handbook of Theory and Research for the Sociology of Education*, New York: Greenwood Press, 1986, pp. 241–58.

Bourdieu, P. *In Other Words: Essays towards a Reflexive Sociology*, Cambridge: Polity Press, 1987/1991.

Bourdieu, P. *The State Nobility: Elite Schools in the Field of Power*, Cambridge: Polity Press, 1989/1997.

Bourdieu, P. 'Social space and symbolic power', *Sociological Theory* **7**(1) (June 1989a), 18–26.

Bourdieu, P. 'The corporatism of the universal: the role of intellectuals in the modern world', *Telos* **81** (Fall 1989b), 99–110.

Bourdieu, P. *Language and Symbolic Power* (edited and with an introduction by John Thompson), Cambridge: Polity Press, 1990.

Bourdieu, P. *The Rules of Art: Genesis and Structure of the Artistic Field*, Cambridge: Polity Press, 1992/1997.

Bourdieu, P. and Wacquant, L.J.D. *An Invitation to Reflexive Sociology*, Chicago: University of Chicago Press, 1992.

Bourdieu, P. *The Field of Cultural Production*, Cambridge: Polity Press; New York: Columbia University Press, 1993.

Bourdieu, P. *et al.*, *The Poverty of Society: A Study in Social Suffering*, Cambridge: Polity Press, 1993/1998.

Bourdieu, P. 'The scholastic point of view', *Cultural Anthropology* **5**(4) (November 1994), 380–91.

Bourdieu, P. *Practical Reasons: On the Theory of Action*, Cambridge: Polity Press, 1994/1998.

Bourdieu, P. 'A Japanese reading of distinction', *Poetics*, 1995.

Bourdieu, P. *Méditations Pascaliennes*, Paris: Editions du Seuil (trans. forthcoming with Polity Press, Cambridge), 1997a.

Bourdieu, P. *Sur la Télévision*, Paris: Editions Liber (trans. forthcoming with The New Press, New York), 1997b.

Bourdieu, P. *Contre-feux: Propos Politiques sur le Capitalisme Sauvage*, Paris: Editions Liber/Raisons d'agir, 1998.

Braun, C. *Max Weber's 'Musiksoziologie'*, Laaber: Laaber-Verlag, 1992.

Breiner, P. *Max Weber and Democratic Politics*, Ithaca: Cornell University Press, 1996.

Bryant, C.G.A. and Jary, D. 'Coming to terms with Anthony Giddens' in *Giddens' Theory of Structuration: A Critical Appreciation*, London: Routledge, 1991.

Burchell, G. 'Peculiar interests: civil society and governing "the system of natural liberty"', in G. Burchell, C. Gordon, and P. Miller (eds) *The Foucault Effect: Studies in Governmentality*, London: Harvester Wheatsheaf, 1991, pp. 119–50.

Burchell, G., Gordon, C., and Miller, P. (eds.) *The Foucault Effect: Studies in Governmentality*, London: Harvester Wheatsheaf, 1991.

Burns, T. *Erving Goffman*, London: Routledge, 1992.

Callinicos, A. *Althusser's Marxism*, London: Pluto, 1976.

Canguilhem, G. *Ideology and Rationality in the History of the Life Sciences*, Cambridge: MIT, 1988.

Castells, M. *The Urban Question*, London: Edward Arnold, 1977.

Cavan, S. *Liquor License*, Chicago: Aldine, 1966.

Chambers, I. and Curti, L. 'When was the "post-colonial"? Thinking at the limits', in *The Post-colonial Question*, London: Routledge, 1996.

Chodorow, N. *The Reproduction of Mothering*, Berkeley: University of California Press, 1978.

Chodorow, N. 'Reply by Nancy Chodorow', *Signs*, (Spring 1981).

Chodorow, N. *Feminism and Psychoanalysis*, New Haven: Yale University Press, 1989.

Chodorow, N. *Feminities, Masculinities and Sexualities: Freud and Beyond*, London: Free Association Books, 1994.

Chodorow, N. 'Gender as a personal and cultural construction', *Signs* (Spring 1995), pp. 516–44.

Cicourel, A. *The Social Organization of Juvenile Justice*, New York: Wiley, 1968.

Clough, P.T. *The Ends of Ethnography*, London: Sage, 1992.

Cohen, I.B. (ed) *Puritanism and the Rise of Modern Science: the Merton Thesis*, New Brunswick, NJ: Rutgers University Press, 1990.

Cohen, I.J. *Structuration Theory. Anthony Giddens and the Constitution of Social Life*, London: Macmillan/New York: St Martin's Press, 1989.

Cohen, I.J. 'Structuration and social order: five issues in brief', in J. Clark, C. Modgil and S. Modgil, *Anthony Giddens: Consensus and Controversy*, London: Falmer Press, 1990, Ch. 4, reprinted in C.G.A. Bryant and D. Jary, *Anthony Giddens: Critical Assessments*, London: Routledge, 1996, Selection 40.

Cohen, I.J. 'Theories of action and praxis', in B.S. Turner (ed.) *The Blackwell Companion to Social Theory*, Oxford: Basil Blackwell, 1996, pp. 111–42.

Coleman, J.S. 'Robert K. Merton as a teacher', in J. Clark, C. Modgil, and S. Modgil (eds) *Robert K. Merton: Consensus and Controversy*, London: Falmer Press, 1990.

Collins, R. *Weberian Sociological Theory*, London: Cambridge University Press, 1986.

Collins, R. 'The Durkheimian tradition in conflict sociology', in J.C. Alexander (ed.) *Durkheimian Sociology*, Cambridge: Cambridge University Press, 1988, pp. 107–28.

Collins, R. and Makowsky, M. *The Discovery of Society*, 5th edn, New York: McGraw-Hill, 1993.

Colomy, P. and Brown, J.D. 'Elaboration, revision, polemic and progress in the second Chicago School', in G.A. Fine (ed.) *A Second Chicago School?*, Chicago: University of Chicago Press, 1995, pp. 17–81.

Coser, L. (ed) *The Idea of Social Structure: Papers in Honour of Robert K. Merton*, New York: Harcourt Brace Jovanovich, 1975.

Craib, I. *Psychoanalysis and Social Theory*, Brighton: Harvester Wheatsheaf, 1989.

Craib, I. *Anthony Giddens*, London: Routledge, 1992.

Craib, I. *The Importance of Disappointment*, London: Routledge, 1994.

Creelan, P. 'The degradation of the sacred: approaches of Cooley and Goffman', *Symbolic Interaction* 10 (1987), 29–56.

Crothers, C. *Robert K. Merton*, Key Sociologists Series, London: Tavistock Publishers, 1987.

Cruz, J. and Lewis, J. (eds) 'Reflections upon the encoding/decoding model: an interview with Stuart Hall', *Viewing, Reading Listening: Audiences and Cultural Reception*, Boulder: Westview Press.

Darwin, C. *The Expression of Emotion in Man and Animals*, New York: Philosophical Library, 1955.

Darwin, C. *The Origin of Species*, Harmondsworth: Penguin, 1968 [1869].

Day, L.H. 'Durkheim on religion and suicide – a demographic critique', *Sociology* **21** (1987), 449–61.

Dean, M. *The Constitution of Poverty: Toward a Genealogy of Liberal Governance*, London: Routledge, 1991.

de Beauvoir, S. *She Came to Stay*, London: Fontana, 1984. First published as *L'Invitée*, Paris: Gallimard, 1943.

de Beauvoir, S. *The Second Sex*, Toronto: Bantam Books, 1964.

de Beauvoir, S. *Old Age*, London: Penguin, 1977.

de Beauvoir, S. *Memoirs of a Dutiful Daughter*, Harmondsworth: Penguin, 1987.

de Beauvoir, S. *Letters to Sartre*, New York: Arcade, 1991.

de Beauvoir, S. *Signs*, Special issue on Simone de Beauvoir **18**(1) 1992.

Deegan, M.J. and Hill, M.R. (eds) *Women and Symbolic Interaction*, Boston: Allen & Unwin, 1987.

Deleuze, G. *Foucault*, Minneapolis: University of Minnesota Press, 1988.

Denzin, N.K. *On Understanding Emotion*, San Francisco: Jossey-Bass, 1984.

Denzin, N.K. 'On understanding emotion: the interpretive-cultural agenda', in T.J. Kemper (ed.) *Research Agendas in the Sociology of Emotions*, New York: State University of New York Press, 1990, pp. 73–85.

Denzin, N.K. *Symbolic Interactionism and Cultural Studies*, Oxford: Blackwell, 1992.

Dewey, J. *Human Nature and Conduct: An Introduction to Social Psychology*, New York: Holt, 1922.

Dewey, J. *The Problems of Men*, New York: Philosphical Library, 1946.

Dews, P. (ed.) *Habermas: Autonomy and Solidarity*, 2nd edn, London: Verso, 1992.

Ditton, J. (ed.) *The View from Goffman*, London: Macmillan, 1980.

Donzelot, J. *The Policing of Families*, Baltimore: The Johns Hopkins University Press, 1979.

Douglas, J. *The Social Meanings of Suicide*, Princeton, NJ: Princeton University Press, 1967.

Drew, P. and Wootton, A. (eds) *Erving Goffman: Exploring the Interaction Order*, Cambridge: Polity Press, 1988.

Drew, P. and Heritage, J. (eds) *Talk at Work*, Cambridge: Cambridge University Press, 1992.

Dreyfus, H. and Rabinow, P. *Michel Foucault: Beyond Structuralism and Hermeneutics*, Chicago: University of Chicago Press, 1982.

Dumm, T. *Michel Foucault and the Politics of Freedom*, Thousand Oaks: Sage, 1996.

Duncombe, J. and Marsden, D. 'Love and intimacy: the gender division of emotion work', *Sociology* **27**(2) (1993), 221–41.

Duncombe, J. and Marsden, D. '"Stepford wives" and "Hollow men": doing emotion work, doing gender and "authenticity" in intimate heterosexual relationships', in G. Bendelow and S.J. Williams (eds) *Emotions in Social Life: Critical Themes and Contemporary Issues*, London: Routledge, 1997, pp. 211–27.

Dunning, E. and Rojek, C. (eds) *Sport and Leisure in the Civilizing Process: Critique and Counter Critique*, Basingstoke: Macmillan, 1992.

Durkheim, E. *Suicide*, Glencoe, IL: Free Press, 1951.

Durkheim, E. *Moral Education*, New York: Free Press, 1961.

Durkheim, E. *The Elementary Forms of the Religious Life*. New York: Free Press, 1965.

Durkheim, E. 'The dualism of human nature and its social conditions', *Emile Durkheim on Morality and Society*, Chicago: The University of Chicago Press, 1973, pp. 149–63.

Durkheim, E. *The Division of Labor in Society,* New York: Free Press, 1984.

Duster, T. 'Herbert Blumer: 1900–1987', *ASA Footnotes* **15**(6) (1987), 16.

Eagleton, T. *Literary Theory: An Introduction*, Minneapolis: University of Minnesota, 1983.

Elias, N. 'Problems of involvement and detachment', *British Journal of Sociology* **7** (1956), 226–52.

Elias, N. *What is Sociology?*, London: Hutchinson (trans. 1978 from original German in 1970).

Elias, N. *The Civilising Process: A History of Manners*, vol. 1, Oxford: Basil Blackwell, 1978.

Elias, N. *State Formation and the Civilising Process*, vol. 2, Oxford: Basil Blackwell, 1982.

Elias, N. 'Knowledge and power: an interview by Peter Ludes', in N. Stehr and V. Meja (eds) *Society and Knowledge*, London: Transaction Books, 1984, pp. 252–91.

Elias, N. 'The retreat of sociologists into the present', *Theory, Culture and Society* **4** (1987), 223–47.

Elias, N. 'Violence and civilization: the state monopoly of physical violence and its infringement' in J. Keane, *Civil Society and the State*, London: Verso, 1988, pp. 177–98.

Elias, N. 'On human beings and their emotions: a process-sociological essay', in M. Featherstone, M. Hepworth and B. Turner (eds) *The Body: Social Process and Cultural Theory*, London: Sage, 1991, pp. 103–25.

Elias, N. *The Civilizing Process*, Oxford: Blackwell (combined edn. 1994, originally published 1939).

Elias, N. and Dunning, E. *Quest for Excitement: Sport and Leisure in the Civilizing Process*, Oxford: Blackwell, 1986.

Elliott, G. *Althusser: The Detour of Theory*, London: Verso, 1987.

Elliott, G. (ed.) *Althusser: A Critical Reader*, Oxford: Blackwell, 1994.

Evans, M. *Simone de Beauvoir*, London: Sage, 1996.

Evans, P.B., Rueschemeyer, D. and Skocpol, T. (eds) *Bringing the State Back In*, Cambridge: Cambridge University Press, 1985.

Fine, G.A. (ed.) Special Issue on Herbert Blumer's Legacy, *Symbolic Interaction* **11**(1) (Spring 1988).

Fine, G.A. 'Symbolic interactionism in the Post-Blumerian age', in G. Ritzer (ed.) *Frontiers of Sociological Theory*, New York: Columbia University Press, 1990, pp. 117–57.

Fineman, S. *Emotions and Organisations*, London: Sage, 1993.

Firestone, S. *The Dialectic of Sex*, New York: Bantam Books, 1970.

Foucault, M. *Madness and Civilization: A History of Insanity in the Age of Reason*. London: Tavistock Publications, 1967.

Foucault, M. *The Archaeology of Knowledge and the Discourse on Language*, London: Tavistock Publications, 1972.

Foucault, M. *The Birth of the Clinic*, London: Tavistock Publications, 1973.

Foucault, M. *The Order of Things: An Archaeology of the Human Sciences*, New York: Vintage Books, 1973.

Foucault, M. *Language, Counter-memory, Practice*, D. Bouchard (ed.), Ithaca: Cornell University Press, 1977.

Foucault, M. *Discipline and Punish: The Birth of the Prison*, New York: Vintage Books, 1979.

Foucault, M. *The History of Sexuality:* vol. 1: *An Introduction*, New York: Vintage Books, 1980.

Foucault, M. *Power/Knowledge: Selected Interviews and Other Writings 1972–1977*, C. Gordon (ed.), New York: Pantheon Books, 1980.

Foucault, M. 'Afterword: the subject and power,' in H. Dreyfus, and P. Rabinow *Michel Foucault: Beyond Structuralism and Hermeneutics*, Chicago: University of Chicago Press, 1982, pp. 208–26.

Foucault, M. *The Foucault Reader*, P. Rabinow (ed.), New York: Pantheon Books, 1984.

Foucault, M. *The Use of Pleasure;* vol. 2 of *The History of Sexuality*, New York: Pantheon Books, 1985.

Foucault, M. *The Care of the Self*, New York: Pantheon Books, 1986.

Foucault, M. 'Kant on enlightenment and revolution', *Economy and Society* **15**(1) (1986), 88–96.

Foucault, M. *Politics, Philosophy, Culture: Interviews and Other Writings, 1977–1984*, L. Kritzman (ed.), New York: Routledge, 1988.

Foucault, M. 'Governmentality', in G. Burchell, C. Gordon, and P. Miller (eds) *The Foucault Effect: Studies in Governmentality*, London: Harvester Wheatsheaf, 1991, pp. 87–104.

Foucault, M. *Ethics: Subjectivity and Truth*, P. Rabinow (ed.), New York: The New Press, 1997.

Freud, S. 'The Ego and the Id', in S. Freud *On Metapsychology*, Harmondsworth: Penguin, 1923/1982.

Freund, P. 'The expressive body: a common ground for the sociology of emotions and health and illness,' *Sociology of Health and Illness* **12**(4) (1990), 452–77.

Freund, P. 'Social performances and their discontents: reflections on the biosocial psychology of role-playing', in G.A. Bendelow and S.J. Williams (eds) *Emotions in Social Life: Critical Themes and Contemporary Issues*, London: Routledge, 1997, pp. 268–94.

Friedman, D.J. 'Marx's perspective on the objective class structure', *Polity* **6** (1974).

Frisby, D. *Simmel and Since: Essays on Georg Simmel's Social Theory*, London: Routledge & Kegan Paul, 1991.

Fullbrook, K. and Fullbrook, E. *Simone de Beauvoir and Jean-Paul Sartre: The Remaking of a Twentieth Century Legend*, London: Wheatsheaf/Harvester, 1993.

Gagnon, J. and Simon, W. *Sexual Conduct: The Social Sources of Human Sexuality*, Chicago: Aldine, 1973.

Garfinkel, H. 'Color trouble,' *Opportunity Magazine* (May 1940). Reprinted in E.J. O'Brien (ed.) *The Best Short Stories of 1941*, pp. 97–119.

Garfinkel, H. 'Research note on inter- and intra-racial homicides,' *Social Forces* **27** (1949), 370–81.

Garfinkel, H. 'A conception of, and experiments with, "trust" as a condition of stable concerted actions', in O.J. Harvey (ed.) *Motivation and Social Interaction*, New York: Ronald Press, 1963.

Garfinkel, H. *Studies in Ethnomethodology*, Englewood Cliffs, NJ: Prentice-Hall, 1967a.

Garfinkel, H. 'Practical sociological reasoning: some features of the work of the Los Angeles Suicide Prevention Center', in E.S. Shneidman (ed.) *Essays in Self-destruction*, New York: International Science Press, 1967b.

Garfinkel, H., Lynch, M. and Livingston, E. 'The work of a discovering science construed with materials from the optically discovered pulsar', *Philosophy of the Social Sciences* **11** (1981), 131–58.

Gerth, H. and Mills, C. Wright (eds) *From Max Weber: Essays in Sociology*, New York: Oxford University Press, 1946.

Gerth, H. and Mills, C. Wright *Character and Social Structure: The Psychology of Social Institutions*, New York: Harcourt, Brace, 1964.

Giddens, A. 'Power in the recent writings of Talcott Parsons', *Sociology* **2** (1968), 257–72.

Giddens, A. *Capitalism and Modern Social Theory: an Analysis of the Writings of Marx, Durkheim and Max Weber*, Cambridge: Cambridge University Press, 1971.

Giddens, A. *New Rules of Sociological Method: A Positive Critique of Interpretive Sociologies*, London: Hutchinson, 1976.

Giddens, A. *Central Problems in Social Theory: Action, Structure and Contradiction in Social Analysis,* London: Macmillan, 1979.

Giddens, A. *A Contemporary Critique of Historical Materialism:* vol. 1: *Power, Property and the State*, London: Macmillan, 1981.

Giddens, A. *The Constitution of Society: Outline of the Theory of Structuration*, Cambridge: Polity Press, 1984.

Giddens, A. *The Nation-State and Violence*, London: Macmillan, 1985.

Giddens, A. 'Erving Goffman as a systematic social theorist', in A. Giddens (ed.) *Social Theory and Modern Sociology*, Cambridge: Polity Press, 1987, pp. 109–39.

Giddens, A. *Social Theory and Modern Sociology*, Cambridge: Polity Press, 1987.

Giddens, A. ' A reply to my critics', in D. Held and J.B. Thompson *Social Theory of Modern Societies: Anthony Giddens and His Critics*, Cambridge: Cambridge University Press, 1989, pp. 249–301.

Giddens, A. *The Consequences of Modernity*, Cambridge: Polity Press, 1990.

Giddens, A. *Modernity and Self-identity: Self and Society in the Late Modern Age*, Cambridge: Polity Press, 1991.

Giddens, A. *The Transformation of Intimacy*, Cambridge: Polity Press, 1992.

Giddens, A. *Beyond Left and Right: The Future of Radical Politics*, Cambridge: Polity Press, 1994.

Giddens, A. 'Living in a post-traditional society', in U. Beck, A. Giddens, and S. Lash *Reflexive Modernization: Politics, Tradition and Aesthetics in the Modern Social Order*, Cambridge: Polity Press, 1994, Ch. 2; reprinted in A. Giddens, *In Defence of Sociology*, Cambridge: Polity Press, 1996, Ch. 1.

Gilligan, C. *In a Different Voice*, Cambridge: Harvard University Press, 1982.

Goffman, E. 'Communcation conduct in an island community'. Dissertation, University of Chicago, 1953.

Goffman, E. *The Presentation of Self in Everyday Life*, New York: Doubleday Anchor/Harmondsworth: Penguin, 1959.

Goffman, E. *Asylums: Essays on the Social Situation of Mental Hospital Patients and Other Inmates*, Harmondsworth: Penguin, 1961.

Goffman, E. *Behaviour in Public Places: Notes on the Social Organisation of Gatherings*, Glencoe: Free Press, 1963.

Goffman, E. *Stigma: Notes on the Management of Spoiled Identity*, Englewood Cliffs, NJ: Prentice-Hall, 1964.

Goffman, E. *Interaction Ritual*, Garden City, NY: Anchor, 1967.

Goffman, E. *Relations in Public*, Harmondsworth: Penguin, 1972.

Goffman, E. *Frame Analysis: An Essay on the Organisation of Experience*, New York: Harper & Row, 1974.

Goffman, E. 'The arrangement between the sexes', *Theory and Society* **4** (1977), 301–32.

Goffman, E. *Gender Advertisments*, London: Macmillan, 1979.

Goffman, E. *Forms of Talk*, Oxford: Blackwell, 1981.

Goffman, E. 'Reply to Denzin and Keller,' *Contemporary Sociology – An International Journal of Reviews* **10** (1981), 60–8.

Goffman, E. 'Felicity's condition', *American Journal of Sociology* **89** (1983), 1–53.

Goffman, E. 'The interaction order', *American Sociological Review* **48** (1983), 1–17.

Goffman, E. 'Erving Goffman's sociology'. Special Issue of *Human Studies* **12** (1 and 2) 1989.

Goldner, V. 'Toward a critical relational theory of gender', *Psychoanalytic Dialogues* **1** (1991), 249–72.

Goldthorpe, J.H., Lockwood, D., Bechhofer, F. and Platt, J. *The Affluent Worker: Industrial Attitudes and Behaviour*, Cambridge: Cambridge University Press, 1968.

Goodman, J. *Tobacco in History*, London: Routledge, 1993, p. 25.

Gordon, C. 'Governmental rationality: an introduction', in G. Burchell, C. Gordon and P. Miller (eds) *The Foucault Effect: Studies in Governmentality*, London: Harvester Wheatsheaf, 1991, pp. 1–51.

Goudsblom, J. 'Elias and Cassirer, sociology and philosophy', *Theory Culture and Society* **12** (1995), 121–6.

Goudsblom, J. *Fire and Civilization,* London: Penguin, 1992.

Gould, S.J. 'Polished pebbles, pretty shells: an appreciation of OTSOG', in Clark, J., Modgil, C. and Modgil, S. (eds) *Robert K. Merton: Consensus and Controversy*, London: Falmer Press, 1990.

Gouldner, A. *The Coming Crisis of Western Sociology*, New York: Basic Books, 1970.

Gouldner, A. *The Coming Crisis of Western Sociology*, London: Heinemann, 1971.

Gramsci, A. *Selections from the Prison Notebooks*, London: Lawrence & Wishart, 1971.

Gutting, G. *Michel Foucault's Archaeology of Scientific Reason*, Cambridge: Cambridge University Press, 1989.

Habermas, J. *Strukturwandel der Öffentlichkeit*, Neuwied/Berlin: Luchterhand, 1962; 2nd edn. Frankfurt: Suhrkamp, 1989 (trans. Thomas Burger as *The Structural Transformation of the Public Sphere*, Cambridge: Polity Press, 1989).

Habermas, J. *Theorie und Praxis*, Neuwied/Berlin: Luchterhand, 1963 (trans. as *Theory and Practice*, London: Heinemann, 1974).

Habermas, J. *Erkenntnis und Interesse*, Frankfurt: Suhrkamp, 1968 (trans. as *Knowledge and Human Interests*, London: Heinemann, 1971).

Habermas, J. *Technik und Wissenschaft als Ideologie*. Frankfurt: Suhrkamp, 1968 (part trans. in J. Habermas *Toward a Rational Society*, London: Heinemann, 1971).

Habermas, J. *Zur Logik der Sozialwissenschaften*, 2nd edn, 1971 (trans. as *On the Logic of the Social Sciences*, Cambridge: MIT Press, 1988).

Habermas, J. *Legitimationsprobleme im Spätkapitalismus*, Frankfurt: Suhrkamp, 1973 (trans. as *Legitimation Crisis*, London: Heinemann, 1976).

Habermas, J. 'What does a crisis mean today?', *Social Research* (Winter 1973), reprinted in P. Connerton (ed.) *Critical Sociology*, London: Penguin, 1976.

Habermas, J. *Zur Rekonstruktion des historischen Materialismus*, Frankfurt: Suhrkamp, 1976 (part trans. in *Communication and the Evolution of Society*, Boston: Beacon Press, 1979).

Habermas, J. *Legitimation Crisis,* Boston: Beacon Press, 1979.

Habermas, J. *Theorie des kommunikativen Handelns*, Frankfurt: Suhrkamp, 1981 (trans. as *Theory of Communicative Action*, London: Heinemann, 1984 and Cambridge: Polity Press, 1987a).

Habermas, J. 'The entwinement of myth and enlightenment', *New German Critique* 26 (1982), 13–20.

Habermas, J. *Moralbewußtsein und kommunikatives Handeln*, Frankfurt: Suhrkamp, 1983 (trans. as *Moral Consciousness and Communicative Action*, Cambridge, MA: MIT Press, 1989).

Habermas, J. *The Theory of Communicative Action*, vol. 1, London: Heinemann, 1984.

Habermas, J. *Der Philosophische Diskurs der Moderne*, Frankfurt: Suhrkamp, 1985 (trans. as *The Philosophical Discourse of Modernity*, Cambridge, MA: MIT Press, 1987b).

Habermas, J. *Die neue Unübersichtlichkeit*, Frankfurt: Suhrkamp, 1985 (trans. as *The New Conservatism*, Cambridge: Polity Press, 1989).

Habermas, J. 'Modernity – an incomplete project', reprinted in H. Foster (ed.) *Postmodern Culture*. London: Pluto Press, 1985.

Habermas, J. *The Theory of Communicative Action*, vol. 2: *Lifeworld and System: A Critique of Functionalist Reason*, Cambridge: Polity Press, 1987.

Habermas, J. *Nachmetaphysisches Denken*, Frankfurt: Suhrkamp, 1988 (trans. as *Postmetaphysical Thinking*, Cambridge: Polity Press, 1992).

Habermas, J. *Moral Consciousness and Communicative Action*, Cambridge: Polity Press, 1990.

Habermas, J. *The Theory of Communicative Action*, vol. 1: *Reason and the Rationalisation of Society*, Cambridge: Polity Press, 1991.

Habermas, J. *Erläuterungen zur Diskursethik*, Frankfurt: Suhrkamp, 1991 (trans. as *Justification and Application*, Cambridge: MIT Press, 1993).

Habermas, J. *Vergangenheit als Zukunft*, M. Heller (ed.) Zürich: Pendo, 1991; 2nd edn, Munich: Piper, 1993 (trans. as *The Past as Future*, Lincoln: University of Nebraska Press, 1994).

Habermas, J. *Faktizität und Geltung*, Frankfurt: Suhrkamp, 1992 (trans. by William Rehg as *Between Facts and Norms*, Cambridge: Polity Press, 1996).

Hall, S. 'Encoding/Decoding', CCCS Working Papers in Cultural Studies, reprinted in S. Hall (ed.) *Culture, Media, Language*, London: Unwin Hyman, 1990; in S. During (ed.) *The Cultural Studies Reader*, London: Routledge, 1993, pp. 90–103.

Hall, S. 'The West and the rest: discourse and power', in S. Hall and B. Gieben (eds) *Formations of Modernity*, Cambridge: Polity/OU Press, 1992, pp. 275–320.

Hall, S. 'When was the post-colonial? Thinking at the limit', in I. Chambers and L. Curti (eds) *The Post-Colonial Question*, London: Routledge, 1996.

Hall, S. 'The spectacle of the "Other"', in S. Hall (ed.) *Representation: Cultural Representations and Signifying Practices*, London: Sage, 1997.

Hall, S. and du Gay, P. (eds) 'Who needs identity', in *Questions of Cultural Identity*, London: Sage, 1996.

Hall, S. and Jacques M. (eds) *The Politics of Thatcherism*, London: Lawrence & Wishart, 1983.

Hall, S., Held, D. and McGrew, T. (eds) *Modernity and its Futures*, Cambridge: Polity/OU Press, 1992.

Hall, S., Hobson, D., Lowe, A. and Willis, P. *Culture, Media, Language*, London: Hutchinson, 1980.

Hamilton, P. *Talcott Parsons*, London/Chichester: Tavistock/Horwood Ellis, 1983.

Hamilton, P. (ed.) *Talcott Parsons: Critical Assessments*, 4 vols, London: Routledge, 1992.

Hamilton, P. 'Systems theory', in B.S. Turner (ed.) *The Blackwell Companion to Social Theory*, Oxford: Blackwell, 1996, pp. 151–9.

Hammersley, M. *The Dilemma of Qualitative Method: Herbert Blumer and the Chicago Tradition*, London: Routledge, 1989.

Haraway, D., see *Primate Visions: Gender, Race and Nature in the World of Modern Science*, New York: Routledge, 1989.

Harding, S. *The Science Question in Feminism*, Ithaca: Cornell University Press, 1986.

Harrington, J. 'Tobacco smoking among the Karuk Indians of California', *Smithsonian Institute Bureau of American Ethnology* **94** (1932), 193–4.

Heath, J. *Simone de Beauvoir*, Hemel Hempstead: Harvester Wheatsheaf, 1989.

Held, D. and Thompson J. (eds) *Habermas: Critical Debates*, London: Macmillan, 1982.

Helle, H. *Simmel on Religion*, Yale University Press (in press).

Heritage, J. *Garfinkel and Ethnomethodology*, Cambridge, Polity Press, 1984.

Heritage, J. and Greatbatch, D. 'Generating applause: a study of rhetoric and response at party political conferences,' *American Journal of Sociology* **92** (1986), 110–57.

Hill Collins, P. 'The social construction of black feminist thought,' *Signs* **14**(4) (1989), 745–73.

Hobsbawm, E. 'Marx and history', *New Left Review* **143** (1984), 39–50.

Hochschild, A.R. 'Emotion work, feeling rules and social structure', *American Journal of Sociology* **85** (1979), 551–75.

Hochschild, A.R. *The Managed Heart: The Commercialization of Human Feeling*, Berkeley, CA: University of California Press, 1983.

Hochschild, A.R. 'Reply to Cas Wouter's review essay on "The Managed Heart"', *Theory, Culture and Society* **6**(3) (1989), 439–45.

Hochschild, A.R. *The Time Bind: When Work Becomes Home and Home Becomes Work*, New York: Metropolitan Press, 1997.

Hochschild, A.R. with Machung, A. *The Second Shift: Working Parents and the Revolution at Home*, London: Piatkus, 1990/[1989].

Holton, R. 'Talcott Parsons and the integration of economic and sociological theory', *Sociological Inquiry* **61**(1) (1991), 102–114.

Holton, R.J. and Turner, B.S. *Talcott Parsons on Economy and Society*, London: Routledge, 1986.

Holub, R.C. *Jürgen Habermas. Critic in the Public Sphere*, London: Routledge, 1991.

Honneth, A. and Joas, H. (eds) *Communicative Action*, Cambridge: Polity Press, 1991.

Husserl, E. *The Crisis of European Sciences and Transcendental Phenomenology* (trans. D. Carr), Evanston, IL: Northwestern University Press, 1970.

James, N. 'Emotional labour: skill and work in the social regulation of feelings', *Sociological Reiew* **37**(1) (1989), 15–42.

James, N. 'Care=organisation+physical labour+emotional labour', *Sociology of Health and Illness* **14**(4) (1992), 488–509.

James, V. and Gabe, J. (eds) *Health and the Sociology of Emotions*, Oxford: Blackwell, 1996.

Jessop, B. *The Capitalist State*, Oxford: Martin Robertson, 1982.

Joas, H. *The Creativity of Action*, Chicago: University of Chicago Press, 1997.

Kahlberg, S. *Max Weber's Comparative-Historical Sociology*, Cambridge: Polity Press, 1994.

Kaplan, E.A. and Sprinker, M. (eds) *The Althusserian Legacy*, London: Verso, 1993.

Käsler, D. *Max Weber: An Introduction to his Life and Work* (trans. P. Hurd), Chicago: University of Chicago Press, 1988.

Kemper, T.J. 'Social relations and emotions: a structural approach', in T.J. Kemper (ed.) *Research Agendas in the Sociology of Emotions*, New York: State University of New York Press, 1990, pp. 207–37.

Kemper, T.J. 'Themes and variations in the sociology of emotions', in T.J. Kemper (ed.) *Research Agendas in the Sociology of Emotions*, New York: State University of New York Press, 1990.

Kilminster, R. 'Introduction to Elias', *Theory Culture and Society* 4 (1987), 213–22.

Kilminster, R. and Wouters, C. 'From philosophy to sociology: Elias and the neo-Kantians (a response to Benjo Maso)', *Theory Culture and Society* 12 (1995), 81–120.

Laclau, E. *New Reflections on the Revolution of Our Time*, London: Verso, 1990.

Laclau, E. and Mouffe, C. *Hegemony and Social Strategy: Towards a Radical Democratic Politics*, London: Verso, 1985.

Lal, B.B. *The Romance of Culture in an Urban Civilization*, London: Routledge, 1990.

Lasch, C. *The Culture of Narcissism*, London: Sphere Books, 1980.

Lawler, J. *Behind the Screens: Nursing, Somology and the Problem of the Body*, Melbourne/Edinburgh: Churchill Livingstone, 1991.

Layder, D. 'Social reality as figuration: a critique of Elias's conception of sociological analysis', *Sociology* 20(3) (1986), 367–86.

Layder, D. 'Contemporary sociological theory', *Sociology* 30(3) (1996), 601–8.

Leach, E. 'Violence', *London Review of Books*, October 1986.

Lemert, C. *The Postmodern Is Not What You Think*, Malden, MA: Blackwell, 1997.

Levine, D. *Georg Simmel: Individuality and Social Forms*, Chicago, IL: Chicago University Press, 1971.

Lichtheim, G. 'Historical and dialectical materialism', in *Dictionary of History of Ideas*, vol. 2, New York: Charles Scribner's Sons, 1973.

Lipietz, A. *Towards a New Economic Order*, Cambridge: Polity Press, 1992.

Lockwood, D. 'Some remarks on the social system', *British Journal of Sociology*, 1956.

Lockwood, D. *The Blackcoated Worker*, London: Allen & Unwin, 1958.

Lockwood, D. 'Social integration and system integration', in G.K. Zollschan and W. Hirsch (eds) *Explorations in Social Change*, London: Routledge & Kegan Paul, 1964, pp. 244–57.

Lockwood, D. *Solidarity and Schism: 'The Problem of Disorder' in Durkheimian and Marxist Sociology*, Oxford: Oxford University Press, 1992.

Lofland, L.H. 'Social life in the public realm: a review', *Journal of Contemporary Ethnography* 17 (1989), 453–82.

Lofland, L. 'Reminiscences of classic Chicago: the Blumer–Hughes talk', *Urban Life* 9(3) (1980), 251–81, reprinted in K. Plummer, *The Chicago School*, vol. 4, London: Routledge, 1997, Ch. 45.

Lukes, S. *Emile Durkheim*, New York: Harper & Row, 1972.

Lyman, S. and Vidich, A. *Social Order and Public Philosophy: The Analysis and Interpretation of the Work of Herbert Blumer*, Fayetteville, AR: University of Arkansas Press, 1988.

Lynch, M. *Scientific Practice and Ordinary Action: Ethnomethodology and Social Studies of Science*, Cambridge, Cambridge University Press, 1996.

Macey, D. *The Lives of Michel Foucault*, London: Vintage, 1994, pp. 413–14.

Macherey, P. *Theory of Literary Production*, London: Routledge & Kegan Paul, 1978.

McIntosh, M. 'The state and the oppression of women', in A. Kuhn and A-M. Wolpe (eds) *Feminism and Materialism*, London: Routledge & Kegan Paul, 1978, pp. 254–89.

MacIntyre, A. 'The self as a work of art', *New Statesman* March, 1969.

MacIntyre, A. *After Virtue*, London: Duckworth, 1981.

McLellan, D. *Karl Marx: His Life and Thought*, Basingstoke: Macmillan, 1974.

Maffesoli, M. *Au Creux Des Apparences*, Paris: Plon, 1990.

Mahon, M. *Foucault's Nietzschean Genealogy: Truth, Power, and the Subject*, Albany: State University of New York Press, 1992.

Maines, D.R. 'Myth, text and interactionist complicity in the neglect of Blumer's macrosicology', *Symbolic Interaction* **11**(1) (1988), 43–57.

Mandel, E. *Late Capitalism*, London: New Left Books, 1975 (first published in German, 1972).

Manning, P. *Erving Goffman and Modern Sociology*, Cambridge: Polity Press, 1992.

Marcuse, H. *Eros and Civilisation*, London: Sphere Books, 1969.

Marks, E. and de Courtivron, I. (eds) *New French Feminisms*, Brighton: Harvester, 1981.

Marx, K. Letter to Weydemeyer, March 5, 1852.

Marx, K. 'Preface' to *A Contribution to the Critique of Political Economy*, 1859.

Marx, K. *The Eighteenth Brumaire of Louis Bonaparte*, 1851, Marx and Engels Collected Works, II.

Marx, K. *Economic and Philosophical Manuscripts of 1844*, trans. M. Milligan, Moscow, 1959.

Marx, K. *Early Writings*, T. Bottomore (ed.), London: 1963.

Marx, K. *Capital*, vol. 2, London: Lawrence & Wishart, 1972.

Marx, K. *Capital*, vol. 3, London: Lawrence & Wishart, 1972.

Marx, K. 'Introduction to a contribution to the critique of political economy', (1857), in M. Nicolaus (ed.) *Gruidrissse*, Harmondsworth: Penguin, 1973.

Marx, K. *Capital*, vols 1–3, London: Lawrence & Wishart, 1976.

Marx, K. and Engels F. *Manifesto of the Communist Party,* Marx and Engels' Collected Works 6, 1975.

Maso, B. 'Riddereer en riddermoed – ontwikkelingen van de aanvalslust in de late middeleeuwen' (Knightly honour and knightly courage: on changes in fighting spirit in the late Middle Ages), *Sociologische Gids* **29**(3–4) (1982), 296–325.

Maso, B. 'Elias and the neo-Kantians: intellectual backgrounds to the civilizing process', *Theory, Culture and Society* **12** (1995), 43–79.

Maso, B. 'The different theoretical layers of the civilizing process: a response to Goudsblom and Kilminster and Wouters', *Theory, Culture and Society* **12** (1995), 127–45.

Mead, G.H. *Mind, Self and Society*, Chicago, IL: Chicago University Press, 1934.

Mennell, S. *All Manners of Food: Eating and Taste in England and France from the Middle Ages to the Present*, London: Blackwell, 1985.

Mennell, S. *Norbert Elias: An Introduction*, Oxford: Blackwell, 1989.

Mennell, S. *Norbert Elias: Civilization and the Human Self-image*, Oxford: Basil Blackwell, 1989.

Merton, R.K. 'The unanticipated consequences of purposive social action', *American Sociological Review* I (1936), 894–904.

Merton, R.K. 'Social structure and anomie', *American Sociological Review* III (1938), 672–82.

Merton, R.K. 'Bureaucratic structure and personality', *Social Forces* XVIII (1939), 560–8.

Merton, R.K. 'Review of Bernal', *American Journal of Sociology* XLVI (1941).

Merton, R.K. *Social Theory and Social Structure*, rev. and enl. edn, Glencoe, IL: Free Press, 1957.

Merton, R.K. *Social Theory and Social Structure*, enl. edn, New York: Free Press, 1968.

Merton, R.K. 'On the history and systematics of sociological theory', *Social Theory and Social Structure*, enl. edn, New York: Free Press, 1968.

Merton, R.K. 'Science, technology and society in seventeenth century England', in *OSIRIS: Studies on the History and Philosophy of Science, History of Learning and Culture*, vol. 4, part 2; G. Sarton (ed.), Bruges, Belgium: St Catherine Press, 1938, pp. 362–632. Reprinted with 'Preface: 1970', New York: Howard Fertig, 1970; New York: Harper & Row, pub. edn, Torchbook 1970.

Merton, R.K. *Sociological Ambivalence and Other Essays*, New York: Free Press, 1976.

Merton, R.K. *Social Research and the Practising Professions*, A. Rosenblatt and T. Gieryn (eds), Cambridge, MA: Abt Books, 1982.

Merton, R.K. *On the Shoulders of Giants: A Shandean Postcript*, vicennial edn, New York: Harcourt Brace Jovanovich, 1985 and 'Post-Italianate Edition', Chicago, IL: University of Chicago Press, 1993.

Merton, R.K. *On Social Structure and Science*, P. Sztompka (ed.), Chicago, IL: University of Chicago Press, 1996.

Merton, R. with Barber, E. 'Sociological ambivalence' in idem. *Sociological Ambivalence and Other Essays*. New York: Free Press, 1976 (1963).

Miles, M.W. 'The writings of Robert K. Merton' in Lewis A. Coser (ed.) *The Idea of Social Structure: Papers in Honor of Robert K. Merton*, New York: Harcourt Brace Jovanovich, 1975.

Miliband, R. 'Marx and the State', *Social Register*, London: Merlin Press, 1965.

Mill, J.S. *On the Subjection of Women*, London: Dent, 1970.

Mill, J.S. *On Liberty and Other Essays*, J. Gray (ed.) Oxford: Oxford University Press, 1991.

Miller, T.G. 'Goffman, social acting, and moral behavior', *Journal for the Theory of Social Behaviour* 14 (1984), 141–63.

Millett, K. *Sexual Politics*, London: Virago, 1977.

Mills, C. Wright *White Collar*, New York: Oxford University Press, 1956.

Mills, C. Wright *The Sociological Imagination*, New York: Oxford University Press/ Harmondsworth: Penguin, 1959.

Mitchell, J. *Psychoanalysis and Feminism*, New York: Vintage Books/Harmondsworth: Penguin, 1975.

Moi, T. *Simone de Beauvoir: The Making of an Intellectual Woman*, Oxford: Blackwell, 1994.

Molière, *Comedies*, vol. 2, no trans. named (Everyman's Library, No 831, Poetry and Drama) London: J.M. Dent and Sons, 1929.

Morley, D. and Chen, K-H. (eds) *Stuart Hall: Critical Dialogues in Cultural Studies*, London: Routledge, 1996.

Mouzelis, N. 'System and social integration: a reconsideration of a fundamental distinction', *British Journal of Sociology* December, 1974.

Mouzelis, N. *Modern Greece: Facets of Underdevelopment*, London: Macmillan, 1978.

Mouzelis, N. *Back to Sociological Theory*, London: Macmillan, 1990.

Mouzelis, N. *Post-Marxist Alternatives*, London: Macmillan, 1990.

Mouzelis, N. *Back to Sociological Theory: The Construction of Social Orders*, London: Macmillan, 1991.

Mouzelis, N. 'Social and system integration: Habermas' view', *British Journal of Sociology* **43**(2) (June 1992), 272–7.

Mouzelis, N. *Sociological Theory: What Went Wrong?* London: Routledge, 1995.

Mouzelis, N. 'Social and system integration: Lockwood, Giddens, Habermas', *Sociology* (forthcoming).

Oakes, G. *Essays on Interpretation in the Social Sciences*, Totowa, NJ: Rowman and Littlefield, 1980.

Okley, J. *Simone de Beauvoir*, London: Virago, 1986.

Osborne, P. and Segal, L. 'Culture and power: Stuart Hall interview', *Radical Philosophy* **86** (November/December 1997).

Outhwaite, W. (ed.) *The Habermas Reader*, Cambridge: Polity Press, 1994.

Outhwaite, W. *Habermas, A Critical Introduction*, Cambridge: Cambridge University Press, 1996.

Owen, D. *Maturity and Modernity: Nietzsche, Weber, Foucault, and the Ambivalence of Reason*, London: Routledge, 1994.

Parkin, F. *Marxism and Class Theory*, London: Tavistock, 1979.

Parsons, T. *Structure of Social Action*, New York: McGraw-Hill, 1937.

Parsons, T. 'The professions and the social structure', *Social Forces* **17** (1939), 457–67.

Parsons, T. *The Structure of Social Action*, 2nd edn, Glencoe, IL: Free Press, 1949.

Parsons, T. *The Social System*, Chicago, IL: Free Press, 1951.

Parsons, T. 'Social structure and dynamic process: the case of modern medical practice', in T. Parsons, *The Social System*, New York: Free Press, 1951.

Parsons, T. 'Illness and the role of the physician: a sociological perspective', *American Journal of Orthopsychiatry* **2** (1957), 452–60.

Parsons, T. 'Evolutionary universals in society', *American Sociological Review* **29**(3) (1964), 339–57.

Parsons, T. 'Some comments on the sociology of Karl Marx', in T. Parsons *Sociological Theory and Modern Society*, New York: Free Press, 1967.

Parsons, T. *The System of Modern Societies*, Englewood Cliffs, NJ: Prentice-Hall, 1971.

Parsons, T. 'The superego and the theory of the social system', in P. Roazen (ed.) *Sigmund Freud*, Englewood Cliffs, NJ: Prentice-Hall, 1973.

Parsons, T. and Shils, E.A. (eds) *Toward a General Theory of Action*, New York: Harper & Row, 1951.

Parsons, T. and Smelser, N. *Economy and Society*, London: Routledge, 1956.

Parsons, T., Bales, R.F. and Shils, E.A. *Working Papers in the Theory of Action*, New York: Free Press, 1953.

Person, E. 'Sexuality as the main stay of identity', *Signs*, 1981.

Plath, S. *The Bell Jar*, London: Faber, 1963.

Plummer, K. *Sexual Stigma*, London: Routledge, 1975.

Plummer, K. (ed.) *Symbolic Interactionism:* 2 volumes, Aldershot: Edward Elgar, 1991.

Plummer, K. *Telling Sexual Stories*, London: Routledge, 1995.

Plummer, K. (ed.) *Chicago Sociology:* 4 volumes, London: Routledge, 1997.

Pollner, M. *Mundane Reason*, Cambridge: Cambridge University Press, 1987.

Pope, W. *Durkheim's 'Suicide'*, Chicago: The University of Chicago Press, 1976.

Poulantzas, N. *Political Power and Social Classes*, London: New Left Books, 1973.

Poulantzas, N. *Classes in Contemporary Capitalism*, London: New Left Books, 1975.

Poulantzas, N. *State, Power, Socialism*, London: Verso, 1978.

Pound, E. *A Lume Spento and Other Early Poems*, New York: New Directions, 1965.

Powell, W.W. and DiMaggio, P. (eds) 'Introduction' in idem, *The New Institutionalism in Organizational Analysis*, Chicago: University of Chicago Press, 1991, pp. 1–38.

Powell, W.W., and DiMaggio, P.J. (eds) *The New Institutionalism in Organizational Analysis*, Chicago: University of Chicago Press, 1991.

Purrhus and Cinéas was first published in 1944 Paris, Gallimard and *The Blood of Others* in 1945, as *Le Sang des Autres*, Paris, Gallimard.

Radcliffe-Brown, A.R. *Structure and Function in Primitive Society*, London: Cohen and West, 1952.

Rajchman, J. *Michel Foucault: The Freedom of Philosophy*, New York: Columbia University Press, 1985.

Ransom, J. *Foucault's Discipline: The Politics of Subjectivity*, Durham: Duke University Press, 1997.

Red-Green Study Group (R-GSG) *What on Earth is to be Done?* R-GSG: 2, Hamilton Road, Manchester, 1995.

Reich, W. *The Sexual Revolution*, London: Vision Press, 1957.

Resch, Robert P. *Althusser and the Renewal of Marxist Social Theory*, Berkeley, Los Angeles and Oxford: University of California, 1992.

Rich, A. *Of Women Born*, London: Virago.

Robertson, R. and Turner, B.S. (eds) *Talcott Parsons: Theorist of Modernity*, London: Sage, 1991.

Rock, P. *The Making of Symbolic Interactionism*, London: Macmillan, 1979.

Roscoe, P.B. 'Practice and centralisation: a new approach to political evolution', *Current Anthropology* 14(2) (April 1993), 111–40.

Rose, N. *Governing the Soul: The Shaping of the Private Self*, London: Routledge, 1989.

Rosenblatt, R. 'No escaping modern times,' US News and World Report, October 2, 1989, pp. 10–11.

Ryan, A. 'Maximising, minimising, moralising', in C. Hookway and P. Pettit (ed.) *Action and Interpretation*, Cambridge: Cambridge University Press, 1978.

Sacks, H. *Lectures on Conversation*, Oxford: Blackwell, 1992.

Sacks, H., Schegloff, E.A. and Jefferson, G. 'A simplest systematics for the organisation of turn-taking in conversation', *Language* **50** (1974), 696–735.

Sartre, J-P. *Witness to My Life*, London: Hamish Hamilton, 1992.

Sayer, A. *Method in Social Science*, London: Hutchinson, 1984.

Scaff, L. *Fleeing the Iron Cage: Culture, Politics and Modernity in the Thought of Max Weber*, Berkeley, CA: University of California Press, 1989.

Schegloff, E.A. 'The routine as achievement', *Human Studies* 9 (1986), 111–51.

Schegloff, E.A. 'Between micro and macro: contexts and other connections', in J.C. Alexander (ed.) *The Micro-Macro Link*, Berkeley, CA: California University Press, 1987, pp. 207–34.

Schegloff, E.A. 'Goffman and the analysis of conversation', in P. Drew and T. Wootton (eds) *Erving Goffman: Exploring the Interaction Order*, Cambridge: Polity Press, 1988.

Schegloff, E.A. 'Reflections on talk and social structure', in D. Boden and D.H. Zimmerman (eds) *Talk and Social Structure: Studies in Ethnomethodology and Conversation Analysis*, Cambridge: Polity Press, 1991, pp. 44–70.

Schegloff, E.A. and H. Sacks 'Opening up closings', *Semiotica* **8** (1973).

Schultz, R.W. 'The improbable adventures of an American scholar: Robert K. Merton,' *The American Sociologist* **26**(1) (Fall 1995), 68–77, (reprinted from *Temple Review* **47**(1) [Spring, 1995]).

Schutz, A. *Collected Papers*, vol. 1: *The Problem of Social Reality*, The Hague: Martinus Nijhoff, 1962.

Seidman, S. 'Classics and contemporaries: the history and systematics of sociology revisited' and the response 'The historicist/presentist dilemma: a composite imputation and a foreknowing response', drawn by the editor from writings of R.K. Merton, *History of Sociology* **6**(1) (Fall 1985), 121–36, 137–52.

Sennett, R. *The Fall of Public Man*, Cambridge: Cambridge University Press, 1977.

Setton, K.M. 'Foreword to the Torchbook edition', in Henry Osborn Taylor, *The Emergence of Christian Culture in the West* (originally, *The Classical Heritage of the Middle Ages*) New York: Harper & Brothers, 1958.

Sewell, W.H. Jr 'A theory of structure: duality, agency, and transformation: dialectic, and history', *American Journal of Sociology* **98**(1) (July 1992), 1–29.

Shalin, D.N. 'G.H. Mead, socialism and the progressive agenda', *American Journal of Sociology* **93**(4) (1988), 913–52.

Sheridan, A. *Michel Foucault: The Will To Truth*, London: Routledge, 1990.

Sica, A. 'Review of R. Bierstedt's "American Sociological Theory: A Critical History"', *American Journal of Sociology* **XCI** (March 1986), 1229–31.

Sills, D.L. and Merton, R.K. (eds) *The Macmillan Book of Social Science Quotations* (also published as vol. 19 of the *International Encyclopaedia of the Social Sciences*) New York: Macmillan, 1991.

Simmel, G. *Conflict and the Web of Group Affiliations*, Glencoe, IL: The Free Press, 1955.

Simmel, G. 'The metropolis and mental life', in D. Levine (ed.) *Georg Simmel on Individuality and Social Forms*, Chicago: Chicago University Press, 1971, pp. 324–39.

Simmel, G. *Les Problèmes de la Philosophie de L'Histoire (1907)*, Paris: PUF, 1984.

Simmel, G. 'Uber sociale differenzierung', *Gesamtausgabe* **2** Suhrkamp: Frankfurt am Main, 1989.

Simmel, G. 'Secret et société secrète', *Circé*, Saulxures, 1992.

Simmel, G. 'Soziologie: untersuchungen über die formen der vergesellschaftung', in *Gesamtausgabe* **11** Suhrkamp, Frankfurt am Main, 1992.

Smart, B. *Michel Foucault*, Chichester: Ellis Horwood, 1985.

Smelser, N.J. and Swedberg, R. 'The sociological perspective on the economy,' in N. Smelser and R. Swedberg (ed.) *The Handbook of Economic Sociology*, Princeton: Princeton University Press, 1994, pp. 3–26.

Smith, D.E. *The Everyday World as Problematic: A Feminist Sociology*, Boston: Northeastern University Press, 1987.

Smith, P. *The Emotional Division of Labour in Nursing*, Basingstoke: Macmillan Educational Books, 1992.

Solow, R.M. 'How did economics get that way and what way did it get?', *Daedalus* **126** (Winter 1997), 39–58.

Stearns C.Z. and Stearns, P. *Emotions and Social Change*, New York: Holmes and Meier, 1988.

Stearns, P. *American Cool: Constructing a Twentieth Century American Style*, New York: New York University Press, 1994.

Stevens, R. (ed.) *Understanding the Self*, London: Sage, 1996.

Stoler, A. *Race and the Education of Desire*, Durham: Duke University Press, 1995.

Stones, R. *Sociological Reasoning: Towards a Past-modern Sociology*, London: Macmillan, 1996.

Strauss, A. *Continual Permutations of Action*, New York: Aldine de Gruyter, 1993.

Suttles, G.D. *The Social Order of the Slum: Ethnicity and Territory in the Inner City*, Chicago: University of Chicago Press, 1968.

Sztompka, P. *Robert K. Merton: An Intellectual Profile*, New York: St Martin's Press, 1986.

Sztompka, P. 'R.K. Merton's Theoretical System: An Overview', in J. Clark, C. Modgil, and S. Modgil (eds) *Robert K. Merton: Consensus and Controversy*, London: Falmer Press, 1990.

Taylor, S. *Durkheim and the Study of Suicide*, London: Macmillan, 1982.

Terray, E. *Marxism and 'Primitive' Societies*, New York: Monthly Review, 1972.

The New Encyclopaedia Britannica, 15th edn. vol. 29. Chicago, Encyclopaedia Britannica, 1993.

Therborn, G. *Science, Class and Society: On the Formation of Sociology and Historical Materialism*, London: New Left Books, 1976.

Thoits, P.A. 'Emotional deviance: research agendas', in T.J. Kemper (ed.) *Research Agendas in the Sociology of Emotions*, New York: State University of New York Press, 1990, pp. 135–52.

Turner, B. *The Blackwell Companion to Social Theory*, Oxford: Blackwell, 1996.

Weber, M. *The Protestant Ethic and the Spirit of Capitalism* (trans. by T. Parsons) London: Allen & Unwin, 1930; New York: Scribner's, 1958.

Weber, M. *From Max Weber: Essays in Sociology*, ed. and trans. by H. Gerth and C. W. Mills, New York: Oxford University Press, 1946.

Weber, M. *The Methodology of the Social Sciences*, ed. and trans. by E. Shils and H. Finch, New York: Free Press, 1949.

Weber, M. *The Rational and Social Foundations of Music* (trans. Martindale *et al.*), Carbondale: Southern Illinois University Press, 1958.

Weber, M. *Economy and Society: An Outline of Interpretive Sociology*, ed. and trans. by G. Roth and C. Wittich, New York: Bedminster, 1968.

Wedderburn, D. and Crompton, R. *Workers' Attitudes and Technology*, Cambridge: Cambridge University Press, 1972.

West, C. and Zimmerman, D. 'Doing gender,' *Gender & Society* 1 (1987), 125–51.

White, S.K. (ed) *The Cambridge Companion to Habermas*, Cambridge: Cambridge University Press, 1994.

Williams, C. *Gender Differences at Work*, Berkeley, CA: University of California Press, 1989.

Williams, R. 'Goffman's sociology of talk', in J. Ditton (ed.) *The View from Goffman*, London: Macmillan, 1980.

Williams, S.J. 'Emotions, cyberspace and the "virtual" body: a critical appraisal', in G. Bendelow and S.J. Williams (eds) *Emotions in Social Life: Critical Themes and Contemporary Issues*, London: Routledge, 1998, pp. 120–32.

Williams, S.J and Bendelow, G. 'Emotions, health and illness: the "missing link" in medical sociology?', in V. James and J. Gabe (eds) *Health and the Sociology of Emotions*, Oxford: Blackwell, 1996, pp. 25–54.

Wittgenstein, L. *Philosophical Investigations*, 2nd edn, Oxford: Basil Blackwell, 1958.

Wollstonecraft, M. *A Vindication of the Rights of Woman*, London: Dent, 1970.

Woolf, J. 'The invisible flaneuse', in J. Woolf *Feminine Sentences*, Cambridge: Polity Press, 1990, pp. 34–50.

Wolff, K. *The Sociology of Georg Simmel*, Glencoe, IL: The Free Press, 1950.

Woolf, V. *The Crowded Dance of Modern Life*, London: Penguin, 1993.

Wouters, C. 'Informalization and the civilizing process', in P.R. Gleichmann, J. Goudsblom and H. Korte (eds) *Human Figurations: Essays for Norbert Elias*, Amsterdam: Stichting Amsterdams Sociologisch Tijdschrift, 1977.

Wouters, C. 'Response to Hochschild's reply', *Theory, Culture and Society* 6(3) (1989), 447–50.

Wouters, C. 'The sociology of emotions and flight attendants: Hochschild's "Managed Heart"', *Theory, Culture and Society* 6(1) (1989), 104–5.

Wright, E.O. *Class, Crisis, and the State*, London: New Left Books, 1978.

Wright, E.O. *Classes*, London: Verso, 1985.

Wright, E.O. *et al. The Debate on Classes*, London: Verso, 1989.

Wrong, D. 'The oversocialised conception of man in modern sociology', *American Sociological Review* 26 (1961), 183–93.

Zweig, F. *The Worker in an Affluent Society*, London: Heinemann, 1961.

Index